Farm Workers
and Agri-business
in California, 1947–1960

Other books by Ernesto Galarza

Plantation Workers in Louisiana
Strangers in Our Fields
*Mexican-Americans in the Southwest (with Herman
    Gallegos and Julian Samora)*
Spiders in the House and Workers in the Field
Barrio Boy
Merchants of Labor
Zoo Risa
Zoo Fun

Farm Workers and Agri-business in California, 1947-1960

ERNESTO GALARZA

UNIVERSITY OF NOTRE DAME PRESS

NOTRE DAME   LONDON

Library of Congress Cataloging in Publication Data

Galarza, Ernesto, 1905–
  Farm workers and agri-business in California, 1947–1960.

  Bibliography: p.
  Includes index.
  1. Trade-unions—Agricultural laborers—California—
History.   I. Title.
HD6515.A292C33   331.88'13'09794   76-51615
ISBN 0-268-00941-4
ISBN 0-268-00942-2 pbk.

To Mae

Publication of this volume
was assisted by a grant from
the John Hay Whitney Foundation

Contents

Contents ix

Preface

In the published history of agricultural workers in California and their efforts to organize, there remains a gap of over a decade. In October 1947 the National Farm Labor Union struck the DiGiorgio Farms located near Arvin; in August 1960 the successor to the NFLU, the National Agricultural Workers Union, disappeared from the scene of organized labor, merged with the Amalgamated Meat Cutters and Butcher Workmen of America. More accurately the NAWU was submerged, its only asset in the transaction having been an AFL charter which gave it jurisdiction over farm workers in the United States.

This book is an endeavor to fill the gap. Within this thirteen-year period there were three stages of response to the situation faced by the Union. The years from 1947 to 1952 were those of an intense, widespread organizational activity that probed deep into the structure of the agricultural industry and the society that lay beneath it. It was a period of close contact with the rural communities where former migrant families were settling down, of a continuous search for stable local leadership and of strikes that produced limited economic gains. By the end of 1952 it had become clear, however, that the corporate farmers against whom most of the action had been directed had organized a formidable deterrent to unionization, the "bracero" system, as the contracting of Mexican citizens for employment in the United States came to be known. They had been experimenting with it since 1942, institutionalizing it through work contracts based on governmental agreements between the United States and Mexico, a system of clearances and logistics worked out between the industry's leaders and government officials, and a large bureaucracy subsidized by the United States. The farm labor market in California and other southwestern states was being redesigned with the intention of making braceros the key to the control of agricultural employment.

Public Law 78, enacted by Congress in July 1951, gave the bracero system the sanction of federal law, creating a farm labor contracting scheme that in time could mobilize the unemployed masses of Mexico to displace domestic farm workers. As the system was perfected and refined in response to the demands of corporate agriculture, it had a

bright and extended future. There was a seemingly inexhaustible reserve of manpower south of the border. Growers had a long experience
in labor manipulation, which could be more efficiently coordinated at
the higher levels of bureaucracy and diplomacy. State and federal agencies were at hand to provide logistic facilities. The farms to which the
braceros were assigned, and on which the encounters with domestic
workers took place, were sufficiently removed from public view to
avoid disturbing the national conscience. And the whole of the process
was represented, insofar as explanations were necessary, as the response of agri-business to the national food shortage, world hunger, and
the crisis of democracy.

To the members of the NFLU the impact of bracero hiring was
immediate and drastic—displacement from steady jobs, disruption of
community life in the rural *barrios* and *colonias*, broken strikes, standby
hiring, lower wages, and forced migration to the cities. To the officers of
the union it was clear, as of 1952, that the problems of organization now
centered on Public Law 78 and its multiple effects. Without opposition,
the bracero system would have a drastic effect on the hiring of domestic
agriculture laborers, except as needed as standbys for emergencies.

The NFLU set for itself the appropriate tasks: to engage that system;
to discover in detail how it worked on the ranches and farms; to bring the
corporation farms to the picket line as often as possible so that their
manipulations of braceros as a massive task force to prevent unionization could be observed; to pursue pliant government agencies
through a devious and prolonged coverup; to document these processes
over sufficient time and make them public; and to redress the imbalance
of forces through nationwide publicity with sufficient force to bring
about the repeal of Public Law 78. The National Agricultural Workers
Union stayed at these tasks through the year 1959.

The third period covered by this narrative—1959–1960—was the
period of liquidation. The "action research" that had been completed
did not, as a union strategy, please the influentials of the labor movement. Technically it was a hopeless deviation from labor's orthodoxy
for organizing, which was profitless unless it resulted in a collective
bargaining contract. Furthermore, as the union's small but active cadres
wrenched from corporation agriculture a picture of the bracero system,
the mesh of American society—government, the universities, the rural
press, diplomacy—was revealed. The accounts from the fields profiled
the structure of power which the bracero system manifested. Since
organized labor had already passed the stage of intellectual or political
interest in the analysis of existing social power, the NAWU's behavior
came to be regarded as deviant, imprudent, and possibly disruptive.

The NAWU disappeared from the scene, its policy of militant opposition in the fields rejected by organized labor. But the momentum of its long campaign against Public Law 78 continued with the final result that Congress terminated the bracero system in 1964.

The system of foreign contract labor was by no means limited to California; braceros played the same role in Texas, Arizona, and some areas of the Midwest. What the sponsors of Public Law 78 were structuring and what the experience of the NAWU everywhere confirmed, was a national scheme of labor importation administered by government on behalf of and for the profit of private industry. But there was no organized opposition to this design other than in California.

The group of men and women responsible for the action of the union between 1952 and 1958—most of them veterans of the strikes of the period from 1947 to 1951—never numbered much more than a hundred. With them the resistance was planned and carried out. I participated in most of those actions, in which it is difficult to separate personal from collective roles. In my encounters with those who administered the bracero system out of public view, the workers had no opportunity to act. In such situations I was often the only adversary, and I see no practical method of reporting these incidents otherwise. If this style suggests a certain nonobjectivity of the narrative, so much the better. The ultimate compass of what men say and write and do are values, which cannot be found anywhere save in their conscience, reflected in every choice of behavior self-servingly characterized as "objective."

The academically minded may find the suggested readings too thin. A solid appendix of published references with a ballast of footnotes will no doubt be provided in time by those who might consider this text insufficient. For the convenience of such, I have given the Stanford University Library all the papers that I and my fellow-unionists collected during the years of action. In addition to the Stanford collection, there is another at the University of North Carolina, dating back to the days of the Southern Tenant Farmers Union, the predecessor of the NAWU.

A book, like a picture frame, is likely to give a false impression of self-containment. Books and pictures might be better left untrimmed, thus suggesting the fabric of life of which they were a part. At least, I hope this one will be so received.

Persons in the Action

Raul and Trinidad *Aguilar*—NAWU volunteer organizers in the Salinas Valley

Saul *Alinsky*—noted radical, community organization strategist, director of the Industrial Areas Foundation

Jose *Ayala*—volunteer organizer in the Salinas Valley, NAWU liaison with government camps in the area, veteran field worker

Dave *Beck*—president of the International Brotherhood of Teamsters, Helpers and Warehousemen, predecessor of James Hoffa

William *Becker*—staff organizer for the National Agricultural Workers Union

Floyd *Behringer*—manager, Progressive Growers Association of Santa Clara County, headquartered in San Jose

Fay *Bennett*—secretary of the National Sharecroppers Fund, the link between the NAWU and its financial supporters

Glenn *Brockway*—regional director, Bureau of Employment Security, U.S. Department of Labor, with central offices in San Francisco

Edmund G. *Brown*—Governor of California, 1959-1966

Wofford B. *Camp*—large scale grower, cattle breeder, and capitalist of Kern County, principal figure in the organization of the planting cottonseed monopoly

Elias *Colunga*—Mexican Consul in Calexico, Imperial County, 1950

R. T. *Creasy*—Assistant Secretary of Labor

Franz *Daniel*—assistant director of organization, AFL-CIO

A. R. *Duarte*—manager, San Joaquin Growers Association

Robert S. *Goodwin*—national director, Employment Security Agency, U.S. Department of Labor, Washington D.C.

Patrick E. *Gorman*—secretary-treasurer, Amalgamated Meat Cutters and Butcher Workmen of America

Cornelius J. *Haggerty*—secretary-treasurer, California State Federation of Labor

Edward F. *Hayes*—chief, Farm Placement Service, California State Department of Employment

B. A. *Harrigan*—manager, Imperial Valley Farmers Association

Henry (Hank) *Hasiwar*—western director of organization, NAWU, principal staff representative in the DiGiorgio strike

Ralph *Helstein*—president, United Packinghouse Workers of America, AFL-CIO

Francisco *Hernandez Cano*—Mexican bracero, member of the NAWU, Soledad Local, Salinas Valley

Goodwin J. *Knight,* governor of California, 1955-1958

Clive *Knowles*—International Representative, United Packinghouse Workers in America

Louis *Krainock*—assistant to Norman Smith and director of public relations of the Agricultural Workers Organizing Committee

Don *Larin*—deputy director, California State Department of Employment in charge of farm labor

John W. *Livingston*—National Director of Organization, AFL-CIO

George *Meany*—president, American Federation of Labor-Congress of Industrial Organizations

Keith *Mets*—president, Imperial Valley Farmers Association

J. J. *Miller*—manager, Agricultural Producers Labor Committee based in Los Angeles and member of the advisory committee to Brockway

H. L. *Mitchell*—co-founder of the Southern Tenant Farmers Union, later the National Farm Labor Union and the National Agricultural Workers Union

Frank L. *Noakes*—official of the Brotherhood of Maintenance of Way Employees and chairman of the U.S. Section of the U.S.–Mexico Joint Trade Union Committee

Willaim *O'Dwyer*—ambassador of the United States to Mexico

Frank *O'Dwyer*—brother of William O'Dwyer and partner of Keith Mets in the Imperial Valley

Max *Osslo*—vice-president, Amalgamated Meat Cutters and the California State Federation of Labor

Phineas *Parks*—lay preacher and member of Local 218, NAWU, participant in the DiGiorgio strike

James *Price*—president, NAWU Local 218, Arvin-Lamont

Bertha *Rankin*—family farmer in the Weedpatch area, donor of NAWU hall, and chief source of information in opposition to the planting cottonseed monopoly

William *Renner*—compliance officer, Bureau of Employment Security in San Joaquin and Stanislaus Counties

Victor *Reuther*—officer of the IUD, brother of Walter Reuther

Walter *Reuther*—president, United Auto Workers and Industrial Union Department AFL-CIO

Charles *Rhodes*—manager, Northern California Growers Association mainly serving growers in Yuba, Sutter, and Butte Counties

William *Schnitzler*—secretary-treasurer, AFL-CIO

Norman *Smith*—director, Agricultural Workers Organizing Committee

Earl *Warren*—governor of California 1943-1952

Bob *Whatley*—first volunteer organizer of the DiGiorgio field and packinghouse employees and active participant in the strike

I: Introduction

The military conquest of western America was completed by the end
of the 1840s. The political and legal consolidation of this vast region into
the institutional structures of the United States continued during half a
century. In its wake the economic rewards of armed expansion were
staked out by the conflicting claims of a populist, agrarian democracy on
the one hand and a profit-centered capitalist corporatism on the other.

What is most striking about the panorama of events during those fifty
years is the sense of motion. New social forms of organization—
industrial production, market penetration and consolidation, a banking
system, corporate property, a public domain subject to private appro-
priation, vigorous enterprises in commerce and trade, a state in command of a regular army and navy—had already propelled the United
States on a course of continental expansion. It was the case of a small
nation thinking big, ready to release the energy of those social forms on a
frontier waiting to be taken. And to take it meant to move.

The motion went forward in many tempos, from the scramble of the
Gold Rush to the crawling persistence of the pioneer homesteaders.
Between the incursions of the U.S cavalry there was the steadying task
of building and defending nuclear sites like trading posts around which a
new society would form. A people was on the move, taking over as the
industrial revolution placed in their hands the instruments, tools, and
weapons for overcoming nomadic Indian tribes and pastoral Mexicans.
The steam locomotive and the Winchester repeating rifle were part of
the industrial hardware that won and held a continental prize.

Apart from the sense of national destiny first expressed by the Mon-
roe Doctrine in 1823, which placed the Western Hemisphere out of
bounds for European intruders, the West was to be a possession for the
American people to have and to hold. Conquest is never civilized. Its
business, while it lasts, is to destroy men and their cultures. The sense of
national destiny is added in order to convey the feeling that the con-
querors, as agents of the destruction, are the precursors of a nobler type
of mankind. The West was to be an extended home for the brave and the
free. The promise of this design lay in that such a society was to be free
more than that it was to be brave, freedom being much less prevalent
among the nations of the earth than courage.

· But to organize a new society, the indispensable condition is stability. A line from the musical *Oklahoma*, composed when it was all over, sang of the restless, high-pitched decades of the winning of the West: "We know we belong to the land/ and the land we belong to is grand."

The movements in quick step that embraced the particular tactics of subjugation, penetration, and occupation—from military control to the substitution of legal systems—were plainly a means to an end. For the settlers the goal was to clear their freeholds of timber, Indians, and Mexicans and thereafter to stabilize a new agrarian society of men belonging to the land in perpetuity.

But an odd thing happened. By the 1900s the profit-centered corporation capitalism that had organized modern industry on the eastern seaboard of the United States, improving on the European model, had taken over the designing of the agricultural economy of the New West. This design required, above all things, mobility—the mobility of capital matched by the mobility of men. To achieve stability, the condition necessary to create stratifications congenial to the new society, would require, like any cultural process, centuries. Men require continuity in their individual lives as well as in their collective experience. Profit-centered corporate capitalism has a more limited view of stability, accepting only so much of it as may be necessary to enforce its claims on a productive society. Socially, men will move only if they are tempted by adventure or by the promise of relief from the pressures of insecurity. Economically, for a system that seeks maximum profits, the essence of mobility is turnover. The frequency of turnover multiplies the return of capital. The object of capital is to maximize itself. Social formations that tend to stabilize interactions so that men may gain some sense of personal and collective purpose and fulfillment, are, from the capitalist point of view, parochial and obstructionist.

Thus the odd thing that happened in the West was that mobility began as a temporary strategy of conquest, provisional to the goals of a national mission, and ended as a basic requirement of the corporate structure of western agriculture. Corporatism, in its broadest sense, was the force that raided the national domain to convert millions of acres of public lands to private ownership. It fought and overcame land squatters who got there last with the least. By technological and financial and marketing integration it reduced the family farm to a sentimental memory.

The descriptive term for the elimination of such parochial forms of social organization as family farming and rural community was coined much later, when the United States government used it to describe its role in the Chilean military junta's coup that resulted in the assassination of President Salvador Allende and the destruction of his government. It was called "de-stabilization." And the casualness with which a process existent in domestic affairs for decades became a principle of American diplomacy was not sufficiently noted.

Once corporate capitalism is exempted from responsibilities to people whose way of life must be drastically de-stabilized to enhance mobility and turnover, the manner of supplying manpower for agricultural production is determined. The work force must be composed of men and women—and often children—perpetually on the move. "We want workers when we need them and we want them out when we don't" became an accurate expression of the demand and a description of the market for labor it created.

Thus the title of Nels Anderson's book *Men on the Move* was more than a reference to the migrant fringe of America's landworkers, the seasonal wayfarers who harvested the crops across the face of the republic. Men on the move became the characteristic of the agricultural sector in western America. California became the prototype of such a labor market, and of such a way of life.

Central to such a market, which economists fell into the habit of describing as "unstructured," was the concept of the labor pool. To be a farm worker, typically, was to have an incidental, sidelong connection with the process of agricultural production. The cash connection between hired hands and farmers lasted no longer than the time necessary to pick a crop of tomatoes or peaches or cotton, and these seasons, brief enough already, were to be shortened even more by scientific plant breeding and mechanical harvesting. In the labor pool, with its constant flux of people, there was no room for social ties. To social de-stabilization there was added social denigration. Employers called their help migrants, transients, vagabonds, bindle stiffs, bums, and winos.

One wonders at the mentality of a social class that could view the laborers so essential to its economy from such heights of scorn. In part this view was encouraged by the total mobility of the labor pool of Chinese, Japanese, Filipinos, Mexicans, Blacks, and Okies, who flowed by turns into and out of the common reservoir of harvesters. The dispossessed of many lands, and of America itself, broke away in desperate migrations that found their way into this labor pool.

From the employer's point of view, it was the most appropriate way of providing short-term manpower for western agriculture. And it had a profound side-effect. It created a subculture within whose depths a future national psychosis was fermenting—anomie, powerlessness, alienation, emotions of people by design permanently disconnected from one another and from the sources of their livelihood. The requirement that men must be kept mobile to match the mobility of capital at first applied only to peons moving north from Mexico and dust bowl refugees moving west from the middle south.[1] It would take nearly three-quarters of a century to demonstrate that advanced training in sophisticated technology would not prevent skilled men and women from being forced into labor pools of their own. Once it became well established in American society that the pattern was acceptable to the mode of capitalist corporate production in the fields, it became the model for all categories of production. And the time would come when there would be isolated labor pools in America of electronic engineers, college professors, skilled tool-and-die makers, credentialed teachers, and even junior executives.

Those sectors of a society that for the moment enjoy some measure of its benefits are prone to miss the historical as well as the moral points of this process. Forced mobility as a model was seemingly prescribed only for farm laborers. Their containment and their exclusion from power was a consequence of their alienation from property as productive wealth. But this condition affected as well the better favored elites above them. And as certain classes of professionals, technicians, and intellectuals became less indispensable to the economic processes of capitalism, they too became more expendable, and they too broke away from their uncertain moorings in the society. To be unconcerned over the fate of those already in the distresses of de-stabilization was the moral expression of historical innocence, the penalty of which succeeding strata of American society were to discover.

In California there was no need for enclosure acts such as country gentlemen of eighteenth-century England used to de-stabilize the village workers. The western lands were vacant, save where wandering Indian tribes and Mexican rancheros occupied them. The ownership and use of the best of these lands went from the sovereign public domain to private speculation on a scale unprecedented in the history of the nation. For decades the West was so abundant, the stage for personal enterprise so inviting, that it seemed to have something for everyone, forever. But the promise could not be kept. The contours of the future society had been set by the scarcity of land for those who would come later; and when they came, in waves of migration induced by land-rich but labor-poor operators, their desperate condition where they came from gave them no choice but to accept the equally desperate condition where they were going.

Too narrow a view of a social process such as this one tends to remain focused on the immediate conditions of labor, with the emphasis on the agricultural scene itself. The story of denial of the promises of American life for so many people has emphasized the misery of their lives, and rightly so. It has missed, however, certain important changes in non-rural society that taken together amounted to requirements for the operation of that process.

One such change was the growth of cities on the Pacific Coast. Themselves the product of forces at work in the nonagricultural sector, large cities became important to the operation of the farm labor pool. There was no room on or near the job site to harbor the migrant harvesters between crops. Where they went was something of a sociological mystery. According to the California Welfare and Institutions Code of 1947, they returned during their "seasons of repose" to their place of residence. But this place was little more than a crowded corner in some city slum, a rented room shared with many others, a flop house, or a deteriorating cottage in a back alley. Out of such cyclical retreats there developed the small towns that grew out of clusters of tents and shacks on dusty byways and unrewarding rock piles. Over the decades these lodgments became the nodal points of a process opposed to the perpetual motion in which the agricultural industry preferred to keep its laborers. In time, if left alone, a counterpart life style would form around them. Even the urban skid rows of San Francisco, Sacramento, Los Angeles, and Fresno, for all their fetor, provided a semblance of sociability against a system determined to destroy it.

In the cities also there was demonstrated the peculiar relationship of city laborers and migrants to one another. Following the cue of the "regular" migrants, city craftsmen—carpenters, day laborers, production workers—would seek jobs on the farms during hard times in the cities, in the role of moonlighters rather than as proletarians moving down the economic ladder permanently. And since in their off seasons the harvesters competed for the more menial urban jobs, they came to be regarded as a threat to the living standards of the lower income city dwellers.

This overlap of occupations of urban and farm workers provided experiences that would have important effects over the long run. Harvest hands had opportunities to participate in and observe trade unionism organization in the cities. Though not a school to sharpen the social insights the farm laborers so badly needed, it taught them enough to provide leadership when they returned to the fields. The interchange also began a process of awareness among the urban trade unionists, alerting them to the threat to their own security represented by the political power of corporate agricultural wealth. The growers associations based in the rural areas were ever prepared to support the latent assault on organized labor always present in the minds of the state's industrial employers. Not the least important aspect of this awareness, moreover, was the climate of sympathy for farm workers that after four decades finally welled into the urban boycott committees of the 1960s.

These were some of the ways in which the urban and rural sectors came to see each other, signifying in the long run that their isolation would diminish and finally end. This was of great importance to the chances of unionism in the fields, appealing as it did to the responsive chords of the American conscience that step by step can grow into an aroused public opinion.

As this isolation and containment gradually broke down, in the rural areas a vital contest was underway between an increasingly integrated industry—bent on keeping the farm labor force mobile, floating, scattered, and in a word socially meaningless—and the persistent search for stability by the working class, including the farm workers. Personally, integration is the process of an individual human being trying to give meaning to his experience and his subjective reactions to it; socially, it is the effort to find a location in relationships with others that offers a way of anticipating and securing psychological and material support. The first step is a hold in the universe closest at hand, a base that can be at the same time the point of departure and the point of return.

The signs of how farm labor families were going about this were observable. A down payment of a few dollars secured a sandlot where assorted rocks, discarded bricks, broken cinder blocks, and chunks of waste concrete could be piled to provide some day the foundations for a permanent dwelling even if it were only a shack. In time the shack would be mended and refurbished into a more proper cottage. This was the base around which families established more stable circuits that would enable them to come back periodically to familiar places and neighbors, and within which ties of family would be least likely to break. Farm labor contractors set up camps in which they assembled followings of seasonal workers with a kind of intermediate identity. Wherever public agencies offered a harbor in an agricultural area, such as government camps, households were attracted and soon formed into communities.

These communities were groping ventures in stability, where dwelling places of discarded materials were made by a people who refused to remain themselves discards of society.

Against these challenges to a completely mobile labor force the industry waged a cold but unrelenting war. Wherever and in whatever form the harvesters showed signs of putting down roots, shallow as they might be, they were condemned to de-stabilization forthwith. Thus the federal government camps built to meet the housing needs of farm workers during World War II did not withstand the political attacks of the farm labor associations, which eventually took possession of them, and managed them into a state of physical deterioration that matched the moral tone of the government agents who submitted to the growers' demands. Pursuing the same ends it became common practice for local police to raid the so-called jungle camps of transients who did not winter on skid row. In the 1950s the skid rows themselves became targets of urban renewal, which eliminated the flop houses and the soup lines of homeless and hungry men who worked occasionally in the crops. These were intermittent mop-ups compared to the massive uprooting that followed the introduction of the bracero system in 1942, by which entire towns in rural areas were gradually deserted, their residents denied the work that the braceros were contracted to do at lower wages.

Each immigrant group that entered the shapeless congestion of the agricultural labor pool responded in a different manner to its dis-couragements. The Japanese, who followed closely on the Chinese, after a brief period of organization as wage workers, developed a tightly knit system of intensive family labor, supported by Japanese financial credit to help them acquire land. The Filipinos modified the structure of gang hiring until it was transformed into a cohesive company of specialized workers with quasi-democratic controls and close ties to the urban centers where they wintered. The Sikhs, who came much later and were fewer in number, settled out of migrancy and into the ranks of the small farmers and orchardists of the upper Central and Imperial valleys.

Outnumbering all these, the Mexicans became the major tributary of the labor reservoir. It is estimated that between 1900 and 1920 the Mexican rural resident population of California increased from some 8,000 to over 88,000, practically all of them land workers. In a pattern that was to endure, they settled principally in the counties of Los Angeles, Imperial, San Bernardino, Orange, and Riverside. These Mex-ican settlements grew almost in geometric progression, their aggregate population probably numbering more than 350,000 by 1940.

Not until mechanization of the farms and the bracero system com-pelled them to do so, beginning in the early 1940s, did the Mexican harvesters begin to turn away from agriculture. As long as they had remained submerged in its labor pool they had protested its abuses only by occasional insurgency, such as the strikes of the 1930s. The Mexican peasants who took refuge in California during the first forty years of the century brought with them no traditional institutions, except those of religion, capable of ameliorating, if not affecting, the terms and condi-tions of work in rural California. They came and they remained agricul-tural proletarians, unable to create within their own ranks material and cultural resources supportive of their own interest. The Mexican emigrants lost the sustaining power of ancestral ideas, the collectivism in the distribution and use of land, and the communitarianism of village life.

In many respects it was no different with the Okies and Arkies who swelled by the hundreds of thousands the farm labor market of the state. They had been kept in subjection by the system of sharecropping after the Civil War. Millions of Blacks had been emancipated from the planters only to remain exploited by them as tenant sharecroppers, whose only cash crop, year in and year out, was cotton. Never noted for their economic insights, the planters nevertheless understood that the source of their wealth was unpaid labor. As one of them stated plainly, "Cotton cannot be grown at a profit if all the labor has to be paid for."[2] The portion of the market value of that labor allowed as the picker's income by the planters was the economic decision upon which the social system of the post-bellum South rested.

By the 1930s the uncertain tenure of the southern landworkers was breaking. The combined force of tractoring and the plowing under of cotton through federal subsidies produced the second colossal dislocation of people in sixty years. As tenancy collapsed, three-quarters of the tenants became wage laborers. Those who had not been tractored out averaged an income of seventy-five dollars a year in the mid-thirties. Those who could not find space in the hill country above the fertile cotton fields moved northward to look for work in New York or Detroit or Chicago. In the ten years beginning in 1940 North Carolina alone lost five hundred thousand residents.[3] Those who could not migrate so far moved to southern cities like Memphis, from which "day hauls" by truck kept them available for picking. The collapse of tenancy forced nearly four million people to leave the South permanently, leaving behind a society as improvident of the poor who stayed as of its soil.

Among those who stood and faced these events, unwilling themselves to become men on the move without protest, was a handful of 'croppers who rallied around H. L. Mitchell, co-founder, with another white man, Clay East, of the Southern Tenant Farmers Union. Mitchell's one-man dry cleaning shop in Tyronza, Arkansas, became the center of earnest discussions of families faced with eviction from the land, the effect of the federal government's Agricultural Adjustment Act being implemented by bulldozers and tractors. From these discussions the call for a meeting was sent out, and in July 1934 some twenty Blacks and Whites assembled to organize in a clapboard building auspiciously called Sunnyside Schoolhouse. They voted to be bi-racial with membership open to tenants, sharecroppers, and small farmers.

Such was the beginning of the revolt of the sharecroppers, which crystallized the anger and disillusion of those who felt themselves about to be removed once again from the basic securities of work and rights of citizenship. For them the dawn of the New Deal had quickly darkened into omens of Section 7-A of the AAA. To palliate the massive dislocations that were wiping out entire communities, Washington created the Relocation Administration, by its title alone a reaffirmation that when capital requires it, men must move.

Planter society saw the peaceable actions of the Sunnyside founders as nothing less than an uprising and they proceeded to break it by systematic terror. The union's organizers lived in constant expectation of violent death at the hands of night-riding planters and their henchmen. Bullets riddled the homes of members. A church where union meetings were held was burned to the ground, another stuffed to the beams with hay.[4] Union sympathizers were flogged and driven out of their cabins and off the plantations. Eviction notices were served in batches, debts were called in, speakers were assaulted.

Firmly committed to nonviolence, the STFU responded to terror by a combination of tactics that added up to what became a classic strategy for insurgents of the soil against overwheming odds. In one 1935 demonstration dozens of evicted families were assembled on a public road, their household goods piled on vehicles of all sorts and aligned to form a continuous barricade. Timely notice to newspaper and radio reporters secured a national audience. A series of strikes that must have caused as much consternation as fury among the planters began, with hundreds of pickers walking out of the fields and encircling them with picket lines and caravans.[5]

Undoubtedly to the southern planters the mere fact that a workers' organization had appeared was revolutionary; but the demands set forth by the striking croppers were for redress, not revolution:

> . . . that no sharecropper be without decent clothing, food, fuel, and shelter. No overcharge for furnished goods. Honest weights and measures. Stop killing of sharecroppers. Cotton picking $1.00 per hundred. Collective bargaining. Union recognition.
>
> —*Sharecropper's Voice*, July 1935

The only living space on earth for the harassed families had been narrowed to the dirt shoulder of a public road, but it proved ground enough to make their protest heard around the nation.

The STFU under Mitchell's guidance, also confronted the planters in the courts and legislative halls. Floggings were investigated and the assailants brought to justice. The planters' self-serving interpretations of the acreage limitation contracts of the AAA were challenged and proposals for reform legislation were placed high on the agenda of the union, where they would not fail to be noticed by congressmen.

Through those dangerous years the STFU generated an élan that soon turned it into a regional influence, if not yet a force. Mitchell, Clay East, Ward Rodgers, and J. R. Butler went about their organizing missions with the zeal of revivalists. Within three years of its founding the union was holding annual conventions with delegates from all the states in the Deep South. The union organ, the *Sharecropper's Voice*, appeared whenever the rickety mimeograph machine was functioning and there were a few dollars in the treasury for paper. It carried not only the news about conditions in the land of cotton that would not appear elsewhere but also the lofty theories of Adam Smith and the doctrines of Henry George and Norman Thomas, for the STFU called itself socialist. It was dedicated to the peaceful termination of the most malevolent system of power saddled upon American farm workers anywhere in America, committed to enlightening the minds of its members no less than to easing their material burdens.

With $509.12 in its treasury the union in 1935 could reach nearly twenty-three thousand nominal members in two hundred local affiliates. In contrast with the southern landowners, this was a powerless base, but it served admirably the aims of Mitchell and his associates—to arouse a current of public opinion that would gain the sharecroppers the sympathy of liberal Americans, create discomfort in the White House and Congress, recruit professional volunteers who would defend them in court, and raise funds with nickels and dimes against an opposition that worked with dollars. In this fashion there was soon created a National Sharecroppers Fund which raised money, provided speakers, and relayed the drumfire of news, pamphlets, and reports of which Mitchell was the principal source.[6] In 1935 a National Sharecroppers Week was staged, and the sharecropper's voice was heard at the convention of the American Federation of Labor, asking for "sympathetic consideration, encouragement, and assistance."

The terror in the South abated and the struggle to awaken the national conscience continued. In its dreamiest moment, the STFU regarded itself as an articulate organization of men "moving irresistibly toward revolution."[7] It was much less—none of the resources and levers of power were passing into its hands. Nevertheless it showed how, in a society like America's, power that cannot be transformed can be resisted and contained. It was a message that came through lightly in the soft speech of men like Mitchell but one that became so magnified that it was still echoing in the marches of the Delano strikes thirty years later.

Such was the union that under a new name, the National Farm

Workers Union, went West in 1947. The STFU had already affected the California farm labor scene. Its persistent publicity led to the creation by the United States Senate of the LaFollette Committee to investigate violations of the civil liberties of agricultural workers. The committee report, published in 1942, traced in fine lines a network of economic and political power as entrenched in its own way as that of the southern planters. At the time the committee was sitting in San Francisco the union had made no contact with workers farther west than New Mexico. Four years later, responding to appeals from dust bowl refugees who had settled in California's San Joaquin Valley, the union stepped boldly into another stronghold of agricultural power.

What propelled the leaders of a union that for all its gallant rebellion in the South had hardly touched the traditional monopoly of power? In part the call of farm workers throughout the nation who had been stirred by the example of the STFU and were sending out pleas for help. The socialist temper of the union's leaders made them responsive to such calls without screening them through the calculated requirements of business unionism. The STFU itself needed the momentum of new campaigns as the one in the South spent itself in legislative maneuvers, litigation, and publicity, not to speak of the taxing effort to educate and train its scattered ranks. The nation was in one of its periodic euphorias of hope and glory—the New Deal—which offered the advocates of the oppressed opportunities to speak and be heard in high places. The STFU, finding a few sympathizers in the upper levels of organized labor, envisioned the prospect of close support by them for organizing on a nationwide scale, toward which the move into California was to be the first step.

These were certainly important elements in the decision to confront corporate capitalist agriculture in the West. Mingled with them were the principles, the attitudes, the strategies, and the techniques which had permitted the STFU to survive, if not to overcome. "Bloodshed and violence are against every principle we hold dear," the *Sharecroppers Voice* had proclaimed, and the union had remained nonviolent, even under savage provocation. Membership was to be open to all classes of landworkers, from day laborers to small farmers. The trade union was the form of organization that could give them negotiating weight among the multiple claims of a pluralistic society. Unionism was the door through which the forgotten toilers of the land could eventually enter the House of Labor, as shareholders in a condominium, not as poor relations lodged in the basement. Collective bargaining was the prime objective of economic action. The decisions, the tactics, the experiences of the collective effort were the educational curriculum of the union, and a measure of its respect for informed minds as the basis of its democracy.

Unlike its appearance in the South, the STFU, in extending itself to California, was not initiating but only continuing a struggle that went back several decades.

There had been more or less organized resistance by the raisin pickers around Fresno in 1901, and in some Central Valley vineyards in 1906. Intermittently "clubs" of Japanese and Filipino harvesters, through slowdowns and stoppages, forced wage settlements with their employers. Though it passed unnoticed because it rarely broke into open conflict, there was a permanent undercurrent of discontent, which was expressed in the late arrival and early departure of migratory workers sufficient to seriously affect harvesting. History began to record these protests when they crested into bloody encounters like that of Wheatland in 1913, of the Imperial Valley in 1928, and the cotton belt in the 1930s. From 1927 to 1939 organized economic actions by workers numbered over 150, no doubt a conservative estimate.[8] Unaccountable numbers of workers invariably joined these protests by staying home or drifting away; but it is not improbable that during those twenty years over two hundred thousand men and women participated in more or less overt forms of protest.

As the number of Mexican farm laborers increased after 1920, they became more active in these strikes. In the rural towns of the Imperial Valley, union organization was preceded by cooperative groups such as mutual aid societies, funeral associations, and patriotic committees. The Confederación de Uniones Obreras Mexicanas appeared in Los Angeles in 1927 and for a short time was also militantly active in the Imperial Valley. The Confederación wavered between revolutionary exhortations and a naive trust that local businessmen would cooperate with it in achieving peaceful reforms. Not infrequently these ends were frustrated by Mexican consuls, who showed no inclination to lead revolutionary struggles against the local Chamber of Commerce. Eventually the unionists realized that their hope of negotiations with the Mexican government to regulate the immigration of Mexican labor into the United States was as unrealistic as their plea for solidarity with the American Federation of Labor.

The indifference of the AFL, the Chambers of Commerce, and the Mexican government to these pleas, and the ever-latent resistance of California agriculture, were more than compensated by the response of the International Workers of the World and the American Communist Party. Between them they accounted for a struggle that was sustained sporadically for thirty years before the successor of the NFLU renewed it. The IWW, until it was clubbed and legislated and prosecuted out of existence, mounted a campaign of direct confrontation through "job actions." It never had and never sought a base of stable resident laborers. A small but highly tempered core of roving organizers appeared wherever the migrant pickers were ready to strike, providing aggressive leadership as long as the ranks held. Their proclaimed goal was a world revolution. When they broke, the IWW cadres moved on to re-form at some other place and another season.

In the settlements that the uprooted landworkers were contriving in the breathing spells allowed them by a pursuing adversary, the IWW ignored them with single-minded scorn.

By the mid 1920s the IWW campaign was spent, its leaders in jail, its followers scattered. The field was open to the Communist party which operated through the Trade Union Unity League, created as a branch of the party in 1929. The purpose of the league was to provide revolutionary direction to the chronic discontent of the rural proletariat. The TUUL spent nearly ten years in this attempt, providing organizers such as Caroline Decker and Pat Chambers, who breasted the organized violence of rural vigilantism with a courage like that of the southern tenant croppers. Finally defeated, the TUUL withdrew in 1937, leaving behind fragments of the league, such as the United Cannery and Packinghouse Workers, predecessor of the United Packinghouse Workers of America. This succession represented the "left wing" of agricultural labor in California, which was to parallel the National Farm Labor Union until both disappeared in the AFL-CIO merger of the 1960s.

Through these turbulent years neither the IWW nor the TUUL attempted to organize a base for power of the farm workers. They saw in the constant flux of migrant labor the signs of a disintegrating capitalist society, taking them as cracks in the system that would widen into cleavages by dint of revolutionary slogans and dangerous organizing in the heartland of agri-business. They scorned the temptations of working within the system, preferring the risks and cost of being the vanguard of what they regarded as its decline and fall. The tiny cadres they sent to the picket lines were not formations on which social power could be set up. There was a revolutionary situation neither in rural America nor among the middle-class urban masses. What spurred the agricultural laborers was not ideology but bread-and-butter desperation. Depicted in its most repulsive aspects, rural poverty appealed to the compassion of a liberal, democratic, Christian, pluralistic society. Middle-class Americans, like farm workers, were not actually the agents of their own history, and were indeed becoming less so in respect to the decisions that controlled the structure of the economic system on which they depended vitally. But neither were they ready to seek new formations of social power to resolve crucial issues of which they were hardly aware. Within these limits of the national mood, the successive stages of farm labor protest were forced to play their roles.

Though they failed in so many respects from the point of view of these efforts from decade to decade, they succeeded in one important respect. The stage on which farm laborers could act became more open, less threatened by violence, and increasingly visible to an enlarging public. As the audience grew, at the expense of the dead of Wheatland and the freedom of militant leaders, it became possible for the later organizers to move about in the Imperial Valley and Salinas without fearing for their lives. Furthermore, through the years there were handed down tried methods and techniques of organization that unions, whether anarchist, communist, socialist, or reformist, adopted. Taken together these divergent styles of unionism proved that farm workers were organizable; that strikes, however incapable of bringing employers to the bargaining table, were invariably economically effective for the militant as well as for the many who did not participate at all; and that trade unionism, to the extent and only to the extent that it appeals to the minds as well as to the self-interests of men, always leaves behind it individuals with ineradicable commitments to keep trying. From 1900 to 1975 unionists reduced the area of unlimited power over people's lives and were able to hold it in check over time. That was the substance of their history through three-quarters of a century.

If their progress is measured by improvements in the conditions of labor and life, it was not spectacular. Wages and housing, the principal and most readily available indexes of the condition of the farm laboring class, were reported by government bodies, journalists, and scholars in a dismal chronicle. The Bureau of Labor Statistics found in the Imperial Valley in 1925 that "growers have made no effort to protect the health and decency of their Mexican workers," who were housed in "filthy shacks on their ranches."[9] A special committee investigating violence against strikers in the valley "found filthy squalor" and "scenes that violate all the recognized standards of living."[10] Mae Stoneman, an officer of the State Federation of Labor, described to its convention in 1938 migrant families "living in river bottoms . . . camped under trees and bluffs under the most revolting conditions."[11] In March 1942 the Fresno *Bee* was moved to promote through its news stories a public collection for families stranded without food, shelter, or transportation in some of the richest cotton country in the nation. The plague of poverty continued year after year. When a state legislative committee observed the same area seven years later it called the west side labor camps of

Fresno, Kern, and Tulare "slums of miserable shacks."[12] Lester Velie, a nationally prominent journalist, wrote in *Collier's Magazine* in April 1950 of "mud-sodden camps and knocked-down trailers—thumbnail sketches of incredible misery." That same year and in another part of the Central Valley a special agent for the state justice department, was amazed to find people living in hovels under "terrible conditions."[13] In Hemet, the center of the apricot country midway between Bakersfield and the Mexican border, the crop was picked that year by hundreds of Mexican families who pitched camp on bare earth and used stone pits for cooking.

On this evidence life and labor in rural California for harvesters remained stagnant and miserable for fifty years. During the 1930s and after, the steady flow of uprooted Mexicans and southerners into the labor pool kept wages low and jobs rationed to guarantee a common lot of near-starvation.

This was the small end of the California cornucopia.

From the large end poured an abundance of wealth into the hands of those who owned the soil, in a distribution appropriate to the contrasting qualities of the propertied and the propertyless classes. It was believed that "the wage workers are for the most part a separate social class from their employers and the permanent residents of the community."[14] Mexicans were set apart because they "fit well on jobs not requiring any great degree of mentality, and do not object to dirt." Demographic containment, a stern judiciary, hostile sheriffs, and local police supervised by county political boards attuned to growers, if not indeed composed of them, stabilized social and economic relations in rural California.

In normal times, that is, when the farm workers were quiescent, Californians were not greatly concerned over these conditions. They survived the occasional protests of indignant government investigators and the stories of prowling newspapermen. But when discontent rose and strikes threatened or broke out, an explanation was necessary. The "red menace" answered the purpose. It was a simple way to raise local hysteria among small farmers, merchants, and the peace-loving citizens who managed to make a living in the shade of corporate agriculture. These mobilizations of vigilantes provided the knuckle power that beat organizers and the trigger-happy gunmen who occasionally shot them to death.

In many respects the suppression of the Salinas strike of lettuce workers in the summer of 1936 was the full-dress demonstration of the resources and skills that the industry could count on to keep its laborers in hand: a citizen's association to legitimize suppression; a headquarters staffed by military experts: private detectives, local police, state patrolmen, and roving goons; importation of strike breakers; armed assaults on farm labor camps; disciplinary pressures on farmers hesitant to join the general panic by depriving them of credit, ice, containers, storage space, and transportation; and a public relations campaign to arouse the urban middle class to the overriding priority of heads of lettuce over human heads.

Considering the history of farm laborers up to Salinas, it was remarkable that they struck so persistently and that the industry showed so little wear and tear after so many encounters. The strikes were episodes in an intermittent insurgency. Over the long run it was a protest taken in hand by a succession of trade unions whose sum total of accomplishment was to wrest some small economic gain, maintain a connection between a million people isolated from the larger society, offer them the prospect of collective bargaining, deflect the most uncivil reprisals, and keep an aggressive propertied class in fear of social ostracism.

These efforts became a serious challenge to corporate agriculture and its institutional supports. Undoubtedly they suffered a loss of moral repute, being put to much expense and ingenuity to maintain a believable public image. As the outrages of the vigilantes became less frequent, they developed more sophisticated controls over the masses of men that worked the fields as well as over the various sections of society—government, the police, the courts, technology, academia, the media—that in one way or another served the system of mobile men and money. The resulting establishment was Agri-businessland, to which we now turn our attention in some detail.

II: Agri-businessland

There is a deceptiveness about social systems that beguiles those who view them, because of fondness, interest, or perversity, as a product exclusively, ignoring them as a process. The present is only the front end of a culture. On its surface it is possible to trace boundaries, categories, types, classes, and settlements that can be isolated for semantic treatment to the delight of scholars and the advantage of politicians. It is like viewing a kaleidoscope clamped firmly in a vice so it will not turn even slightly and scatter the charmingly frozen image. There is a certain peace of mind in peering at such images, as there is in gazing at seemingly immovable social institutions.

From a distant perspective, Agri-businessland had that look when the Southern Tenant Farmers Union under its new name, the National Farm Workers Union, went west. It came upon one of those cultural artifacts fashioned over time by the winners of the West, the agri-businessmen. They had worked diligently, appropriating, discarding, adapting, inventing, shaping, sharpening, and remolding the many facets of a new economy and a new polity. Each of these was a component of the long process originally propelled by the self-interests of particular actors, none of whom had a grand design, all of whom had license to hunt freely in a perpetual open season the resources of the West. In time they became cunningly articulated, more abundant in the human debris they left behind them, more efficiently integrated, upward and crosswise. What they had in common was a prowling search to simplify, articulate, discard, and combine more and more until a multifaceted agri-business would look like the model of the multinational corporation. Abstracting them for a closer view, these components can be identified.

The Land

John Milton never saw California, but his poetic vision of the promised land could have been written from the peak of Mount Shasta looking south:

> It was a mountain at whose verdant feet
> A spacious plain outstretched in circuit wide
> Lay pleasant; from his side two rivers flowed,
> The one winding, the other straight, and left between
> Fair Campaign, with less rivers interveined,
> Then meeting joined their tribute to the sea.

The "rich furred garden of yellow," as naturalist John Muir saw it in 1912, was some twenty thousand square miles of unstaked Paradise.

With the 1848 change in sovereignty California was opened to as many as were ready, able, and willing to acquire a piece of it by settlement, possession, work, purchase, force, or fraud. The State of California, before 1880, disposed of more than eight million acres in these various ways. The Homestead Act of 1862 was intended to prevent monopoly from becoming the dominant form of land ownership but Congress, trying to give something to everybody, provided the single-family homesteaders with the stimulating competition of corporations starting in business with hundreds of thousands of acres in assets. When the scramble for land was over, railway corporations held more than eleven million acres of what had been public domain. The effect of this competition did not become clear for another half century. There was enough open space as late as 1914 to permit homestead entries for nearly five million acres with twenty-one million acres of vacant public lands still available.[15]

Small farmers could remain competitive in urban markets that were nearby and not across the continent. Proximity to such markets enable family farming to produce and deliver independently and to delay the integration into the web of agri-business. As long as mechanization of agricultural production was occupied with the simpler operations, such as plowing and hauling, even small farms could profitably substitute horsepower for manpower. University extension information and counseling services seemed to be keeping the small man abreast of the big one. When seasonal harvesters were necessary the small farmer found ways of dipping into the labor pool. Statistically, the small units of ownership and production were holding their ground well into the mid-1950s when over 120,000 of them were counted.

The count suggested that homesteading was surviving, but not much more. The grants of land and the provision of services by the government were even more generous to corporations moving toward monopoly. In contrast to the way of life of the farm family, theirs was a way to profit. Large landholdings became the backbone of the agricultural industry, producing the greatest value of crops, employing the largest number of seasonal wage workers, and applying the most horse-power through machines.

It was on these holdings that the economies of business management could be applied, the barriers to efficiency removed, and the factors of success—technical, managerial, financial, and political—coordinated.

These strongholds of corporate property were not marked on the landscape by plantation mansions or turreted castles. They were nonetheless centers of a dominant system of getting things done. The di Giorgio Fruit Corporation, the largest single producer and shipper of fresh fruits and vegetables in the United States, operated 11,000 acres in Arvin and 5,000 acres in Delano. The 97,000-acre Irvine ranch straddled the southern California country from the hills to the sea, its citrus plantings alone covering 6,000 acres.[16] El Tejon ranch, sprawled over the Tehachapi range, began with a Mexican grant of 1843 and in the 1960s had expanded from its original 97,000 acres to 300,000. The Kern County Land Company, a corporation with more than 12,000 stock-holders, owned more than 1,900,000 acres in four western states, of which 75,000 were under cultivation. The company owned and operated its own system of irrigation canals. The Newhall-Saugus Land and Farming Company carried on intensive cultivation of produce on thousands of acres within an hour by truck of Los Angeles. The central part of the state had its own green giants. The Spreckels Sugar Company, the successor of another Mexican grant, with its refinery dominated the Salinas Valley. In 1952 the Boswell Company, engaged in cotton growing and cattle feeding, owned or controlled 100,000 acres. The Salyer Farms, based in Corcoran in the lower west side of the Central Valley, in 1959 farmed 30,000 acres, some its own land and some under lease, the base for multiple operations that made it the economic government de facto of the area. In northern California the units were not so large in acreage but were nonetheless outstanding. Corporations and partnerships dominated the rich delta of the San Joaquin-Sacramento river with tracts of as many as 4,000 acres in one crop, such as asparagus. Not far to the south the Coit ranch of Mendota had 8,000 acres in cantaloups, alfalfa, cotton, and barley. In rice production, centered around Colusa County, farming was carried on in units of thousands of acres in a sweeping panorama specked by an occasional farmhouse.

Such holdings, standing by themselves, did not fully show the base on which capitalist agri-corporatism rested. They were often linked to larger patterns that emphasized even more their corporate character and their strategic position as an economic reserve of large-scale private enterprise. The Boston Land Company, the Southern Pacific Railroad, and twelve other enterprises in the west Central Valley owned over

81,000 acres of land in active or potential cultivation. The Standard Oil Company of California in the 1940s held over 200,000 acres. The largest of these operations, by which some of the most sophisticated of America's industrial and financial private enterprises became involved in rural California, was that of the Southern Pacific Company. In 1958 it managed some 4,000,000 acres in California, Nevada, and Utah, 165,000 acres of which were devoted to the most advanced practices in agriculture.

Direct ownership provided the core of control but was supplemented by leasing in two principal forms. The large operators found it expedient to acquire rights by rental or to grant such rights by leasing to tenants. Such arrangements made it extremely difficult to locate even the approximate boundaries of actual control over the disposition of land or the uses to which it was put at any given time. Leasing also became a device by which small farmers unwilling to be squeezed out sought to keep themselves competitive. It was their way of attempting to equalize the difference in unit costs between them and those who had received the lion's share of federal public lands.

In another way the large grantees had a remarkable advantage that improved with time. Their holdings were strategically located in the paths of future facilities constructed with public funds that added to the value of rural land, such as irrigation projects, reclamation, and roads. These facilities capitalized the land reserves of the large properties, which were in a position to take advantage of them. In Fresno County, the heart of Agri-businessland, agricultural acreage increased an average of 5 percent each decade in the first half of the twentieth century. Lands that had been passed by until the 1940s in favor of the bonanza flats of the valleys were now brought within the range of profitable operation by those who could work them on a large scale. In the 1960s such a new frontier was opened by the construction of the San Luis Dam on the western rim of the Central Valley.

As California agriculture became more and more commercial actual monopoly of ownership was held in check by the official policy of maintaining the balance between the homestead and the corporation. One threat against this balance was thwarted by the Alien Land Law of 1913—"to prevent aliens who are ineligible for citizenship from owning land in California." Going further, Congress limited holdings served by federally financed irrigation projects to 160 acres, intended to set a limit to corporate encroachment. Repeal of that law became the major objective of a campaign pitched to the theme that acreage limitation is "a form of vassalage . . . an archaic and ridiculous device to impose petty political tyranny on agriculture."[17]

In the 125 years that followed the American occupation of California,

agriculture continued indisputably as the base of its economy. Corporation farms held the most productive and advantageous portions of the
land. These units dominated the production of food, bending it to the
requirements of corporate business enterprise. Next in importance to
the land was water.

Water

John Muir's "rich furred garden of yellow" on second inspection
presented as many problems as promises. Great spots in the Central
Valley were sandy wastes. Rivers were numerous but their courses, dry
beds in some seasons, became rampaging floods when heavy snow
packs in the Sierra Nevada melted in the spring thaws. In the lesser
valleys that ringed the great central bowl, like the Salinas and Imperial,
rich soil deposits received either too much water or too little. For all its
poetic glamour much of the state was an arid pocket beset by scorching
summers. Altogether it contained some nineteen million acres of potential farm land, but to make them productive required water, rationed,
reliable, and plentiful.

On a scale determined by the size of mission lands and the character of
their production, the Catholic priests who opened California to Spanish
settlement in the 1760s introduced irrigation, adopted from a Mexican
and Spanish tradition. From these early predecessors private entrepreneurs took their cue and organized local private irrigation systems that
were in the course of time extended or consolidated into larger ones. For
the next three quarters of a century they dominated the scene. Taken
together, these private establishments—Kern County Land Company,
Fresno Consolidated Canals, Sacramento Valley Irrigation Company,
and others—gained control of hundreds of thousands of acres of the
most desirable land in the state.[18]

This was the American competitive system in its best form. Where
water rights conflicted the contest was fought with guns., lawsuits,
bribes, political wile, and legislative corruption. By the 1920s the larger
canal companies had spheres of influence in various sections of the
state, none of them capable of responding to the "Water Problem" of

the state as a whole. Up to 1890 only one million acres were under irrigation, clearly too slow a pace for an industry eager to feed the world and make money.

American free enterprise has been a progress marked by spacious cycles from private capitalist accumulation asking nothing but to be left alone to public funding of large undertakings which are too costly, too green, or too ripe for private risk. The former case is called "providing the infrastructure", the latter, "subsidizing ailing corporations." From the standpoint of water-short agriculturists California irrigation was in the first of these stages: too inadequate, too risky, too expensive, and too slow. Over seventy million dollars in capital had gone into the hundreds of private networks of canals and dams. In 1930 less than one percent of the irrigated acreage had been developed through federal financing.[19] Only half the farms were supplied with water and the twenty-one thousand miles of ditches of all types were insufficient to service the rest.[20] It was time for the next gigantic thrust of infrastructuring.

Out of this emerged the California water plan of 1931, from which no major agricultural area was excluded. Eventually all the valleys were to be joined in a network of reservoirs, grand canals, pumping stations, percolation pools, and the hydroelectric power plants necessary to set the whole in motion.

The plan, floated on federal appropriations, was well under way by 1960, and the state was becoming, in the glowing phrase of the California Blue Book, "one huge reclamation project," with some eight million acres served and the capital investment climbing into the billions of dollars. In the integrated project nearly a thousand reservoirs stored forty-two million acre feet between seasons.[21]

The two outstanding exhibits of this engineering feat were the Imperial Valley Irrigation District and the Central Valley Project. To convert Imperial into a winter garden of fresh vegetables the federal government damned the Colorado River well back into the mountains, regulated the flow, and delivered it by gravity through mains and laterals that spilled into thousands of acres of wasteland. From the air the cultivated valley became a baize of greens of every hue trimly marked except along the edges where the desert chewed persistently on the neat carpet of vegetation. With more than enough water for its own needs, Imperial stretched its canals northward, taking water to the shady date gardens, grapefruit groves, and vineyards of the Coachella Valley.

Vast in scale compared with the Imperial Valley Irrigation District, the Central Valley Project undertook nothing less than to balance land and water resources between the northern and southern areas of the Sacramento and San Joaquin basins. Two-thirds of the irrigable land lay in the south and two-thirds of the water originated in the north. Using combined state and federal funds, the Central Valley Project was scheduled to bring water to sixty thousand more acres a year, enough to create 21,500 new farms. By December 1959 $634,000,000 had been spent on construction. The projected final cost rose from $900,000,000 to nearly two billion dollars. As it grew the CVP left its mark everywhere on the Central Valley—the level crest of the Shasta Dam, the battery of huge penstocks of the Tracy pumping plant, the white ribbons of con-crete of the two canals that flanked the valley on the west side, and the terminal pool from which the water was lifted hundreds of feet and emptied into the canyons of the Tehachapi on its way to Los Angeles.

The goal of all this was not only to make water available but to provide it at a cost low enough to permit its users to convert it into profitable cash crops. With interest-free loans for ditching and pumping and with water at $14 per acre foot, the value of farm income on the west side of the Central Valley could maintain a level of $80,000,000 a year; without government subsidies it could fall as low as $25,000,000. In a southern district like Blythe, water was sold by the government at even lower rates, $10 to $12 per acre foot. The White Rock Dam was counted on to reduce irrigation costs from $485 to $50, with the expectation that the cost could be reduced further to $10 per acre foot.[22]

As old production units increased in value because of the availability and the subsidized price of water, new and hitherto unprofitable tracts were planted with cash crops. The upland meadows of Pacheco Pass, where underground veins of moisture had fed serpentines of poppies, watercress, and bluebells, resplendent but unmarketable, became or-chards and irrigated stands of grain; between 1940 and 1960 more than 225,000 acres of pasture and stubble land were converted to fruit and vegetable production.

To match so vast a gift of land with an equally generous gift of water became the goal of the engineers, the promoters, and the politicians of the 1930s. The goal was accomplished in less than thirty years. It was as if Achsah again had said to Caleb: "Thou hast given me a southland, give me also springs of water."[23]

Public enterprise having done so well at infrastructuring itself at public expense, the agricultural industry was now ready to swing toward private control of irrigation; or if not private control, at least to a transfer of jurisdiction to the government of the State of California, which was judged to be more responsive than the federal. Senator Sheridan Dow-ney spoke strenuously for the repeal of the Draconian 160-acre limita-tion law. *Business Week* as far back as 1954 suggested some possible strategies for recapturing the largest and most valuable asset of the state next to the land. These included giving the U.S. Army Corps of Engineers more control over water projects, which the government was developing gratis for the wealthy producers who could afford the necessary but expensive pumps; and the purchase outright of the entire Central Valley Project by the State of California. As experience had demonstrated, in transactions involving the transfer of public property to private hands on such a scale the state government was amenable to settling for ten cents on the dollar of the original cost. Senator Downey's campaign was given a welcome boost in 1958, when Attorney General Edmund G. Brown interpreted a 1933 ruling of Secretary of the Interior Ray Lyman Wilbur to the effect that the acreage limitation law did not apply to the Imperial Valley Irrigation District.

As surveyors mark elevations and land levels on their maps and engineers locate gradients for canals, so political scientists could mark the lines of power which in California was compounded of soil and water. On them Agri-businessland rested and prospered and was content.

Labor

When the National Agricultural Workers Union made its first contact with California farm laborers these were loosely stratified in three types—domestics, braceros, and undocumented migrants without legal status of any kind. Vast differences in culture and ethos separated these groups despite their common class status as rural proletarians.

The total number of persons who participated in harvesting in the late 1940s was probably close to 500,000 including family farmers of whom 140,000 were "local" wage laborers. For present purposes no account is taken of the labor inputs of farm families or of year-round employees, of which there were in those years some 100,000 and 120,000 respectively. Half a million persons available at the peak of the harvest cycle was the number considered necessary to move the crops, roughly one-third of them families moving within contracting circles of intrastate seasonal migrancy.

The Domestic Workers

The domestic workers were in the broadest sense those available for farm employment in any section of the labor market of the United States. Within the continuous reshuffling of two million or more laborers of this general type there was a tendency in California, as in other parts of the Southwest, to reduce the circles of migration and to stabilize them. It was as if farm workers as a national class were so many steel filings on a sheet of paper, under which there moved the magnetic influence of available jobs. Where the magnet paused seasonally, recognizable patterns appeared. These workers moved in a constant flux, but many remained in one area for increasingly long periods of precarious residence, choosing to wait out the "seasons of repose" between harvests. This was the sector of the farm laboring class that more and more came to identify itself as the domestics. For the Spanish-speaking Mexicans the word was *locales*. The process can be compared to floating islands in the labor pool that eventually anchored themselves in shallow spots over silting mudbanks. Considering the physical conditions in which thousands of families lived during the cold and rainy winters, the metaphor is not as forced as might at first appear.

The domestic was the core of the labor pool and manifested all its characteristics. He tended to become less mobile, resisting the drift around him. Like his more transient contemporaries he was a marginal laborer. As an interchangeable unit he was replaceable; his mobility was horizonal, in and out of the migrant force, not upward and out of it. He was competitive with his own children, with prison labor, with students on summer vacations, and with the urban unemployed. The agricultural employers had long ago settled upon the formula that "two or three men for each job is about right.[24] To maintain this ratio they had flung their networks of recruitment far and wide to China, Japan, the Philippines, Mexico, and the Deep South. In due course the domestics became an assortment of races, colors, and cultures, all of them detached from their original territorial base, and all seeking in common a new one.

Viewed as a minority within the larger society, the domestics served a number of roles. Ethnically and culturally their settlements were the natural ports of entry for new arrivals. In that way the labor pool was constantly replenished and conditioned to the ways of American employers. In the Mexican *colonias* and the Filipino clubs acculturation of the newcomers began and the skills required by highly specialized cropping were passed on. It was from the ranks of domestics that the industry recruited row bosses, field foremen, checkers, and camp overseers. These were the pacesetters on whom the employers relied for efficient field operations. This seasonal host could not be totally mobile and transient without reducing productivity. The best equipped were the domestics who had attained the know-how of harvesting. Only those who persisted in stereotyping all harvest hands as "unskilled" failed to acknowledge the many skills that proper handling of tomatoes or canta- loups or peaches required. These skills, practiced with the economy of motion and effort that only experience can bring and refined into a kind of wisdom of work, the domestics possessed.

With respect to the working class of the industrial sector, the domes- tics played an equally important role. Into their ranks unemployed urban workers retreated during the cyclical crises of the nation. Harvesting was the training ground for packing shed and cannery workers; without recruits from the fields the processing would have become a bottleneck. Since they were not organized for economic bargaining, the domestics could not press upon the industry demands that would have brought economic benefits equal to those of the teamsters who moved the crops from the fields or of the cannery workers who processed them. Trade- union economics reflected trade-union power, and the wages of poverty in the fields became a condition of economic improvement for the workers in the other branches of the industry.

These important functions of the domestics were out of proportion to their numbers in the total labor force of the state. In 1958, according to official data of the California Department of Employment, of 4,487,000 employed persons 422,000 were in agriculture, forestry, and fishing. At most 300,000 of these would have been farm workers.

The point to which this brief reference to the domestic workers must return, so that its importance is not missed, is that they represented the tendency to bring social form and structure to the formlessness of the labor pool. What John Steinbeck wrote of the migrants of the Salinas Valley was true of all the domestics in their early stages—"they lacked almost every necessity that reason demanded they should have to put down roots in such a hostile environment." But in time they did, and these grew into towns like Arvin, Delano, Mendota, Olivehurst, and Soledad. Settlements like these absorbed even the massive tide of dust bowl refugees, of whom some 250,000 entered California between 1930 and 1940. It was their resilience in sharing poverty that absorbed the seasonal collapse of jobs, which in Fresno County, for example, fell from a peak of 32,000 in September to less than 500 in the winter. It was in these agricultural towns that most of the news passed from mouth to mouth about crop conditions, wages, and availability of housing, prompting families to stay in place or to move temporarily.

Workers who did not have their own transportation and would have

been limited to local job markets provided a commuter population for
the day hauls. In the larger cities as well as in the rural towns day
laborers converged on staging points where they boarded fleets of trucks
in various stages of deterioration for a day's work in the fields and
orchards. There were dozens of these pick-up points throughout the
state, providing thousands of harvesters who "shaped up" at dawn and
disbanded at dusk. Round trips of more than a hundred miles were not
unusual, often starting at 3:00 A.M. and ending after dark. For such
transportation the fares varied from 50 cents to a dollar or more, the
premium paid to obtain a day's wages for fifteen hours at work and on
the road.

The major day-haul terminals, such as those of Fresno, Sacramento,
and Oakland, became so-called "skid rows," where transiency was the
way of life. These were rows of run-down rooming houses where single
wanderers could "flop" for a night or longer, shuffling out in the early
morning darkness to make sidewalk deals with the truckers who operated the day haul. Job offers were hawked by foremen and growers who
pulled away when a gang was aboard. As daylight came over the dismal
scene the crowd on the sidewalks thinned, leaving stragglers who filed
out of sight into dingy shops for bad coffee and cheap wine. Occasionally
a police patrol car would circle the area, marking the limits within which
idle skid-rowers could wander. At night the trucks returned, spilling
along the row tired men who disappeared into dank rooms smelling of
disinfectant or shuffled to the evening handout of food under the il-
lumined cross of the Salvation Army which said with persistent compassion: "Jesus Saves."

Not all the participants who sought jobs in the skid row labor market
were single, out-of-town transients; as many as one out of five might be
local residents who walked for miles for day-haul work when nothing
else was to be had. Their presence indicated how uncertain were the
boundaries between the different stages of mobility of the domestics.

The stereotype of the skid row hiring system became the "wino,"
whose image of alcoholic degradation continued a long tradition of
contempt for the most mobile and the least favored of the harvesters. It
was adopted by the industry as the synonym for "lazy bums" and was
commonly applied to any workers who demanded higher wages or
joined a union or picketed a farm. Just as the Chinese, Japanese,
Filipinos, and Mexicans had been stamped with images that explained
their unsuitability when a cheaper source of labor appeared, so now the
domestics, by association, were classed as "winos"—unworthy, unreliable, and unproductive.

Skid row, behind all its squalor, was a dramatic sign of the direction in which domestic workers as a class were moving in a mechanized, gasoline-powered agriculture. The direction was down, skid row being the ultimate illustration of men considered as residues of an industrial process. At this level the word *domestic* lost its vague suggestion of rights of residence, seniority, merit, and claims of consideration for services.

That the domestics as part of the farm labor force tended to move not up but down the agricultural ladder made it obvious that the laws of the land did not recognize such rights. In fact the industry had gone to extremes of violence to prevent such recognition in collective contracts. The domestics in the 1940s numbered perhaps one hundred thousand, were destined for replacement and relocation to cities that were already crowded with their own poor.

Alien Contract Workers—the Braceros

Since the bracero system is described in considerable detail in my book *Merchants of Labor,*[25] here only enough will be said on the subject to place it in this context of Agri-businessland.

Pursuing their traditional search for new supplies of manpower, California farm employers had reason to intensify it with the outbreak of World War II. The full employment that war always brings raised foreign labor importation to the level of an urgent measure of national defense. Railway and agricultural corporations were quick to see the opportunity and they turned southward for manpower. It was hardly necessary for Congressman Cranford to remind them that "the two real sources of raw labor in the Western Hemisphere" were Mexico and Puerto Rico.[26] Senator Ellender of Louisiana agreed; raw labor from south of the border had been found appropriate "to make available an ample supply" of agricultural manpower.

Amplitude was to be understood to mean sufficient numbers to take the place of the thousands of domestics who were seeking higher wages in wartime industries throughout the Southwest—and sufficient also to displace them permanently when the pressure of war would disappear and the labor force would be thrown into another of those massive reversals that Congress seemed never to foresee.

To the sense of urgency created by the war there were added shrewd hopes of corporate farmers who had endured decades of disappointment beginning with the "heathen Chinese" and culminating with the American winos. Like Clemens Horst, on whose hop ranch the bloody Wheatland strike had occurred, they continued to search for a system of employment by which the growers could improve their position. The American Farm Bureau Federation stressed that "Mexican workers [braceros] unaccompanied by wives and families . . . can fill our seasonal peaks and return home . . . without creating difficult social problems." To an Assistant Secretary of Agriculture the braceros appeared as "a highly mobile task force" that could be moved "from one area to another as they are needed." An attorney speaking for the industry told a state legislative committee that the bracero legislation "completely removes the possibility" of the bracero ever becoming a part of the American labor movement. The California Farm Bureau Federation pointed out that the domestics in contrast with "braceros" were free men and could seek employment elsewhere when working conditions dissatisfied them.

In July 1951 Congress formalized its approval in Public Law 78. It was to be what Congressman Poage described as an orderly method of employment under the law, "to provide employment for the citizens of a friendly republic, safeguard the living standards of the laboring people of the United States, and protect human rights."[27] On these grounds the United States government began subsidizing bracero recruiting in 1942.

With the authority that Congress delegated to it and that the courts were later to sustain, the U.S. Department of Labor became, on behalf of corporation agriculture, the prime contractor for braceros.

In the decade preceding the enactment of Public Law 78 bracero hiring was a somewhat erratic experiment in mixed management, with growers determining the need and the federal government providing financial support and administrative facilities. After 1951 the balance of responsibility shifted toward the government, the object being to stabilize the supply of men by means of tri-lateral negotiations, understandings, agreements, and contracts. The three participants were the growers, the United States government, and the Mexican government. The bracero himself was a participant after the fact—he was permitted to sign his individual work contract after its terms had been approved.

Under these arrangements nearly 40,000 braceros were contracted in California in 1952; 90,000 in 1959. These men were a part of a larger host recruited for Texas and other southwestern states. Nevada, Arizona, and California together accounted for 171,000 braceros in 1955. Altogether an estimated 2,000,000 Mexicans under contract passed through California between 1942 and 1960. As growers became more certain that they had a guaranteed source of manpower and as they discovered how to apply it advantageously to an increasing variety of operations, the use of braceros in many crops increased at the expense of the domestics. In 1957, of the harvest force that picked tomatoes in

San Joaquin Valley 92 percent were braceros; 93 percent in the lettuce harvest of Imperial County; 94 percent in celery in San Diego County. In central and northern California the percentages were smaller, but increased toward eventual domination of the harvest labor market for the entire state.

The braceros came from all parts of Mexico, principally from rural areas. Among them were small farmers who had abandoned some hillside patch of corn in Guanajuato, *ejidatarios* from the collective farms of Sonora, day laborers from Zacatecas, and sharecroppers from Nuevo Leon. Not all were landworkers, however. Recruiting attracted men from towns and cities—taxi drivers, mill hands, porters, and elevator operators. Rumors that in these occupations pay was far less in a year than in three months as a bracero swept over Mexico like a warm and inviting breeze. So widespread and enticing were the reports that they added almost a new dimension to the national awareness.

The spell not only cut across occupational differences but also through cultural and ethnic borders. Indians from Tlaxcala, small wiry men who spoke only the tribal tongue, showed up in Yuba City. Mountain men from Guerrero, accustomed to a life of steep ups and downs, found themselves chopping cotton or weeding beets on the sweeping flats of the Central Valley. The first-timers were usually men under forty, more likely to have come from isolated *rancherias*. The repeaters, who had two or more turns as contractees, became the sophisticates of the camps, the ones to whom cultural impact came not only as wonder over the technical ingeniousness of their gringo bosses but also as a resentful discovery of their devices for getting the most work out of the least pay. For a tiny minority of the repeaters, new prospects for advancement were opened by employers who promoted the more agile and dexterous and obsequious to the rank of checker, row overseer, truck tender, or camp helper. For the bracero, these steps pointed to the favored place in the employer's esteem, longer contracts, and possibly a permanent job on the ranch in the category of a "special."

As a form of labor management the braceros represented a nearly ideal combination of reliability during the harvest, guaranteeing "the men will be here Monday morning," and the mobility that removed them from the scene "when we no longer want them." If the time, the route, the direction, the pace, and the purpose of moving about are dimensions of the freedom of men, the braceros enjoyed a type of directed, supervised freedom. They did move about, but only within the boundaries of the authorized area of employment and for the duration of the work. At other times they were based in camps and provided with barracks, cabins or tents. On rainy days or during lulls in the harvest the men lay on their cots under improvised indoor clotheslines strung with everything from socks to overalls. On such days the mood in the bunk-houses tended to be as gloomy as the weather, giving the men time to mull over what they would be charged for meals, and what they would lose in earnings during the lay-off. They secured their foot lockers as well as they could; the petty thieves and the card sharks invaded the security of the men's meager possesssions just as the open dormitories did the privacy of their lives.

The braceros were marked off from the domestics insofar as they could be managed as a separate component of the labor force. The work assignments were arbitrary, lodgings were shuffled capriciously, meals were priced by a cost formula known only to the managers, payroll records were coded. The individual work contract that each bracero was given contained four pages of small print that set forth all the ways in which he was separate and more equal than the domestic worker.

In reality the world of the braceros was not as insulated as the industry wanted it. On shopping trips to the towns they mingled with the Mexican *locales* in restaurants, stores, bars, and wherever Spanish was spoken. Hundreds of repeaters broke ranks before their contracts ended; they became "skips" on the official records. By skipping they became "libres" (free men), getting lost among the thousands of fellow Mexicans who made up the clandestine part of the labor force. Cultural similarities prevailed where class distinctions were arbitrarily drawn and imperfectly controlled. Thus there developed an interchange between braceros who became wetbacks, illegals who returned to Mexico to be contracted, domestics who abandoned the struggle and returned to Mexico, to begin again in the land of their birth or of their ancestors. Sometimes all three—braceros illegals, and domestics—worked side by side in temporary gangs formed by chance or by design of employers.

While the braceros came and went with the seasons, the view of the growers, that as a system they were becoming an integral part of the farm labor market, turned from a fond hope to a firm conviction. The trade journals of Agri-businessland affirmed it in their editorials and government officials said it privately. In spite of the report of a national commission created by President Truman in June 1950, which documented the social dislocations that were already appearing, the permanent supply of braceros became a central goal of corporate farming.

This was understandable. The demand for Mexican laborers, originally justified by a war emergency, over twenty years revealed the many possibilities for exploiting them. At different levels of the system these opportunities ranged from the petty to the gross; taken together they created a combination of interests bent on perpetuating the conditions and practices that had evolved around the administration of Public Law 78.

A labor force that could be expanded or contracted at will enabled the industry to increase crops that offered larger profits or to diminish those that threatened losses by overproduction. Braceros made possible the increase in strawberry plantings from some seven thousand acres in 1951 to more than twenty thousand in 1957. Speculation in agriculture, always cumbersome and languid compared to other forms of entering and taking, became more agile with the flexible inputs of alien contract labor at its disposal. Significant savings in the wage outlay for harvesting became possible by discarding domestics and lowering wage scales to more economical ratios with fertilizer, machinery, fuel, and other non-human inputs. The services which were provided by the employers without direct charge to the workers and which became indirect labor costs enabled growers to hold down the subsistence levels of the braceros with which the domestic, who did not receive such free services, was not able to compete. Bracero wages fell so low that employers could pay contracting fees and graft to Mexican government officials without disturbing the margin of costs for braceros as compared with domestics. The artichoke producers of Castroville reduced picking costs by more than half. Beet growers who learned to combine braceros with machines harvested an acre at $13 instead of $32.

These were some of the forms of more profitable exploitation practiced on high management levels. In addition the braceros were mulcted in numerous and petty ways, through overcharges for merchandise in the camps, fees for cashing pay checks, and the perennial chiseling on the price and quality of meals.

The cost-benefit audit of bracero hiring explains why braceros were considered an asset in Agri-businessland.

Outcast Labor—the Wetbacks

When individuals or groups qualify for the statistical attention of society, counted by the census takers and tabulated by demographers, they achieve recognition and a degree of identity. A society which counts its members by the millions must of necessity periodically locate them, describing their various roles and attributes. Invariably some get lost in the count, by choice or by accident. Anonymity of this kind points to a defect in the census system that governments usually strive to keep within the bounds of statistical reasonableness.

The exceptions were rare. One of them was the rule among the census takers in Imperial to the effect that "wetbacks who live in as domestic servants can be counted . . . even if they live in a small apartment in the rear." Since the information was confidential no reports were made to the Immigration Service; and the advantage was that, to cite an example, "the City of El Centro will receive from various state funds six dollars for every name in excess of the 1950 population; . . . these wetbacks will be providing the city with some revenue."[28]

In the farm labor force of California there was regularly present a large sector that was always absent from the census returns. These workers, men and women, came to be known variously as "wetbacks," "line jumpers," or "illegals." They were Mexican citizens who entered the United States clandestinely in search of jobs and who lived in perpetual alert against arrest and deportation. They did not wish to be counted, and government agencies and employers tacitly agreed that they were indeed numerous and important, but regrettably not identifiable. Behind this official anonymity there existed an extra-legal labor market that operated side by side with that of domestics and braceros, one that was continuously dissolving and reforming. In such a situation totally devoid of social form or structure the illegals lived in a vacuum of American society—economic, legal, moral.

The increase of illegal entries into the United States from Mexico beginning with the 1920s can be described as a demographic spill caused by the increasingly sharp differences in economic and social opportunity south and north of the Rio Grande. The Mexican revolution was beginning to fail its promise of land and liberty for the Mexican *campesino*; at the same time large-scale agriculture in California and other southwestern states was reclaiming the West and searching for wage laborers. This imbalance was partly corrected as more and more Mexicans found their way northward through an open border. The Mexican population increased, political instability continued, and living standards tilted more sharply in favor of the United States. By the time the Border Patrol was created in 1924 these and other factors had fixed a pattern of supply and demand for farm labor that could not be easily contained by a line of police. The currents of migration in both countries had established channels byways through which they continued to seek their own course. Just as in the Central Valley most of the water was in the north and most of the land in the south, so in the Southwest most of the unemployed were in Mexico and most of the work was in the United States.

The flaws in census taking concealed the number of illegals, but there were other clues. Agencies like the California Farm Placement Service could not ignore their presence altogether. Oblique references and guarded sources provided an elastic measure for this sector of the agricultural labor force. In 1948, for example, it was estimated that there were between thirty-five and sixty thousand illegals throughout California, four to six thousand of them in the Imperial Valley alone. Sophisticated guesses by the Border Patrol indicated that, in March 1950, ten thousand Mexicans crossed the border surreptitiously.[29] Even the figures on deportations indirectly suggested the volume of illegal movements. In 1956 over eighty thousand were granted the right of voluntary departure; the total number of deportees probably numbered half as many again. Though the figures were never precise, they were sufficient to indicate that wetbacks constituted a significant and permanent part of the farm labor market. During the tomato harvest of 1951 a confidential check made by an official of the Wage Stabilization Board and based on interviews with growers indicated that 60 percent of the labor was provided by illegals.[30]

Since there was no statistical evidence as to employed illegals, there were no official data as to their wages. Here again only random contacts with the illegals themselves and highly unreliable reports provided occasional clues. These included wages collected by state labor commissioners and sometimes even by the Immigration Service on behalf of arrested aliens before deportation. Destitution and fear of the police forced some wetbacks to accept wages as low as fifteen cents per hour. Employment agents advertised in Mexico that hardworking farmers were ready to accept minimum pay in exchange for employers' assistance to enter and remain in the United States. The minimum could range from a few cents to half the going wages paid domestics for similar work. In 1952 illegals worked as irrigators in the Imperial Valley for as little as thirty cents an hour. Just as braceros could be substituted for domestics at rates of pay that sometimes represented a difference of 30 cents an hour or more, so wetbacks were available to displace braceros at half or less what the braceros were guaranteed by contract. These were accurate indicators of the differences in levels of living of the three types of workers,—a difference which gave a rough measure of differential profits of the employers.

The uses, misuses and abuses to which the wetback labor market gave rise existed in a corner of the American scene incredibly deviant from normal American standards and values, devoid of sources of information, demanding of overriding proof. These conditions have been amply documented by journalists, government agencies, and social scientists.

As a footnote to the bleak record it may be noted that even the law took its toll of unpaid labor. In one instance a group of illegals who were detained at the Border Patrol compound in El Centro were put to work, without wages, constructing a small building on the premises.[31] It became necessary to order economy-minded border patrolmen to stop the forced labor of detainees.[32]

After repeated entries into California, illegals became familiar enough with the underground detours to find work far north of the border. The industry, however, could not rely on the uncertainties of self-help. Something approaching mass transportation was required, something that could work outside the law yet within the short-term requirements of harvesting. By the 1950s the logistics of contraband manpower had been worked out—a phantom fleet of run-down school buses and rattling trucks, staging depots, overnight stops and relays and pickup points serving the entire state. Experienced drivers knew the side roads where the Border Patrol was least likely to intercept them. The fares varied from fifty to a hundred dollars or more from the border to receiving points as far as five hundred miles away. The traffic was totally unscheduled, depending as it did on so many contingencies, but it regularly moved hundreds of men at the peak of harvesting. The distribution points were towns like Westmoreland, Indio, Cucamonga, Huron, Delano, Tracy, Alviso, Soledad, and Yuba City.

The movement of men in such numbers and on so large a scale was a public secret shared by growers, contractors, food purveyors, camp followers, and the Immigration Service. An intolerable evil had become, by its sheer proportions, moderately acceptable. "Yes, we have always had wet Mexicans. We have no doubt that both farmers and the Immigration Service look the other way," said the farm journal *Pacific Rural Press*, on June 17, 1949. It was a source of income for all those who provided mobility, supervision, shelter, food, liquor, and prostitutes. The mood of toleration was set by the farm employers, to whom the exploitation of illegals had become very nearly an iron law of economics. It spread to the local police and to the Immigration Service itself, which eased its conscience by reasoning that if all the wetbacks in California were placed under arrest the jails would be packed, the administrative machinery would become jammed, and the transportation system of the service itself paralyzed.

Among the illegals a different temper prevailed. As men who lived outside the law and passed their days under the watch of surly camp bosses, they combined the outward demeanor of human beings willing to submit to any indignity with an inward mettle that enabled them to survive. It was what Mexican peasants called "aguante," the ability to live through trying times, touched with a subtle pride that their mean, backbreaking tasks would exhaust other men. What was generally interpreted as fatalism by those who viewed the wetback casually on closer look proved to be patience under stress. Outwardly these were men intent on losing their identity, changing their names frequently, giving false addresses, producing forged birth certificates. As their behavior plainly showed, however, they were not persons who as a class were sickened by the loss of selfhood of the truly alienated. Among the illegals there were many with a hard core of awareness and ingenuity equal to the unending strains of survival. The Border Patrol had ample evidence of this in the cleverly camouflaged bush huts, the foxholes, the screened hollows in stacks of baled hay, the overnight billets in irrigation drains, the padlocks ostentatiously placed on doors of rooms into which weary wetbacks crawled through loose planks in the floor, the sandal tracks in the dust made by walking backwards, pointing toward Mexico.

The black market in Mexican farm labor flourished because it was provided with self-renewing mechanisms. South of the border illegal entry was facilitated by rings of smugglers who evaded Mexican immigration laws with as much ease as they violated those in the north. It was a felony in the United States to cross the border a second time, but in proportion to the mass of deportees the number prosecuted for second offenses was infinitesimal. Ways were found by the U.S. departments of Justice, State, and Labor to transform wetbacks into braceros without the formality of returning them to Mexico. Federal raids, airlifts, and massive roundups were tokens of enforcement that did little more than inconvenience the unlawful traffic.

The illegals as a class could have well served as a model of functional reduction of men to sheer utility more advantageous in some respects than slavery. Their disconnection from society was as complete as anything yet produced by capitalism, bountifully supplied with poor by a neighboring people. In California the social cost of their misfortunes was lifted from the industry and placed on unsuspecting taxpayers; returning to Mexico they were again nothing more that units in the free reserve of manpower on which corporate agriculture so heavily relied.

Because of its many irregularities, that part of the farm labor market supplied by illegals came closest to fitting the description of recruiting and hiring for harvesting as an "unstructured" labor market. By comparison with the collective bargaining that American workers had wrested from employers through unionism, the terms of the wage bargain in agriculture were indeed unregulated. Those who spoke for the industry saw no place for enforceable rules that limited the absolute control of labor as the prime factor in moving perishable crops. Employers exercised the right to set wages, conditions of production, work qualifications, standards of performance, hours, size and composition of crews, and procedures for measuring and recording work performance. On the laborer's side, there was indeed an alternative. He could refuse to work and take to the road again.

In point of fact, the farm labor market was not as unstructured as it appeared. Within each of the major sectors of disposable supply of manpower—domestics, braceros, and illegals—there had evolved over a period of fifty years certain mechanisms of direction and control suitable to the requirements of the free agricultural enterprise.

These mechanisms, respectively, were the Farm Placement Service, the associations of growers and shippers, and the farm labor contractors. The nature and operation of each of these must be noted separately, although in reality they functioned in complement. The boundaries between them reflected practical, informal understandings that made the manipulation of the three sectors of the labor force easier. The interests of shippers, growers, and processors dictated that under certain conditions the Farm Placement Service, created to serve domestics, could decisively affect the number and distribution of braceros; that the associations could preempt certain functions of the Farm Placement Service; and that illegals could be floated between contractors and the associations.

The Farm Placement Service

In accordance with the provisions of the Wagner-Peyser Act of 1933,[33] there was created the United States Employment Service, responsible for the organization and direction of farm placement. In order to operate within the State of California approval by the legislature was required and this was forthcoming in June 1933. It was one of the rare instances of inclusion in a federal statute of provisions relating to agricultural labor. It was acceptable to employers for two reasons. First, the act did not protect workers with respect to wages, housing, transportation, or other sensitive matters. Second, farm placement services were to be provided at no cost to the farmers since funding was to come from taxes levied for unemployment insurance, to which neither workers nor employers in agriculture contributed.

Except for an interval of three years, the FPS remained in the Department of Labor, the executive branch of the federal government charged with statutory and administrative supervision of legislation concerning the welfare of working people. From 1943 to 1946 the FPS was operated within the Agricultural Extension Service of the University of California, which in turn was subordinate to the U.S. Department of Agriculture. Under these auspices the FPS developed by 1946 into an establishment of over ninety permanent field offices reaching into forty-five counties and with a budget of $860,000. From its permanent offices it deployed mobile units that served as temporary information and referral stations as the harvests shifted.

Control of FPS operations centered in a Chief, who became the most powerful single individual in the state's farm labor market. The lines of administrative authority that were in his hands, the daily contacts of area supervisors and field men with those who owned the land and disposed of jobs, the total absence of such connections with workers, the recruitment of personnel from a class of small landholders and modest gentlemen farmers provided the framework of an administrative structure for the reservoir of seasonal domestics. Set up by federal and state legislation, the system provided growers channels of information on the current state of the crops, access to the highest levels of the bureaucracies on which employers were never hesitant to impress their requirements, and monitoring of organizational activities in the fields. The whole apparatus was subsidized by the federal government.

Social process is a continuous and fluid joining of actions that serve the particular needs and interests of men, who, if they are free to act, devise forms of association that serve them. Each element of the process has a history of its own and tends to appear as a straight line of events in a chain of causes and effects. Motion forward is the essence of events, and history is inconceivable without it. When a powerful enough incentive is present among a particular class of men at the appropriate moment, the lines join in a pattern, driven by need and purpose, the partner of motivation. The pattern completed and its goals achieved, it is consecrated by custom and law and becomes a structure, to which forward motion is disturbing. The only allowable cause thenceforth is the will of those who dominate the structure; the only permissible effect, its security. Given enough time the structure hardens into an institution. Out of a consortium of institutions comes a civilization for which history on all appearances has come to rest.

The Farm Placement Service was already in that stage when the National Farm Labor Union appeared in California. Since the union was setting out to organize domestic farm laborers, contact with the FPS was immediate and inevitable. The aim of the union was to introduce a process into the agricultural manpower supply to secure collective representation, bargaining, higher wages, and generally more favorable work-living conditions.

In theory, the union and the FPS were substantially on the same course. In 1942 a congressional committee report on the matter[34] listed among the aims and purposes of the FPS the following: to direct agricultural workers to seasonal opportunities for employment; to minimize wasteful and fruitless travel in search of jobs; to stabilize work opportunities and thus reduce migration; to provide adequate income for the workers; and to eliminate irresponsible farm labor contractors. Legally, it could be argued that since the FPS was administered by the Secretary of Labor such aims were to be pursued on behalf of the workers.

If such was indeed the legislative intent originally, in the course of time it became fouled. Exactly how this happened has never been researched by historians in the linear tradition. There are only clues but they are persuasive. In September 1948 it was already the view of the Chief of the FPS that its assignment was "to insure adequate labor for the harvest of any crop in California."[35] As it hardened from a structure to an institution the FPS regarded itself increasingly as the guarantor of "a more favorable supply" of workers in the labor pool.[36] This is how it eventually came to be regarded by employers, who added that the labor supply must not only be ample but fluid.[37]

Whatever Congress had intended, the FPS developed its own image as a government agency. "We are a public service organization charged with the assistance to employers and employees alike."[38] It was an image of pure neutrality from which class interest and institutional bias had been purged, but behind that screen the FPS was transformed into an effective tool of both. The Service regarded its offices as friendly clubs where farmers could advise and be advised, where they could "share experience and knowledge and to discuss prospective operating policies and procedures."[39]

From business to conviviality was a short step. It became the custom of the top officials of the FPS to dine and drink with the leaders of the industry across the street from the state capitol at the El Mirador Hotel and other comfortable watering places. No doubt on these occasions the leaders congratulated one another, as they did in print, on their courage and truthfulness on matters agricultural.[40] So notorious did these happy hours become that in 1953 special orders were issued to staff members to avoid dinner courtesies tendered by grower representatives. Here and there a local field man would decline the drinks and instead recall to the attention of growers the original assignment of the FPS. Such employees did not rise to influential positions.

To make certain that in its view all its interests were compatible with those of growers, the FPS set up the machinery by which they could register their advice and consent with the management of the agency[41] Even as it was being organized, the California State Chamber of Commerce advised that it be staffed with persons properly trained in the social orientation of the Extension Service, itself a product of the U.S. Department of Agriculture. Staffing proceeded so agreeably that the advisory function became a part of the system. A statewide Agriculture Advisory Council was appointed in 1948, preliminary to the creation of County Farm Placement Committees, of which there were thirty-four the following year. These committees were composed of the local leaders of the industry to whom, for all practical purposes, the agency employees became staff assistants. By 1958 the advisory network had grown to forty-nine local committees with more than 350 members, which included eminent figures of Agri-businessland—Phil Bancroft president of the Associated Farmers; B. A. Harrigan, Secretary of the Imperial Valley Farmers Association; Keith Mets, business partner of the brother of the American ambassador to Mexico; W. B. Camp, one of the organizers of the cotton seed monopoly in the state; and Jack Bias, manager of the Salinas Vegetable Growers Association.[42]

These advisory connections, without legislative or executive authorization, gradually assumed the typical shape of a bureaucratic pyramid, at the top of which appeared the State Board of Agriculture. Unlike the Wagner-Peyser Act, as interpreted by the FPS, the State Agriculture Code plainly recognized the Board as the spokesman for and guardian of the industry. Its role in influencing the FPS affected all the levels of consultation, advice, and decision of the local committees.

With the same easy informality by which all this was accomplished, the Farm Placement Service assumed functions of vital consequence to the domestic workers who were presumably the chief objects of its concern. The most important of these was the determination of need—not the needs of laborers for steady work and better pay, but the need of the industry to keep them fluid and abundant. Once this was settled, determination became a politcal process, behind a facade of research the nature of which was betrayed by the fumbling syntax of the experts in shortages. For example: "We discount the fact that if we had 4,000 people only 1,200 will show up and some of these will not work more than a day or so and some will work all through the season, and come up with the best estimate we can of how much actual labor will be provided by what labor supply we can count on in the community and match that against our estimate of how much labor will be required to handle the crop and the difference is the shortage."[43]

The mathematics of establishing labor shortages were as weird as their results were necessary for the maintenance of the labor pool. The view of the industry was accepted without question by the FPS, that the labor supply would always be inadequate. The pool could never be flooded, but would always be in varying stages of deficit. It was agreed that the industry was under perpetual threat of disaster; to avert it the FPS placed no limits on its guessing game. In the Imperial Valley where the total labor force averaged about 15,000 persons—domestics, braceros, and illegals—the declared shortage in 1956 was 15,000.[44] For the entire state in that same year the deficit in manpower for the harvests was estimated at over 111,000, roughly equivalent to all the domestics. This was a high water mark in comparison with the normal range of predictions released over the years—45,000 to 75,000. After 1950, when the forecasting of shortages had become more sophisticated, year in and year out ruin threatened the major crops like grapes and tomatoes, and many of the minor ones like broccoli and dates.

If the economics of disaster as practiced by the Farm Placement Service were dismal, they were by no means devoid of touches of charm and pathos. In Brentwood, center of a rich farming area, apricot growers calculated their shortages of pickers five to ten days after the trees reached full bloom, the blossoms bringing bright promises of sunshine and shortages. Small farmers were pictured wandering despondently through orchards among ripe peaches that had dropped and rotted from a lack of harvesters.

In bureaucracies pervaded by a climate of deceit the most melancholy effect is not moral lapse but mental weakening. Men of sharp minds who have risen to the top of public agencies fail to notice facts that do not fit into what they must pretend is the true state of affairs. This happened in the Farm Placement Service. Its most prestigious technicians missed the view of themselves that outsiders would eventually have, as sorcerers able to predict from three to nine months in advance a labor shortage of one hundred to nine thousand harvesters.[45] Neither did they hesitate to exclude from their estimates the thousands of illegals of whose presence the Farm Placement staff was fully aware. In 1952 when the distribution of illegals was reported as "normal," union organizers estimated their number at forty thousand, a figure almost exactly equal to the official labor shortage. With illegals available in such precise ratios of demand to supply it was still possible for the FPS to negotiate on behalf of the industry contracts for supplementary braceros to fill twice over the declared vacuum in the labor supply.

In truth all this pathetic make-believe was merely the reflection of a political arrangement legitimized as research. The shortages were little more than state totals based on the partial reports of the local advisory committees, whose data derived from official deficits for previous years, late blooming apricots, the annoying fugacity of wetbacks, and the traditional proposition that there could never be too many harvest hands. The elite farmers who dominated the advisory committees invoked the forecasts of the FPS as scientific proof of shortages and the FPS hedged its guesses by ultimately deferring to the advisory committees.

Upon this close interaction depended the certification of need for braceros, which also moved by steps from the advisory committees to the local Farm Placement staffs, to the central offices in Sacramento, to the regional headquarters of the Department of Labor in San Francisco, and finally to Washington, and then through diplomatic channels to Mexico City and the recruiting centers in various parts of the country.

The proof of the operation, end to end, was the delivery of braceros to the fields. *Agricultural Life,* a spokesman for the industry, quoted officials of the FPS to the effect that in 1956 the supply of domestic farm workers had fallen short by a hundred thousand. The deficiency had been made up through the importation of braceros.[46] It was perhaps unnecessary to adorn the economic facts, but officials and employers could not desist. James G. Bryant, informing the Governor's Council of California, tripped his colleagues in the FPS when he said that forecasts of shortages were based on previous understandings that substantial numbers of braceros would be available. "We can count on these men," Bryant said.[47] Hank Strobel, a horny-handed dirt farmer who had helped break a strike with axe handles and not a man practiced in deception, reasoned matter-of-factly that the best proof that California had been short thirty-six thousand workers in 1951 was that exactly that number of braceros had been used.

Power is both cumulative and polivalent. Those who possess it tend to enlarge it. It can be exerted in ways surprisingly different from its original puposes. When it can be applied by those who have it without accountability, power becomes nearly absolute. That it can be applied indirectly, even covertly, enhances its effect. Such was the case of the Farm Placement Service. As surrogate for corporate agriculture, it exercised power with respect to farm laborers, giving it two thrusts. It undercut efforts to improve the conditions of living and working; and it deliberately avoided and ignored the presence of the National Farm Labor Union.

For years it had been known that an excess number of job applicants in the harvests was one of the causes of low earnings and wasteful management; the FPS distributed leaflets intended to encourage saturation. Employers accepted collective negotiations with crews only under extreme pressure from the workers; the FPS made it a policy not to refer groups, that is, self-organized crews. Area hearings on wage proposals were at one point considered by the U.S. Department of Labor; but the FPS refused to attend after the hearings were attacked by the growers associations. The Secretary of Labor at one time was ready to prescribe standards relating to housing for migrant workers; the growers rejected them; the FPS kept a prudent neutrality.

When a ranch was struck, the FPS moved slowly in discontinuing referrals. It steadfastly refused to take notice of strikes except as "labor disturbances," which pleased employers and avoided legal implications. It declared that "it would not be helpful" to admit labor representatives to the local advisory committees. It kept employers advised on union activity in the fields. Acting as informer, it was presumably aware of the existence of the union. Yet in 1956 it went so far as to assure high officials of the Department of Labor that the NFLU had no desire to be represented in the meetings in which vital matters concerning wages were discussed by growers and public officials.[48]

The role of the FPS in the politics of Agri-businessland was not altogether a discovery of the union. Two congressional committees chaired by Senator LaFollette and Senator Tolan had looked at the agency in the early 1940s. The LaFollette Committee concluded that in no substantial way did the agency try to place workers in accordance with actual need for them. In the Tolan hearings it was described as notoriously incompetent and virtually a tool of employers.

One method of weighing power is to observe how little it is moved by criticism from those who speak with merely formal authority, however prestigious, but who do not bring vested interest swiftly to accountability. In the congressional hearings the FPS stood accused but not indicted, much less convicted. In the rare instance of criticism or demurral by some conscientious federal official the FPS was even less disturbed. It had come a long way since the passage of the Wagner-Peyser Act.

The Growers Associations

In California diversified agriculture never meant the type of farm intended primarily for the subsistence of the rural family. Such a model for an agricultural economy was the result of the conditions forced on pioneer farmers advancing along the isolated borders of the expanding West. When roads were opened and markets began to appear, exchange became the norm rather than the exception and specialized farming took over. The variations of soil and climate, together with economic opportunities for profitable sale in expanding markets and the appearance of financial and credit institutions, affected the size of the agricultural unit. Localized specialization in California was the result, creating the Peach Bowl of Yuba, the Salad Bowl of Salinas, the Citrus Belt of Riverside, the Date Gardens of Coachella. The state became a mosaic of such specializations and only of the state as a whole could it be said that California farming was diversified.

Within a statewide range of material production there appeared a diversity of interests among growers. As commodity specialists the growers competed with one another for credit, for markets, for shipping facilities, and for labor. On the other hand, as the volume of agricultural production rose until it passed the three billion dollar level by the 1950s, the agricultural producers, small and large, found themselves pulled between what each wanted to take away from the others, and what all had to do together to gain certain benefits for themselves as a class. These common benefits were: securing at public expense construction of enormous irrigation systems that would bring them subsidized water; eliminating alien entry into the property system, as had been threatened by the Japanese in the early 1900s; receiving the services of agencies such as the extension and farm placement services; obtaining the benefits of research and development through a state university system that kept agriculturists informed on the latest progress of technology and science affecting them; preventing the passage of state and federal legislation that would extend to farm workers such benefits as the minimum wage and unemployment insurance; discouraging government-sponsored housing for migrants; and replenishing the labor pool. To secure these common benefits there evolved a network of associations whose primary aim was the control and regulation of harvest labor.

It is important to note that there was competitiveness as well as cooperation among agricultural producers, reflecting the balance of weights between the large producers and the small. The state had over a hundred thousand farm units in 1920, among which consensus was indispensable as the only way to obtain agreement among such a large constituency, still composed mainly of small farmers. The day of vertical integration had not yet arrived and until it did the dominant corporations, perforce identifying themselves as dirt farmers, set the goals, planned the public relations campaigns, and worked out the political understandings with state and federal legislatures and agencies. In short, within what to all appearances was a functioning democracy achieving benefits for all, there was, as always in large social groups, a central grid of information, funds, decisions, and connections.

Horizontal combinations of producers banding to serve some special crop interest began in the 1860s with the wool growers and wine makers; their example was followed in the next hundred years by producers of practically every speciality crop in the state. They saw themselves primarily as bargaining associations striving to inform their members as to market conditions, prices, cultural practices, sales promotion, freight rates, and related matters. Typically there were the Central California Beet Growers Association, established in 1931; the California Tomato Growers Association, the California Asparagus Growers Association, the Diamond Walnut Growers, which processed and shipped 70 percent of the national production, and the California Cotton Producers, which spoke for 3,800 members. Similarly there was a free-stone as well as a cling peach association. The Sunkist Growers, which regarded itself as the most successful cooperative enterprise of its kind in the world, operated 132 packing sheds and employed over twelve thousand packers at the peak of the citrus harvest. Sunkist provided field service men, arranged loans, supervised picking and packing, maintained storage facilities, managed processing plants, and advertised and sold on behalf of their members. It was the imagination and the knack with lilting slogans of these promoters that acquainted the nation with the romance of navels and the gentle laxative effect of the California prune. Sunkist alone spent a million dollars on national advertising in 1959.

Parallel to these private organizations were publicly supported service agencies that formed another system of interconnections. These were the irrigation districts established to promote local water projects, of which there were seventy in the state in 1923; the agricultural commissioners, assigned to all but a few of the counties as promoters of agricultural associations, also composed of local farm leaders and mainly concerned with the oversight of the annual county fairs. In all these contexts industry's dominant figures found additional opportunities to be seen, heard, and attended.

But it was through the associations of growers and shippers that the commodity interests and services evolved into a political power structure.

The configuration of that power arose when farm units of the corporate type began to overshadow in size, value of production, profitability, and general efficiency the smaller ones. The big vegetable and fruit properties established their own picking and processing plants, to which smaller producers were forced to turn. The grower-shippers who handled not only their own but their neighbor's produce were not slow to recognize the integrating possibilities of their superior position, and gradually the larger operators came together in that tendency to nucleation that all power exhibits.

Labor procurement never ceased to be the primary function of these grower-shipper associations, and as early as 1926 they began to function as labor bureaus. Their experience with the braceros in 1942, and finally the enactment of Public Law 78, provided the opportunity for the associations to perfect their role as labor brokers on an unprecedented scale. They operated as nonprofit associations inasmuch as they were devoted to make profits for their members only as producers and not as members.[49] They were careful to write into their charters that they were set up "solely to provide an agency for contracting and negotiating with U.S. government agencies for the importation of farm labor."[50] In 1959 there were fifty-nine such associations with a membership of over twelve thousand growers.

As they grew in importance by reason of their role as intermediaries in the bracero system, they refined their traditional practices of leveling wage rates, such as policing farmers to enforce them, and using their connections with freight handlers, field inspectors, processors, banks, and suppliers to enforce compliance on any who might be inclined to break ranks. Since the inner circle of the association formed an overlapping community of interests with those who operated in the higher centers of finance, shipping, and distribution, it was at the level of national marketing that the shape of production was more and more determined.

The geographic spheres of influence of the association's power were the Imperial Valley, San Diego, Kern County, Ventura, Salinas, Fresno, Stockton, Yuba, and Santa Clara. In these areas the association managers, appointed by boards dominated by the larger operators, moved commandingly at their assigned tasks—to procure braceros, regulate their distribution, provide legal counsel, promote public sympathy for the industry, coordinate with other protective organizations, and maintain liaison with political elements.[51] In all important respects the managers supervised the governance of the harvest labor market when it became dominated by braceros. They were, indeed, the government.

To provide for certain emergencies requiring quick action and the enlistment of broader public support, there were created from time to time special liaison groups. Such were the California Farmers Emergency Food Committee and the Diversified Farmers. When representations were necessary at the highest levels of government, the local association joined hands through councils like the Agricultural Producers Labor Committee, based in Los Angeles.

The role of local farm advisory committees from which the Farm Placement Service obtained its statistics on shortages has already been noted. Their advice was transmitted to the governor and the state legislature through the Board of Agriculture. Finally there was a Special Farm Labor Committee composed of representatives from forty-eight states who carried the message to the Secretary of Labor and Congress. At this level the overriding common interest was the procurement of foreign labor on the positive side, and on the negative the prevention of administrative or legislative interference with its day-to-day operation. The basic economic interests affected by tariffs, subsidies, regulation of commerce, crop allotments, and foreign trade were watched over by lobbies like that of the American Farm Bureau Federation.

Orchestrated into the division of labor among agricultural interests was the California Farm Bureau, the state affiliate of the AFBF. Its structure, too, was a pyramid of connections that reached out to the countryside through more than fifty county agencies, with some five hundred local affiliates claiming sixty-five thousand members. The bureau joined hands with the Agricultural Committee of the State Chamber of Commerce through men like Frank M. Shay, who in 1956 was also vice-president of the State Board of Agriculture. At its headquarters on the edge of the University of California campus in Berkeley the bureau maintained a radio network beamed at a farm audience, a speakers' bureau, and a good will service which arranged social affairs for country and city folks to demonstrate the underlying unity of interests of both, on behalf of "renewed dedication to the great future that lies ahead for all Americans."[52] Ten commodity departments provided legal advice, research, bulletins, and other sorts of technical support to local affiliates.

Specialized farming as a highly competitive individualized system of ownership and management generated serious problems. It was speculative in that each farm operator was dependent on marketing factors that were beyond his control; its erratic behavior was reflected in the cyclical gluts and shortages of typical capitalist production. For these producers the central problem soon became one of abundance, not of scarcity. An unusually good crop depressed prices, forcing acreage reductions and other equally unwholesome measures from which even the bonanza crops, such as peaches and grapes, were not exempt.

It was the threatening abundance of oranges that led to the organization of the citrus protective associations such as the Southern California Fruit Exchanges (1893) and the California Fruit Growers Exchange (1905). Their example was soon followed by other specialty crops and by the 1930s regulatory cooperatives of this type were numerous. Their principal purposes were to exercise control over the volume of production, to deal collectively with large buyers such as chain stores, and to bargain favorably with canners and other processors. The regulatory cooperatives usually included in their purposes the suppression of unfair and fraudulent practices in the buying and selling of fresh fruits and vegetables. From the sixty-five that existed in 1900, marketing associations of various kinds increased to over five hundred in 1937.

Appropriate state legislation was passed to permit self-regulation without risk of prosecution for violation of federal statutes on restraint of trade, authorizing ways to operate lawfully in restraint of abundance. Producers and handlers of farm products were "authorized and encouraged to combine," as one industry magazine put it simply and to the point.[53] They did so through referenda in which growers voted upon proposals for regulation, approval of which led to the promulgation of marketing orders. In addition to authorizing crop limitation, these orders set forth the conditions with which all participants were bound to comply. For each regulated crop there was appointed an advisory board with a paid manager. Assessments were levied to meet the costs of management, research, promotion, and compliance. The marketing agreements were subject to approval by the U.S. Department of Agriculture. In 1960 there were thirty-five boards with 952 participating members overseeing regulation in a variety of crops that included lettuce, pears, peaches, potatoes, strawberries, tomatoes, and cantaloups.

The number of marketing orders fluctuated from year to year. Old ones were dropped and new ones were added in accordance with the prevailing prices in particular crops, and the degree to which producers found it more profitable to be curbed than to be free was bringing the era of individualism to an end. Such a system of voluntary regimentation affected more than forty-five thousand growers in 1960.

The marketing orders legalized the practice of systematic destruction of fruits and vegetables when production volume threatened the price structure. The practice known as "green drop"—by which peaches were allowed to ripen and fall to rot on the ground—accounted for the planned waste of thousands of tons of fruit that normally would have been processed and delivered to trade channels. In Kern County potatoes were pulverized to be sold as hog feed. In the citrus country of Southern California trucks dripped golden rivulets of orange juice as they made their way to the dump. When the ticker tapes of Salinas lettuce growers showed that too much lettuce was moving toward the terminals of the great eastern markets, discing machines destroyed enough acreage to re-establish scarcity. In years too slack to provide vineyardists with returns at or above production costs, they would allow thousands of tons of grapes to spoil unpicked.

The immediate object of the regulatory associations was to protect growers from the processors, canners, and chain store buyers. These, too, had long been ranged in associations of their own, collective bargainers who stood between the grower and the consumer. The Canners League of California with its forty member corporations and companies represented 85 percent of the food-processing capacity of the state in 1959. The members of the producers Cotton Oil Company represented the ownership and management of sixty cotton gins. The California Packing Corporation through a contract system had established itself not only as an economic power among processors but also as an important decision maker in field and orchard.

On still another level the organization of the industry proceeded. From 1943 to 1947 there existed a California Farm Production Council, financed out of public funds, and whose function was to coordinate the interests of agriculturists. Other private organizations appeared on the scene to act as advisors and lobbyists. Such were the California Grape and Tree Fruit League, the Agricultural Council of California, and the Council of California Growers. These organizations, like the advisory committees and the marketing associations, provided additional escalators into the higher spheres of politics and banking. Charles F. Wente was both chairman of the board of the Council of California Growers and chairman of the State Fish and Game Commission. He was also director of Fireman's Insurance Fund, whose holdings included the Bank of America, California Packing Corporation, Crown Zellerback Paper Company, and Kern County Land Company. These councils, leagues, chambers, and bureaus also facilitated access directly to the state and federal bureaucracies.

Coordination of interests on behalf of corporate agriculture did not end here. It was also a function of the California State Chamber of Commerce, described by one of its past presidents as follows: "The California State Chamber of Commerce, Agriculture and Industry . . . combines into one organization both urban and rural areas . . . [and] the agricultural, commercial, and industrial elements in the entire State of California."[54]

Considering the scope and depth of this mesh of interests, strikes in the fields were not the local employer-worker conflicts that they appeared to be on the surface. Higher wages increased harvesting costs except as they could be countered by mechanization in the long run. Passing these costs from growers to processors to shippers meant creating ripples if not waves of apprehension that eventually reached even the board rooms of banks. From this point of view it can be understood why strikes, threatened or actual, were of interest to enterprises as distant from one another as Associated Seed Growers, the Southern Pacific Company, and Trans Lux Products Corporation. Not all the strikes were the effect of union organization, but all were seen as such; this was reason enough to explain the general hostility to union organization of varying intensity from the growers to board rooms. These were the odds against unionization, and they ranged themselves sometimes overtly, sometimes in quiet supportive ways. A few examples from a history of fifty years illustrate the point.

The Salinas Vegetable Growers Association played an important role in the smashing of the lettuce cutters strike in 1936, abetting violence that approached civil war.[55] Gin managers gathered and passed on information about the cotton strikes of the early 1950s. The Farm Bureau saw one of its important functions to be "protection as to labor movements in agriculture,"[56] and to train farmers in the techniques of avoiding traps laid by wily union organizers. As a public service the Council of California Growers compiled a manual for farmers threatened by strikes, advising them to call immediately on the most experienced experts in such matters. These included former Chief of the Farm Placement Service Edward F. Hayes. For advice on ways to avoid wage increases the Apple Growers Association went to the Farm Placement Service itself.[57] The manager of the Asparagus Growers Association regularly reported to his clients developments "in the labor picture so that we could be able to take care of your interests."[58] The Western Growers Association, in its campaign to prevent legislation that would have interfered with its freedom, in its magazine berated "sensitive souls who shrink from using heat to cure the union blight."[59] The

Council of California Growers, established to meet the threat of minimum wage legislation, helped to rally in the halls of the state legislature a thousand shouting lobbyists, among them representatives of industry and business.[60] The Agricultual Producers Labor Committee rallied to its support the Inter-Association Unemployment Insurance Committee, the Western Oil and Gas Association, California Portland Cement Company, Pacific Gas and Electric Company, Rexall Drug Company, Southern California Edison, California Trucking Association, Pacific Maritime Association, and Pacific Telegraph and Telephone. Funds for these activities were provided through acreage assessments, volunteer contributions, quotas, dues, and membership fees.[61]

The classic example of aggressive specialization on strike prevention and wage control was that of the Associated Farmers of California. Founded in 1934, the AF was the successor of the Farmers Protective League which in 1915 had kept watch over farm interests in thirty-two counties. Through the efforts of Joseph DiGiorgio, the AF enlisted the financial support of California Packing Corporation, Canners League of California, Southern Pacific Company, Standard Oil, Bank of America, and Pacific Gas and Electric. It remained a frontline service agency wherever labor organization threatened, led the statewide campaign for the enactment of a right-to-work law, dealt with farmers who fell out of step on predetermined wage scales at harvest time, denounced the hiring hall and the closed shop, and generally "fostered and encouraged respect for law and order." In plainer language *Fortune Magazine* described the AF as "run by big growers but supported and manned by the little ones who pay dues and wield pick handles and rifles in case of trouble. . . ."[62] In the late 1940s the AF probably had some twenty thousand members, nominal and active, in thirty-seven counties.

The techniques borrowed from the past by the Associated Farmers, together with those of its own invention and those improved by its successors, constituted the arsenal of anti-unionism, coordinated at so many levels with dispatch. The catalogue is not a short one: violence by Citizens Committees; communist slurs on union organizers; expulsion of union members from town; police harassment; disruption of meetings; use of tear gas; undercover intelligence; recruiting and hiring of strike breakers; anti-union publicity in the metropolitan and local newspapers; injunctions; firing workers who joined a union; refusal to bargain; lobbying; appearances before legislative committees; interchange of information with local police; litigation; armed escorts; assaults on camps; and solicitation of funds for these purposes.

By 1950 the image of the AF as dirt farmers battling to save the nation from hunger and communist infiltration was fading. It gave way after a quarter of a century to more sophisticated organizations such as the California Council of Growers. It left behind a record of farm workers beaten, jailed, and slain and strikes crushed.

Farm Labor Contractors

The third important agent by which the harvest labor force was regulated was that of the private labor contractor. Like the Farm Placement Service he was subordinate to the grower associations, labor bureaus, and labor exchanges, as they were variously called. The decisions made by growers through their associations shaped labor management in all important aspects, and to these decisions both the FPS and contractors conformed, the former because it was a bureaucratic instrument of the industry, the latter because they were dependent upon the grower.

Contracting grew out of both economic proximity and cultural distance. There was a labor pool of Chinese, Japanese, Filipinos, and Mexicans in California, created to serve an expanding agriculture on the Pacific Coast. Because of differences of language, customs, social forms, and living styles and of the practical problems of the cyclical demand of workers, intermediaries became necessary. When the Blacks and southern Whites arrived belatedly to enter the pool the contracting system was well established and for them, too, provided a way, often the only one, to jobs.

In every ethnic group there were always some individuals who achieved a more permanent social location between those who were looking for work and those who had it to offer. Storekeepers in shanty towns did contracting on the side for their customers. Straw bosses learned enough about production and management to set up in business for themselves as labor procurers. Lay preachers found time to help their congregations find pastures on earth as well as in heaven. Publicans found their taverns, flop houses, and restaurants natural gathering places for job seekers. These were the persons and places that provided domestic migrants with access to the labor market.

The labor contractor not only closed the cultural gap but more importantly he assumed certain responsibilities that the grower found too costly or inconvenient to discharge himself. He thus avoided establishing bonds between himself and the worker that might become formal and eventually compromising. Since the contractor himself was an economic dependent and only partly removed from the insecurities of farm employment, around him there could not evolve forms of social stability in the farm labor community.

The relationship between the contractor and the grower was based on a contract, verbal or written. By its terms the employer retained certain rights, such as the location of the work, the amount of production, timing of the operation, general oversight, and sometimes the right of dismissal. Typically the contractors agreed to recruit manpower; provide housing, transportation, and food; keep work records and make payments of wages; and manage camps. Contractors also hired at their own expense the necessary personnel for the details of crew management, such as checking and bookkeeping. Gradually contractors specialized as to the type of employer served and crops harvested, based on the extent and reliability of their connections on the one hand with employers and on the other with workers. If he could regularly fulfill expectations of this kind year in and year out, a contractor could become a personage of sorts in his chosen area of operations. He would buy a house in town and manage a payroll of as much as two hundred thousand dollars a year. Since contracting was highly competitive, his preserves were constantly raided by outside cut-rate bidders.

Mindful of the historic evils of private labor contracting in agriculture, the California State Legislature included the farm contractor in regulatory legislation. Section 1682 of the Labor Code defined him as "any person who, for a fee, employs workers to render personal services in connection with the production of farm products." He was required to obtain a license and post a bond. In December 1950 over twelve hundred persons held licenses; double that number operated without them. Approximately 40 percent of them were Spanish surnamed. They were active in all the major and most of the minor crops, dominating the labor supply in some counties.

Experience proved that the Labor Code was far from adequate to prevent the systematic exploitation of workers practiced by the contractors. The amount of the bond—one thousand dollars—was too low to deter licensed swindlers who absconded with many times that amount in pay due the harvesters. Those caught operating without a license got off with light fines and short raps in the county jail. The employer-employee relationship was never clearly defined by law, permitting both growers and contractors to evade responsibility of nonpayment of wages and unsanitary conditions in the camps. The legislature was benevolently indifferent to a situation which the growers did not want disturbed.

Some of the abuses practiced by contractors were notorious, while others were merely a part of the routine of petty larceny. In the camps the contractor served food of the poorest quality and charged what the traffic would bear. If he collected premiums for social security, which many did, and failed to pay them over to the government, the risk of discovery was minimal and the chances that a worker would complain were even more unlikely. Cool water was not provided in the fields in the hot summer days in order to favor a concessionaire, usually a relative of the contractor, who sold bottled cold drinks at marked-up prices. Transportation accidents took a heavy toll in injuries and fatalities, but contractors continued to carry thousands of harvesters in what must have been the most dilapidated fleet of carriers in the nation. An important part of the traffic in drugs that entered California from Mexico moved north through labor camps, contributing its share to the business of prostitution and liquor. And in the matter of short weights the tricks of the contractor were notorious.

Free to practice mean extortion and chicanery in the camps, the contractors acted as agents of growers in other respects. It was they who passed on to the crews the mendacious reports on the depressed state of the market which made it necessary for employers to pay low wages. Occasionally a contractor would appear at growers' wage-fixing meetings to speak approvingly in the name of the workers. When strikes occurred contractors, stimulated by premium commissions, were always available to replenish the labor supply from distant areas.

Because he operated in the twilight zone of the law, the contractor was able to exploit domestics, illegals, and braceros according to opportunities offered at any given time. He was familiar with the rural towns where the domestics were settling where he recruited for local day hauls. He was closely acquainted with the sources of illegals and their availability, shielding the growers from responsibility for the disreputable traffic. And even though the law forbade contractors from participating in the bracero system, they did so because of their managerial experience in housing, feeding, transporting, and supervising. The growers associations admitted them to membership, thus making them subcontractors of braceros in fact, sometimes qualified as member-users under the terms of Public Law 78 and the agreements with Mexico. Since many contractors had no scruples about using mixed crews of braceros and illegals, through them associations were able to draw on the wetback reserve.

The associations soon recognized that only the largest of the Mexican contractors could serve their interests in the supervision of braceros. Favoritism developed, excluding the smaller contractors from bracero allotments. Had the bracero system become permanent, it would have finally eliminated all but a select cadre of contractors, and these would have been assimilated as unofficial adjuncts of the associations. This process was laconically revealed by a small contractor who had been forced out because braceros had supplanted domestics in the fields and he was not admitted to the local growers association. When asked his occupation, he replied, "My job is not." Such individuals withdrew permanently from recruiting, or went back to former employment as crew pushers, field foremen, bus drivers, and camp managers.

On their account, contractors as a class became even more alienated from domestics. In the earlier stages of the bracero program it was the Mexican contractors who had served the grand strategy of displacing the *locales*. The contractors served their own interests by substituting braceros for domestics, denying them housing, allotting them the worst fields, terminating the employment of women, and collaborating with the Farm Placement Service.

Farm labor contracting at no time ceased being other then a convenient arrangement with considerable moral, legal, economic, and social flexibility working to the advantage of farm employers. It would probably never disappear completely from the scene.

Wages

To instill in the domestic workers the fear that "they might not have a job tomorrow" was one of the objects of keeping the labor pool flooded. "It is the only thing they react to," as one employer stated it.[63] The importance of this psychological grip on the work force explained the uncompromising resistance of growers to collective bargaining, which would have placed the harvesters in a position to demand a larger share of wage payments. As production practices became more mechanized and more dependent on chemicals and other products of industry, and as agriculturists were forced to surrender more of their profits to railways and distributors, arbitrary control of their wage costs became vital. The wage decision had to be kept unilateral, left to the ingenuity and rapacity of particular employers. A work force kept in leash by fear was the solution to the widely lamented "squeeze" of which the industry persistently complained.

The growers' most effective device for setting wage rates was the "fair price" meeting for particular crops.[64] Before competitive bidding could set in as the harvest approached, growers met to determine wage scales, in effect setting a ceiling on earnings. By gentlemen's agreement, the grower set a standard for chiseling contractors, staged ceremonial displays of fairness and economic justice, and presented a public show of solidarity among those who owned the land.

Touches of rationality were added to this process. A uniform wage, it was argued, saved the harvesters from travelling needlessly in search of more favorable conditions.[65] The term "wage fixing" was studiously avoided. The stress was rather on wage uniformity, which in no way created the basis for collective bargaining with workers. Government participation in the process was carefully avoided. Cotton growers refused to attend a public discussion on picking rates that Governor Olson attempted to call in the fall of 1959. Wage levels tended over the years to stay significantly close to the uniformities declared by growers.

The "fair" and "uniform" rates thus determined were clouded over by other terms that had as little relevance to the economic factors, such as the "going rate" and the "base wage rate." The latter term was defined by Joseph DiGiorgio as the rate thought to be acceptable to one's neighbors. Less common was the use of the term "community wage," another way of referring to the consensus of the growers, especially the larger ones. And finally there was the "prevailing wage," the yardstick approved by government agencies that administered the bracero program, and that was held to be the "most common wage" reported to the Farm Placement Service by growers.

It should be noticed how easily these euphemisms glided into the language of the literature from the press handouts of the growers meetings to the testimony in legislative hearings and the official reports of government agencies. Academics, with few exceptions, borrowed freely from these sources, under which were buried the details of the agricultural wage transaction, such as actual payments made on hourly and piece rates, payments made to hand harvesters as distinguished from foremen, machine operators, and haulers, and unit costs of harvested crops.

The prevailing wage concept for determining bracero wages had several advantages. It was an officially declared rate, which permitted employers to shrug off criticism by pointing out that not they but the government determined it. The FPS field men merely circulated among the harvesters recording the wages they were receiving. The rates thus reported as the "most common wage" had an air of spontaneity if not of coincidence. But the coincidence lay in that the FPS and the employers had agreed privately on the level of the prevailing wage before it was announced publicly.[66] These understandings were arrived at without regard for the provisions of the Labor Code which did not apply to agriculture. The prevailing wage was in fact the bracero wage.[67]

Even more flexible were the various scales that agricultural experts devised from time to time to cover the inconsistencies of rates—"going," "base," "common," or "prevailing." In 1958 tomato growers set up a sliding scale for piece wages according to yield per acre, taking into consideration such variables as the method of harvesting and the variety of the fruit picked, distance between rows and length of "claims" assigned to each worker. The object was to provide a technical screen to reduce rates, which was the case in the tomato harvest in 1952, described below.

Whatever they were called, the stabilized scales made no provision or allowance for the most significant variable of all, namely, the short weights on which payments were based at the point of delivery of the work measured by units—the cotton sack, the tomato lug, and string bean hamper. Potatoes were picked into a stub, a canvas sack with a black line on the outside at the 50-pound level. The rate of pay in Kern County in 1950 was 6 cents a stub containing 50 pounds. Contractors insisted on "topping," which could bring the actual weight to 60 or 65 pounds. Since the contractors were paid by the ton, topping yielded them a profit of 15 to 20 percent over the wages actually paid. In the harvest of that year, Kern County potato pickers probably lost a quarter of a million dollars in this manner. In cotton picking the classic trick was for the weigher to turn the face of the scales away from the worker, crediting the picker with a few pounds less than actually delivered. Some operators adjusted the scales beforehand, making the sleight-of-hand technique unnecessary. These were alleged to be methods of compensating the employers for the trash and stones that pickers supposedly threw into their sacks to tip the scales in their favor. In the snap bean harvest pay was on the basis of 30-pound baskets. When full the minimum acceptable weight was 34 pounds, with the allowance for tare. If the weather was damp or foggy, some checkers raised the tare to 36 pounds to compensate for the moisture absorbed by the wicker containers. Some checkers paid off at each weighing with small change laid down at the far end of the weigh-in counter. Counting it held the picker's attention while his basket was on the scales. Added to these devices was the requirement in some bean fields that the picker "throw in" an extra pound or two as topping. The Mexican workers had a name for this—*el pilon,* "forced tribute," The English speakers called it "chiseling."

When cotton was delivered to the gins payment to the growers was based on tonnage. Packing sheds kept records of packed-out crates; canneries, of fruit delivered at the docks. These receipts were the ultimate record of what the pickers put out in the fields and orchards on piece wages and what the producers delivered to the processors. Receipts were exchanged at the terminal end of these transactions, but not at their beginning. In one instance beet cutters complained that they had received credit for delivery of a load of 36 tons that had been recorded at the refinery at 76 tons. Since much of the harvesting was done by gangs that re-formed every day rather than by steady crews with responsible leaders, the argument that there was no one to receive production receipts anyway had a ring of plausibility. Individual workers resorted to tallying their work units on bits of paper, cigarette wrappers, brown paper bags, or grocery slips, but with these no picker could win an argument against a foreman or a contractor.

Another device was the deduction of the "bonus," an amount held back until the end of the harvest to discourage early departure. In agriculture the bonus was not a premium for satisfactory performances but a deduction from the earned wages, which provided another opportunity for short changing. Workers could be discouraged by assignment to less productive parts of a field, or by harassment, or by bad food. Those who left in anger or disgust forfeited their bonus.

In carrot harvesting a form of wage clipping closely related to the bonus was to charge the tiers for the cost of Twist-ems, wires covered with thin strips of gaily colored paper printed with the grower's brand. Twist-ems were necessary equipment for tying carrots in bunches. The ususal explanation for the practice of deducting the cost of Twist-ems was that it discouraged waste.

Until mechanization was able to displace hand labor in a given operation, the favored method of payment of wages was by piece rates. This method reduced supervision costs to a minimum, made possible the use of family labor, provided the maximum of flexibility in hiring, and lowered standards of performance and requirements of skill without affecting volume or quality. It also concealed a variety of practices by which the harvesters delivered more work than they were paid for. Cotton pickers, along with the bolls they stuffed into their sacks as they dragged their way along the rows, also delivered cotton seed, which the grower sold but for which the picker received no pay. Weighing in, whether in cotton or snap beans, was arduous work, but the time and effort expended by the harvester were not recorded or paid for. Carrying empty lugs and scattering them was in some operations required as part of the picker's routine. When vegetables or fruit were returned by the cannery for failure to meet quality standards or size it was the pickers who re-sorted the load without pay. Jobs were not differentiated; for instance, tomato pickers would have to carry lugs weighing as much as sixty pounds the length of the row to roadside stacks for loading. In one day a worker could carry as much as two and half tons, yet be paid only for picking. Still another method of economizing on piece rates was to change the capacity of the bucket, the lug, the sack, or the basket by adding a few inches to its cubic dimensions.

The piece rate system was by no means rigid, being interchangeable with hourly rates at the discretion of the employer. Such shifts from piece to hourly rates or in reverse were used to regulate the day's earnings, another way of softening the impact of field wages on the total harvest costs. Shifts could be ordered on the spot without prior notice and if confusion resulted as to how much had been done on piece rates and how much by the hour, doubts were settled by the records in the possession of the management.

In this matter of records the prevailing disregard for verifiable facts appeared at all levels. State and federal agencies entrusted with gathering statistics "relating to the conditions of labor in the state"[68] never developed methods of reporting to reveal the peculiarities of the distribution of wealth in the state's most important industry, which boasted of paying the highest farm wages in the country. But it was impossible to separate wages paid for actual harvesting tasks and wages paid for loading, hauling, grading, packing, and supervision, so that the high farm wages turned out to be an inflated bag of all these. The state of affairs was such that when one field investigator accidently came by a genuine cost report on tomato picking, he advised his superiors to mark the extraordinary document. If in the tranquil quarters of public agencies there was so little concern for accurate data, it was understandable that in the fields distinctions as to the actual compensation of harvesters should be ignored. In their place falsified payroll records, short weights, deceptive containers, denial of receipts, inaccurate time books, and misleading classification of work became standard operating procedures.

Housing

Next to wages the most important factor that determined what kind of workers would be available, and in what numbers, was the housing. Family labor in the fields required shelter for the adult workers, men and women, as well as for their children. If the family had a home base to which it could return between harvests, its requirements for living away from home were minimal. Many took to the road in their own mobile homes of canvas or planks fixed to trucks that needed only parking space under trees or in some by-way close to the job. Those who could not move with their household equipment depended entirely on the employers to supply them with a place to live. The supply and quality of housing were determined by the grower and were important factors in the wage bargain itself. To him it was an unavoidable labor cost necessary to attract and hold a work force; to the laborer with a family it represented a concession on wages necessary to obtain shelter.

The large number of farm production units, their range in size and profitability and climatic factors, produced individual or local variations in what was called on-farm housing. Off the ranch there were the camps operated by labor contractors and by the federal government, supplemented by low-rent auto courts. For migrants who could not manage otherwise there were isolated groves and sheltered spots under bridges and in dry river bottoms where housekeeping could be managed for a while. Another type of off-farm housing was that of seasonal workers who were town dwellers within commuting distance of the farms; this type included the skid rows.

The character of the labor force in an agricultural district could be judged by the kinds, the amount, and the quality of dwellings for its labor. In the rice country of the northern Sacramento Valley, sweeps of cultivated acreage without a single farm house indicated an economy of six-thousand-acre ranches, skilled machine operators, extensive mechanization, and a nontransient labor force. At the other end of the state, in the Coachella Valley, sprawling rural ghettos among sand hills and rocky wastes provided the catch basins into which the labor pool poured its idle seasonal surplus. In between, the shoestring settlements along the ditch banks of Fresno County, the shanty towns of the Central

Valley's western piedmont, and the poverty pockets along the Sacramento River, told of perishable crops, extreme seasonal peaks of demand, an intermediary system of recruiting, and long gray seasons of
unemployment.

There never was a housing policy for the state, but rather a wide
variety of types in a multiplicity of conditions. In the long run, economic
characteristics of the industry determined the kind of housing offered. In
1950 40 percent of the job applicants at Farm Placement Service field
offices were not referred for lack of offers that included housing.[69] The
shortage of family housing that became chronic in the 1950s reflected the
massive substitution of domestics by braceros. Since this was the policy
of the industry, dictated by the corporate influentials, ratified by state
and federal governments, and carried out by the growers associations, in
the determination of housing standards the corporate producers prevailed. Assured of alien labor, they set the trend toward the elimination
of on-farm housing and the substitution of barracks for braceros.

Once the pattern was established the smaller producers followed it,
eliminating family housing and with it family labor. Domestics were
discouraged from applying for work in the tomato fields of San Joaquin
County in 1951—"no housing available."[70] In San Luis Obispo and
Santa Barbara counties free or low-cost family housing vanished. In
Merced County more than half of the family on-farm shelters were
closed, demolished, or reconditioned to more productive uses as
chicken coops, hog pens, and barns.[71]

Individual growers had their own ways of encouraging families to
move on. Jobs were advertised "for adults only—no children." No
Parking signs were placed where migrants were likely to stop. The city
of Corcoran discontinued access to the town pump, the only source of
water available to many families living outside the city limits under
squatter conditions. Black migrants were advised that bunks would not
suit them because they had been made to fit the smaller Mexican
braceros. Rents were raised, lights and butane were metered. Single
men were billeted in the same cabin with families.

Such measures appeared reasonable to many growers. Single worker
housing was less expensive. Families often brought with them two or
three nonworkers and these had to be accommodated also. Urban
encroachment on farm land in the vicinity of large cities made long-term
investment in family housing too risky. These rationalizations were
backed up by sympathetic boards of supervisors of unincorporated
areas. Campsites that had by custom been open to migrants were declared to be unsanitary and occupancy was forbidden. In the Almaden
Valley of Santa Clara County Mexican farm labor families that had

year-round tenure in exchange for guaranteed harvest service to the farmer were turned out by their employers as metropolitan San Jose advanced on the countryside.[72]

To accommodate braceros, eviction notices were likewise served on domestic families housed in government camps. This happened in the Salinas Valley, in Imperial, and in the Westly area of the San Joaquin. On July 15, 1955, a notice bearing the letterhead of the California Department of Employment and signed by the manager of the Patterson Camp, advised some forty families of domestic Mexicans to vacate in anticipation of the arrival of braceros for the fall harvest.

Changes in family life followed these dislocations. Long absences from the family, increased commuting distances for the breadwinner, and doubling up with city relatives were only some of the preliminaries to the mass migration to the cities of the 1960s. Families working as units, a characteristic of harvesting for decades, were discouraged. Until a family could relocate in town, yearly earnings became more precarious. The young turned toward the city. These were not just manifestations of housing policy; they were indicators of how an industry could perpetuate the mobility of people it no longer wanted. First their wages were reduced, and then they were deprived of shelter.

The methods to accomplish these drastic changes were quietly persuasive as between those who lived in possession and those who lived in fear. But the final measure, eviction, was also resorted to. In the gullies and river beds of the central coast counties, such as San Benito and Salinas, deputy sheriffs kept migrant families on the move. Health and building codes were invoked to force out seasonal squatters from improvised shelters along ditch banks. Their places as harvesters were filled by braceros day-hauled out of the county fairgrounds in Stockton.[73]

These were the effects of internal changes within the industry, economic in their origin, social in their effects. There were other factors at work causing family farm housing to disappear.

The leasing of crop lands by owners to short-term speculators created a class of seasonal managers who had no interest in a stable labor supply and therefore no need for permanent housing. For example, the three-year lessees of tomato farms in San Joaquin and Tulare counties preferred braceros, matching transient labor with transient profit taking.[74] Metropolitan sprawls like that of San Francisco reached into rural areas, not only pricing farm land into higher urban brackets, but also taking with them the tracts of bedroom suburbs that overran old *barrios* and *colonias*. Such powerful social forces in motion included agricultural mechanization. "Where the harvest [of cotton] is now almost completely mechanized, many growers have torn down their camps.''[75]

As to the housing that was left for domestics, standards fell as growers vigorously discouraged the intervention of federal and state agencies in the process described above. Louis A. Rozzoni, speaking for the Farm Bureau Federation, protested administrative regulation of housing by the U.S. Department of Labor, pointing out that ''the sixty-three thousand members of the Bureau employed the majority of braceros in California.''[76] The department agreed to leave to the growers the determination of housing policy, public or private.[77] Denied a place to live, domestic farm laborers discovered yet again that their powerlessness economically was matched by their powerlessness politically.

Mechanization

''The revolution has come,'' exclaimed a large wheat farmer, referring to the mechanical headers that in 1879 harvested twenty-nine million bushels, placing California seventh in rank as a wheat-producing state. It was a revolution that never stopped. The twenty million acres of tillable land, stretching tantalizingly to the horizons and into the future, were an invitation to devise ways to grow and deliver increasing quantities of produce faster and cheaper, to tame deserts, swing rivers around, cut corners in gathering, sorting, storing, and preserving everything from almonds to zucchini. Machinery became indispensable to the industry, its perfection and use a running resistance to increasing costs of the farm, such as transportation. Specialized farming produced torrents of food and fiber whose very mass was a perpetual goad to cut unit costs. Into the brief duration of the harvests were compressed a multitude of techniques and a pace of production that pulsed through every ''deal,'' the term used in Agri-businessland to signify the grand finale of the cycle of planting, cultivating, gathering, and selling a crop. In 1944 in Kern County alone there were over 3,300 tractors on farms, some of them equipped with headlights so that work could go on through the night. Machinery became awesome, like the motorized cotton picker; graceful, like the spidery walnut pruner; delicate, like the electronic lemon sorter; or spectral, like the eighty-foot land leveler moving through clouds of its own dust.

The mechanical revolution was a joint product of the ingenuity of farmer-mechanics tinkering in their garages and of methodical research. Promising ideas born on the farm, nagging problems demanding better ways of getting things done, were referred to laboratories in the state universities where the skills of agricultural engineers, plant scientists, entomologists, and soil physicists were enlisted. What they brought forth changed planting patterns, cultural practices, the shape of fruit trees, and the uses of manpower. These teams of searching minds set themselves tasks such as inducing a snap bean plant to set its pods high on the stalk and to release them with less pull, or to condition millions of tons of tomatoes to ripen by the calendar. The caprices of nature could be controlled enough to warrant the expense of research and development.

Technological advance into harvesting became pervasive.

Irrigation, as the vital partner of the earth itself, had to be rationalized. Rivers that rampaged and dried up by turns were channeled into reservoirs and pools from which the water was fed by gravity or pumping into sprinkling systems that delivered rain on call. Mounted on large wheels, pipe assemblies anchored to portable towers could creep and wheel by electronic control, watering a thousand acres at a time, their thin jets tracing arches of sunlit spray against the sky. Supplementing the channel water, deep wells were sunk that could deliver thousands of gallons per minute. Irrigation engineers eventually laced a system of ditches, control gates, settling ponds, pipes, siphons, pumps, and sluices that constrained water to do anything, even to flow uphill.

With the water tamed, men perfected contraptions into refined tools for gathering the harvests.

In the fields, a potato-digging machine tested in the Edison district of Kern County in 1951 was soon on the market; it dug, sorted, and packed "without the touch of human hands . . ."[78] Onions were dug, lifted, and windrowed in one continuous operation. Corn was no longer picked by hand but by an apparatus that husked the ears, picked the kernels, chopped the stalks, delivered the grain to escorting trucks, and spat the debris along its path. In the lettuce fields a vacuum process was developed and installed by which hundreds of packed heads could be cooled in steel tunnels with a capacity of five railway carloads per hour, ready for loading in refrigerated cars at the sheds. Forage crops were harvested by fleets of mowers moving in close formation with trucks, into which they spewed the chopped grass through six-foot pipes that moved in echelons like huge ungainly geese. A "hoe with a brain" could weed a beet field faster than twenty men, using an electronic eye to distinguish between wild grass and beet leaves.

The mechanization of the sugar beet crop showed how close the dovetailing of harvesting could become. It began with the seeds being planted with automatic drills to secure evenly spaced stands. Precision planting was matched by the precision harvesting machine, a tractor on which was mounted a perpendicular wheel bristling with long spikes that skewered the beets out of the ground. By 1952 over 80 percent of the state's beet crop was harvested in this manner. One machine could collect as much as forty tons an hour.

Along with machines that could pound their way across a field, there were those that could be tender, almost solicitous, in their address. Such was the harvester that lifted, washed, bundled, and packed celery before the morning dew evaporated from the green fronds. Asparagus, that most delicate of all vegetables, long resisted the touch of steel, but eventually cutting devices were tested that eliminated the stooping trot of the Filipino hand cutters. In 1958 progress was being made on heating for asparagus beds by means of an electric blanket of wires laid underground to coax the spears to an early start. A crate delivered by air freight in New York in early January could bring as much as $35.00, compared to the $7.50 it would fetch a month later, when it was in season.

In the orchards also machines were taking over. Lemon groves were trimmed by hedging machines that maneuvered a bank of circular saws fourteen inches in diameter arranged on a metal beam that moved them around and above the trees, giving them crew cuts that left them handier for picking. The lemons themselves, after being sorted and graded by electronic eyes, could be handled and packed in bulk, eliminating expensive hand-wrapping. An electronic sorter could separate 2,200 lemons into four shades of green and pack them in boxes. The modern way to pick dates in the cool, stately gardens of Coachella was to raise a crew of six to eight pickers on elevated catwalks sixty feet in the air within reach of the clusters. Mechanical cutters were tried even on the sensitive apricot, but not with notable success. Peaches, one of the state's leading crops, and a fruit with a very low tolerance for manhandling, were poured gently into bins, cradled onto trucks by forklifts, floated in tanks of water where they lost their fuzz before sorting for the pack. And so it was with pears and plums which were wafted into boxes, settled into firm but gentle compactness by vibration, and held in place by soft pads under tightly fastened lids.

In the rice fields of the northern Sacramento it was not a matter of delicate touch and tender loving care, but of space and sweep. There were rice harvesters capable of delivering two thousand hundred-weight of grain in a day. The fields were seeded and fertilized by aircraft of the type that became common as dusters and sprayers of orchards and cotton fields.

Mechanization in cotton, tomatoes, and grapes, three of the most important cash crops, employed armies of harvest hands and set the pace of the industry, in the unrelenting thrust of automation.

In 1927 John Rust discovered that moistened spindles made of steel spring wire rotating as they combed a cotton plant could pick the boles like human fingers. Ten years later Rust's machine could pick not pounds but bales by the day. By 1949 mechanical cotton picking was a demonstrated success. The improved version of Rust's original model looked like "an assembly out of science fiction,"[79] at its forward end a perpendicular slot between two baffles that embraced the stalks as the machine advanced, passing them through the wet spindles, sucking them through vacuum tubes upward and into a wire cage that topped the wierd contraption. The operator, sitting high and forward, tilted the cage sidewise into a waiting gondola that carried the cotton to the gin. For first picking the machine could maintain a working speed of 2.5 miles per hour and comb a field with better than 90 percent efficiency. The mechanical partners of the Rust machine were the planter-cultivator that covered four rows simultaneously, and the scrapper that salvaged the bolls left at the ends of the field where the picker was not able to maneuver. Over a level field of the Central Valley eight or more machines could move in formation, sweeping through hundreds of acres of cotton fluff like a rumbling herd of trunkless elephants. There were over 1,400 of these machines in the Central Valley in 1950. They accounted for 35 percent of the cotton picked that year in that area; six years later it was 70 percent, 260,000 bales. For the entire state the figures were 90 percent, 821,000 bales. And in the final stage the cotton gin was perfected to the point where five hundred-pound bales did not vary more than twelve ounces.

Like cotton, tomatoes offered the same incentives to mechanization: acreages in the thousands, a huge demand by processors, a level terrain, and a system of planting that arranged the plants conveniently. Experimental models of machines were being tested by 1951; and by 1961 there were five commercial machines in the fields, with forty-five more on the drawing boards for the following year. The operation consisted of cutting the whole tomato vine at the roots, raising it by a conveyor belt, shaking the fruit loose, sorting it by hand on a moving rig, and loading on trucks moving alongside. In sixteen minutes one machine could load four thousand pounds on a trailer. Tomato growing became a matter of staggered plantings and controlled ripening.

Grape production was ready for mechanization in the early 1960s. A grape planter was developed that could cover fifteen acres in one day with three men. The old hand shears gave way to pneumatic cutters which enabled eight men to prune from six to eight hundred acres in a day, better than three times the rate of pruning by hand. Conveyor loading and the use of plastic baskets emptied into metal barrels and gondolas began to take the place of lug boxes. With a forklift four men could load a two-ton gondola in one hour.

In corporate agriculture lower unit costs were of course the driving incentive to mechanization. Harvesting costs in tomatoes were reduced by $5 to $7 per ton, amounting to $200 an acre or more at normal rates of yield. Comparative cost studies showed that in cotton picking, machine as against hand operations favored the machine by a wide margin of $20 a bale, discounting loss of grade. Even though accurate unit cost data were a private affair with the industry, from the figures on displaced manpower it was clear that this was the incentive to mechanize. The object of technology in agriculture was the same as in industry—to eliminate people from production.

Mass displacement of workers was regarded by the industry as a mark of efficiency and its data were not screened from the public. They revealed the following typical cases: One cotton machine could do the work of 25 hand pickers. The labor force for cotton dropped from 85,000 in 1950 to fewer than 35,000 in 1960. Before the grape-cutting machine was fully developed for commercial production, its designers were confidently claiming that one machine would be able to pick as much as 65 workers could. Scientists called it "wonderful. It's so economical that 100,000 grape pickers may no longer be needed."[80] The prospect in tomatoes was similar. One machine with a crew of 13 could accomplish the work of 60 hand pickers. By 1965 more than 478,000 man-hours of hand harvesting had been eliminated by mechanization. By 1960 over 90 percent of beet harvesting was done by machine.

Considered by themselves, the figures on gross displacement of people from harvesting did not indicate the multiple effects of mechanization. It reduced the duration of the cotton picking season by eight to ten weeks, eliminating a source of income for pickers who could thus tide themselves between the end of cotton and the beginning of the spring cycle. The use of belt loaders and gondolas eliminated swampers and loaders in grapes and potatoes. Women were substituted for men sorters on the moving tomato rigs. "These women," it was said, "were dependable. They do not come to work with a wine bottle in their pocket. They give a full day's work for a day's pay."[81] Mechanization changed planting patterns, stressed recruitment of men with experience in handling machinery, and tended to promote more regular year-round employment for a much smaller number of persons. Piece rates gave way to hourly rates as machinery made work more predictable and supervision more exacting. As packing operations moved from town sheds to movable assemblies on wheels they were reclassified as field work with lower rates of pay and many fewer workers. Mechanization also meant the final disappearance of family labor.

The effects of technology in the fields affected other economic relationships. As higher skills were required and the labor force was drastically reduced, a form of ethnic discrimination set in, disfavoring Mexicans, Filipinos, and Blacks. It set the stage for a process of selection that reflected long-standing racial bias, a certain ethnic elitism, and the interest of the International Brotherhood of Teamsters in claiming "everything on wheels." The cost of machinery, and the requirement of large acreages to make it economically attractive, made the corporate farms the pacesetters in a race to reduce unit costs that only they could win. Massive use of machinery called for merchandising on a large scale, which in turn marked the decline of "mom and pop" stores in the metropolitan markets. Psychologically, the use of machines spread a comforting euphoria throughout Agri-businessland. "Labor could never be in a position to ruin the California tomato industry . . . either through availability or price."[82]

Mechanization went hand in hand with planned waste, legalized under the marketing orders described above. Unharvested grapes exceeded national consumption by 350,000 tons in 1954; raisins went on the block at 2 cents a pound. Top grade Irish potatoes were ground and sacked for cattle feed for one cent a pound. Peach growers agreed to destroy 10 percent of the harvest amounting to 650,000 tons.[83] Only nonperishables and produce that could be canned and stored into the next season escaped waste on such a scale.

The resulting surplus of people, too, was of major proportions. Hand labor would never disappear entirely, because there would be a demand for it where mechanization was unprofitable or tasks were still beyond the ingenuity of engineers. Yet improvements in technology led the *Imperial Valley Press* to observe that "we may be on the verge of plowing under another big chunk of manpower—the American migrant worker." However inconvenient this effect might be for the migrant laborers, accountability for it could not be traced to any government agency. "It's not a problem for the U.S. Department of Agriculture anyway."[84]

Along with surpluses of food and people, technology was also producing a surplus in family farms. Mechanization was reducing unit costs below the competition level of the small farmer.

Family Farms

Among the stereotypes that have survived reality in American history probably none has endured longer or more tenaciously than that of the yeoman farmer. The Jeffersonian ideal of democratic agrarianism was the model of a political structure resting on access for all men to the economic opportunities of ownership of the soil. The nation that was visualized was one of farms that would provide the main source of income of the family, all of whose members participated regularly in supplying a substantial part of the labor and making the managerial decisions. Jefferson asked only "that as few shall be without a little portion of the land," secure in their status as "the most precious part of the state."[85] And it seemed as if in California the ideal had been taken seriously. The State Commission on Land Colonization had the avowed purpose of settling laborers on small farms. The Central Valley Project, designed to bring dependable irrigation to millions of idle acres, would generate, it was said, fifty thousand new farms for 250,000 people. Federal policy, stated in the rhetoric of classic agrarianism, was pledged to establish, protect, and enhance the family type farm as the pattern for American life.

It never happened in California. What did happen was that the corporate form of property ownership and management already fully developed in the industrial East, was equipped and eager to take over the agrarian West. But social systems are not contrived overnight. Capital, immigrants, technology, the powers of the state, market opportunities, and science, all must move in the same direction and at last fall into the places assigned to them by men of determined will and single-minded purpose. The framework of a corporate society was erected and maintained as the open spaces became scarcer. A certain articulation had to be imposed on the loose parts, the wanderer of the migrant stream and the independence of yeomen land workers. The process took a hundred years. One of its objects was the reorganization of land tenure into the image of corporatism. The intermediate casualty was the family farm.

Technology tipped the scales heavily against it. To establish a farm of forty acres in the 1940s required capital of $85,000; a vineyard of fifty acres, $60,000; a modest poultry farm, $30,000. The most economical rice producers in northern California were units of several thousand acres on which the investment in machinery represented more than half of the capital. With less than two hundred acres no almond grower could justify spending the $25,000 necessary to compete with those who had mechanized, and whose harvesting costs were only 10 percent of those who had not. Custom harvesting, a form of cooperative mechanization, offered only limited relief for growers who were too small to buy their own equipment. In crops like cotton, subject to notorious variations in acreage caused by erratic prices, the man least likely to succeed was the small grower. It was the bigger operators who could take advantage of high market prices in the early period of perishable "deals," as in asparagus and lettuce. "It takes money to make money," the Bank of American advertised to its prospective customers. And money was what there was the least of among the 150,000 small farmers and their families in California in the 1950s.

It was against the labor costs of the financially and technically inte-grated units that the family farmer had to match the value of his personal labor power. Both were reduced to a common denominator when they met in the price competition of the market. The preponderance of hired labor was on the large ranches, whose aim was to mechanize pro-gressively and to minimize the wages of hired workers to the limit. Furthermore, when the value of the personal labor of a one-man opera-tion was determined in the market place it tended to level with the wages of braceros and illegals. It was the margin of value determined by the cost of men and machines, retained by those who had most advantage from both, that sealed the fate of the family farm. Only those who by luck or wit found themselves in the middle zone where mechanization was economical were able to hold their ground. Even they, however, remained at the mercy of the dominant corporate units, for it was not only in production that the test of survival had to be met, but also in the competition for credit and marketing facilities, the areas in which corpo-rate farm managements had notable advantages.

Just as braceros by their numbers and wage levels came to dominate the labor market as against the domestics, so the large ranches pressed upon the small ones by the additional advantages of industrial and financial integration. The facilities for storage, shipping, field trans-portation, credit, and quality control were in the hands of grower-shipper associations. Through contracts the canneries intervened more and more in the managerial decisions of tomato harvesting. Cotton ginners made crop loans whose terms made the small grower an eco-nomic satellite. All this resulted in a psychological as well as material servitude that led the small farmers to organize strikebreaking mobs in the early days of vigilantism, and in the more urbane period of public relations to march on the state capitol to demand that wages be kept unregulated by law. These same farmers in moments of more sober reflection lamented that their labor was worth only what an illegal or a bracero was paid. The agricultural escalator was working in reverse. Small farmers became tenants. Tenants became day laborers. Day laborers became unemployables.

Allowing for the statistical effect of what constitutes a farm as defined by the U.S. Department of Agriculture,[86] it was clear that they were on the way out. In round numbers there were 150,000 of them in 1935, some 123,000 in 1954, and fewer than 100,000 in the 1960s. The trend pointed to the disappearance of another 30,000 by the end of the 1960s. The operators of the small farms that remained statistically alive either enjoyed a sheltered position because of climate, soil, or proximity to market, or they combined farm work with seasonal jobs elsewhere. For the rest a losing battle for survival went on. In the vicinity of large cities they were forced out by rising assessments, or by the installation of an automobile assembly plant, or the construction of an eight-lane freeway. Along the country roads that once served farming communities like Florin, Livermore, Santa Rosa, and Bakersfield, farm houses weathered away, their windmills clanking softly on twisted and rusty frames leaning away from the prevailing winds.

These were the remains of what California's Senator Sheridan Downey called "that highly prized institution, the family farm." They gave point to the unanimous prophecies voiced by agri-businessmen in the *Western Grower and Shipper*[87]: "The small farmer is already gone"; the Los Angeles Chamber of Commerce: "The old fashioned hired man is a thing of the past"; Dr. George L. Mehrens of the University of California: "Our traditional farming is finished": Alan T. Rains, vice-president of the United Fruit and Vegetable Association: "Small truck farms must yield to larger and stronger hands"; and Robert W. Long, official of the Bank of America: "The disappearance of the family farmer is a requirement of the new technology."

How the requirements of the new technology, in combination with the new politics and the new structures of Agri-businessland, hastened the inevitable fate of the small farmer, was illustrated in the case of the cotton industry.

The California Planting Cotton Seed Distributors, Inc.

As one of the important cotton producing states of the nation, California presented in the 1950s a distribution of land tenure of contrasts and extremes. There were holdings, relatively few in number, of thousands of acres each, constituting the core of diversified enterprises owned by corporations or individuals of great wealth. Side by side with these there were hundreds of units representing the specialty cropping of small operators whose cash income was derived solely from cotton. One marketing association alone, Cal-Cot, had over 3,800 members in 1957. In the earlier days of the industry, small-scale cotton planting was typical in the Central Valley, as for example in Kern County, where the 1939 reports showed 66,470 acres under cultivation by 1,082 farmers with less than one hundred bales production per farm. There were only 26 farms that produced over five hundred bales in the county that year.

Cotton growing was a chancy business, subject to the uncertainties of speculation and changes in price supports, causing sudden expansions and contractions in acreage. Cotton plantings rose from 341,000 in 1941 to 948,000 in 1949. The fate of the small planter hung on the operation of distant forces beyond his control from congressional politics to war.[88] On these premises alone, single cropping on small acreages was not the most promising way to attain the Jeffersonian ideal. The agronomic foundations of cotton culture made it even less likely.

All cotton planted in the state was of the single variety known as Acala 4.42, long-fibered, wilt-resistant, and early maturing especially favored by the climate of California. It had been bred in the late 1920s at the U.S. Department of Agriculture's experimental farm in Shafter under the direction of Wofford B. Camp. Camp was familiar with cotton cultural practices in the southern states, and when he left the department to join the Bank of America he turned over the unfinished experiments with Acala to his successor, George H. Harrison.[89]

Harrison, a painstaking scientist, devised a process for multiplying the handful of precious seeds that were gathered in his plots. Pollen was carried by hand, temperatures were controlled, deviant stalks rigorously discarded, survivors isolated with intense care. By stages of transplantings, the parent seed out of the Shafter nursery was multiplied into registered seed, certified as such by the California State Department of Agriculture. In turn it was increased to planting seed, which could now be reckoned by the ton instead of the pound. Only at this stage could the registered seed be sold to the commercial planter.

Harrison laid down exacting rules for the process by which the seed from his plots passed from hand to hand. A bag of not more than 16 to 20 pounds was turned over to each of 16 selected growers, who agreed to follow Harrison's instructions. The privileged 16 planted their allotments which yielded hundreds of pounds of seed, which they distributed to 300 chosen planters. These in turn produced the certified seed that was sold to the 12,000 growers of the state. By 1959 there were 900,000 acres in cotton, all of it of the Acala variety.

It was Agriculture Department policy to encourage the planting of a single variety to prevent cross pollinization of different strains in a given area. The aim was uniformity in quality of the fiber. The strain that did best in California was Acala. The next step was to prohibit the planting of all other varieties throughout the state. Camp and his associates addressed themselves to this problem when they met in Riverside in March 1924, organized the California Cotton Growers Association, and drafted a bill, which they presented to the legislature. It was passed in May 1925. Thereafter it became unlawful "to plant, possess for planting, pick, harvest, or gin" any variety of cotton other than Acala.[90]

What had been designed as a cornucopia became a funnel and then a bottleneck of great expectations for Camp and his associates.

There existed at the time a Kern County Farm Bureau which included hundreds of cotton growers and which had adopted and promoted the single-variety policy. The Farm Bureau, as an affiliate of the state organization, theoretically was controlled through democratic participation of all its dues-paying members. The local farm bureau was legally a cooperative for the distribution of Acala in the county.

In April 1936 some of the large cotton planters who were members of the bureau met and there occurred what may be called a cotton coup. Without due notice to the membership of the bureau, they organized a private enterprise which incorporated as the California Planting Cotton Seed Distributors, Inc. By a contract with the U.S. Department of Agriculture, the C.P.C.S.D. became the sole receiver of the seed developed at Shafter.

As such the C.P.C.S.D. became the arbiter of the multiplier process, influencing if not controlling the selection of the favored recipients at the various stages on increase until the certified seed was placed on sale. Thenceforth the directors set the price of planting seed. In 1951 it was $160 per ton, five dollars higher than the previous year. Sales of 23,252 tons produced a revenue of $3,720,000.[91] Research now continued under the sponsorship of the Distributors, which in four years gave the University of California at Davis $225,000 for that purpose.[92]

There is no record of organized protest or resistance to the bold moves of Camp and his associates, if indeed there was general public knowledge of their actions. The single protestor was Mrs. Bertha Rankin, a retired nurse and widow of a small farmer near Arvin. Mrs. Rankin held that the transfer of control of Acala from the Farm Bureau to the C.P.C.S.D. was highly irregular and contrary to the interests of the small farmers in her community. She believed that such private control was in violation of the antimonopoly provisions of the California Business and Professional Code. Three governors of the state—Warren, Knight, and Brown—ignored or evaded her demands for an investigation. Nor had there been any outcry from the yeoman farmers; they were dependents of the cotton ginning companies, without whose credit, trailers, and processing their cotton would not get to market. The gin managers, themselves a highly concentrated branch of the cotton business, represented a financial hard core, a network of information, a front line of resistance to liberal legislation, and were accustomed to speak of "my growers."

The emplacement of a perfect monopoly within the agricultural system of California attracted no attention. As a possible model for the future, it showed that commodity associations were capable of attaining the ultimate in integration. There was no more inclination in the Department of Agriculture than there was in the governor's office to investigate the monopoly. The department refused Mrs. Rankin's request for a copy of its contract with C.P.C.S.D., responding, "We have to have the consent of the person on the other side of the contract. If we didn't we'd lose his business."

Thirteen years after the cotton coup, Camp told a congressional committee that he "had nothing to do with the distribution of a particular type of cotton seed in California."[93] The Pacific Gas and Electric Company, commenting editorially in one of its periodic success stories in Agri-businessland, said that the single variety law had not been adopted "to regiment growers."[94]

It was not an explanation difficult to believe. Rather than regimentation it had produced great wealth funneled to a small group. Among its members were Wofford Camp and his brother Saul, operators in cotton, cattle, oil, trucks, land leasing, and ginning. On the flat plains of Kern County their monuments were the pyramids of cotton seed, the tribute to and symbol of their power.

Fittingly, the PG & E chronicle closed with a tribute to George Harrison, the modest civil servant who made cotton king in California.

He retired with a distinguished service award from the Farm Bureau
Federation, cited as the man who was putting an extra twenty-five
million dollars a year into the pockets of California farmers. In his
well-earned retirement he could watch "the loyal subjects of King
Cotton grow rich and grateful."[95]

The cotton seed affair demonstrated how monopolistic control could
be established in a sector of California agriculture. Two circumstances
favored this, the strength of those in the innermost circles of agribusiness representing a commodity interest, and the inability of small
farmers to challenge them. Although unusual both in the manner in
which it was accomplished and the circumstances that made it possible,
the cotton coup gave dramatic point to the direction in which the
agrarian economy was moving. The DiGiorgio Fruit Corporation had
already moved far toward controlling the auction markets of the eastern
seaboard. A federal antitrust action was necessary to stop it. In the wine
industry names like Wente and Gallo were emerging as most powerful.
Amadeo Giannini had made the Bank of America the dominant farm
creditor of the state. In production, bottlenecks like the one that Camp
had devised for cotton would be unusual; but it was a model that had
potential emulators in crops such as cantaloups, lettuce, and carrots. It
also revealed that men with hard wills could penetrate the soft bureaucratic structures of government concerned with agricultural affairs.

The State Establishment

The state capitol in Sacramento with it golden dome resting on tiers of
Greek columns and a classic pediment gleams over one of the most
charming public parks in the West. Set among pines, magnolias, and
giant camelias, the seat of the political power is flanked by expensive
hotels, fancy restaurants, and dim lounges where lobbyists practice
their calling. Farther back are the highrise complexes of the bureaucracies. In California, the most important of these agencies deals with
agriculture, with regulation, research, information, education,
irrigation—any and all matters affecting the interests of farming. The
State Department of Agriculture, once described by Professor Claude

B. Hutchinson of the University of California as "the farmers' own organization," interlocked with powerful men who played dual roles in government and the industry. In it the attributes of economic and political government became integrated producing a form of public administration in which checks and balances did not operate.

The State Board of Agriculture was the body officially charged with promoting the progress and prosperity of the industry. Its technical character was clear as the administrative arm of the state in agricultural matters such as marketing, commodity agreements, weights and measures, livestock diseases, and pest control. The members were appointed by the governor to speak for every major branch of the industry. Each member represented in his own right the elite levels of such branches as dairying and tree fruits. Together they formed a council of private powers based on the wealth of rural California. Appointments were rotated among men of the stature of Frank M. Shay, John S. Watson, Saul Camp, and Louis A. Rozzoni, the voices of the Farm Bureau, the Associated Farmers, the grower-shipper associations, and the cotton integrators.[96]

Governor Earl Warren assigned this body the additional responsibility to act as advisor to the Farm Placement Service in order, as it was directed, to facilitate close cooperation between the departments of Agriculture and Employment. This was in accord with the mandate under the Wagner-Peyser Act, that every state agency receiving federal funds for the administration of the national employment service should create a state advisory council.[97] Under Warren's order and in accord with the organizational scheme approved by the board, the chief of the Farm Placement Service reported to the board in its advisory capacity. Taking part in FPS policy decisions affecting harvesters were men like Shay, who was also chairman of the Agricultural Committee of the State Chamber of Commerce and president of the California Prune and Apricot Growers Association, and John V. Newman, member of the National Advisory Committee on Farm Placement.

On the next lower level were the various local committees that kept watch over the county agricultural commissioners, the field offices of the Farm Placement Service, and the federal Extension Service. A subcommittee of the Los Angeles Chamber of Commerce advised on recruiting and hiring of foreign labor.

The subjects of the advice that the leaders of the industry gave at all levels of the state government were not set forth in any laws or regulations. Nor was it intimated that they had any policy-making authority. It was only necessary to place them in some formal relationship with the agencies that affected vital employer interests, avoiding the need for clandestine communication between the courtiers and courtesans of power.

There was also a corps of agriculture commissioners, one for each of the fifty-eight counties, which offered another facility for contacts between officials and growers. Their role was straightforward—to promote the interests of farmers. Reporting to both the county boards of supervisors and the State Board of Agriculture, the commissioners were the servants of agriculture, as they were described by A. A. Brock in 1945.

The most effectual servant of agriculture was, of course, the Farm Placement Service itself, the agency cited in 1948 by the Agricultural Labor Bureau of San Joaquin for its "almost perfect coordination of weather and labor." Other state agencies were not as finely tuned to the needs of growers as the FPS, because it was in this agency that the responsibility to recruit workers rested. The other agencies, more remotely connected with needs and more clearly responsible for regulation of safety, housing, and the like, were not so closely subject to pressure. Nevertheless, there was a pervading sensitivity to other types of grower needs—the need to be excused from providing privies for field workers or from close enforcement of child labor laws, or the need to be left unmolested by inspectors of trucks and buses not in compliance with safety regulations.

Officially, the state agencies were neutral with regard to the conflicting interests of workers and employers. The standing orders of the State Department of Employment were to serve both agricultural employers and workers fairly and efficiently. The tone of administration was one of prudence leaning toward realism in dealing with grower power. The department advised growers that its procedures had been designed to give them maximum control over the hiring of braceros. When striking domestics complained that outsiders were being referred by the Farm Placement Service, the reply from one department chief was that the burden of proof rested on the workers. The view in the field among agricultural agents was that crop strikes should be treated differently from industrial disputes. So should the health problems of migrant workers. The Board of Supervisors of Orange County, with the health officer concurring, expressed deep concern over state intervention "in an area of service that has historically been provided by local government alone."

The Office of the Attorney General did not count among its many duties that of questioning the institutional tilt of government against farm laborers, nor that of investigating the cotton seed affair. One attorney general concluded that for purposes of employment "agriculture is not a trade or an industry."

In the office of the governor, farm workers could not expect partisanship in their favor; their solicitations were always received with formal interest, correct but not exuberant. A succession of governors appointed functionaries whose chief merit was the sponsorship of the Farm Bureau or the Board of Agriculture. The governors were responsive to the needs of agriculture. In his message to the legislature of January 1949, Governor Warren extolled the industry as "the foundation of our economy," observing that "our many specialty crops have not had the protection of subsidies and supports that has been provided for the more staple crops of the nation." He exhorted "that we be alert to any change of economic conditions that might disrupt agriculture." Governor Knight, discarding neutrality between labor and management, publicly endorsed the false information reported to him by the Farm Placement Service. Governor Brown, nettled by criticism that he was unresponsive to complaints of an eminent member of the Board of Agriculture, replied: "I am as concerned about fruit rotting in the fields as you are. We would not interfere with normal economic processes."[98] The cry that fruit was rotting in the orchards set the stage for growers to call up political pressure dramatizing the perennial FPS reports of labor shortages. The normal economic processes to which Governor Brown referred included the planned destruction of farm products.

The Federal Establishment

The federal agenicies that most immediately affected agricultural laborers were, in order of importance, the U.S. Departments of Labor, Agriculture, Justice, and State. Of these four divisions of executive power, two were essentially protective—Labor of the interests of working people and Agriculture of farmers. The laws that created them reflected the advocacy of those interests by Congress. Because of the national origin of so many farm laborers—emigrants, permanent or temporary, from Mexico and Asia—the Department of Justice, through the Immigration and Naturalization Service, affected their lives in important ways. The Department of State played a critical role with regard to the bracero system, the existence of which depended on diplomatic understandings with the government of Mexico.

The twenty years following the initiation of the bracero program in 1942 were in effect years of experimentation with and perfection of a labor market radically different from that in which American industrial workers had struggled toward collective bargaining. The most important characteristics of the bracero system were that it applied after 1945 exclusively to farm laborers; the worker-employer relationship was defined initially in an international agreement and secondarily in individual work contracts; the terms of both were the subject of formal negotiation between representatives of both governments; in the logistics of moving hundreds of thousands of seasonal harvesters back and forth, certain costs were financed mainly by the government of the United States; field supervision and compliance were delegated to the U.S. Department of Labor and its agent, the California Department of Employment. In effect Public Law 78 was the congressional authorization to restructure the farm labor market of the nation, and the federal departments became its executors. The departments of Labor, Justice, State, and Agriculture together represented the federal establishment with which domestic workers had to reckon.

The direction taken by the administration of PL 78 was due in part to congressional negligence and in part to the peculiar climate of Washington politics. From its highest to its lowest levels the Department of Labor was less an advocate of workers than a sensitive barometer of the powerful forces that focus in the national capital. Like all the other executive departments, bureaucratic rivalries with the other elements of the establishment occupied much of its time and it was continuously exposed to the ever-present lobbies of farm employers.

Once, in 1934, a special commission investigating the Imperial Valley strikes had included in its report the following curious recommendation: "Specifically . . . that the U.S. Department of Labor send representatives who can speak Spanish to aid the Mexican and Filipino groups and others to organize for the purposes of collective bargaining."[99] The history of the department thereafter was entirely the reverse of such advocacy. A posture of neutrality was maintained through a succession of secretaries of labor who were contemporaries of the bracero system. One of them, Arthur J. Goldberg, took the position that the department should not be regarded as the representative of any special interest group but of all sections and interests. Secretary of Labor Durkin, himself an experienced trade-union leader, instructed his staff to the effect that "it is important that we do not lend assistance directly or indirectly to efforts to organize workers or to interfere with such efforts."[100]

There were, nevertheless, precedents of bureaucratic partisanship.

The United States Employment Service, in a Joint Interpretation with the Mexican government of the bracero agreement, committed itself to the following policy: "The U.S.E.S. will, through its good offices, advise and urge each Employer who is not a member of any association . . . to either join an existing association or to form an association with other associated Employers in the interest of facilitating the recruitment of workers. . . . The U.S.E.S. will also undertake informational and educational programs directed at achieving this objective."[101] Disavowing neutrality in respect to the bracero system, the department explained that it was "in line with long-established policy and the source of the most satisfactory performance."[102]

In the Department of Agriculture there were no legal obligations or moral commitments to farm "hands." Among the needs of farm employers that it recognized was that of plentiful manpower. This did not call for administrative interference with the jurisdiction of the Department of Labor. Its role was rather that of an alternate administrator of Public Law 78 should Labor become, in the eyes of the industry, too benevolent toward braceros and domestics. Assistant Secretary of Agriculture Mervin L. McLain, addressing a meeting of the California State Chamber of Commerce, spoke on the subject of "the role of government as the hired hand on the farm."[103]

The record of administrative decisions in Labor, Agriculture, Justice, and State, as it unfolded during the two decades of the bracero system, fulfilled the philosophy of the prudent mean, the uncommitted middle. One grower spokesman praised it for this neutrality: "It is not the proper funtion of government agencies to either organize or aid in establishing citizen organizations or to attempt to influence or control such groups."[104] "We believe," declared the Farm Bureau Federation of California, "that the government's place in the picture should be primarily one of opening the door so that farmers and their organizations can do the job for themselves."[105]

As noted above, in California for many years an advisory relationship had existed between grower spokesmen and officials of the Department of Employment and the State Board of Agriculture. The advisory technique was easily adapted to the bracero system. A Special Farm Labor Advisory Committee was created, through which the department was able to consult periodically with the most important farm leaders from every state of the nation. The Special Committee had a subcommittee on Mexican Labor; important California leaders were on both. No information regarding the meetings of the Special Committee or the business transacted was reported to the public. Evidence of them came from other sources.

A counterpart advisory committee of eighteen representatives of organized labor was set up in response to their demands for a voice in these deliberations.

The two advisory committees and department representatives never met together and the department was careful not to provide the labor committee with information on such important matters as the agenda of the Special Committee, the rules of its proceedings, or anything else that would permit the labor representatives to know what was taking place at these high levels of the department. It decided on the agenda, presented it to the labor advisors on the shortest possible notice, communicated privately with those on the committee judged to be least sympathetic to farm workers, and reserved the right to veto nominations made by the president of the American Federation of Labor. Advisory meetings with labor were called once a year for one day and were principally discussions of matters settled months before.

These were the visible formalities of consultation. Behind them an entirely different relationship was maintained between the federal agencies and the spokesmen of the industry. In confidential conversations from which labor representatives were excluded industrial power spoke and bureaucrats listened. These consultations dealt primarily with three matters: the negotiation of the terms of the international agreements with Mexico, policy concerning the administration of the bracero system, and wages.

With respect to the terms of the agreements, the American negotiators met with their Mexican counterparts only after they had been carefully briefed by grower representatives. The evidence that this was the real decision-making process is abundant. The 1949 agreement "was the result of several months of negotiations by both governments and by all interested private parties."[106] The terms of the 1954 bracero contracts were discussed and agreed upon by labor users and Department of Labor officials in Washington for a week "in an attempt to draft a contract that will give farmers a reasonable deal."[107] "A group organized to stabilize farm labor supply . . . was instrumental in working out various treaties and agreements with Mexico."[108] Attorneys for the growers associations and members of the Mexican subcommittee "actually participated in the drafting of some of the language."[109] Since it was impossible for growers to anticipate the multiple details of the administration of the program, periodic meetings were held to review these.[110] Because farmers felt strongly that they "must harvest the crops," the terms of labor recruiting were arrived at by frequent exchanges between them and the Departments of Labor, Justice, and Agriculture.[111] The most important policy matter of all—the fixing of wage rates—was likewise resolved at the highest levels, including the Secretary of Labor. It was the secretary "and the ranchers who agreed that wages should be fixed at 50 cents an hour" in 1958.[112]

Having avoided the appearance of partisan bias by holding formal consultations with bilateral national advisory committees, the Department of Labor nevertheless stressed that it was indeed impartial. In connection with the Mexican negotiations the department gave assurances that "equal opportunities for consultation will be given to organized labor and management."[113] The promise was not kept and became in effect a deliberate lie.

Concealment of how the bracero system was molded according to the interests of the labor users greatly eased their anxieties. Public Law 78 was a purified version of the wetback traffic, about which publicity was becoming more intense and embarrassing. Plantation owners in the South and farmers in the Midwest brought pressure on Congress to provide cheap labor from Mexico for them, pointing to the advantage to the border users of California and Texas. They demanded a share in the impressive benefits of alien labor. The bracero system permitted the industry to pass on considerable administrative costs to the federal treasury; it guaranteed an abundant flow of manpower; it cleansed the industry of the stains of the illegal black market; and it provided from the sonorous texts of the agreements a rhetoric that made it appear close to a model of collective bargaining.

There was a risk to the industry to be weighed against these considerable advantages. It consisted of the possibility that certan provisions of the Mexican agreements might bring to bear certain federal statutes for the protection of American citizen workers.

The Mexican agreements rested upon the principle that braceros were to be paid the prevailing wage received by domestics, a legal concept that had been clearly defined by Congress. The language of the Public Works Contracts Act of 1936 defined the prevailing wage as that wage paid to workers similarly employed as specified in existing contracts between employers and unions and arrived at through direct negotiation between them. And the Wagner-Peyser Act of 1933 mandated that "the Department of Labor . . . shall foster, promote, and develop the welfare of the wage earners of the United States, to improve their working conditions and to advance their opportunities for profitable employment." It was under these provisions that there was created the Bureau of Employment Security, from which were derived the powers and the funding of field agencies such as the Farm Placement Service of the California Department of Employment. The Wagner-Peyser Act created a national system of employment; and this the bracero system was fast becoming. In short, legislative standards such as the prevailing wage and the improvement of working conditions were being strained by a double standard that was in fact emerging in the fields.

The discrepancy was resolved by the institution of private partisan consultation, the acquiesence of Congress, and the servility of the bureaucracies. The bureau agreed with the growers that its role was "to provide adequate numbers of workers at all times and as soon as needed.[114] It substituted for the prevailing wage principle of the Act of 1936 the nebulous formulas worked out by growers and public officials meeting in private. While the international agreements recognized the procedures by which braceros could form unions, the Department of Labor laid down conditions that totally prevented such an eventuality.[115] The department nullified the right of domestic workers displaced by braceros to administrative hearings. In every essential aspect of the administration of the bracero system the shadow economic government of the industry lay over the law. Senator Richard M. Nixon, campaigning for the vice-presidency in 1952, had said that "the program should be controlled to the greatest extent possible by the growers themselves."[116] It was. That control remained unquestioned through the administrations of Harry Truman, Dwight Eisenhower, and John F. Kennedy in the White House; of Earl Warren, Goodwin Knight, and Edmund G. Brown in the State Capitol in Sacramento; of Maurice Tobin, Martin Durkin, and James P. Mitchell as secretaries of labor.

It was in California that the techniques of private manipulation were perfected. There was created, as requested by growers and approved by the department, the Regional Foreign Labor Operations Committee, composed of high officials of the Bureau of Employment Security, the Farm Placement Service, and representatives of agri-business. Through this committee the BES agreed to share responsibility "in the manning of the agricultural industry of this state." It was intended as "an intelligence medium for the entire agricultural industry and government agencies involved." As such it became the channel through which information and power were passed from the highest federal levels to the growers associations that commanded both.[117] The administrative facilities of the department were placed at the disposal of labor users "to move forward their recommendations."[118] It agreed to exclude labor unions from its discussions. It pledged itself not to deviate from the instructions it received from growers. It endorsed the self-regulation of the associations with respect to contract compliance. It favored the integration of private and public administrative powers at the state and local operating levels.

The vertical integration of government with private interest, shrouded in confidentiality, required a particular type of civil servant. In their rare encounters with domestic workers they affected a cordiality that disarmed criticism and evaded the issues. They acted as the growers expected them to but with the earnest demeanor of men who had to exemplify the uprightness of those clothed with public authority. At congressional hearings they were unctuous and touched by the miseries of domestic harvesters they were duty bound to alleviate. On the whole they were a bland lot of caretakers of the bracero system, the soft facade of Agri-businessland.

Wage rates fixed by growers were ratified, in keeping with the view of a Department of Labor solicitor who said, "We do not want the employer to pay any higher wages."[119] In the face of a farm labor strike, department agents stalled their investigations until the workers broke ranks in desperation. Their records were closed to public inspection on the grounds that the Mexican agreements fell within the class of matters affecting foreign affairs. Referrals of worker's grievances went from the Department of Labor to the Department of Employment to the Department of Justice to the Mexican consuls and eventually to the files.

Legislation and the Harvesters

The weaknesses of the bureaucrats merely reflected a political system in which farm workers as a class had been set apart from the American workers. The National Labor Relations Act of 1935 excluded them from collective bargaining. In the House of Representatives, jurisdiction over legislative matters concerning agricultural labor was assigned to the Committee on Agriculture, which also dealt in the problems of pest control, livestock, and commodity subsidies. In Congress officials of the Department of Labor, State, and Justice were congratulated "for trying to represent the American farmer." A Secretary of Labor with a realistic sense of the traditional lines of power in these matters instructed his agents to maintain "close working relationships with the U.S. Department of Agriculture."[120] One U.S.D.A. official had said that farm workers displaced by mechanization were not a problem for his department.[121]

Such close harmony between the various branches of the federal establishment was not the result of conspiracies or models of deceit skillfully achieved. The black slave, the sharecropper, the hired hand, the migratory harvester, the wetback, the bracero, and all the intermediate types of land workers in America never had any institutional connections with government because they had never possessed land. At the base of social injustice lay the denial of participation in the national wealth. Their protest could find expression only in appeals to the Christian-democratic ethic of the republic. It could not reach into the mechanisms of control in any of the three branches of government.

The legislative branch of state government, like the executive, reflected faithfully the social composition of rural California. Whatever the professional or occupational character of the legislators from the so-called "cow counties," they shared the traditional attitudes toward laborers of alien stock. These attitudes were conditioned for generations by the anti-alien mood that characterized the politics of the state after the 1870s. The state constitution itself empowered cities and towns to move Chinese outside city limits as a quarantine against Asiatic Coolieism. Class hostility did not stop at ethnic boundaries. The state legislature passed criminal syndicalist laws under which English-speaking White labor organizers of American ancestry were sent to jail. Decades of anti-Oriental agitation left an imprint on the legislature, to which no farm workers were ever elected. It was in this tradition that legislators excluded California farm workers from compulsory workmen's compensation, unemployment insurance, and other protective benefits that industrial labor was steadily winning.

The scope of coverage of state laws was trimmed by opinions of the state attorney general, who held that for purposes of defining employment "the terms trade and industry . . . do not connote agricultural work.[122] "It may be an occupation," he conceded, "if it is the principal means of making a living."[123] The privileged position accorded the agricultural industry was reinforced by statute. The legislature "recognized that agriculture is characterized by individual production in contrast to the group or factory system that characterizes other forms of individual production."[124] This was the legislative expression of the first article of faith in Agri-businessland, that farming is different, so different that the rules of social responsibility generally recognized for employers were inapplicable to it. Contradictions in the legislative philosophy posed no problems. Marketing orders legalized the destruction of crop surpluses while in another part of the Agricultural Code it was declared public policy to prevent waste. Among the statutes of 1947 was one enacted "for the purpose of preserving tranquility of its citizens . . . to insure the unobstructed production and distribution of our factories and fields . . . and the preservation of our democratic way of life.''[125] The language bore a striking similarity to that of the declaration of aims and purposes of the Associated Farmers of California.

County government was even more sensitive to the interests of farmers. At this level the supervisors were perennially occupied in discouraging permanent residence of destitute migrants and in setting limits to the exercise of rural democracy. It was the harvest laborers who were directly affected by the restrictions on public assistance, by the enforcement of vagrancy laws, and by antipicketing ordinances which were in effect in thirty-four counties at the end of the 1930s. The San Joaquin County ordinance prohibited the utterance, publication, or use of seditious language; loitering, standing, or sitting on public highways; besetting or picketing the premises of another where any person is employed or seeks employment. More than preventing citizens from beating one another, keeping the peace in these counties meant suppressing disturbances of the economic order such as pickets calling on harvesters to join a strike.

The police power in rural California became less prone to ostentatious violence after the LaFollette report of 1942. The panic of the 1930s had subsided and was followed by a decade unbroken by any major strike. Wetbacks and braceros began to displace domestics, the only potential recruits for unionism. Had there been a need to show force, its principal elements were available—the sheriffs, their deputies, and the California Highway Patrol. As in the past the police intelligence and that of the growers associations were sufficient to monitor the moods and movements of the harvesters. Supplementing these regulars there were the field foremen and other personnel who could be deputized. As a last resort, citizen farmers could be armed with clubs and sidearms and marched through towns beleaguered by unionists. In the tranquil fields of the Imperial and Central Valleys stability and consolidation and integration went on apace, requiring little more than a permanent alert against unionist subversion. The collective police mentality was not far from that expressed by one sheriff: "We protect our farmers here in Kern County. They are our best people. They put us in here and they can put us out again."[126]

The major exception to the bias of the legislature was Article 923 of the Labor Code, and a departure from the social climate of the times. It read:

> Governmental authority has permitted and encouraged employers to organize in the corporate and other forms of capital control . . . The individual unorganized worker is helpless to exercise actual liberty of contract and to protect his freedom of labor. . . . There-

fore it is necessary that the individual workman have full freedom of association and designation of representatives of their own choosing . . . free from the interference, restraint or coercion of employers.

Lacking the economic base that California industrial workers had developed, farm workers were never able to make this policy effective. The courts repeatedly upheld its constitutional validity, calling it an affirmative objective of State policy to equalize the bargaining power as between labor and management by encouraging effective unions. But no administrative agency was ever created to enforce this policy, and farm workers invoked Article 923 in vain against the adamant contention that agriculture was different.

Mindful of the preferred status that the legislature had granted it, the agricultural industry watched over the governmental processes in Sacramento to keep itself in favor and to prevent workers from sharing that status. The farm lobby that waited upon the legislators, the governors, and the bureaucrats was an effective one. It consisted of representatives of the commodity groups as well as the councils and bureaus that looked after the public relations of the industry as a whole. National policies enacted by Congress, such as the National Labor Relations Act, the National Defense Act, and the Wagner-Peyser Act, were effectively neutralized, safeguarding "the great difference between conditions affecting agriculture and those affecting industry." So far as farm labor legislation was concerned the agri-business advocates were unopposed. It was not the least important card in a full hand drawn from a cold deck.

Academia and the Rural Poor

The land, the water, the technology, the bureaucracies, the police, these factors of power moved into place over the course of time needed an appropriate intellectual expression, and this was provided by the state universities. Science and technology were the disciplines of an economic transformation that was reclaiming millions of idle acres, eliminating the family farm, facilitating drastic displacements in the labor force, and smoothing the way for the integration of farming with the corporate structure of the American system. Research was carried on principally at the College of Agriculture of the University of California at Davis with public funds supplemented by donations from private sources. In the 1930s contributors included the Canners League of California, California Walnut Growers Association, Holly Sugar Company, and United Prune Growers. Beginning in the 1920s this research was intensified and oriented toward the efficiency of agriculture as a big business. Support for research at Davis was forthcoming from nonfarming enterprises such as Carbide and Chemical Corporation, Armour and Company, Kaiser Aluminum, Dow Chemical, the Beet Sugar Development Foundation, Del Monte Corporation, Safeway Stores, and the Bank of America. Commodity associations joined in encouraging research on technical problems that concerned those who marketed as well as those who grew a multitude of crops. Select professional talent was assigned to develop varieties of fruits and vegetables adapted to handling in bins, defoliants, precision drill seeding, electronic selection, flotation, heating, hedge pruning, shaking, cradling, and packaging.

Since its foundation in 1868 the College of Agriculture had been regarded as one of the forces creating a new agricultural economy. It was given deserved credit "for the significant innovations that have advanced farm productivity and for educating farmers up to them"[127] Dean Hutchinson of Davis, considered it as the scientific planning board for farmers. Its 1947 budget of $7,252,000 was spent for laboratories, field stations, and publications at Davis and the related facilities of the University on the Berkeley campus. On the Berkeley campus there was the prestigious library of the Giannini Foundation, endowed by the founder of the Bank of America, Amadeo Giannini.

The single-minded aim of research and development and scholarship was, in the words of Dean Hutchinson, "to serve adequately the agriculture of a highly developed commercial civilization such as characterizes California today," and its maintenance "on the highest profitable basis in the face of surpluses." By their own definition the academicians excluded any concern for the effects of such a civilization on the wage earners who depended on it but owned no part of it. It was not, however, an entirely negative bias. Concerning labor certain obligations were recognized. Another dean, Dr. Daniel Aldrich, suggested that better policies were needed to protect the farmer at the peak of harvests. Professor George L. Mehren saw the need for seasonal labor as massive and critical. The Farm Bureau Federation noted with appreciation the urgency with which the Davis researchers were developing a tomato variety suitable for mechanical harvesting in the face of rising labor costs.[128] Newspaper reporters went to the point more directly, observing "the extensive efforts among farm scientists to seek ways and means to eliminate the jobs of farm workers."[129]

That those hundreds of thousands of workers were a part of agricultural society the academic specialists were ready to acknowledge. Dean Hutchinson had himself identified the items of information that the industry required—the amounts and kinds of labor needed by changing production patterns, wage rates per day, numbers and location of harvesters seeking work, and availability of housing. Even this practical agenda was never acted upon.

It was not altogether the fault of this particular sector of academia that its devotion to the progress and profit of commercial agriculture excluded a curriculum on the resulting human conditions. From the beginning researchers and extension agents had no formal commitment to any other sector of rural society. Furthermore, other agencies of the state were responsible for the gathering of such data as Hutchinson had listed. These were the Department of Industrial Relations and its subdivisions, principally that of Labor Statistics and Research. From their beginnings these agencies were hampered by niggardly funding, limited staffing, and an absence of intellectual curiosity in the pursuit of data. In the classification of the various sectors of California's labor force agriculture, forestry, and fishing were lumped.[130] The twenty-second biennial report of the Bureau of Labor Statistics for 1926 contained no data whatever on farm labor. Statistical abstracts of economic and social data on the California labor force did not mention hourly rates and weekly earnings; the Department of Industrial Relations never compiled information on farm labor wages.[131] It was not until 1969 that anything like a comprehensive and scientifically valid survey of agricultural labor was published, and this report dealt only with the enumeration of workers.[132] It did not venture into such areas as the documentation of man-hour inputs. Neither did the State Department of Agriculture have any interest in clarifying such a vital matter, considering itself solely a regulatory and service agency for the industry.

There were two important consequences of this neglect. One was that the official state agencies never challenged the resistance of farm employers to provide the data. Such record keeping was considered by the industry as an unnecessary increase in the cost of doing business. The second consequence was that the statistical data on social conditions were left to the imagination of the Farm Placement Service and its grower advisory committees.

In this manner academic specialization, bureaucratic inadequacy, and audacious pretense left a void in the cultural history of California. It was one of those empty spaces in which vital issues of public policy were ignored or lost. This void the industry proceeded to fill with its own self-serving articles of faith, its own description of the way of life in rural California.

The Ideology of Agri-business

An ideology can be thought of as "a manner or content of thinking of an individual or class . . . a systematic scheme of ideas about life." By this definition there was in California an ideology of agri-business consisting of a set of statements or propositions purporting to explain and justify its role in society.

That of agri-business differed from classical ideologies in that its only ideologues were the academicians who provided it with applied science and technology. These persons were concerned with carrying out practical assignments for efficient production, and to them the only significant action was that of the men and the forces that had molded a commercial civilization.

The pervasiveness of the ideology of agri-business was unquestionable. The industry claimed a privileged position as the foundation of the economy of the state. It was exempt from the social legislation that had slowly extended protection to other occupations. The gap between these and farm laborers as to wages and living conditions was glaring and becoming more so. Periodically the rural peace was disrupted by protest and insurgency, which called attention to conditions which many citizens decried. The material benefits agri-business received from government were on a grand scale, representing over the long run the transfer of enormous wealth from the public to the private domain. A climate of public opinion that would favor the continuation of such benefits was essential. Agri-business addressed itself to that opinion through a widely advertised series of propositions which represented the ideology of the industry:

— Agri-business is the world provider of food and fiber, the productive cornerstone of an America beleaguered by hostile powers, where freedom can survive only by the forces of democracy abundantly fed and clothed. Food could win wars; those who provided it on so vast a scale could well be honored as the provisioners of victory.

— Agri-businessmen are farmers, men of earthy minds and bodies dressed in overalls, the direct descendants of the Jeffersonian yeomen, the élite of the republic.

— The farmer's calling is a singular one, subject to the uncertainties of the weather, the ravages of pests, and all the other hazards of nature against which, for all his smudge pots and sprays, he must struggle.

— Agri-business has devised and harmonized a multitude of production units into a marketing system that regulates abundance and cushions prices. This is cooperative enterprise, a sociological model of economic democracy.

— The American consumer reaps the benefits of this devotion, organizing talent, and cooperative competence. As Americans shifted from rural to urban residence more food had to be delivered by fewer producers and at prices consistent with the national aspiration of rising levels of living for everyone.

— The mission of agri-business is accomplished without benefit of subsidies from government. It is a risky but successful record "of independent operators who do not receive one penny in federal crop payments or government subsidies in any form whatsoever."[133] The accomplishments of the industry are all the more remarkable because it has to rely on an unskilled labor force. Risking loss, it is willing to hire persons unemployable elsewhere, saving them from morally debilitating charity.

— Because of its vital needs, the industry must continuously seek field labor in the reservoirs of Mexican, Blacks, southern Whites, and Asians. American workers find stoop labor unattractive and simply will not accept it.

— Whatever its defects, the domestic labor market represents the best American tradition of unregimented men working at well paid tasks. The harvesters find opportunity in "a free labor pool, operating democratically like all other American institutions."[134]

— In such a self-regulated labor market there is a chronic shortage of domestic workers. There are not now and never will be enough such workers to harvest the crops. To keep them in plentiful supply is an essential condition of agricultural free enterprise.[135]

— Failure of government agencies and public opinion to understand this is responsible for the periodic loss of crops. It is the shortage of harvest labor that forces farmers to disc under lettuce and leave fruit unpicked.

— The industry is not responsible for labor shortages, since it pays the highest wages of any agricultural state in the nation. "The average farm rate being paid in states which are our major competitors is 48 percent less than paid by California farmers."[136]

— A seasonal labor force to provide stoop labor can be guaranteed only through the bracero program. The stabilization of this labor supply through international agreements is indispensable for the operation of an industry whose gross annual production is valued at nearly three billion dollars.

— Braceros are strictly supplementary to the domestic workers. Their labor is more costly because of free services that employers are obligated to provide. They are hired only after certification of need by the Department of Labor. Contract compliance is strictly supervised by the department which also protects the braceros from exploitation.[137]

— Hiring of illegals is not countenanced by the industry, and in any event growers generally cannot tell the difference between a wetback and a legal resident of Mexican ancestry. The industry wholeheartedly supports the Immigration Service in its efforts to discourage the traffic.

— In agriculture there are no strikes, only labor disturbances. Disputes between workers and growers are personal matters and they are fairly resolved through direct dealings between the employer and individual workers.

— Labor disturbances are in most instances caused by outside agitators under the influence of the Communist party, which is controlled by the Soviet government.

— The industry recognizes the right of farm workers to join unions, but no particular union ever fulfills the requirements of genuine representation that employers are bound to respect. "This does not mean that growers are indifferent to the just grievances expressed by the workers; it means only that they are unwilling to give recognition to the union."[138] Farmers have no quarrel with legitimate industrial unions.

— Associations of growers are authorized to act in an employer-employee relationship on behalf of their members in contracting braceros; but no such relationship exists between those associations and domestic laborers.

— The terms of employment of braceros are set forth in detail in the contracts, the provisions of which are the best evidence that collective bargaining exists in the industry. But such contracts with domestic workers would drive growers out of business.

— Collective bargaining and social legislation to protect farm workers cannot be administered without imposing costly recordkeeping on growers. This would absorb the narrow margin of profit under which the industry is forced to operate by costs not subject to its control, such as the cost of transportation.

— The industry must be vigilant with respect to misguided federal agencies, which from time to time advance proposals to unionize farm workers and extend collective bargaining to them.

— The social problems of farm workers are not caused by worker-employer relationships in the industry. The industry accepts its responsibility in that it offers work to those who are too unskilled or too unfortunate to find jobs in other sectors of the economy.

These were the principal tenets of agri-business that justified its role in American society and its views on labor policy. Brought together in such an outline they give the impression of a systematic arrangement of ideas, a corpus of doctrine representing the intellectual statement of those who had shaped the society of California.

This was far from the truth. These propositions were not intended to explain a social system but to promote a favorable public image. They appeared scattered in newspaper advertisements, confidential memoranda, congressional hearings, legal briefs, and learned papers called up to meet a legislative crisis or to counteract unfavorable publicity. All of them raised sharp issues of fact, but none could be brought to the test of proof. Neither examined in the universities nor researched by the public agencies, by repetition and emphasis they became the accepted non-thought of both. Their critique was left to journalists like Carey McWilliams, scholars like Paul Taylor and Varden Fuller, foreign researchers like Stuart Jamieson, and congressional advocates like Senator Robert LaFollette.

Unquestioned in the main, agri-business ideology was widely believed, especially with regard to the bracero system. Its services were invaluable through a half-century of crises which included the Wheatland strike of 1913, the Imperial Valley vigilantism of 1928, and the Central Valley strikes of the 1930s, notably that of cotton pickers in October 1933. It countered the effect of the investigation authorized by President Truman in 1950 and provided the arguments that many congressmen accepted, making possible the crowning achievement of the charter of the bracero system, Public Law 78. And it proved one of the most effective of the weapons of agri-business in resisting and eventually destroying the challenge of the National Farm Workers Union to its long domination.

It is now necessary to turn to that encounter.

III: The Encounters— 1947-1952

The DiGiorgio Strike

California covers an area 775 miles from north to south and 235 miles east and west at its widest latitude. On the map it looks like a thick misshaped bracket marking the place where the western tide of American history was contained. At its center nature provided a maritime shelter in San Francisco Bay and in the south a gently sloping plain open to the sea and ringed by mountains; in these places developed the state's two largest cities.

Agri-businessland was the back country of metropolitan Los Angeles and San Francisco. Back country but not backward; it possessed sophisticated types of social organizations appropriate to, as indicated in the previous sections, the requirements of corporate agriculture. The interior cities like Fresno, Bakersfield, Stockton, and Sacramento became the hubs of what Californians liked to call their Inland Empires—the Imperial and the great Central valleys. Of these the Central Valley was the masterpiece of nature's design, surrounded by satellite pockets like the Salinas and Napa, and jewels like the Ojai.

Ranged according to size, wealth, scale, variety of production, and the other qualities by which the inland empires commonly measured themselves, Kern County was one of the flourishing provinces of agribusiness. The value of its crops had risen from $26,500,000 to $166,500,000 in the decade preceding 1950. Cotton, potatoes, and grapes accounted for market sales of more than $100,000,000 in 1949. At that time its cotton plantings of 213,000 acres were among the largest in the Central Valley. Oil pumping had been an important industry since 1910.

Kern County was the southern terminal of the irrigation network of dams and canals stretching to Shasta in the north, carrying a steady supply of water to its semi-desert lands. Water created "the richest county in the richest state of the richest nation."

This wealth was distributed in the conventional manner. The Kern County Land Company was the base of a domain of one million acres in four states, developed from the original land grants in California dating back to 1890. To irrigate its own lands and those of more than two hundred tenants it owned and operated some eight hundred miles of canals and ditches. The net income of the company in 1956 was $11,745,000 from oil, cotton, cattle, and crops. Lying astride the main highway from Los Angeles to the Central Valley, it waited for the additional bonanza of the urban overflow that time was certain to bring.

Here, too, was the home base of the DiGiorgio Fruit Corporation, whose principal holdings were the DiGiorgio Farms near Arvin and the Sierra Vista ranch north of Delano. These operations had been developed as part of a system of production and distribution that made DiGiorgio the prototype of the successful agri-businessman. DiGiorgio's annual sales climbed to $18,000,000 in 1946 and continued upward and in five years its twenty-one directors and officers were paid $1,500,000. Corporation president Joseph DiGiorgio lived on the Arvin farm, where he dispensed economic justice from his front porch; he enjoyed a reputation for his business talent and philanthropy, unblemished by a federal anti-trust suit in 1942. "A man of kind and generous heart," he had been known "to keep old and faithful employees for months during an illness or ill fortune."[139] The corporation performed its good works, such as donating two slabs of beef to the P.T.A. barbecue, quietly, but still left an imprint on the countryside. There was a DiGiorgio Road and a DiGiorgio Park.

Even less ostentatious was the DiGiorgio power. DiGiorgio had risen on the great tides of change that had transformed California—motor transportation, reclamation, technology, banking, and population. Locally, Joseph DiGiorgio was the major statesman of a circle that included Wofford Camp and Lloyd W. Frick, the representative men of economic power. From Kern County the lines of communication and interest connected DiGiorgio with the state's establishments in banking, insurance, food processing, finance, and retail trade—the Bank of America, Firemen's Fund Insurance, Lockheed Aircraft Corporation, and Pacific Gas and Electric.

To the richest county in the nation came some of its poorest people— black and white sharecroppers from Oklahoma and the Deep South, and brown Mexicans from Texas and the border counties. Around Bakersfield, the county seat of thirty-five thousand population in 1950, they created new communities in the pockets of an agricultural economy, open stretches of sand and brush and saline flats too costly to reclaim. Wasco, Carversville, Weedpatch, Cottonwood Road, Lamont, and Arvin were put together with cardboard, metal scraps, and used lumber salvaged from a long migration. Mixtures of shacks, lean-tos, cabins, and tents, these new towns had a transient look, as if their occupants were not sure that this was their last stop. Some of the neighborhoods had bright names like Mayfair, Sunset, Columbine Colony, and Paradise Acres.

Here the dispossessed formed a new community. From these shanty towns they shuttled to their work as field day laborers, swampers, irrigators, packers, tractor drivers, and handymen. They worked a land "whose amazing productivity is making it famous all over the country."[140] In the summer the sun beat down on the vineyards and orchards at 110 degrees of ground temperature, and a fine dust settled on everything. In the winter when the rains sogged the land and everything on it a grey solitude fell on countryside.

In the towns lived people loosely sorted according to ethnic and cultural similarities. Carversville and Cottonwood Road were settled by Blacks, Delano and the outskirts of Bakersfield by Mexicans, Arvin and Lamont by Okies. Among the Oklahomans the ties of kinship remained strong. Their social life centered on the church; their politics were dominated by the local squires like DiGiorgio and Camp.

The towns were the labor pools from which the farmers drew their manpower. The two closest to the eleven thousand acre DiGiorgio Farms were Arvin and Lamont, typical western settlements strung along wide streets that began and ended abruptly in open fields. The churches, the weekly auction, the "smokehouses" where beer and cheer were dispensed, and the general stores were the community centers where the talk of the town was exchanged. The inhabitants were of types like Johnny Sheldon, whose Barrymore profile and iron muscles become all the more commanding when he was liquored; Hattie Shadowens, who had been a waitress for 10 cents an hour, serving union talk over the counter to her Okie customers; the Chavez family, refugees from Texas who pitched their tent and their hopes on a windy sand lot near Weedpatch; and Tim Parker, an alert, easy-talking Black who was beginning to understand the effects of racial and ethnic lines between working men.

With the exception of Blacks, these were the "hands" of the DiGiorgio Farms. Among them Jim Harron had worked for sixteen years, a minister of the Gospel who had lost the promised land back in Oklahoma but who could still say, "I ain't carried a licking yet." Like his friends and neighbors, the Adays, the Swearingens, the Skaags, and the Mitchells, they were no longer migrants. They had lived long enough in Kern County to have settled into the confidence and support of neighbors, friends, and kinfolk.

For some years before 1948 they had talked about conditions on the DiGiorgio Farms. Men with families to support and who had started working for DiGiorgio for 30 cents an hour were earning only 80 cents fifteen years later. Skilled irrigators worked twelve-hour shifts for 85 cents an hour; they ate lunch as they worked. There was extra time but no overtime, meaning that the work day could be lengthened to fourteen or fifteen hours at the base wage rate. There was no premium pay for night work either, and crews were subject to call-in all week, including Sundays. There was no seniority in the fields or in the packing shed, and workers could be fired on the spot by merely being handed a termination slip. From the decisions of field supervisors there was no appeal to higher levels of management since, as Mr. DiGiorgio himself held, "there is nothing to discuss."

Part of the labor force was housed in camps located on the ranch in segregated bunkhouses and cottages for Mexicans, Okies, and Filipinos. Some cottages rented to families were a constant source of irritation to the tenants, the corporation requiring that they pay for their maintenance in return for the low rents. A few workers were housed in discarded refrigerator cars. And off the Farms, the "incredible eyesores that dotted the surrounding towns of Arvin and Weedpatch and Lamont"[141] were mute witness to the low level of living DiGiorgio provided for his employees.

These matters had long been the talk of the town when Robert E. (Bob) Whatley, a one-armed veteran labor organizer out of Oklahoma, wrote to the National Farm Labor Union asking for "a good speaker and some literature." The letter was written on May 5, 1947, and was addressed to the president of the NFLU, H. L. Mitchell. On this slender lead, Mitchell and his lieutenant, Hank Hasiwar, went to California, did a quick tour of the state, and concluded that Hasiwar should remain in Bakersfield to work with Whatley.

In the summer of the same year organizing was proceeding in earnest. Whatley, with a puckered face like a bleached raisin and a pint flask always in the pocket of his neatly pressed pants, was a frail Jimmy Higgins, the classic union organizer prototype, who "talked union" always and everywhere. The tall, husky Hasiwar loomed large over Whatley as the two walked the streets of Arvin and the rows of tents and cabins in the labor camps. A graduate of roughhouse organizing in New York, Hasiwar had a style of easy manners and ready pugnacity. Around these two gathered volunteers who were to form the core of Local 218 of the National Farm Labor Union. By August 1947, 1,200 authorization cards had been signed by Bakersfield area farm workers, the majority of them employees of the DiGiorgio Fruit Corporation. The rest were men and women who made wages seasonally in cotton picking and in the potato fields around Edison and Wasco.

As the summer advanced field workers turned to the union for organized pressure to demand higher wages in cotton and potatoes, and the possibilities of strike action also raised the expectations of the DiGiorgio employees. During more than a decade the growers associations had continued to set wages, reducing them when they calculated that workers' resistance was soft. Mexican braceros were becoming more numerous as competitors for harvest jobs and as irrigators and loaders. The appearance of the union provided a focus for these grievances and brought the lull to an end.

Arvin Local 218 had already been organized, with James Price, a DiGiorgio shed foreman, as president. The other five members of the executive committee were from states where the sharecroppers before them had withstood the terror of the 1930s—Phineas Parks, Hattie Shadowens, William Swearingen, Riley Watson, and Mervin Kerr, from Oklahoma, Arkansas, and Missouri. Price was a lean man whose corded sinews and spare muscles had been tempered by hard labor, and whose ready smile persisted through grim recitals of conditions at DiGiorgio's.

On September 22, 1947, Hasiwar sent a letter to Joseph DiGiorgio advising him that Kern County Farm Labor Union Local 218 had been designated by a majority of his employees as their collective bargaining representative. Hasiwar requested a conference to discuss wages and working conditions, and recognition of the union "as of this date."[142] The union claimed that there were 1,345 employees of the Farms, of whom the 858 paid members represented a majority. The union requested a 10-cent per hour wage increase, seniority rights, and a grievance procedure.

DiGiorgio ignored the letter. Unionism meant strikes at harvest time, an intolerable threat because "trees, vines, and plants are growing, living things."[143] Offers of the union to submit the signed authorization cards to an impartial arbiter were spurned.

The challenge had been made and accepted.

Hasiwar issued a call for a meeting at Weedpatch on September 30, at which a vote to strike was taken and approved by a large majority. The strike began on October 1. Strike headquarters were opened in an old trailer parked in the backyard of a union member.

Early that morning pickets were posted at the gates and the main approaches to the Farms. The mass walkout left DiGiorgio with some two hundred workers behind the picket lines, many of whom lived in nearby towns or were quartered in the company camps. The stoppage was not complete but it was sufficient to cripple the field and shed operations. From that moment it was to be a contest of endurance and maneuver.

On October 15 DiGiorgio refused to attend a meeting with union spokesmen and government conciliators in Bakersfield, the corporation contending steadfastly that there was no strike. Strict orders had been issued to the local manager of the Farms to refuse all contact with the union. Nor would the corporation consent to an election. The organizers of the strike, it held, were "outsiders intent to make themselves the bosses of Kern County and eventually of all California agriculture."[144] The insiders who were thus denying the local character of the strike were members of the Board of Directors of the corporation, some of whom resided in New York, Chicago, Havana, San Francisco, and Winter Haven. Firings began with Price, the vice-president of Local 218, the Reverend Parks, and veterans like Edgar Brown, deacon of the Assembly of God of Lamont.

At the ranch gates Sheriff John Loustalot stationed patrol cars with two uniformed police in each. The deputies, equipped with riot weapons and tear gas, were parked inside the ranch. Besides personally supervising the forces of law, order, and property along the half-mile front of active picketing, the sheriff found time to appear before the Board of Supervisors to oppose the granting of a mobile loudspeaker permit. The board agreed with Loustalot that the equipment was "a dangerous thing" and denied the request.

The reduction of DiGiorgio's labor force by two-thirds on the first day of the strike was a major feat for the union. But it was only a partial success. Although seriously hurt, the corporation continued in production with a substantial core of manpower. Its immediate objective was to hold the strikebreaking crews and replenish them as rapidly as possible. The attention of both DiGiorgio and the union turned at once to the braceros who had been working regularly on the Farms up to October 1, 1947.

There were 130 of them when the union placed its mass picket line the morning of the first. The corporation had been a user of foreign contract labor in all its operations throughout the state, and some of the braceros at DiGiorgio Farms had been there as long as five years. Among them were a number of "specials," meaning that they had been trained for work other than stoop labor. All of them refused to report for work on the first day of the strike, which meant that for the moment the mainstay of DiGiorgio's field operations had collapsed.

The corporation marshalled its political power, calling in a representative of the U.S. Department of Agriculture and the sheriff. Together they persuaded the braceros to return to work, which they did on October 3.

The character of the persuasion can be surmised from the situation in which the braceros found themselves. They were cut off completely from the strikers and had no information other than what the corporation wanted them to know. All of the men, particularly the specials, hoped their contracts would be renewed. Failure to work meant immediate deportation. There was a display of police force within the ranch. The Mexican consul had not appeared to advise them. The chances of being recontracted in Mexico would be small. It was a totally captive group of workers with no choice but to bow to the advice of the United States government and the sheriff of Kern County,[145] which amounted to an order to return to work. The only witnesses to these events were the senior corporation officers on the ranch.

The role of the Department of Agriculture in persuading the braceros to return to work was appealed by the union to the Mexican Embassy in Washington, after the department failed to respond to the union's protest. Vacilating, the embassy filed a request with the Department of State to withdraw the braceros. The department waited, the *Los Angeles Times* reported, "until it got orders from a higher source."[146] While reporting to his superiors that he was "energetically pursuing" his demand through the Department of State, embassy secretary Sanchez Gavito explained matters differently to the union. On October 23, responding to questions from H. L. Mitchell, the embassy spokesman said the braceros were happy in their work. The Mexican consul in Fresno had told the braceros that they had nothing to do with "labor troubles" in the United States, but that he was not advising them to stay on the job. In any case, the Mexican representatives felt the issue was a political one for the United States government to resolve. Sanchez Gavito emphasized that the embassy did not agree with the position of the Department of Agriculture, but he did rely on official reports passed on by the department from the corporation to the effect that only fifteen braceros had refused to cross the picket lines.

As long as no higher source decided otherwise, the Department of Agriculture held to the position explained in a telephone conversation with union officials on October 14. It was to the effect that the department had no legal authority to withdraw the braceros; that the Mexican consul had directed the men to remain at work; that since DiGiorgio had recruited 800 strike-breakers, the 130 braceros did not represent an important part of the work force on the ranch; and that in any case their contracts would lapse by the end of December.

Union pressure on the department continued through public statements by the union and a sympathetic congressman, Representative John F. Shelley. Mitchell spread the word through the Washington labor lobby. The department was in fact justifying the use of alien workers as necessary "scabs," a position that the corporation would find difficult to defend publicly. On this course eventually the issue could grow into a major controversy in the press and possibly in Congress. Undoubtedly, also, it could not have escaped the Department of State that the diplomatic cover provided by the Mexican embassy was not unlimited. Neither was the evasion of bureaucratic responsibility for the situation.

That the tactics of evading the issue were being coordinated from behind the scenes was evident from the pattern of the lines of communication. When pressed by the union for explanations, the Department of Agriculture and the embassy relied necessarily on information that could have been supplied only by the corporation and the sheriff of Kern County. During the six weeks that followed the calling of the strike, federal agents initiated no contacts with the union. Nor was there any attempt by them to verify statements regarding the strike made by DiGiorgio and contradicted by information possessed by the union. The intelligence in possession of government officials and diplomats was transmitted through a closed circuit. None of it had been obtained from the union, and its existence was only grudgingly admitted under Mitchell's persistence.

Under these circumstances it served neither the corporation nor the bureaucrats in Washington to prolong the controversy over the strike-breaking braceros merely on principle. The practical consideration was to prevent the withdrawal of contract Mexicans long enough to allow the corporation time to reform its work force. This it did by recruiting transients and wetbacks to add to the core of braceros and local domestics who had refused to join the strike. The Department of Agriculture, its mission accomplished, ordered the cancellation of all contracts and terminated its agreement with the corporation to provide braceros, who left Bakersfield on November 10, 1947.[147]

The six-week delay in removing the braceros was crucial to the breaking of the strike. Braceros and wetbacks together provided sufficient field crews to maintain a semblance of production until reinforcements could be brought in. After the harvests of fruit and vegetables, pruning began, and for this operation there were enough non-union replacements to provide an emergency work force. Only much later did the Department of Labor circulate a statement of official federal policy for such situations: "to insure as far as possible that the Mexican labor program is not used to hamper or defeat legitimate efforts to organize or to win economic benefits for farm workers."[148]

The union now had to turn its attention to another government agency which was assisting the corporation with recruiting. This was the Farm Labor Office of Bakersfield, the local agency of the California Farm Placement Service.

Federal regulations under the Wagner-Peyser Act prohibited referrals for employment where a strike was in progress. Hasiwar was informed that the Bakersfield office had refused to post notices that a strike was in effect as DiGiorgio Farms and that is was referring applicants there. The local farm placement manager held that since applicants could not read, the notices would serve no purpose. On November 20, Hasiwar placed pickets in front of the Farm Labor Office to provide applicants with the information that the agency thought unnecessary. Although the Farm Placement Service was not a major supplier of workers, the union's move signified that it was ready to obstruct if not to close official channels of labor supply to DiGiorgio. DiGiorgio's indignant protests were echoed by the Bakersfield Chamber of Commerce.

Since the strike had not started at the peak of DiGiorgio's harvest needs for labor, the strategy of the corporation was to resupply a minimum force in the fields and in the packing shed, prolonging the strike long enough to drain the financial resources and morale of the union. Short of total stoppage of work the corporation could carry on through the winter months. Necessity would force some of the strikers to come back. Retaliation would take care of the rest.

On November 26 complaints for unlawful detainer were issued by Justice of the Peace O. F. Parrish and served on sixteen union families who were living on the ranch. Their employment had been terminated on October 5. Their belongings were deposited on the county road. The costs of improvements of the cottages paid for by the tenants were not reimbursed "for obvious reasons," the corporation explained. The cause of action given in the complaints was willful refusal to work.[149]

By this time the corporation was able to more than compensate for the loss of braceros and farm placement referrals through recruitment by its own agents. One of them, Walter Palladino, appeared in El Paso, Texas, to sign up field workers for what he described as a large farm near Bakersfield, which offered good working conditions, good food, good housing, and prospects of permanent employment. No mention was made of the strike. A contingent of some fifty recruits, mostly Mexicans, arrived in Bakersfield early in December. Defectors told the story in a sworn statement to the union. They complained of cold living quarters, infested mattresses, poor food, and excessive charges for blankets. On the basis of this testimony the union obtained warrants for the arrest of the corporation agents who had assisted in recruiting applicants.

By the end of 1947 the picket line was no longer the center of the contest, which more and more became one of public relations. Apropos of Thanksgiving, Secretary of the Interior Harold Ickes published in a syndicated newspaper column his views on the desperate plight of migrant farm workers, the "notorious Associated Farmers," and the DiGiorgio strike. In response the Kern County Special Citizens Committee made its appearance speaking for the leaders of the community in agriculture, industry, finance, and newspaper publishing. The committee released a lengthy pamphlet titled *A Community Aroused,* in which the Ickes column was denounced. The economic life of Kern County, the pamphlet said, depended on uninterrupted production. The strike was an invasion of the community by outsiders who threatened "the pioneers who built Kern County . . . the people who made America great."[150] Ickes's "miserable propaganda" was brought to the attention of Congress, and the overtones of the DiGiorgio strike became more resonantly political and national.

Three months after the strike was called, it was clear that the corporation's operations could not be curtailed enough to force it to negotiate. As of late December 1947 there were still some 350 pruners at work in the DiGiorgio vineyards. But on the broader public relations front the strike was no longer regarded as an isolated contest between a corporation and a union. It had turned into a symbolic struggle to keep unions out of agriculture, on the one hand, and on the other to establish a local base for bargaining on behalf of agricultural laborers. By personal visits to the ranch, public statements, and appeals to Congress the leaders of agri-business expressed their support of DiGiorgio. Time favored the corporation once it had survived the surprising strength of the union at its gates on October 1. In only one respect could DiGiorgio lose ground, and that irretrievably. The image of corporate paternalism, exemplified by Joseph DiGiorgio, was being demolished by the publicity which gradually became the mainstay of union strategy. It was in this that the union hoped for some success, if at some point the corporation decided to sacrifice profits to reputation.

For the NFLU this strategy was a choice without options. Its cash assets as of November 30 amounted to $2,512. Its total income for 1947 was under $43,000, less than one half from dues and the rest from contributions of sympathizers and other unions. Along with the DiGiorgio strike the NFLU was maintaining organizing activity of sorts in the South, and even probing into the eastern seaboard and the Midwest. Crucial as the DiGiorgio encounter was for the fortunes of the union in the West, it never fully engaged its meager resources either in manpower or money there.

Local 218 called the strike without means for a long encounter. Its members, like all farm laborers, lived from one paycheck to the next— when these stopped groceries could no longer be charged in the stores and the union had to assume the burden of paying rents, medical bills, and automobile payments, in addition to the usual emergencies of the poor. On December 18 there were 248 persons on the strike relief list of the union. The strike leaders had been fired.

Calling a strike on an empty treasury was not the only departure from orthodox trade-unionism. From the outset Local 218 refused to draw ethnic lines between its members, taking the risk of offending some rank-and-filers who talked of Local 218 as an "Okie union." It challenged a powerful corporation in one of the most tightly controlled counties of the state. Within weeks after the picket lines appeared it denounced federal and state government agencies as collaborators of the corporation. Instead of accepting the traditional and misplaced image of destitute wanderers here today and gone tomorrow, they counted themselves as the forerunners of a potentially new type of farm laborer, former migrants who had stabilized their residence, reduced their dependency on seasonal jobs, and maintained a positive cultural identity.

The style of economic action changed correspondingly. Instead of the roving, hit-and-run job actions of the I.W.W. and the communists of the earlier days, the strike was to be more like a siege by local residents, supported initially by the established trade-union movement of the state.

Hasiwar enlisted this support. The Central Labor Council of Bakersfield endorsed the strike and placed DiGiorgio products on its boycott list. DiGiorgio products also appeared on the boycott lists of the major labor councils, including those of Los Angeles and San Francisco. Local teamsters, supported by the winery workers, struck the ranch, refused to deliver supplies, and joined the picket line. On October 26 the Executive Council of the California State Federation of Labor voted a thousand dollars for the strike fund and issued a statewide appeal to all its affiliates.[151] The federation also assigned its attorneys to represent the evicted families.

These endorsements paved the way for the collection of a strike fund administered by a three-man committee appointed by the Kern County Central Labor Council. By the middle of December 1947 nearly $20,000 had been received. Up to March 1949 the committee collected and disbursed $87,749 and distributed $20,000 in food, medical supplies and clothing. The cash contributions came from all sectors of the labor movement throughout the nation.

By the beginning of 1948 the strike had become an endurance contest between DiGiorgio and Local 218. It can best be described by a brief view of the activities of the union and the corporation during that year. The course of the union's tactics will be followed by an account of how the corporation fought off the siege.

The union's position in late February was described as "strong" by the State Conciliation Service, which had made futile attempts to induce DiGiorgio to talk. Support from organized labor continued as the strike passed through its first winter. The Teamsters honored the farm workers' picket lines. On February 27 the Retail Clerks Union of Los Angeles notified the corporation that it had instructed its members not to handle its products, declaring them to be "hot cargo." Truckloads of potatoes, plums, and other produce from the DiGiorgio Farms were being returned from terminals in Los Angeles, flagged by pickets from Arvin who appeared intermittently throughout the year. The State Federation of Labor assigned representatives to keep affiliated unions advised and to coordinate their support.

By early spring the union was able to initiate its own research to deal with the immediate problems of action in the fields and to supply its growing nationwide audience with running accounts of the progress of the strike. The National Sharecroppers Fund, supported by nationally known religious and lay leaders, responded to the Kern County Special Citizen's Committee.

Local 218 was kept well informed on conditions within the ranch. Union members followed DiGiorgio's recruiters to the shape-up points out of which the day hauls operated. A count showed that forty-two men and women were on duty on the picket line, handing out leaflets and exchanging scowls with scabs and the police who escorted them. The union's charges of substandard housing in the camps were upheld in August when state inspectors ordered some units closed as unfit for human occupancy.

By midsummer organizational activity had been extended throughout Kern County and into Tulare and Fresno. Even though it was engaged in a struggle for its existence, Local 218 began registering voters and setting up political committees. In his progress report for 1948 President Mitchell announced with self-assurance and a touch of the grandiose, "We propose to keep a picket line about the DiGiorgio Ranch indefinitely and turn our attention to other areas of the state to break through the solid front of the agricultural employers."

Mitchell's words reflected genuinely the mood of determination that pervaded Local 218 throughout the first full year of the strike. It was bolstered by the food caravans to Arvin organized by unionists from San Francisco and Los Angeles. The March caravan was formed by over three hundred automobiles and trucks bringing food and clothing for distribution by the strike relief committee.

In May the union began construction of its own hall on an acre of land donated by Mrs. Bertha Rankin, by now a well known union sympathizer. On one corner of the union acre the small frame building was raised, where the Reverend Parks opened meetings with prayer and Hasiwar closed them with exhortation.

Throughout 1948 the union pressed its campaign on another front, the

employment of wetbacks by the corporation on the big ranch. In violation of his agreement with the Department of Agriculture, DiGiorgio
regularly hired illegals along with braceros. In its leaflets the union
appealed to the illegals to support the union by getting out of the area.
Some did and as regularly the corporation continued to bring more in,
replacing them from the hundreds of illegals who were available in Kern
County. Occasionally one of these workers would report his grievances
to the union representative, volunteering information on the situation
inside the ranch. Persistent demands by the union for the removal of
wetback strikebreakers resulted in roundups by the immigration agents.
Forty-five were removed on February 28, thirty on April 1.[152]

The October walkout of nearly nine hundred workers still left the
corporation with a work force of more than two hundred nonunionist
field and shed workers. These included Filipinos, braceros, wetbacks,
and local domestics who lived in Arvin and other nearby communities.
As the strike dragged through 1948 the corporation's recruiting proved
effective. Denied braceros, the corporation fell back on the abundant
labor pool of domesitcs in California, supplemented by Texas migrants.
Minors with special work permits began to appear among the crews and
the recycling of wetbacks continued. A higher than usual turnover was
reported by union watchers, who gleaned intelligence from workers who
had stayed on; word leaked out that the corporation had increased the
pace of work, tightened security around the bunkhouses, required double duty from truck drivers, and discouraged visits to relatives off the
ranch. The corporation was thus able to retain a large core of regulars
who eventually replaced all the strikers.

The manpower situation secure and improving, the corporation
struck back, its arsenal of tactics ranging from violence to litigation.

On February 8, 1948, five pickets were assaulted by attackers who
rushed them from inside the ranch, armed with chains and irons. Three
of the pickets were hospitalized. Word of the assault spread and unionists appeared in front of the ranch armed and ready to storm the camps.
It was one of Hasiwar's worst moments. Himself a man of strong
temperament, he nevertheless risked his leadership of the strike to
restrain the militant Okies, who had no fear of the law ranged against
them with automatic weapons and tear gas. DiGiorgio had drawn blood.
A month before, the corporation had sworn charges against four unionists that they had cut down fruit trees in the night, and against seven
others for felonious assault when a rock hit a DiGiorgio truck. A discriminating judge fixed bail in the rock throwing incident at $70,000 and
in the picket line beating at $250 for each of the attackers.

Provocation to violence was the least sophisticated of Joseph DiGiorgio's resources. In February he called on the California Senate Fact-finding Committee on Unamerican Activities.

The committee had been in existence since 1941. Its chairman at the time of the strike was State Senator Jack B. Tenney, best known as composer of "Mexicali Rose." Tenney and his committee were the senatorial watchdogs of Agri-businessland, charged with the surveillance of labor organizers and their supporters and abettors. The groundwork for the intervention of the committee was laid step by step. On February 2 the Associated Farmers released a bulletin in San Francisco warning American Federation of Labor officials that they were being used as "suckers for a handful of out-of-state men who are using communist front groups" seeking control of the agricultural industry.[153] On February 6 the Kern County Special Citizens Committee in a paid advertisement characterized H. L. Mitchell as "formerly an official of a communist-dominated CIO union." And on February 9, Joseph DiGiorgio personally announced that "all this agitation is communist inspired by subversive elements."[154] The message was pointedly aimed and Tenney received it. Among the citizen advisors to his committee there were prominent agri-businessmen like Frank M. Shay, Philip Bancroft, and Parker Friselle.

Tenney moved swiftly, summoning his witnesses and hearing them in Los Angeles in mid-February. Among them were Mitchell and Hasiwar. Senator Hugh Burns, vice-chairman of the committee, credited the investigation to Joseph DiGiorgio, whose charges had set the agenda.[155]

If the Associated Farmers and DiGiorgio had hoped to ignite another red scare in rural California, they were disappointed. The committee found no evidence of communist interference and had in its record the uncontradicted testimony of Mitchell that no officer of the union had ever been a member of the Communist party. Joseph DiGiorgio was also summoned but failed to appear. The testimony was notable in that DiGiorgio's ranch superintendent confirmed that over half of the employees had refused to work on October 1, a fact which the union had published and the corporation had strenuously denied. The testimony also failed to bring out that the Food, Tobacco, Agricultural, and Allied Workers Union had distributed leaflets to the pickets inviting them to join "a real militant union." The FTA was a remnant of Communist party activity ten years before. Its invitation was ignored.

Immediately after testimony closed Tenney announced, on February 19, that he had found no evidence of communist domination of the strike.[156] For what comfort DiGiorgio could find in it, the committee's report stated that the National Sharecroppers Fund, a long-time financial supporter of the NFLU, was "a communist front organization."

DiGiorgio's ineffectual harassment then shifted from political to legal ground. DiGiorgio's attorneys, holding that union picketing of deliveries to the Los Angeles markets was a secondary boycott in violation of the National Labor Relations Act, petitioned the NLR Board, which issued a complaint. The defendants named, apart from the NFLU, were the Teamsters and Winery Workers locals. Pending the hearing of the case and on petition of the NLRB, early in July Judge Pierson Hall of the Los Angeles Federal District Court granted an injunction restraining the unions from picketing. During the four months between the original petition of the corporation in March and the restraining injunction of July the strike continued officially on other fronts.

Hasiwar, attempting to meet the corporation on its own terms, requested registration of Local 218 with the board, and filed a petition for an election, a demand for back pay, and charges of unfair labor practices for failure to bargain collectively.

DiGiorgio appeared to be taking a tantalizing risk. In passing the NLRA, the intent of Congress, reflecting traditional pressures of the agricultural industry, was to exclude farm laborers from coverage. The effect of DiGiorgio's complaint was to invoke such coverage naming Local 218. The corporation's lawyers were proceeding upon a law that said nothing about coverage, trusting they would be upheld without setting a dangerous precedent that, if extended, could have opened agriculture to collective bargaining under federal mandate. Of immediate advantage to the corporation, this would have undercut what the industry as a whole regarded as an inviolable principle.

The maneuver failed. A trial examiner for the board held, in a decision released in July 1948, that farm workers were not employees within the meaning of the Act. Local 218 was held inappropriate as a unit for collective bargaining. By the same rule Hasiwar's petition for registration was dismissed. DiGiorgio's lawyers were indignant when the board refused to hold with them that the law could punish but not protect members of a farm labor union.

While lawyers were exchanging arguments in court, the strikers themselves were literally drawing fire. The strike was in its eighth month. Union organizers were being stopped by the police in the streets and searched for weapons. Arguments and fist fights broke out, the tensions of the picket line spreading to the towns. The effectiveness of the strike now depended on barely a hundred men and women who attended meetings, did picket duty, paid dues, and "talked union" aggressively on the streets and in the restaurants and bars. It was a hard core of survivors of months of deprivation and harassment, violence and policing, around which it seemed that the strike would continue indefinitely, led by the militant strike committee.

On the night of May 17 a meeting of the strike committee was being held in its cottage headquarters. Price, Hasiwar, and five other committeemen were sitting in the front room.

It was 9:30 P.M. In the midst of the discussion there was a fusilade in the darkened street. From a passing car five shots were fired. The attackers sped away, leaving Price lying on the floor in a pool of blood from a head would. The gunmen remained unknown.

As the summer of 1948 passed into autumn and the strike reached its first anniversary neither the determination of the unionists to maintain it nor of the corporation to break it had staled. Both sides published full-page statements in the local newspapers. Hasiwar continued to offer the signed authorization cards which proved he had enlisted a majority of employees and the corporation continued to refuse to look at them. Congressman Philipps moved the controversy to the *Congressional Record,* where he entered a petition signed by 650 persons to show that operations were back to normal at the ranch. Some of the signers were company officials identified as workers. Later another list was released through the *Record,* this time with over 1,100 names, including those of known wetbacks.[157]

But contrived petitions and padded lists were not necessary to prove that the ranch was maintaining a sufficient volume of production to diminish its losses and give a convincing appearance of business as usual. Similarly with the union. Picketing became more of a device around which it could continue to rally trade-union support and public sympathy, to justify appeals for funds, and to legitimize its arguments before legislative bodies. However small their number the pickets were a continuing reminder to Congress, the state legislature, and the public that more than eight hundred farm workers had struck against a system as well as an employer.

As the economic position of the corporation improved and that of the union worsened, the maneuvers on both sides became more remote, a desultory give-and-take that wore the patience of the union's friends, drained its finances, often puzzled its members, and allowed the corporation to bide its time.

The time came on November 12 and 13, 1949. A subcommittee of the House of Representatives Education and Labor Committee convened in Bakersfield to investigate the strike. The preliminaries for the hearings had been laid by Congressman Elliot, who had demanded the investigation in March 1948. The details of this, the last stage of the DiGiorgio, strike are set forth in *Spiders in the House.*[158]

DiGiorgio's lawyers, exploiting a perfect setting, walked into the Bakersfield hearings and served a complaint for libel on Mitchell and other union officers. The cause of action was the showing of a film produced by the Hollywood Film Council, *Poverty in the Valley of Plenty*. The amount of damages asked was two million dollars.

Mitchell could not raise funds to contest this suit. He was advised by the State Federation of Labor to settle out of court. The publication of a false report concerning the film, fabricated by DiGiorgio's congressional friends, including Congressman Richard Nixon, completed the disaster.

By the settlement the corporation agreed to reduce its demand in damages to one dollar, and the union agreed to recall all prints of the film and to end the strike.

On May 9, 1950, Mitchell telegraphed Hasiwar instructing him to withdraw the pickets immediately. The strike was over.

An assessment of the failure of the strike must begin with the fact that it was not a strike against a ranch but against an economic empire. The size of DiGiorgio Farms and their major role in the operation of the corporation made it the keystone of the business. For that reason it was all the more important to immunize it against collective bargaining. A total work stoppage of a few weeks could have forced it to deal with the union. But the braceros provided a crucial interval for the reorganization of the work force, as did the readily available wetbacks. Limited losses could be absorbed by such a diversified enterprise with its farms in other parts of California and Florida and auction houses in several eastern cities. Moreover, the strictly economic interests of the corporation would not stand alone in weighing the effects of bargaining with Local 218. The longer the strike lasted the more DiGiorgio felt the pressure of his peers in the industry, which they did not hesitate to exert by personal appearances at the ranch and by inciting statements through all the media on DiGiorgio's behalf. In a business world where moral commitments had no place there were nevertheless class obligations that Joseph DiGiorgio could not flout. Agri-business had stabilized social relationships in rural California and collective bargaining had no place in them. To accept it would have strained DiGiorgio's connections with those who controlled the banking, transportation, marketing, and political sectors of the industry. He could count on the agencies of government, the sheriff and his deputies, the county supervisors, the Farm Placement Service, and the United States Department of Agriculture. In Congress itself the corporation found men willing to collaborate in a conspiracy to serve its ends.

These decisive weights were skillfully brought to bear, and together they broke the strike, in spite of the failure to revive the "red scare," or of the provocations to violence.

On the union side, the strike was an extension to California of the psychological and moral commitments that had been generated in its leadership during the decade of struggle in the South. Terror had made resistance unavoidable, in which there was no room for avoidance of risk. If there was little calculation in the minds of Mitchell and Hasiwar there was even less in those of the Arvin workers. They had borne indignities and exploitation without protest for more than a decade. The National Farm Workers Union was unprepared financially for the strike and remained so for its duration. It counted on donations from other unions knowing that these would come only after the strike was declared and under way. By early 1949 Price was sending out special appeals as the relief fund became exhausted. Calling the strike when the peak of picking in the orchards and vineyards was over was untimely. The hope that DiGiorgio would respect the majority of his employees who signed authorization cards proved to be false. Respect for the consensus of employees was the end result of a struggle in industry that was only beginning in agriculture.

As they were fired from their jobs and gradually dispersed throughout the state, the members of Local 218 carried with them recollections of disappointment, sometimes bitter ones. But in many ways they had done better than they knew. They had not only put to rest the prevalent view, expressed with great persistence and not a little satisfaction by farmers as well as bureaucrats, that farm workers were unorganizable, with the corollary that they could not withstand encounters of more than a few days. When they struck they had already transplanted to their last refuge in the lower San Joaquin Valley not only a class but also a culture, whose ties helped them resist intimidation and prolonged want. Ethnic differences were overcome even though it had been predicted that they would divide the union. Both the leadership and the rank and file of Local 218 proved equal to the tests of the strike, improvising organizing techniques or adapting them from the traditions of organized labor. Thus the union was able to generate pressures in distant places and remote centers of influence.

The long duration of the strike itself called for a reassessment of conditions affecting the organization of agricultural laborers in California. One of these was that the settled farm workers who struck DiGiorgio for almost three years were not the socially splintered migrants of old. They differed in a number of significant ways. Among the adults of the families that made up the rank and file of Local 218 there were likely to be truck drivers, waitresses, service tradesmen, mechanics, and even small merchants. Some of these were members of established unions. The result was a network of connections, informal as well as institutional, reinforced by ties of family and kinship. This accounted in part for the close bonds of organized farm workers with other trade-unionists in the local community, a rapport that did not exist with the upper level of labor councils and federations. Moreover, Local 218 soon made contacts with small farmers who found themselves without effective institutional defenses against the domination of corporate agriculture. Such individuals did not represent, in the late 1940s, any weight of opinion among small farmers as a class, pressured as they were by economic necessity into conformity against self-interest. But they were men and women, like Bertha Rankin, with whom dialogue could be opened and to whom an organized farm labor union appeared as a useful model of collective action and a source of support. Mrs. Rankin's gift of a corner of her ranch suggested the idea of a Union Acre in each of the major agricultural areas of the state where laborers could find the union and the union could assemble them. The strike also showed the importance of women as participants in economic struggle and not merely as units in the family work team. Local 218 offered such women, black, white, and brown, roles which they fulfilled on the picket line and in the community.

From the Southern Tenant Farmers Union the NFLU received a tradition of promoting the education of its members. Local 218 maintained this tradition, which became a part of all organization throughout the state. It was a curriculum for understanding agri-business, explaining the successes and failures of a struggle in a context that widened continuously. Delegates of Local 218, rank-and-filers, men and women, returned from fund raising and propaganda assignments in Los Angeles, Sacramento, and Washington with reports to the membership meetings like these: "Hell, man, I seen grapes selling for ten cents a pound in Los Angeles, now figure it out how much you get for pickin' a lug-full"; "Me and Brother Hasiwar was at the Farm Labor Office and they jes' hands you a piece of paper with the wages laid out and the feller says 'take it' "; "I seen myself the deal down at Calexico, they's a million Mexicans por as hell waitin' to put in time with DieGeorge"; and "I seen the trainload of grapes rollin' into the auction market. That guy DieGeorge makes more money off'n them as eats 'em than off'n them as picks 'em." These were flashes in the minds of human beings who were not supposed to possess minds at all. These insights grew into a sense of understanding of "where we are at," as the Okies put it.

This was the prime stuff of the morale that carried Local 218 through many disappointments. The most disturbing of these was the limited commitment of organized labor. It took ten more years to fully assess the causes of this; to the workers the evidence of it came as a series of shocking disappointments. The California State Federation of Labor leadership was intimidated by DiGiorgio by the filing of the lawsuit, the subsequent congressional hoax, and the resulting publicity. It declined to confront the corporation in the courts. The federation did not advocate a legislative program for farm workers to counter the aggressiveness of the agri-business lobby in Sacramento. Labor's influence in the state capital was well known, but it was not brought to bear on Governor Warren's promise to investigate the shooting of Price.

The defeat suffered by the NFLU in its first encounter offered lessons that would not be fully grasped until they were repeated elsewhere in the state. Mitchell called off the pickets with a flourish when he said, "We are just ending the first round." The aim of establishing a self-sustaining base for the union in the Central Valley had been thwarted, but the union emerged from its failure with a certain prestige among farm laborers. "No strike in labor's history received such a variety of widespread sustained publicity as that following the walkout three years ago."[159]

Many of the most active strikers left Kern County to settle in farm communities throughout the state. They carried the feeling of veteranship and confidence that men have when they fix not on how small they were but on how big their antagonist and how well they had stood up to him. Throughout the years that followed they were to be found in the midst of all the encounters that are narrated in the following pages. They did not again act on the scale of the Arvin strike, but they spread into all the strongholds of agri-business—El Centro, Coachella, Borrego Valley, Delano, Fresno, Salinas, Santa Clara, Stockton, Tracy, and Yuba City, "talking union" in all of them.

Limited Action—the Potato Pickers

Even before the DiGiorgio strike began, Local 218 became the clearing house of grievances of farm workers who shifted from crop to crop. Many of the DiGiorgio employees returned to these jobs with the sense of support they felt in the presence of a farm labor union in Kern County. From Arvin and Lamont union members made the seasonal circuit in potato and cotton and fruit picking. Some moved permanently out of the county, establishing new contacts and creating expectations that prompted calls for extending the organizing activity. By the end of 1948 the influence of the union had spread to the towns in the southern end of the San Joaquin Valley—MacFarland, Tulare, Farmersville, Corcoran, and Fresno. Unionism was stirring in the counties that had the largest single concentration of farm laborers in California. Appeals like Whatley's came to union headquarters in Bakersfield from Coachella and El Centro, two hundred miles to the south.

Responding to these calls in the midst of the DiGiorgio crisis, the staff of the NFLU probed behind the seamy facade of Agri-businessland, finding what neither Mitchell nor Hasiwar had suspected when they had made their tour of the state in 1947. After DiGiorgio the NFLU staff in California consisted of Hasiwar, William Becker, and myself as full-time organizers. Part-time paid and volunteer assistants were added or subtracted as the finances of the national office teetered between subsistence and insolvency. They drove through the longest stretch of rural slums in America, talking with Black families stranded in Indio, Okies passing the winter in the gullies of San Luis Obispo, and Mexicans living in tar-paper hovels on ditch banks in Corcoran. From all these quarters came tales of destitution and pleas for help. As the light of Local 218 dimmed at Arvin, it seemed to shine more brightly abroad.

The predicament faced by the NFLU was obvious. To respond everywhere at the same time was to thin resources already strained by the demands of the DiGiorgio strike. To stake everything on the single struggle was in effect to box the union in one corner of Kern County. DiGiorgio and his Associated Farmer friends had set in motion the propaganda and political resources of the industry throughout the state, prompting the grower associations to look with even more favor on the use of braceros and wetbacks, to offer the domestics only the most deteriorated housing, to ignore demands for wage adjustments, and to perpetuate the short-weight system of the labor contractors. The scene of the encounter was no longer the DiGiorgio Farms; it was almost the whole of rural California and into it the NFLU was drawn step by step.

It moved into the potato harvest of 1950.

The center of production lay north of Bakersfield, around the towns of Wasco, Shafter, and McFarland. It was a mixed system of landholdings, with numerous small farmers and a dominant minority of large-scale producers, on the scale of the W. B. Camp holdings, the Coberly West Company, and the Shafter Farms. Customarily the large producers agreed on the wage scales to be paid in the upcoming harvest. In March 1949 it was announced in the name of eighty-four growers and packers that wages would be 6 cents per stub.[160]

Machines turned up the potatoes, the rows of which were marked out in "spaces" for the individual pickers, a space varying in length and yield. The picker proceeded down the row, the heavy stub hooked to his belt. The stub was marked with a wide black line indicating the level to which it was to be filled, theoretically at a maximum weight of fifty-three pounds. Stooped over the furrow and dragging the ever heavier stub between his legs, the picker disengaged the bag when he had filled it, leaving it standing between the rows. If the digging machines were moving about, clouds of dust added to the discomfort of the drag and the sun.

By the spring of 1950 preparations began to organize the potato pickers, most of whom usually moved out of the area when the harvest was over. With this typical pattern of convergence-and-dispersion the union could rely for contacts only upon those pickers who lived permanently in towns like Arvin.

It was decided to attempt organization through the labor contractors, the most stable link in so fluid a labor force. Enough contractors responded to provide a test of whether the union could organize harvesters through so dubious a coalition. Contractors were allowed to join the union but could not be elected to office. By April 1950 several written contracts were negotiated. By these agreements, with the contractors acting as middlemen, the stub payment of 6 cents was agreed to and the union was recognized as the sole bargaining agent. The ultimate aim was to develop enough show of strength to approach the Potato Growers Association with the agreements.

Well in advance of the harvest the union distributed leaflets throughout the county, avoiding the issue of wages and concentrating on the notorious practice of short weights. Contractors demanded stubs filled with sixty pounds or more, but paid only for fifty-three. Since potatoes were weighed at the shed by the ton, the contractors benefited through the difference, less whatever the shed cheated by shortening its own weights. Also, the determination of the "spaces" was elastic, resulting in penalties that were even less apparent than in work measured by the stub.

In proposing the elimination of these abuses the union hoped to place the larger growers in a position of defending what amounted to grand larceny of earned wages. It was also an indirect appeal to the smaller growers who were less inclined to condone it but who would have been aroused by a straight wage demand.

Avoiding the appearances of preparing for a strike, union men monitored the potato fields where picking was in progress. Stubs were weighed on portable scales, proving the union's contention that some were filled by as much as ten pounds over the black stripe. These sample checks were the basis of a rough calculation that as much as 20 percent of the labor was unpaid for in some fields. As this information was spread through the area, contractors and field foremen became less exacting. The effect was noticeable even from the roadside—the packed stubs were folded at the black stripe rather than well above it. The presence of a union representative stopping by for a friendly chat with resting pickers was enough to discourage flagrant short weights that could be verified on the spot.

Altogether these were little more than feints that counted more heavily on exposure than on genuine organization. The immediate beneficiaries were hundreds of seasonal workers who would soon disperse beyond contact, and but a few of whom would pay union dues and come back next year to act as field stewards with some experience in organizational techniques.

The most effective of these techniques was the spot rest, a harmless name for the stoppage of picking when the overseers ignored protests over speed up or excessive fills. Work would slow down while negotiations were concluded between union stewards and supervisors. If it became necessary for work to stop completely it was usually resumed in two or three hours. It was a reasonable method short of striking to punish employers who persisted in offering dishonest pay for honest work. It was the first effort of the union with mobile and untried workers in the potato "deal."

The experiment with the contractors failed and remained a warning to the union for years to come. Few of them responded to the union's invitation to plan a more rational organization of picking with a better wage return. In the long run the union was a competitive hiring agent in that it proposed to organize the supply of harvesters, posing in addition the threat of organizing services such as transportation from which contractors profited at the expense of their crews. In such an event the union would have moved in the direction of agreements with farmers themselves, who provided the wage funds in the first place. The attacks of the union on the weight shortages were obliquely aimed at the contractors themselves, who were thoroughly familiar with the practice. The habit of chiseling on one another as well as on farmers was too ingrained, the system too disorderly to permit the NFLU to make lasting connections with it.

Probably more forethought and preparation went into the planning of the potato trial run strike than into the DiGiorgio action. The union's aims went no further than the bread-and-butter issues that were foremost in the workers' minds. If wages could be raised by making weights honest the workers would also learn a lesson in collective bargaining.

Yet it was clear that the bread-and-butter issues were only the beginning of a process of engagement that could go beyond pork-chop unionism. The road to collective bargaining would be a long one. At the end the workers would still find themselves bound through their union by conventional obligations that left the structure of power and the right of exploitation intact. In the potato operation the NFLU began to measure its role as the potential threat to a system of which a powerful corporation was only a part.

The Cotton Strike of 1949

As the DiGiorgio strike dragged on, the union was drawn to a larger stage of confrontations. Strikers who were fired by the corporation returned to seasonal work, principally in potato and cotton picking. Kern County had large plantings in both. The cotton belt, extending two hundred miles north of Bakersfield and south to the Tehachapi range, was an economic subsystem in its own right, with well-defined population centers around which harvest workers tended to stabilize, such as Corcoran, Hanford, Fresno, and Mendota. Responding to the acute expansions and contractions of seasonal demand for labor, thousands of harvesters moved cyclically within a territory able to hold them somewhat above the level of destitution. Arvin and Lamont were the result of this process. Employment at DiGiorgio was a step up from the irregular income of field work, and for many members of Local 218 dismissal forced them a step back. Among the thousands who drifted in and out of cotton picking there were, by the end of the 1940s, hundreds with roots capable of surviving the blight of poverty from one year to the next.

Like the DiGiorgio strikers, these people too had grievances, but they were against a crop, not a corporation. Picking cotton meant stooping and crawling and stuffing bolls into a narrow eight-foot canvas bag until it weighed seventy to eighty pounds. When pickers were ordered into a field that had been irrigated the day before, brown muck slowed their progress. In a sunbaked stretch, those who could afford them wore knee pads to ease their way. Carried like a huge sausage up a rickety ladder, the bag had to be emptied into a trailer after weighing. Pay was by the pound weighed on scales that could be tampered with. Hiring was on the spot, the crews forming anew every morning and scattering again in the evening after being paid off. During the harvest thousands of pickers shifted from field to field, as the rumors of better working conditions attracted them elsewhere.

The California cotton belt was known by those who owned it as the Inland Empire. Its subjects, when they were not wanted, disappeared into winter havens like Corcoran or Dos Palos, towns of straggling rows of shacks put together with flattened tin cans and sealed with newspapers. Cooking was on brick and stone fire pits. Windows were few, and those were boarded up until warm weather made outdoor living possible.

By September 1949 the union had opened seven additional locals in the cotton counties reaching as far north as Fresno. In all of them the expectation was rising that the union would take the lead against the traditional methods of wage fixing, typically by a conference of growers under the sponsorship of the San Joaquin Valley Agricultural Labor Bureau.

As had been its custom the bureau called such a meeting in Fresno on September 2. The bureau announced that the conference was in the interests of pickers as well as growers. According to preestablished rules, only growers could vote. Motions to set wages were not debatable, and only growers could make them. Pickers attending the meeting were admonished to make their comments brief. In all respects it was the annual routine procedure by which the largest growers made known to the smaller ones and to the pickers what the wage scale would be.

Hasiwar took a different view of these formalities and presented himself with three other union representatives at the Fresno conference. Ten years before the pickers had asked the bureau to discuss, not to impose, the wage rate. The growers ignored the request. The presence of the union delegation was a gesture of defiance that increased the probability of a clash over the wage issue. The preplanned results of the conference made such a clash certain. The growers voted to reduce the rate to $2.50 per hundred pounds, fifty cents lower than in 1948. It was the rate that was to prevail in Kern, Kings, Tulare, Fresno, Madera, and Merced counties. Notices of the cut were posted throughout the area. Some growers made no secret of their preference for an even lower rate, encouraged by the availability of braceros.[161] The previous year the manager of the San Joaquin Valley Agricultural Labor Bureau, Ralph Bunje, had met an anticipated wage demand with the statement that the bureau was prepared to contract five thousand braceros.

Cotton picking began in the fall of 1949 amid signs that the pickers were ready to challenge the bureau. Left to themselves they would have walked away in spontaneous stoppages, which had occurred in practically all previous years, and which, totally lacking coordination, were regarded by the pickers themselves as wildcatting. The impetus to action already was in the fields, and the union accepted the role of providing leadership for it. It became the articulator of the demands of harvesters who had never attended a union meeting.

The union began by distributing a wage ballot to all pickers. Some ten thousand were handed out with the question "What do you think would be a fair wage?" The returns showed that the pickers would stand on a demand for three dollars per hundred.

As an organizing device the ballot gave the union an initial mandate that could be opposed to that of the bureau's wage conference. Its distribution occasioned meetings and discussions throughout the area. For the small locals of the cotton belt it provided the opportunity to reach into the flux of harvesters and turn it into concerted action. The organization of wage committees was encouraged, through which the union broadcast information and gathered reports. A wage council composed of the elected chairmen of these committees was projected but never materialized. Like so many of the techniques that the union tried the committees and councils depended upon a core of veteran organizers that did not yet exist.

The strike was under way by the first week of September, its ragged segments brought together by Local 218. The first strike bulletin announced that the local had assumed leadership of what in effect had already become a region-wide walk-off, with entire fields emptied of pickers who stayed home without giving notice or who merely vanished overnight. Rallies were scheduled daily to keep contact with idle workers, who were scattered over an area of more than two thousand square miles with little more communication than that provided by the rumors of the "grapevine."

The effects of the strike were apparent in the attendance at strike meetings that served as daily briefing sessions for the organizing teams. The number of empty trailers, the count of newly-ginned bales standing in the yards, the turnout of strikers for the early morning hauls of contractors, the half-empty trucks transporting workers to and from camps, and the drafts on the skid rows of Los Angeles and Fresno showed that the stoppage, though not complete, was effective. By September 22 union pickets were standing watch on the main highways north and south of Bakersfield, stopping truckloads of workers bound for the cotton fields.

The scenario of the strike that was being improvised by the NFLU proved difficult for the Labor Bureau and its agri-business associates to read. They expected and predicted violence against strikebreakers and damage to property, but there was none of either. That would have been the signal for the revival of armed attacks in the style of the vigilantism of the 1930s. The principal weapons of the strike were the call of the union to stay at home, and the caravans. Columns of automobiles and trucks formed daily after early morning meetings and moved over the country-side, stopping where picking was in progress. To the din of horns and the beating of fists on truck panels and the clang of tire irons, the strikers shouted invitations to those in the field to join them. The measure of success was the number of pickers who folded their sacks and left or swung their own cars to the rear of the column as it moved on.

The roving picket lines were moving from Madera County in the north to the foot of Grapevine Pass in the south. By September 28 caravaning had been extended to Fresno County. The strike front was now over 150 miles north and south through the heart of the San Joaquin Valley. Deputy sheriffs, state highway patrols, and local police trailed the caravans, which also came under the surveillance of aircraft circling overhead.

When a caravan was forced by the police to keep moving, its effectiveness was reduced, and even more so by the enforcement of antinoise ordinances, which curtailed the use of loudspeakers and censored the language that strikers could use over the bullhorns. A Kern County ordinance, approved by the Board of Supervisors on March 3, 1947, made it unlawful for anyone other than law enforcement or governmental agents to use a loudspeaker mounted on a vehicle to address any persons from a public highway without first obtaining a permit issued by the sheriff, and then only if it appeared to the supervisors that it would not lead to a breach of the peace, rioting, or property damage. The written applications were required to set forth information amounting to a preview of union tactics and timely warning to growers—time and place where the equipment was to be used and identification of the persons to be addressed. San Joaquin County ordinance number 526 of March 14, 1949, required a statement of the precise locations where the loudspeakers were to be used, and prescribed that "the human speech and music amplified shall not be profane, lewd, indecent, or slanderous." Orders of this type were in force throughout the California cotton belt.

The county supervisors, by regulating the conditions under which farm laborers could move and speak their grievances, allowed the police to harass the caravaners. On September 22 a union organizer, William Trafton, was arrested in Farmersville for leading a column. On September 26 James Price and eleven other roving pickets were arrested in Kings County as they attempted to pull crews out of the Boswell Corporation fields near Corcoran. These arrests and the impounding of automobiles and trucks disbanded the caravan.[162] At the time of the arrests a local theater was showing the film *The Grapes of Wrath.*

By the end of September caravaning had slowed down. The expense of fuel was draining union resources. In Fesno County enforcement of parking regulations along country roads and the rigorous protection of the tranquil countryside from lewd and indecent exhortations brought motorized picketing to a standstill. Gin managers called meetings of growers indebted to them for crop loans to urge resistance to the union's demands.[163] To discourage the strikers the Farm Placement Office of Fresno announced that there were twenty thousand pickers in the fields as of September 23, with a large backlog waiting for jobs.[164]

In less than four weeks the momentum of the strike was spent. Hasiwar, preparing a withdrawal, requested that a representative of the State Conciliation Service be sent to the area. No negotiations were attempted, but the service found that many growers were meeting the union demand for three dollars per hundred. The major holdout was the San Joaquin Valley Agricultural Labor Bureau, the stronghold of the corporation farms and the cottonseed distributors. Word was passed back to the union that an easing of tensions could induce more growers to meet the union rate. At arm's length the union and the anonymous farmers exchanged an understanding that the union would suspend the caravans and all other types of picketing. The growers would cease stimulating police action and would encourage wider acceptance of the three dollar rate. On October 4 the service announced its withdrawal from the scene because not enough growers had responded.[165]

An oblique maneuver of Hasiwar's nevertheless helped to weaken grower resistance. In announcing the strike, he had said that the union "stands ready to meet with small growers to determine wage and working agreements based upon a recognition that the small growers cannot enjoy many of the advantages of the corporation farmers through their control of the industry."[166] Going further, Hasiwar called for more equitable government support of "forty-acre farmers," and public regulation of cottonseed distribution.[167] In return for agreement on work rules, the union proposed that small farmers join with it in eliminating contractors' fees and false weights.

These proposals were made in the face of the compulsions on the small producers to accept the wage determinations announced by the bureau—the crop liens held by the gins, their control of the supply of trailers and storage facilities, the high cost of mechanical harvesting, and the control by growers associations of the manpower market through the Farm Placement Service. Nevertheless, they produced friendly contacts with some small growers, who recognized the narrow economic gap between them and farm wage labor. These contacts pointed to the possibility of a coalition that might loosen the grip of corporate agri-business upon both.

Such a theory of union strategy could hardly be put to any practical test at the first encounter. Events were moving faster than theory. In the important cotton district of Firebaugh in the northwest part of the San Joaquin Valley brief stoppages stimulated by the course of the strike were preparing the ground for a mass stoppage. Recognizing the threat, early in October growers representing over forty thousand acres of plantings quietly started paying the three dollar rate. By mid-October this was clearly the trend of the picking scale throughout the area, and on October 18 the union declared the strike officially over.

Judged by the tests of orthodox trade-unionism the strike was an organizational failure. There was no way to count the pickers who had walked out of the fields, joined the caravans, stayed home, or left the area for the season. But in all probability not fewer than ten thousand persons had participated in these ways. They had been mobilized in an effective, large-scale economic action by fewer than three hundred union members in ten locals. Hasiwar estimated that the pickers earned five million dollars more than they would have without the strike. The failure of the Labor Bureau to accurately assess the capability of the union and the mood of the pickers in breaking the $2.50 wage ceiling put an end to wage-setting conferences. Evidently large numbers of unorganized workers placed their faith in the union and its insistence on nonviolence, for they gave the lurking Associated Farmers no occasion to make armed attacks in the classic manner.

These were significant gains for the workers, but not necessarily for the union. Potential dues-paying members moved on with the passing of the harvest. The NFLU could raise no funds until the strike was well under way; when it did issue an appeal on September 21 the response was disappointing, barely enough to keep the caravans supplied with gasoline for a few days. However large the number of strikers who walked out, there remained enough mechanical pickers to supply the gins. Other workers, such as irrigators and drivers and warehousemen, who had no interest in the issues raised by the union, remained at work to keep the industry running. The pickers' strike was a case of agricultural craft unionism in its weakest form.

Two elements had caused it to fail.

The first was the persistent insurgency of cotton pickers year in and year out, manifested by techniques of passive resistance such as wild-catting, staying at home, or quiet migration out of the area. The second was, for all its ability to lead, articulate demands, and provide a common strategy, the union had no public forum, just a minimum of institutional support, and no secondary line of men and women with experience in a strike. The 1949 action was a massive stir of harvesters within which a small core of workers could gain some experience in leadership.

But it was not so much the lessons learned as the sense of accomplishment that carried over into the cotton harvest of 1950. With less formality than the previous year, the union was better prepared to respond to the aroused mood of returning pickers. An organizing council of locals made preparations to submit a demand for a wage scale of $4.00 per hundred. Small caravans began moving in Fresno and Kern counties during the first week of October, and again the ordinances were invoked. Arrests and confiscations of equipment followed. The scale rose to $3.50 on some farms, starting a trend that satisfied most pickers, who straggled back to the fields and brought the strike to a desultory end.

The union's tactics did not change and the growers made only ostentatious improvements in theirs. The fields were thickly posted with No Trespassing signs, a legal prerequisite to arrests on the picket line. On one large corporation ranch in Kings County the local police mounted a machine gun by the roadside, with ammunition boxes and canisters of tear gas. As caravans approached, crews were moved deeper into the fields. With the wage scale on some of the farms now one dollar above the maximum offered by the Labor Bureau in 1948, the union was holding a strong position.

A position but not a membership. On October 20, 1950, the union's Valley Organizing Council decided that in the future it would take on no strikes until and unless there was a substantial membership among the group of workers involved. As the union had outwitted the growers, so had the workers outbargained the union.

The benefits conferred by the NFLU did not stop with wage increases. The union went on to challenge the antinoise ordinances in the courts. Complaints by growers, like the one that the union had been guilty of making "loud and raucous noises" on a quiet country road not far from the town of Tranquillity, were appealed by attorneys assigned by the State Federation of Labor. In response to a suit filed by the Tulare–Kings County Labor Council a permanent injunction was granted in June 1950 against the Tulare County Board of Supervisors on grounds that the ordinance violated constitutional rights of free speech. Three years later the State Appellate Court declared the Kings County ordinance unconstitutional.

Farm Labor Camps, Unionism, and Agri-business

The DiGiorgio strike, the potato actions and the cotton strike were precipitated by longstanding discontents over wages and sharp work practices that deprived harvesters of a part of their earned wages. The strike demands of the workers were initially a challenge to the most obvious evils of the wage system but not to their institutional roots. When wages did rise, at most they represented a higher threshold from which to begin next season. This progress for the working man in the fields was a step-by-step ascent on a ladder of immediate economic benefits. Though a latecomer to the American labor movement, the agricultural worker was thus conditioning himself to become a fullfledged unionist ever gaining skill in the approved system of business unionism.

Undoubtedly at the lower economic level of the agricultural employers this also tended to be the view of the nature of labor organization. But at the higher levels, to which the influential corporate leaders had risen and around whom the multiple and intricate connections of interlocking interests were woven, strikes of the size and intensity and duration of those occurring in Kern County and the cotton belt were bound to appear in an alarmingly different light. To them it was the beginning of a process they had always opposed and long contained, and which, if allowed to gain headway, might loosen the connections of the system itself.

This is the sum of all the advantages of those who hold power. The parochialism of the individual entrepreneur gives way to the broad view, and the sense of class. Coalitions of large interests require and develop a sort of statesmanship of their own, practiced by the select minority whose success has given them the opportunity of seeing the system steadily and seeing it whole. Such was the immense distance in points of view that separated James Price, testifying at the Bakersfield congressional investigation of the strike he was leading, and the Special Citizens of Kern County, who were in the audience listening to him.

Far removed from the picket lines a counter strategy was being devised. Its objective was the de-stabilization of the labor communities that had begun to form in the government camps and from which many of the strike leaders had emerged.

In 1935 Congress had authorized the construction of housing facilities for farm workers in areas of high seasonal demand. It was a nationwide program which in California created a chain of such camps extending from Yuba to Imperial counties, reaching into every major agricultural section of the state. In 1948 there were twenty-one camps of 4,450 individual family units with a capacity for 20,467 occupants. At their best the units were small homes with garden plots; at their worst, one-room metal and wooden shelters mounted on concrete slabs. Filled to capacity at the peak of harvesting, these farm labor supply centers, as they were called, retained between seasons a population of between 8,000 and 10,000.

In comparison with the on-farm housing offered by employers the farm labor camps represented a considerable improvement in living conditions. Rents were nominal and facilities such as assembly halls, clinics, and laundries were provided. Managers appointed by the federal government maintained close and in many cases friendly relations with the tenants. In the flux of perpetual migration the farm labor supply centers were emerging as stations of repose from which harvesters could take a broader and more tranquil look at their condition.

But the broader view is reserved for those who hold power, and sharing it with those who came and went with the seasons was totally contrary to the lessons of business experience. The growers associations and labor bureaus were reading the disturbing signs. A farm labor camp was located in Arvin, another in Lamont. Among their residents Bob Whatley and Jim Price had found their first converts to Local 218. The Cochrans, a union family, had lived in the Arvin camp since 1942, and by the time the DiGiorgio strike began they were camp neighbors to more than thirty others who carried union buttons. In Camp McCallum of the Salinas Valley a frail and work-worn counterpart of Whatley, Jose Ayala, made his cabin the center of union propaganda. Driving an ancient "fotingo," Ayala covered the Valley handing out union leaflets and posting signs of union meetings. In the Firebaugh camp of Fresno County there was Isola Redd, who began to organize the nucleus of a union local with Black workers.

The intent of Congress to encourage a more rational supply of harvest labor was turning into a trend toward the rationalization of a labor union. The sense of solidarity had found a base, its best expression the camp councils that had been established by the Farm Security Administration, which managed the camps. The councils were intended to give the residents a voice in management and operation and were composed of representatives elected by the residents. They voted on rules concerning sanitation, recreation, education, safety, and other matters of self-government. Carey McWilliams had seen these councils as significant agents for social organization among a rootless people "foreshadowing a new social order." To the residents themselves they looked rather more like the old-fashioned town meeting. Those of Camp McCallum, in regular assembly, produced in 1947 a document that read: "We, the people of Camp McCallum Farm Labor Supply Center . . . in order to form a democratic self-government, establish justice, insure peaceful relations among ourselves and with others, promote the general welfare, and take part in the privileges and responsibilities given us by the Constitution of the United States of America . . . do ordain and establish this constitution for our camp."

The agricultural industry of California had itself experimented with farm labor supply centers in the early 1940s and had found them acceptable as long as they were financed by the State of California and controlled by growers associations. These camps were eventually sold to employers at bargain prices.

The Farm Security Administration camps with their councils and constitutions and their hospitality for union organizers prompted the campaign to neutralize the union threat from this quarter. The significance of this threat as it appeared to the growers can be surmised from the mathematics of the situation. In the harvests of 1948 there were in the fields and orchards probably close to 250,000 seasonal workers, of whom some 10,000 were stable residents of farm labor supply centers. Of these fewer than 1,000 were union members and active sympathizers. In so small a number agri-business saw on the horizon a cloud no bigger than a man's fist. They moved to dispel it.

The Farm Security Administration, the federal agency in charge of farm labor supply centers, had been vigorously opposed by the industry since the first camps were built in 1935. The explanation given by the Kern County Department of Health, one of the regular sounding boards of the Special Citizens of the agri-community, was to the point: "The growers do not favor camp facilities provided by federal or state agencies. . . . Families residing on property of the operators and subject to the selection of an experienced foreman are usually dependable and loyal. They will behave themselves, take the thin with the thick, the poor picking with the good, with minimum complaint. . . . Occupants of government controlled camps owe no allegiance to any growers."[168]

Operating deficits in the hundreds of thousands of dollars were attributed to unnecessary medical and other social services. Resolutions demanding the end of the FSA camps were passed in conventions of agri-business organizations during the fifteen years preceding the Kern County strikes. The resolution of the Associated Farmers of that county, passed in 1938, was typical, declaring that "farmers can take care of their own labor." When they reached Congress, as they invariably did, these resolutions laid the foundation for a final and decisive attack.

This began in June 1947 when the U.S. Department of Agriculture decided that because of budgetary limitations it would no longer be able to operate and maintain farm labor supply centers beyond September of that year. Congress thereupon authorized the department to dispose of the centers within two years. In its report on the matter the House Committee on Agriculture concurred in the disposition of the camps to public or semipublic agencies or nonprofit associations of farmers "in the best interests of agriculture."[169] A few months later the camps were transferred from Agriculture to the Public Housing Administration.

On notice of these preliminaries to the State of California, Governor Warren appointed a committee of five directors of state departments, which held meetings "with all interested" parties except farm workers. The governor concluded that he had no authority to bid for the camps for the state, noting that the legislature itself had failed to act, which was not surprising since he had not made any recommendation in his budget message to the legislators.

Sensitive politicians in Sacramento did not fail to receive the message that was coming from farm employers. The Associated Farmers of California resolved that the camps should not be bought by the state government, and that they be disposed of to nonprofit farmers associations for nominal sums. The State Chamber of Commerce went on record against precipitate action for public operation. The growers associations then demanded that the state abstain from bidding for the camps and that they be turned over to them "in the interest of the community that surrounds them."

The members of Local 218 had reason to take notice of these events. They represented an oblique attack on the union whose activity in the camps around DiGiorgio had been undisguised. With freedom of assembly the camps offered immediate contacts with hundreds of farm workers. The regularity of such contacts, their interracial composition, the social discipline that the councils fostered, marked the government camps as prime targets for hostile action.

The NFLU recognized the threat but had neither the funds nor the resources to meet it effectively. In Washington, the attacks of the industry had met no opposition from organized labor, whose own lobby was respected in both Houses of Congress. In political terms the actions of the Congress with regard to the camps between 1947 and 1949 amounted to a legislative blitz. The national press, through which the union had learned, since the first days of Mitchell's activity in the South, to trade verbal barrages with southern planters and western tycoons like DiGiorgio, did not find, in this issue, any of the drama of picket lines. Local 218 had no other means to protest publicly the decisions that were being made in Sacramento and Washington.

The effectiveness that the growers, led by their power elite in the structures of Agri-businessland, showed in their deliberate attack on the FSA camps was unmatched by any support that Hasiwar could summon in the labor movement of California. Shuttling between the House of Labor and the State Capitol, he failed to convince Governor Warren that the state should purchase the camps and keep them open, or the State Federation of Labor that it should make a major issue of the question. The proposal that a loan be floated to bid against the growers associations, at least for the camps that were crucial to the union's efforts, met with a cool reception. The American Federation of Labor was not interested in so unorthodox a venture, which might have required as much as a $600,000 investment for all the camps. It would not even endorse the mild resolution of the Executive Board of the NFLU calling for the return of the camps to the jurisdiction of the federal government. The 1947 convention of the California State Federation avoided the issue by merely authorizing its officers to encourage community participation in promoting proper housing for the migrant farm worker and his family.[170] In the light of the prevailing power alignments in Sacramento, organized labor blinked and looked the other way.

The agents of agri-business moved with efficiency and dispatch. On January 9, 1949, they met in Bakersfield to set up the Farm Labor Camps Association, which sent Lloyd W. Frick, a Kern County associate of DiGiorgio and Camp, to Washington. The association offered the federal government fifteen cents on the dollar for properties valued at six million. Negotiations were assigned to Ralph Bunje, author of the $2.50 cotton picking wage scale of the previous year. All areas of the state were represented in these maneuvers. Working in unison, they argued that the tenants had no objections to grower management; the associations would be in a position to invest their capital gains by reason of the bargain rates at which they expected to acquire the camps; government red tape would be eliminated; and management would be transferred to local citizens groups familiar with the needs of the camp population.

In the summer of 1947 the phasing out of government operation began. Without waiting for actual purchase, the federal government negotiated revocable use permits under which the growers associations took temporary possession.

As auctioneer in a market with no competitive bidding, the federal government did little more than accept the highest offers of the association. Typically, the Arvin camp, valued at $697,000, went on the block at $104,000. The Arvin–Lamont Agricultural Labor Housing Association was formed, with sixty farmers of the area as its members. Its officers included special citizens Joseph DiGiorgio, Lloyd W. Frick, and Harold Pomeroy, associate of W. B. Camp. Before the end of 1947 negotiations were well advanced for the transfer of the five labor camps located in Kern County to private control.

Throughout the state the same process was taking place. In El Centro, the Imperial Valley Farmers Association bought a camp that housed 850 men. In Firebaugh the West Side Growers Association took control of a labor supply center with a capacity of 1,500 persons. Management of the Butte County camp at Gridley passed to an association composed of prominent local merchants and growers. In Blythe, Westley, Patterson, El Centro, Soledad, and Marysville the camps fell into the hands of the growers in the classic manner of toppling dominos.

In some cases the takeover was immediate and at a price that was attractive to the growers. In others it was slow, lasting into the mid-1950s and culminating in no price at all. In August 1957 the sixty-three-acre Sutter County Farm Labor Center was turned over free of cost to the Sutter County Housing Authority,[171] a front for local agri-business. As a portent of things to come, in 1945 the Yuba camp was already housing Mexican braceros.

While growers associations were assuming control, changes in management policies were made. Rents were increased in some camps from $4.50 to $7.50 per month. In others the increases amounted to a hundred percent. Applicants were turned away on the pretext that cabins were being repaired or that the camp was crowded. In the Westley camp eviction notices were served on union activists. Some managers, obedient to the new rules issued by the associations, demanded work slips proving the occupant was employed by a farmer in good standing. Child care centers, recreation centers, and clinics were closed and community facilities allowed to deteriorate. In Yuba expenditures for camp maintenance were opposed by the new landlords on the ground that "substandard people live in substandard homes."[172] Failure to pay the rent promptly brought notices to vacate. "Bad camper" lists were passed from one camp to another by dutiful managers, "bad" campers being those who were delinquent with rents or who "were undesirable from some other standpoint." Camp councils ceased to meet.

By the middle of 1949 the majority of the camps were in a run-down condition.[173] After less than three years of operating the Arvin–Lamont camps the growers decided to phase them out even faster on the grounds that private farm housing was more plentiful and that mechanization of harvesting was reducing the demand for shelter.[174] Eventually many of the units were totally abandoned, as on the Gridley Camp in Butte County, which deteriorated to the point of being declared unfit for human habitation.

Whether the NFLU could have in fact developed a durable base in the camps had they remained under federal administration was never more than a distant possibility feared by the employers and hoped for by the union. The point was obvious: In an agrarian society inwardly tuned as delicately as Agri-businessland, a farm workers' strike was not simply a strike but an alarm that activated reprisals such as the campaign to close the farm labor centers. Deeper than the issue of wages was that of the potential challenge to the structure of power, no part of which could be disturbed without endangering the equilibrium of the whole. Confronted with these recoils the NFLU could not cope. Like others that were to arise later, these were not issues that were of the union's making, and its inability to address them foreshadowed its undoing.

The Tracy Tomato Strike—1950

Specialized cropping impressed on California a uniformity of land use and economic activity which were the result of experience with soil conditions, climate, reclamation, and irrigation. Measured in terms of decades, the changes in crop patterns were gradual, their characteristics permanent enough to identify certain localities, such as Salinas, the Salad Bowl not only of California but of the United States. In the northern part of the great Central Valley specialization was on tomatoes, the dominant farm product in large portions of Tulare, San Joaquin, Sacramento, and Yolo counties.

On the economic map these huge tracts appeared like capricious arrangements of human activity determined by marginal differences in the production of wealth. In a highly speculative crop like tomatoes acreage was likely to expand or shrink dramatically from one season to the next, depending on factors like the quantity of the cannery pack carried over from the previous year. The tomato country of the upper

San Joaquin was less a bowl than an irregular sprawl reflecting the caprices of the market and the calculations of processors, distributors, and bankers.

Special crops, with rare exceptions, are highly perishable, and tomatoes particularly so. Once they ripen they must be quickly picked and canned. Deep in the background of the economics of perishables is a labyrinth of inventory controls, cost projections, demand predictions, export fluctuations, yield estimates, weather forecasts, storage capacities, and contract commitments. The common denominator being profit and the mean temperature the heat of speculation, the tomato "deal" was a fever of activity. A nervous energy tensed every step of the operation. Teletypes clattered day and night in the offices of the brokers and shippers. Truck and railroad terminals rumbled with traffic. Over the highways twenty-ton loads of lugs and bins rolled steadily to processing plants, their exhausts roaring in round-the-clock operations. Contractors pushed their crews to the limit, and machines moved deliberately along the rows uprooting the plants with a forward speed regulated to so many feet per second. Field communications were maintained by radio, jeeps, and pick-up trucks, and in the dimly lighted warehouses columns of canned fruit and juice rose in stacks thirty feet high.

At the height of the "deal" the participants looked alert and slightly angry, especially in the field. If picking slowed down or stalled the entire apparatus would go into shock.

By these signs the harvest of 1950 in San Joaquin and Tulare counties was going forward normally. The first picking began late in August and would last through October or until rain or frost ended it. In the district of which the town of Tracy was the trading center there were over twenty-three thousand acres planted to tomatoes. In Modesto, Stockton, San Jose, Sacramento, and Oakland canneries like Flotill and Libby McNeil were geared for peak production. Together the processors in the twelve northern counties turned out 95 percent of the state's output. The three Flotill plants alone employed more than four thousand persons and packed four million cases a year, which represented a gross revenue of over twenty million dollars in 1952. The president of Flotill Canneries, Mrs. Tillie Lewis, had begun canning in her kitchen with the dream of "building an industrial empire for myself," and she did.

The tomatoes were supplied to the processing plants during their eight to ten week season by a field force of harvesters that in some years numbered more than fifty thousand people. They came mainly from other parts of California; less than 10 percent of them were out-of-state migrants. Except for day-haul pickers recruited on the skid rows of

Stockton, Sacramento, and Oakland and the residents of nearby towns like Tracy and Manteca, they crowded into camps operated by labor contractors. These camps were nondescript collections of tents, shacks, and metal cabins, rented for the season. A mess hall and a general store provided contractors with profitable sidelines of groceries, hard liquor, beer, and drugs. Screened by rows of trees, contractors sought out-of-the-way locations posted against trespassing the better to shield themselves from prying observers. In the extended Tracy area some twenty contractors, mostly Mexicans, managed several thousand pickers, approximately 20 percent of the labor force at its peak. Families that could not find housing or afford to pay rent pitched camp along the levees and groves of the San Joaquin River.

An important part of the picking was done by families, many of them following the circuit of prune harvesting in Santa Clara, peaches in Yuba City, carrots in Salinas, lemons in Ventura, and figs in Fresno. They set up housekeeping with a remarkable economy of effort. In such families life moved with the seasons and the crops, though they owned neither the earth nor its fruits. When asked about her young children a mother was likely as not to say that "this one was born in the cotton, this one in the grapes, that one in the cherries, and I expect the next one in the tomatoes."

For those who cared to look for them, there were continuities between the yearly ebbs and flows of thousands of men, women, and children who came to the area year after year. To those who were busy building empires out of tomatoes, these threads of sociability were invisible and in any case irrelevant. Nor were they of greater concern to the members of the Tomato Growers Association, which set the wage scale for picking.

The contrasting worlds of growers and workers met fleetingly in the short span of the picking. The wage terms in the harvest of 1950 were at the rate of 18 cents for a fifty-pound lug box and a withholding of 2 cents per box called euphemistically a "bonus." The 18-cent rate applied to the first picking and was raised by as much as 10 cents for the second and third pickings. The "bonus" was a source of abuses such as harassing the workers into leaving before the picking was over thereby losing the wages withheld, or delaying their computation until the crews had dispersed, or the disappearance of bookkeepers and checkers. Such withholding was illegal; a legitimate bonus, as defined by law, was a "payment by way of compensation or a consideration in addition to that which the recipients would ordinarily be entitled to."[175]

Before the harvest began the word was passed along by recruiters, crew leaders, camp bosses, and growers that the "bonus" would remain at 2 cents and that the wage scale would be reduced to 12 cents per box. It aroused the resident workers in Tracy who customarily picked tomatoes between other seasonal jobs.

Among them was Ignacio Guerrero who lived with his wife and thirteen children on the outskirts of town. A former migrant, Guerrero, like many of his neighbors, settled his family and built for them on a rocky parcel of flood land a house of salvaged lumber and other second-hand building materials.

Guerrero talked with his friends and showed them union leaflets that had come from Kern County telling of the DiGiorgio, the potato, and the cotton actions. Contact with the union was made and in Guerrero's kitchen the first organizing meetings of a local were held. Before picking began in the fall of 1950 Local 300 of the NFLU was chartered with a handful of members who proceeded to make it the center of propaganda against the "bonus" and the rallying point against the drastic wage cut ordained by the Tomato Growers Association.

Meetings like those in Guerrero's home were held in the surrounding communities where settled families could be located. To them earnings in the tomato harvest represented an important part of the yearly income, vital against a return to migrancy. Through them a network of information was established among seasonal harvesters. From these centers contacts were made with the camps through storekeepers, relatives, truck drivers, and friends gathered for talk in the bars, barber shops, restaurants, and pool halls. The word was that Local 300 was preparing to resist.

The setting was that of a crop strike like those already experienced by the union in Kern County. Considering the weaknesses of Local 300, such a strike should not have been called. The Tomato Growers Association was locked into the superstructures that profited from the wage system in the fields—the canners, processors, contractors, food purveyors, bankers, and transporters. Against them Local 300, like Local 218, was organizing a resistance with no treasury, no strike fund, no regular staff, and only a token membership base.

As experience had already shown, in such situations the objective was not a collective bargaining contract, notwithstanding the stress on this demand in the union propaganda. It was collective action within the limited duration of a perishable harvest by thousands of harvesters who were totally unorganized and who would arrive penniless in dozens of camps and stay there only at the sufferance of hostile camp bosses.

In the weeks preceding the harvest, I discussed strategy with domestics like Guerrero. It was agreed that intensive contact in an area encompassing fifteen thousand acres of plantings centered in Tracy would be maintained daily. Leaflet distribution would be extended north, east, and south gradually to give the organizational activity the appearance of wider reach. Members of Local 300 would take turns in staffing the office that had been rented in a vacant building in Tracy. Families were to be instructed to stay in camp and demand the legal thirty-days' notice if they were threatened with eviction. There was to be no violence against persons or property. All members of the local were to stand watch where pickers gathered in town. No strike action was to be taken until Local 300 could assemble a minimum of 250 pickers from designated areas, and representing the distribution of the labor force around Tracy. Special efforts were to be made to maintain contact with small growers who were on friendly terms with resident worker families.

Caravans were to be used principally to publicize the union action at the outset, or where field crews were notoriously unresponsive. Local 300 was to begin and direct the action on the understanding that a team of experienced organizers from Kern County would join me if necessary.

The assumptions of such a strategy were that among the tomato pickers there would be an experienced core familiar with the walk-away, fade-out, and stay-home methods of protest that had long characterized spontaneous wildcatting. Lines of communication could be maintained with such workers and through them with enough others to make a stoppage significant. By limiting costly caravaning and staying in camp, families could stretch their means over several weeks. The illegals who were in the area were to be regarded at first as fellow workers, appealed to and asked to leave the area voluntarily; if wetback scabbing became serious, Local 300 would denounce employers who were using illegals. Enough of them would automatically flee the strike area, as they always had, creating a problem for the growers. Information on union activity provided through leaflets and couriers to every tomato production area in Northern California would distract the attention of the growers and stimulate union talk where no action was intended. Inspections of farm labor camps, where even minimum requirements of sanitation and safety were disregarded, would make contractors more understanding. Recruiting of strikebreakers by the Farm Placement Office could be effectively stopped by picketing. Small growers would feel the manpower pinch sooner and Local 300 would undertake to supply crews to farmers who would agree to abolish the "bonus" and pay 18 cents. If cannery supplies were sufficiently reduced the canners would at a point use economic persuasion on growers to avoid a prolonged contest. If the growers resorted to heavy use of braceros, risks would have to be taken and the situation dealt with.

The chances of failure were not overlooked; but taking part in meetings that weighed them awakened motivations as propelling as economic gain: seeing their own practical experience respected as a factor in important judgments, learning techniques of cooperative action, sharing the responsibility of improvising new ones, hoping that they could compete with the contractors for influence upon the conditions of their labor, and realizing that thousands of pickers would be watching them for cues. The handful of charter members of Local 300 who took part in those kitchen caucuses grew in the confidence they needed for the task.

Preliminary meetings to plan the strike were held in different parts of the area in August 1950 until the local was ready to test its drawing power through camp delegates. These brought together pickers from various camps, from Stockton, and from Tracy, to fill the union hall with over 250 men and women. Fewer than 30 were members of the union.

The first specific assignment to them was the distribution early in September of a wage ballot, in which pickers were informed of the decision to cut their wages by one-third and to maintain the 2-cent "bonus." They were asked to state on the ballot their opinion of a fair wage. Eleven hundred signed ballots were returned. They voted to keep the 1948 wage scale of 18 cents. The "bonus" was unanimously condemned and the position of Local 300 for its abolition was supported.

On September 5 the first union bulletin was distributed in camps, grocery stores, shops, gasoline stations, restaurants, and staging points of field crews. They appeared thereafter as the principal medium of instruction and information, giving hundreds of pickers a paper in hand with which to counteract the rumors spread by contractors. On September 6 camp delegates gathered at union headquarters in Tracy and approved a formal demand for an 18-cent scale and the immediate termination of the "bonus." The following day a mass meeting of over three hundred pickers endorsed the demand and agreed to begin the walkout.

The strike began without the usual formalities of advising employers. Contractors had been invited to meet with the Executive Committee of Local 300 earlier. Out of sixteen invitations only three were accepted, the contractors maintaining that they could not discuss conditions of work without consulting the canneries and the growers. Previously the union had asked for a public hearing on the proposed wage scale by the State Agricultural Resources Committee. The request was denied on the ground that the members of the committee were "extremely busy persons" and in any case enough facts were already in hand that "typify conditions of agricultural workers throughout the state."[176] Letters to individual growers and the Tomato Growers Association were unanswered.

On September 6 there were twelve camp delegations reporting. They estimated that crews in the critical strike area around Tracy were down from one third to one half. The most reliable index was the number of idle workers who were reporting in from the Westley area, ten miles to the south; Patterson, Manteca, French Camp, and Brentwood asked for more leaflets. Car pools substituted for caravans and the strike became newsworthy.

At the end of the first week the action had become a major slowdown. It was agreed that families that had completely exhausted their funds could send a member into the fields for intermittent picking, and to do so by agreement with the camp committee. Spot checks of unloadings at the canneries indicated that operations had not been stopped, but that they were crippled sufficiently to alarm both growers and canners.

Briefing meetings and rallies were held daily, maintaining a constant rotation of pickers between headquarters and the camps. Substandard housing conditions were reported at meetings and demands for inspections announced publicly. Membership in Local 300 rose to two hundred, the majority of them residents of the central strike area. From among these there was elected a negotiating committee representing the camps to reinforce the executive committee of the local. Local merchants were approached with information on the effect of the proposed wage reduction on the community. The wives of some of the committee members requested representation and formed themselves into a committee to picket and gather information. By mid-September most of the two hundred regular participants in rallies were on strike duty.

Local 300 had been cautioned not to expect a total or even a major response to the strike call. How the pickers themselves rated the response was indicated by their high morale in the first two weeks of the action. Individual reports were checked by field inspections, and these showed contractors moving half-empty buses to and from work, quantities of empty lug boxes lying scattered in the roadways, packing shed crews waiting for fruit.

Contractors whose domestic crews refused to work fell back on illegals, reinforced by recruits from the thousands who were available in the Central Valley alone. By leaflets and word of mouth these workers were invited to support the strike, and the union identified the camps and ranches where they continued to pick, demanding that the Immigration Service remove them. Some raids followed and were publicized to keep the strikebreakers in check. Impartiality required that the service also interrupt union meetings by the sudden appearance of agents who demanded identification of all present who were obviously Mexicans. The service also responded to the Tomato Growers Association by citing me to appear at its headquarters in Stockton to produce evidence of American citizenship—a mere formality, I was assured, to lay to rest misleading tips that had been provided the service by employers.

By September 18 there were pickets throughout San Joaquin and Stanislaus counties, carrying signs composed by pickers with a working knowledge of English that said succinctly: 18 Cents—No Bones. It was estimated by the camp delegates that between 3,500 and 4,000 pickers were idle, which meant that some eight million pounds a day of ripe tomatoes were not reaching the canneries. In some fields the reduction of tonnage delivered roadside was calculated at 80 percent. The decision to limit the strike to a critical area proved a sound one. A daily loss of this size might have been absorbed if spread over the thousands of acres in all the northern counties. Weighed against the maximum production of the fifteen thousand acres under direct pressure from Local 300, such a loss was impressive. The dawn patrols of the strikers could see the scraggles of crews and smell the sour bouquet of tomatoes that would never be picked. At the height of the action there were over three hundred pickets on duty, all of them at camp gates, none at the ranches. Foremen paced the rows with pistols at their belts, racing between fields with hunting rifles and shotguns on the gun racks of their pickup trucks.

There were invariably signs of an itch for violence and an impatience to scratch it with bullets. One evening a thoroughly drunk contractor stalked into a bar adjoining the union headquarters, carefully stood a row of bullets on a table next to his automatic, mumbling, "This one is for Guerrero, this one is for Galarza." The drunk was a well-known labor broker. His soliloquy was immediately reported next door and it was decided to interview him on the spot. A committee of five unionists joined him in the bar, sitting close to his armament, broken beer bottles within reach. The conversation was amiable, ending in an agreement that the bullets were to be returned to the clip, which was to be entrusted to the bartender until the alcohol and the belligerence wore off.

On another occasion a lanky stranger in hip boots and western garb appeared at the union hall exhibiting a brace of hand guns and offering his services to the union as a guard. He was disarmed and asked not to return. One camp boss sent an invitation to me to negotiate a private settlement of the strike as to his crews. The camp was located two miles north of Tracy in a section heavily populated with wetbacks. On the way to the rendezvous two of them intercepted me with the information that a rifleman had been concealed in the camp office. An argument was to be provoked, the fight would move outside to the driveway, and the contractor's bodyguard would go into action in self-defense. I took two members with me, stopped the car in the middle of the road, and waited. Two No Trespassing signs flanked the entrance to the camp. We took out our signs and picketed for a few minutes. There were cars in the driveway but no one came out. The interview was over.

These were hazards of strike action no more serious than those the pickets faced at the camp gates. They were on constant alert to avoid being run down by trucks turning sharply at high speeds; they refused to respond to taunts from the armed guards; they stood watch in the sun waiting for the relief picket and the coffee break.

Seeing that the strike was effective and could not be dealt with by provocations to violence, the growers dealt two heavy blows—the intervention of the Teamsters Union and the recruitment of braceros in large numbers.

In mid-September Hasiwar placed a picket line in front of the Heinz processing plant in Tracy, which was receiving loads of canning to-matoes. The drivers pulled up and their rigs began to form a line along the highway, in plain view of hundreds of passing motorists. In the tradition of union solidarity they were honoring the picket line. En-thusiastic pickers gathered to view the scene.

It did not last long. As the steam exhausts of the plant sputtered over the plant and company guards watched, a black limousine pulled up in front of the gates. Teamster officials from Stockton and San Francisco got out, walked up and down the line of trucks talking to the drivers, and began waving them into the yard of the plant. Within minutes several thousand tons of tomatoes were rolling to the Heinz loading docks. Previously the Teamster representatives had toured the fields and had found that an effective strike was indeed under way.

On October 2 Harry Hanson, Secretary of the Central Labor Council of San Joaquin County, informed Local 300 by letter that sanction of the strike, which had been given previously by the council, "was limited to the picking of crops in the fields, and [did not include] permission to picket canneries or packing sheds." A Teamster business agent who had agreed to speak at a rally in Tracy telephoned his regrets after the Heinz episode. He explained that the Teamsters had contracts with the can-neries that they were bound to honor.

Simultaneously braceros began to appear in large numbers through-out the strike area. They were contracted by the Mexican government to the San Joaquin Growers Association, which maintained a labor pool in the Stockton County Fair Grounds. On September 18 hundreds of these men were sighted in trucks on the highways, and in heavily reinforced crews in the fields. Mingled with wetbacks they represented a con-tingent of between eight hundred and a thousand scabs. Before the end of the month braceros were deployed to the camps in the struck area. They moved under escort of highway patrol cars, sheriff's deputies, and growers. Private police were stationed at camp gates, replacing the camp overseers who had been armed and deputized. The influx of braceros made it necessary for the Department of Interior to permit growers to house them in a vacant camp near Vernalis, which, when previously requested by the union for use of displaced domestic families had been judged by the department to be too deteriorated for human occupancy.

Mobilization of braceros on such a scale did not halt the union. The government decision makers in Sacramento, San Francisco, Washington, and Mexico City were beyond its reach. Instead, union men infiltrated the bracero camps, informing the men that in the event of a union victory their pay would be increased from 12 to 18 cents per box. Surreptitiously, braceros began to pass back information, sometimes asking for advice on their own grievances, often inquiring how they might assist the strike.

Three months before the Tracy action began Hasiwar had met with state and federal officials. Hasiwar, bearing in mind the DiGiorgio episode, had been assured by Hayes, Chief of the Farm Placement Service, that qualified workers would be referred to employers of Mexican braceros, and at the same meeting Glenn Brockway, Director of Region IX of the Bureau of Employment Security, had guaranteed that braceros would not displace or otherwise prejudice the employment of qualified domestic workers.[177]

Teamster intervention and bracero mobilization did not demoralize the striking pickers. Neither did the harassing of the police or the contractors. As eviction notices were served and dispossession was threatened, the union arranged for the rental of tents and a vacant lot on which to pitch them. The wetback raids continued. Braceros were assisted to present demands for the 18-cent rate. By the end of September, five hundred pickers applied for membership, some paying a month's dues of two dollars, others making token payments of small change. And the canneries were still unable to meet their daily quotas of ripe fruit.

The first signs of spring have no more charm than the first indications of a favorable break in a crop strike. On September 27 there were still approximately fifteen thousand acres of planted fields under union pressure. A grower with two hundred acres near Tracy walked into the union office to say he would accept the 18-cent rate and elimination of the "bonus" in exchange for a crew to report that afternoon. As the word spread camp delegates asked for instructions on similar offers from growers who had had enough. By October 4 the prevailing wage was 18 cents and the "bonus" was abolished. In their haste to attract pickers some growers raised wages to 29 cents for first picking. Bundles of leaflets mailed throughout the state to all NFLU locals said, "The Bonus is dead. *Ganamos la huelga.*"

Through October as the harvest came to an end and the workers dispersed the active membership of Local 300 was reduced to a handful of dues-paying members, not all of them residents of the area. The task of creating a permanent base for the union again had to be faced. At most fifteen or twenty members could be counted on to maintain a core for the Local. They would need continuing financial assistance and counseling from the national office. Support would have to be provided against the inevitable reprisals of growers and contractors. Among the hundreds of domestics living permanently within a radius of twenty-five miles of Tracy a sustained recruiting and education effort would have to be made. The special conditions of employment in the fruit and vegetable crops of the area would have to be researched. Relations with the industrial and service trade unions of the area would have to be cultivated. Ways would have to be found by which the local could negotiate with the harvesters themselves as they moved into the area the terms and conditions on which the local would lead them into organized representation and if need be, resistance.

The experiences of the strike were vivid, its lessons clear. Among them was the certainty that the momentum of the 1950 action would carry over into the 1951 harvest. Insurgency had proved successful again and the returning pickers would remember it. But so would the growers, and the interval between harvests would be a time of planning for the second round. But as in the potato action, Local 300 was unable to make good use of the interval, as events were to prove.

To begin with, the risks of a crop strike could be assumed by the union only once. Essentially it was demonstrated to the harvesters that the union was capable of giving their spontaneous protests successful direction. The 1950 action had brought some ten thousand acres of plantings under union work conditions. Less than 20 percent of production had been affected but it was enough to compel drastic changes in the wage terms. After they returned to work it was estimated that the gain in the pickers' income was over $300,000. "Bonus" deductions were eliminated on more than two million boxes. The strike had cost nearly $1,800, of which the national office of the NFLU had sent $300 and the rest had been raised from out-of-pocket contributions by organizers and from the Los Angeles Central Labor Council, which donated $465 for relief.

As to the immediate economic benefits for the harvesters, the union again demonstrated that even with a minimum of preparation and resources it could raise wage levels. But such successes did not conceal the instability and lack of continuity of union action. A local emerging out of a crop strike would need supervision, assistance, and support for two to three years after the initial contest. The anchor of the organization would have to be among resident farm labor families with which year-round contact could be maintained. Any local action was bound to provoke reprisals from growers on levels of influence and power—Sacramento and Washington—progressively more remote from the field of action, and on these levels the union must respond. Unless it did so its local efforts would be overwhelmingly outmatched and its gains cancelled.

This was the background to the events of 1951.

During the spring and summer of that year the bracero labor force was increased, controlled by the San Joaquin Valley Growers Association with base camps in Stockton, Tracy, and Westley. The number of available harvesters was thereby increased from nine thousand to seventeen thousand. The number of illegals also increased, their role as a stand-by supply of manpower facilitated by the cooperative arrangements between labor contractors and the association. The labor shortage of 1950 created by Local 300 also prompted the Farm Placement Office in Stockton to coordinate more closely with the association its recruitment of outside harvesters. For this cooperation it was cited by the Tomato Growers Association.[178]

The 18-cent scale for first picking was also undermined by federal wage stabilization orders, one of which, issued by the Wage Stabilization Board, fixed a ceiling of 20 cents for all pickings, which in effect lowered the rate for the first. In October 1951 some bracero and wetback crews began picking at wages from 2 cents to 4 cents below the union scale of the previous year. Many contractors interpreted the stabilization order as a restoration of the "bonus." The right to request reviews of wage orders on grounds of hardship was limited to employers, and the right of appeal of workers was ignored. In the wage order nothing was said about the excessive filling of lug boxes, although the 20-cent maximum was based on the fifty-pound fill. Government agencies as facilitators of ways to cancel strike gains were hailed for their effectiveness in holding "wage troubles" to a minimum,[179] and the growers praised the wage orders for enabling growers "to pick first and second pickings at a much lower rate than had been anticipated."[180]

The pickers again turned to Local 300. The scale was lower for all pickings, drastically so for the third. Whether or not the "bonus" was enforced depended on the caprice of the individual contractor. Again mass meetings were called, pickets were posted, caravaning was attempted in the face of police harassment. And again the State Conciliation Service was rebuffed by the association with the standard comment that "there is no strike."

The conditions of action in 1950 were significantly changed and Local 300 had not been able to call up reserves to deal with them. The national organization as usual was in financial trouble. The State Federation of Labor ignored appeals for help. Ignacio Guerrero moved his family to seek work outside the area. Local 300 dissolved.

A frustrating pattern was emerging from these episodes. In each of them the flame of unionism was applied to the frozen structures of power, but it was like trying to melt an iceberg with a candle. At the conclusion of the strikes there were neither members nor contracts. The major gain, over the long run,, was that a system was being revealed in the specific manifestations of its power where agri-business had set up its domains in grapes, cotton, tomatoes, and other large-scale commercial crops. The spreading resistance to that power, pervading the entire agricultural economy of California, became an undertow of protest that moved through the harvesters of those crops. The NFLU, carried by the momentum it had helped to create, tried again, this time in the Imperial Valley.

Three Years in the Imperial Valley

In the southeastern corner of California is a desert plain surrounded by mountains, bounded on the east by the Colorado River and on the south by Mexico. The Imperial Valley is a scoop in the sandy wasteland, level at the center and sloping gently to the Salton Sea on the north where it falls 235 feet below sea level. It is one of the natural bowls of California agriculture, into which men began to channel the waters of the river in 1901. Four years later the river ran wild, a disaster that prompted the construction of Boulder Dam in 1935 at the headwaters of the Colorado, and in 1940 the All-American Canal downstream, together representing one of the most costly and impressive engineering systems in the west.

As water flowed into the Valley from the east human sweat poured into it from the south, the sweat of Mexicans emigrating north in flight from chronic poverty and the turmoil of the Mexican Revolution.

With such endowments the Valley became a cradle of wealth. By 1951 its irrigated lands were valued at $600,000,000. Over 4,800 farm operators cultivated more than seventy different crops, thirty-seven of them of the garden variety. The value of many of these crops was calculated in multimillions of dollars.

By the time water was delivered from the Colorado down the fretwork of canals to the rich alluvial soil bank of the Valley, the pattern of land ownership had become fixed, more than 40 percent held by less than 7 percent of the operators. The sagas of wealth became interwoven with romantic tales of how this remote corner of the West had been wrested by man against nature, with men betting their shirts on the desert, as the *Saturday Evening Post* phrased it. They bet and won. The wager was in blue chips—federal water and Mexican refugees—and the winnings were high. On nineteen acres of lettuce one small operator invested $3,800 and produced a crop that he sold for $20,000;[181] a tomato grower paid off the mortgage on his newly purchased land with the profits of one season.[182] Towering over a featureless landscape the refinery of the Holly Sugar Company drew on twenty-thousand acres of sugar beets.

Among the bonanza products of the Valley cantaloups figured prominently, with nearly thirteen thousand acres of plantings in 1950 yielding an average of 128 crates per acre. That year market shipments by railway amounted to 3,668 cars, exclusive of truck shipments. Over 40 percent of the acreage was owned or operated by ten grower-shippers, such as American Fruit Growers, The Arena Company, H. B. Murphy, and Fred R. Bright.

As a subsystem of the national economy, Imperial's agriculture was well served by public facilities. Basic to them all was the Imperial Valley Irrigation District, delivering water through more than 3,000 miles of canals and electric power over more than 2,500 miles of distribution lines. The Department of Employment, through the Farm Labor Office, kept the labor pool of domestics and illegals at optimum level by routinely approving the estimates of manpower needs of the growers. A field station of the University of California near Brawley pursued pests that nibbled on the profits of cropping. On the perimeter of the Valley the Border Patrol of the Immigration Service maintained a flexible cordon restraining the wetbacks from wandering farther north. From the Planters Hotel in Brawley the Market News Service of the U.S. Department of Agriculture issued reports gathered over radio and telephone on the vital statistics of the major deals—market prices, deliveries at terminal markets, railway loadings, truck shipments, and destinations. There was a symmetry and an operational efficiency about these services that was reflected in the local press, in the maintenance of law and order, in the courts, and in the spacious aloofness of the ranch houses of the successful.

The orderly arrangement of this society was even better shown by the institution that transposed economic into political power. This was the Imperial Valley Farmers Association, which in 1950 had 480 members representing 90 percent of the planted acreage in the Valley. The core of these was composed of grower-shippers who controlled 50 percent of the acreage, among them Danny Dannenberg, Joe Maggio Company, Bud Antle, Keith Mets, Garin Kantro, and Arena. Some of these operators also had holdings in the Salinas Valley and the Yuma Valley of Arizona. The minor growers, three thousand of them, clustered around the majors, dependent on their decisions as to wages, manpower, legislative advocacy, credit, relations with government agencies, and marketing.

In 1950 the tight structure of the IVFA centered in B. A. Harrigan, its Secretary-Treasurer and also agricultural commissioner for Imperial County, Sealer of Weights and Measures, and President of the Board of Trade. In the name of the association he was the exclusive negotiator and contractor of Mexican braceros. He was a portly man of medium stature, inclined to comfortable obesity, with a Stetson style of haberdashery that did a great deal for his personality. Powerful but unpretentious, he was inclined to kindliness, to which his unpublicized gift of a steer on the hoof to a Catholic priest for a barbecue in a bracero camp bore witness. On the rare occasions when he appeared at public hearings dealing with affairs of the association, he preferred a back seat in a corner of the hotel lobby, filling a lounge chair to capacity and scanning the scene from under the wide brim of his jaunty hat. Harrigan spoke quietly but his words reverberated through the Farm Placement Office and the U.S. Department of Labor, for his voice was the voice of O'Dwyer and Mets, of Bruce Church, Inc., of D'Arrigo Brothers, and of their peers.

Harrigan in effect made the decisions that maintained a labor pool arranged in three segments or layers, complementary and competitive, reflecting the tidiness of the social arrangements of Imperial agribusiness.

In the order in which they had arrived in the Valley, the first of these were the domestics or *locales*. They had formed *barrios* or *colonias* such as those of Calexico, El Centro, Brawley, Calipatria, Westmoreland, and Holtville. From them they migrated seasonally to the northern harvests, returning in the fall.

The *locales* were men and women inured to the most punishing living conditions in all of California agriculture. In the dark of the early morning they walked under the stars to climb into trucks and buses so they could be at work an hour or two ahead of the sun. They gathered watermelons in total darkness, testing them for ripeness before wrenching them from the vine by the sound of a middle finger triggered from the thumb against the rind. They topped onions all day, squatting on the rough ground, their shears making a fine drizzle of tinkling music over the baked field. By ten o'clock the cantaloup pickers had done most of the day's work, carrying sacks that weighed as much as eighty pounds a hundred yards down the row to the trailers in temperatures of 120 degrees. For them the Valley was a universe of heat and dust, of short-handled hoes, overloaded crates, sixty-pound lug boxes stacked six and seven high, that conditioned their bodies to the strains of heavy work. The veterans of such harvesting measured their days by the thousands of strokes weeding a field, by the endless rows of white conical caps placed gently over young melon plants, or by the bundles of carrots tied with wire Twist-ems. Their talk was that of people who knew the fields by their first names.

As a community of settled families paying taxes and meeting their modest expenses, such as those of sending their children to school, their economic position was under constant pressure. There were levels of living even lower than their own, those of the illegals and the braceros, and these differences were clearly expressed in the wages that each of these were willing to work for in competition with the domestics. There were differentials also with regard to working conditions, concerning which the domestics resisted demands for performance that braceros and illegals were forced to accept. For example, crews of domestics in the melon harvest demanded a count of the trailer loads that left the field, the number of crates packed out from each trailer load, packing house receipts for trailers delivered, and a count of the fruit discarded at the shed. All of these were devices by which unpaid labor was siphoned from their daily toil; only the domestics recognized their importance.

The enactment of Public Law 78 in 1952 provided the growers of the Valley with the choice between the rising expectations of the domestics and the markedly lower demands of braceros with respect to both wages and working conditions. It brought about displacement and dismissal of women workers, the first to go as the braceros advanced; the introduction of the short-handled hoe, which many of the domestics at first rejected; the substitution of hourly for piece rates; the increase in time lost in moving from field to field; the distribution of work among larger crews and the discriminatory assignment of field spaces; the use of production quotas on piecework to weed out the "slow" workers. Men who had worked in the fields for twenty years or more, some of them veterans of America's foreign wars, were retired in their prime. Those who were retained were assigned as lead men or pushers for green braceros or illegals.

In the years that it took a domestic harvester to equate the level of his wages with that of his family's living, he learned to pace his work within tolerable limits of human endurance. He noticed the ways in which he was cheated by the contrived shrinkage of his work product between the time he delivered it and the computation of his weekly paycheck by the company clerks. Knowledgeable in these matters, he became a marked man, progressively less desirable than illegals and braceros. To the ten thousand domestics who had settled in the Imperial Valley by 1950, half of whom made their living entirely as field workers, the signs that their tenure as residents of the Winter Garden was coming to an end were unmistakable. Those who read them early and decided that the open road was more hospitable than the closed Valley boarded their houses and migrated farther north.

The competitive disadvantages of the domestics that were forcing them out of their communities did not result from the free play of market forces. They were the effects of a deliberate design to dislocate them in order to make room for the braceros. In twenty years, these, too would develop work experience awareness and social stabilities of their own. Psychologically, they too would become *locales,* but another decade or two would have passed; and since the Mexican reservoir south of the border remained inexhaustible and open, the recycling of poverty in the Imperial could go on indefinitely. The terms and conditions of life and work in the Valley must now be viewed from the angle of illegals and braceros.

The names "wetbacks" (*mojados*), "line jumpers" (*alambristas*), and "illegals" (*chúntaros*) were originally the colorful linguistics of working-class border residents which later came into general use. These wetbacks, line jumpers, and illegals outwitted national sovereignties, ignored boundaries, and avoided legal requirements designed to contain them. Free passage over the earth had been an ancient right. In the American Southwest it was maintained, clandestinely to be sure but effectively nonetheless, by the men and women who were in perpetual flight from hopeless poverty.

Not that entry into the Imperial Valley was free. Many paid for it in cash to the runners who bootlegged them into the United States, as many others paid for it with their lives. It was not entirely an individual matter. A system of penetration had developed in response to a system of containment, whose weakness the wetbacks discovered, such as the relaxed surveillance of the Border Patrol during peak harvest seasons, the transportation service of contractors, the underground shelters along the main routes operated in many cases by ex-illegals, and the comparative safety of ranches on which the growers provided housing of sorts.

In 1950 there were in the Valley an estimated five thousand wetbacks, who made up approximately one-third of the agricultural labor force. Hundreds of them lived in scrubby hideouts along the banks of the main canals, and in the gullied desert around Heber, Holtville, and Westmoreland. They dug caves behind screens of brush, cooked over open pits, spread their clothes to dry on stones, left their retreats before sunup to be picked up by growers and contractors who took them to the fields, and returned at night by the light of the moon to rest by tiny campfires. They fashioned straw huts shaped like pup tents, tying the stalks with Twist-ems purloined from their employers, and from which it was possible to tell for whom they worked. An abandoned farmhouse, standing desolate in mid-desert and surrounded by dusty poplars or cottonwood trees, on close inspection showed all the signs of occupancy by illegals. Beneath loose floor planks there were dugouts, under an innocent pile of trash cooking utensils were kept wrapped in old newspapers, in back of the house an escape route. Water for these encampments was taken from irrigation ditches, fuel gathered from isolated woodlots.

This was the life style of thousands of Imperial Valley illegals whose minimal requirements fixed their level of living. In 1950 the median pay was between 40 and 50 cents an hour, with piece rates correspondingly lower. Wetbacks doing their first stint in the Valley could be found working for 35 cents an hour. The few who had won the favor of growers and had gained experience in evasion could expect to make as much as 70 cents for skilled work, such as driving tractors, irrigating, feeding cattle, or repairing machinery.

Midway between the illegals and the domestics the braceros provided a third economic alternative to the growers. By the spring of 1950 bracero wages had been standardized at 70 cents per hour, an increase of 10 cents over a decade. This was the wage scale for all harvest tasks, including thinning, cutting, loading, and field packing. Irrigators, truck drivers, sorters, and camp helpers were also paid 70 cents an hour, if they were braceros. In the melon harvest with pay by the hour rather than by the crate, there was no need for shed receipts and crate counts. Among the braceros there were many who had been recontracted repeatedly and on these some of the domestics' sophistication about working conditions rubbed off. For this reason growers found it expedient to raise the standard wage to retain their more experienced men, but this was done quietly and on a selective basis. The premium braceros continued to be the inexperienced ones, preferably younger men from the less developed rural areas of Mexico. They set the bench mark from which the Imperial Valley Growers Association measured the intervals of wage costs upward toward the domestics and downward toward the illegals.

The end of the DiGiorgio strike was still months away when appeals began to reach Local 218 from Imperial Valley for assistance. Late in 1949 organizers from Arvin responded, their observations confirming the complaints of the domestics in those areas, and by the spring of 1950 the NFLU was well on the way to a major encounter two hundred miles south of Kern County. Local residents were being systematically denied jobs and others with longstanding records as steady workers were being fired. As the Farm Labor Office continued to certify the Imperial Association for more Mexican contract labor, the number of unemployed domestics grew. Among them were the veterans of many harvests, men who could level a field by their sense of the tractor, or estimate accurately the number of crates or sacks or boxes a planting would yield from the roadside. Such were the men who were sidelined as hundreds of braceros rolled by on the way to work.

By mid-April of 1950 the NFLU had organized groups in the Valley, starting with the El Centro Local, Number 280. From it were issued the first documented complaints on behalf of domestics who were joining the union, filed with the governor of the state, the Farm Placement Office, and the U.S. Department of Labor's Regional Office in San Francisco. These authorities were requested to investigate the drastic reduction in wages in the fields following the arrival of the spring contingents of braceros.

When the union appeared in the Valley, Harrigan's offensive against the domestics was already under way. Union organizing hastened it. Beginning in March there was unusual activity by Mexican contractors moving busloads of illegals into the Valley from northern counties. They were crowded into isolated ranches, barracks, and camps that were normally used as depots in the underground supply routes of bootleg labor. Preparations were already being made at high official levels of government to "adjust the status" of these reinforcements, converting them into braceros and legalizing their presence in the Valley. By the end of 1950 over four thousand braceros already working in the Valley had been recontracted. Late in March 1951 another 1,200 contracts were renewed by the Imperial Valley Farmers Association, and on the eve of the strike Keith Mets, the president of the association, announced that the association had been authorized to contract five hundred more braceros.[183]

In El Centro, Brawley, and Calexico, where the three new locals of the NFLU had been established, the replacement of domestics continued. The women were the first fired; young union members were next. Workers known to be active members of the locals, or reported attending union meetings by the ubiquitous *soplones* (the Mexican translation for "informers"), found it increasingly difficult to find work as the spring of 1951 passed.

The denial of jobs and the dismissal of veteran workers went hand in hand with the systematic disruption, by agreement between the Farm Placement Service and Harrigan's association, of the crew system of melon picking that had existed for many years.

The practice of contracting between individual employers and self-organized crews of pickers dated back to the beginnings of the Imperial bonanza, agreements having been recorded as early as 1933. Like the artels of czarist Russia, they were elementary forms of worker associations based partly on kinship ties, partly on long-standing neighborliness, partly on ethnic sympathies, and partly on common interests in the work process and its conditions. Participation was voluntary, the size of the crews limited to fewer than twenty members. The crew formed itself before the harvest, with its leader a worker with a reputation for honesty and reliability as well as proven skill as a harvester, a pacesetter whose example promoted gainful production through cooperative mutual assistance. The leader scouted for the job and negotiated its terms. At the outset and throughout the operation he spoke for the crew. An agreement in writing was negotiated by the employer and signed by every member of the crew. It specified the scale to be paid, who was to provide the picking bags, the manner of payment, and compensation additional to the piece rate in the form of a bonus at the conclusion of the harvest.

These standard picking agreements or contracts were a limited form of collective bargaining. An employer might have various crews under separate agreements. The pay was distributed in equal parts for which reason the crew leader was relied upon to accept members with comparable diligence, experience, trustworthiness, and reliability. The crew leader received no extra pay for his role, worked side by side with his peers, exercised no authority over them, and was responsible for recording the production of his group day by day. Production records were verifiable and open to all. Earnings were equally shared. Wages were paid weekly to the crew leader and distributed by him on the spot. A grievance procedure operated informally based on the expectation of good faith by both parties to the bargain. Associations of this type tended to continue from season to season. The characteristics of the crew system contrasted sharply with hiring out by individual workers as well as with the contracting system of the braceros.

The destruction of these relationships began systematically during the harvest of 1950 and was completed by 1952. No standard picking agreements with crews of domestics were signed in those years. Efforts of crew leaders to make preseason arrangements for crew employment were rebuffed by both growers and the Farm Placement Offices in the Valley centers. Members of the union who were known throughout the Valley as crew leaders could not find work as field hands. Since the crews had become natural organizing units of the union, their disruption suited the displacement of all domestics by braceros, as well as the urgency to stop the union before it could gather headway.

A Diplomatic Confrontation

While organizing was progressing in the Valley, the NFLU was forced to deal with the association at higher levels.

In January 1951 negotiations began in Mexico City for renewal of the international agreement between the United States and Mexico for bracero contracting. The settled policy of both governments was that such negotiations were to be conducted exclusively through diplomatic channels. For the United States this meant the Department of State, for Mexico the Secretaria de Relaciones Exteriores.

It had also been settled that the U.S. Department of Labor would give the associated farmers throughout the country ample opportunity to brief the department on the terms that the growers wanted written into the agreements. Private meetings were arranged for such briefings. The Agricultural Labor Users Committee, which included Harrigan's association, had demanded that all international agreements be subject to prior consultation with representatives of bracero employers. The United States government agreed to this demand and held discussions with various regional associations, which were scheduled at times and places convenient to them. Officials of the Department of State, the Immigration and Naturalization Service, the Department of Agriculture, and occasionally of the Mexican government attended them.[184]

To make certain that in the 1951 negotiations the continuity of these briefings would be maintained the growers were invited to send an advisory delegation to Mexico City, which met privately with the American officials for a daily exchange of information and views. On the official delegation and available for the advice and consent of the grower spokesmen were Senator Ellender of Louisiana and Congressman Poage of Texas, both of whom had long records of opposition to farm labor unionism.

Mitchell attempted to obtain an official invitation to the NFLU to send an official observer to Mexico City, but he was ignored, except for the suggestion, made by low-echelon officials, that the union be represented unofficially. It was decided that I should go, notwithstanding the poor prospects of such a mission, the costs of which the NFLU was in no position to defray. Some reassurance was provided by the fact that the Railway Brotherhood of Maintenance of Way Employees was sending one of its officials, Frank Noakes, to make certain that the agreement did not include contracting of braceros in its jurisdiction.

The negotiations began late in January. Both Noakes and I approached Robert S. Creasy, a former trade unionist who had risen to the position of Assistant Secretary of Labor. Creasy pointedly ignored me. Noakes and I jointly addressed a letter to Creasy. We requested a daily briefing in writing from him. Meeting privately with Noakes, Creasy offered to keep him informed generally on the progress of the negotiations. Noakes waited from day to day for Creasy to communicate, failing which Noakes settled for an informal commitment that there would be no discussion of bracero contracts for railway employment.

Normally this would have been the end of Noakes's assignment, but he did not stop there. Noakes was a dapper dresser, in whom the dignity of his Brotherhood blended with a fond recollection of his early days as a trade unionist, when he walked the tracks signing up members. Happily, also, his low-key style clashed subtly with Creasy's pomposity. Noakes readily agreed to stay on a few days and help me deflate it. While he remained in Mexico City he paid for my dinners and allowed me the use of his hotel suite.

The negotiations proceeded into the first week of February behind closed doors. We failed in our efforts to reach the U.S. delegation directly with a request that no final agreement be signed until it had been submitted to the NFLU for comment.

With Noakes in agreement, I decided to make contact with Mexican labor organizations in Mexico City, to address public meetings of hundreds of applicant braceros who had gathered from all parts of the country, and to talk with newspaper reporters. I wrote a second letter to

Creasy, rejecting his claims that as Assistant Secretary of Labor he represented the members of the NFLU, with respect to agreements that affected their working conditions. The Mexican Confederation of Workers (Confederacion de Tabajadores de Mexico), the most influential labor body in the country, advised me not to interfere with the Mexican government's conduct of the negotiations. Among the bracero applicants the response was more positive. Arrangements were made for me to address them in a mass meeting in one of the working-class districts of the capital. I then called a press conference on the Paseo de la Reforma, complete with refreshments, partly paid for by Noakes. At the press conference a roomfull of correspondents received copies of documents I had brought with me concerning wages and working conditions of braceros who had returned from California and asked the NFLU to assist them in pressing grievances they had left pending and which neither government had resolved. I pointed out to the reporters that the NFLU was offering this information in view of the tight security that the Secretaria de Relaciones had placed on the negotiations. There had been no official communiques on the subject. The metropolitan press, including dailies like *Excelsior* and *El Universal*, had been unable to break the story. *Ultimas Noticias* railed against the Secretaria for its "infantile and hostile attitude toward the press in failing to keep it informed."[185]

The publicity resulting from the press conference and the leaflets announcing the mass meetings, with Noakes and me as the guest speakers, aroused the Mexican government. The Secretaria de Gobernacion, which in the Mexican system has control over political security, picked up two of the organizers of the mass meeting, advised them to cancel it or face jail, and to pass the word to me that unless I desisted I would be deported under Article 33 of the constitution, which provides for the summary expulsion of undesirable aliens. I had become an American citizen in 1939.

The mass meeting was called off, but it was agreed that I would meet with the small groups of applicant braceros who gathered daily in the national stadium and some of the public parks. I then asked Noakes to fly back immediately to Washington and stand by to continue the press conferences there if necessary, but to meet me with a committee of trade unionists at the border in case I was deported. Noakes understood that as a Mexican-born American citizen I would present the Mexican government with peculiar problems with respect to Article 33, and that my deportation would be the best way to call international attention to what was happening in Mexico City.

Noakes left for the United States and I continued my course. The most that the Secretaria de Gobernacion did was to station in my hotel lobby two agents who followed me on my extended walks through the city to talk with bracero applicants.

After Noakes had left I received word from the American embassy that my request for an interview with the ambassador would be granted. The Honorable William O'Dwyer received me alone. I stated briefly that the purpose of my presence in Mexico City was to make known to both governments and to the public the position of the NFLU on the bracero system and to protest the singular manner in which the negotiations were being conducted.

The ambassador heard me out. Then he proceeded to explain matters as follows: It was the Mexican government which had insisted on a small delegation, secret conversations, and no publicity. For these reasons outsiders like myself could not be admitted to them. Negotiations of this type are always very sensitive. The Mexican government has the upper hand and dictates the terms and the procedure. The NFLU should work out its problems in the United States rather than as a participant in international negotiations. George Meany could vouch for the sympathetic interest of the ambassador in labor's problems, since organized labor helped elect him mayor of New York. Creasy's presence on the delegation meant that it was representative of all interests, including those of farm workers. Once a United States government agency determines that there is a need for braceros, that settles the matter and negotiations can properly proceed.

The ambassador sat across from me at his wide desk, high on a leather chair, as if on a throne. He was framed in drapes, plaques, photographs of the famous, great seals, and the perpendicular folds of an American flag at rest on a polished mast. I imagined behind these props a distant montage of the powers that had brought him to such eminence.

As I listened closely to his lecture, I was aware that the man speaking was the ambassador of the United States of America to the Republic of Mexico. But he was also the brother of Frank O'Dwyer, partner of Keith Mets, President of the Imperial Valley Farmers Association, associate of B. A. Harrigan, employer of more than five thousand braceros. William had been appointed to his post by President Truman in the midst of an investigation of police graft.

I returned to the Imperial Valley to help in the preparations for the 1951 melon harvest.

Imperial Valley — 1951

By mid-February the three locals were chartered and enlisting mem-

bers in Calexico, El Centro, and Brawley. Hasiwar had already requested the State Department of Industrial Relations to detail more
agents to the Valley for investigation of unlicensed labor contractors.
Organizers moved through the hideouts of the wetbacks, advising them
to leave the area in the event of a strike. Petitions began to come in from
the *barrio* residents, men and women who were working for 35 cents an
hour. The locals assembled and collated reports, letters, declarations,
dismissal notices, and other documents for presentation to the Department of Labor as proof of the situation of domestics in the area. Letters
went out to the merchants of the principal towns whose trade depended
mainly on resident harvesters.

The union soon discovered that its relations with the Department of
Labor were not likely to be fruitful. Union men reported that in a field
operated by Frank O'Dwyer and Keith Mets wetbacks and braceros
were working in a mixed crew of over two hundred men. This was a
practice prohibited by the international agreement and punishable by
cancellation of permission to use braceros. The union filed charges and
asked for a hearing to present witnesses. Instead, the department officials from regional headquarters in San Francisco met privately with
Mets and Colunga, the Mexican consul in Calexico, refusing to give the
union a copy of the transcript or minutes of the meeting.[186] The department's position was that the agreement provided that complaints of that
nature must be heard in closed administrative meetings. The agreement,
the department held, said nothing about procedures on complaints by
domestic workers of adverse effects on them. It left such procedures to
the discretion of department officials, who would neither recognize the
domestic workers as an adverse party nor follow due process to hear
them. Into this secret chamber of administrative discretion all union
complaints were thenceforth to be consigned.

By the middle of May, as the harvest began, the NFLU had all its
California organizers in the Imperial Valley. Besides Hasiwar there
were William Becker, William Swearingen, Carl Lara, and myself. In
each of the three locals there was a team of volunteers, altogether some
twenty-five men and women, to mobilize a labor force of fifteen
thousand domestics, braceros and illegals. To reach them information
leaflets were issued regularly, with a circulation of 1,500 to all corners of
the Valley. In the leaflets the union dealt not only with working conditions in the fields for domestics but also with the grievances of braceros
and illegals, violations of transportation safety regulations, and the like.
It was an intensive educational campaign on matters that had not been
publicly aired in the Valley ever before.

Mitchell signalled to proceed with plans for action, and wrote on May

17, "Go ahead on credit until we can get some cash there."[187] At that point the budget for strike preparations amounted to five hundred dollars.

As Director of Organization for the NFLU in California, Hasiwar addressed a letter to the Board of Supervisors asking it to mediate a meeting with the association. The request was dismissed with a reference to the international agreement which as a matter of form guaranteed that no braceros would be hired until all domestic workers had been placed. The board took no action on the matter.

On April 26 Hasiwar wrote a letter to the association advising it that the union represented farm workers in Calexico, El Centro, and Brawley, that on their behalf the NFLU wished to discuss wages and working conditions, and that the union was willing to invite the State Conciliation Service to participate in the discussions as a third party. Since the association had already negotiated the bracero contracts in Mexico City, it did not respond. Demands were thereupon served on the association consisting of (1) preferential employment for domestic workers, (2) hourly wages of $1.00 (3) an increase in pay for melon picking from 20 to 25 cents a crate, (4) no discrimination against members of the union, and (5) no employment of illegals.[188] Taken together they represented a demand for recognition of the union for purposes of bargaining. Demands were not served on individual employers, since the association was the sole party to bracero contracts.

Harrigan answered through the press. The position of the association was that on these matters it could not bargain with the union. It had no authority from its members to negotiate employment terms for domestic workers. Its only function was to facilitate the contracting of braceros.[189]

A crucial issue was raised: whether the association was a legitimate negotiating body, and whether it could legally choose to represent its members in one case and not the other. The association was settling these issues arbitrarily, yet they rested on the provisions of the international agreement, the terms of the contracts, the legislative history of bracero legislation, the declarations of the secretary of labor, the solemn assurances of Congress, and the articles of incorporation of the association itself.

This was the point at which the union should have started an aggressive legal attack; but the NFLU, as usual, had no funds for costly litigation. By default the association was permitted to retreat behind a legal fiction and an administrative myth, that it was under the rigorous supervision of the U.S. Department of Labor.

As the melon harvest gathered momentum the association pressed its advantages. Along with the other associations of the state it had obtained all it wanted in Mexico City. The Immigration Service was prepared to "readjust the status" of hundreds of wetbacks, who were being transported to the Imperial Valley from the north by labor contractors. The Mexican Consul was ready to legitimize the process. The Department of Labor had already shown its bias by covering up the O'Dwyer–Mets charges. The melon growers had purged themselves of domestic pickers to the point that toward the end of May twenty-five employers had on their payrolls 374 domestics and 1,055 braceros.[190] One company had 65 braceros and no domestics. Harrigan remained unchallenged as the judge of his own case.

There matters stood when the American Fruit Company fired all its domestic workers on May 23. None was given cause for dismissal. Some had worked for the company for ten years.

That evening all members were called to a meeting at Hidalgo Hall in Brawley, with more than three hundred workers present. They voted to strike.

At 3:00 A.M. on May 24 more than four hundred pickets appeared in front of packing sheds that were receiving fruit from fields picked by braceros and illegals, and at the gates of the camp in El Centro where the association housed several hundred braceros, as well as various other camps in Calexico and Brawley. Where trucks or buses loaded with braceros stopped by the wayside or at gasoline stations they were approached by pickets and urged to go back to camp. Leaflets were left where illegals would find them and be informed of what was occurring. The organizing teams of volunteers became strike committees. Where illegals were known to be concentrated under surveillance to be converted for a fee into dried-out wetbacks, union delegates appeared to confront the contractors. In one contingent alone two hundred illegals were intercepted in Calexico as they arrived from Ventura County, 275 miles to the north.

On the first day of the picketing the packers in three sheds refused to cross the picket lines. They were members of the United Packinghouse Workers Union of America. Growers and contractors shifted their loading points for illegals from the customary locations in the towns to private camps and even isolated spots in the bush country around the Valley. An unusual number of trailers were standing empty in the fields and shed yards. On May 25 the strength of the union consisted of five hundred active participants and probably twice as many more who remained at home. Shipments of melons on May 28 stood at 404 compared to 1,978 for the same date in 1950.

At all hours of the day and night new faces appeared at the union halls, to join or to carry back news and leaflets. It seemed as if the whole social fabric of the *locales* had tightened in an effort to preserve itself against the determination of the associated growers to destroy it. It was more than individual melon pickers who were on strike; it was a community.

The signs that the NFLU was most anxiously scanning were not, however, on the picket lines or in the response of the townspeople. They were in the position that the other unions, most importantly the Teamsters, would take on the strike. Undoubtedly it was also the crucial point in the strategy of the association, reflected in the editorial comment of the *Imperial Valley Weekly* on May 24: "The biggest club the union holds is the possibility that the Teamsters Union will recognize the strike."

There were reasons for the NFLU to expect such support. The Imperial Valley Central Labor Council, with the Teamsters Union participating, had sanctioned the strike. Teamster members had picketed in the DiGiorgio action. Perhaps more encouraging, the Teamsters had agreed with the NFLU that the organizing campaign was to be extended to the beet fields, on the understanding with the local that drivers of beet trucks were to be in the Teamster jurisdiction. On the other hand there was the precedent of the Western Conference of Teamsters officials who had waved Teamsters through the picket lines in Tracy.

The rank-and-file reaction of both drivers and shed workers on the first morning of the strike was in the trade-union tradition. A work stoppage began to develop in some of the sheds. Drivers on the roads and at the terminals stopped and asked questions of the union pickets.

But whatever was happening in the ranks of workers of different crafts living in the same community, it was contrary to policy at the high levels of Teamster authority. On May 24 and 25 newspapers in Sacramento, Los Angeles, and the Valley published wire service reports that Verne Cannon, legislative representative of the Teamsters in Sacramento, had declared that the strike was a wildcatter, that it was unauthorized, and that the Teamsters would not support it.[191] Local Teamster officials in El Centro announced immediately that they would abide by all contracts with the Western Growers Association and other employers, which provided that the union would not strike, slow down, or take any other job action for the duration of the agreement.

The business agent of the Packinghouse union followed suit at once, stating to the press that it would abide by its own agreements, which also contained a no-strike clause.[192] Thereupon all sheds resumed packing operations, their supply of fruit coming almost exclusively from illegal and bracero scabs.

The news struck the union. The background of the blow was as follows:

The Associated Farmers and their fellow lobbyists had introduced bills in both the state Assembly and Senate prohibiting the controversial "hot cargo" boycotts. The Teamsters Union regarded itself as the chief target of these bills, and prevention of their passage was the first item on its legislative agenda. The bills had the highest priority for the Associated Farmers, too. The two exchanged views in the customary manner of sophisticated lobbyists. Each side was prepared to arrive at a compromise, especially if it could be accomplished at the expense of third parties not present, such as farm workers and consumers.

In the midst of these negotiations the melon pickers struck and the door to such a compromise was suddenly opened. The Teamsters' worries about possible hot cargo legislation were evenly matched by the concern of the Associated Farmers, Harrigan's association included, over the threat posed by the NFLU in the Imperial Valley. It must have appeared formidable to them, much more so than the union was able to guess.

In the resulting deal the Teamsters agreed to disavow the strike if the growers would consent to call off their legislative dogs. They did. Teamster president Dave Beck wired the sponsors of the bill in the Senate stating that he had ordered Teamster officials in the Imperial Valley to abide by all contracts. He gave assurances that all products harvested would be transported "regardless of any labor interference or other alibis." Beck emphasized that the picket lines of Imperial were to be breached "under my orders."

Both parties to the deal kept their word. By the morning of May 25 trucks and trailers were moving melons in and out of the sheds across the picket lines, and inside the sheds CIO workers were packing them.

Undoubtedly the progress of the negotiations in Sacramento was reported regularly to California State Federation of Labor Secretary–Treasurer C. J. Haggerty. That he was thoroughly briefed was shown by his testimony before the assembly committee that killed the controversial bills. He commended the Teamsters for their willingness to confer with the Associated Farmers, offering to join in the consultation. Referring to the Imperial Valley strike, then it its early stages, Haggerty merely deplored the sad condition of the wetbacks, lamenting the continuation of "Grapes of Wrath conditions."

The most complete account of these events was that of the Teamsters themselves, which appeared in the *Southern California Teamster* of June 13, 1951.

The growers understandably gave these matters wide publicity. They took the action of the Teamsters and the UPWA as an endorsement, stressing with satisfaction, as did Keith Mets, that even the box makers of the Carpenters Union had disregarded the "so-called picketing."[193]

There was nothing left for the NFLU but to express its contempt to the Teamsters for their behavior. I sent the following telegram to Teamster legislative agent Cannon: "This is the most severe finking blow which our union has yet received from a sister union."

Standing alone as they now were, the union ranks did not collapse. Through the next four weeks picket lines were maintained at the sheds and posted at some of the larger ranches. The mood of the workers was bitter, but the orders against violence were not relaxed. Police escorted trucks and buses filled with illegals and braceros, and between these assignments they stationed themselves across the street from union halls, chatting over their radios, passing on intelligence to headquarters and to Harrigan. Crew supervisors appeared in some fields in the dual capacity of company employees and deputy sheriffs, carrying side arms. Women unionists boarded trucks in Calexico in the early morning hours, stalling them until they were arrested. They patrolled day-haul staging points, routing contractors from them. On the seventh day of the strike, and six days after the Teamster detente with the Associated Farmers, sixteen pickets were jailed, thirteen of them women. The picket lines were thinner by now, but the number of participants in the strike remained steady. They were now covering packing sheds, labor camps, the Holly sugar refinery, terminals, and the ranches of the most notorious antiunion corporations.

The Calexico local was assigned the task of picketing the international boundary to dissuade border jumpers and to keep watch on the trucks and buses manned by growers and contractors that kept predawn rendezvous with them. Ten crossing points along the border were guarded, extending over a distance of more than eight miles. These positions were the terminals of paths on the Mexican side over which the foot traffic moved, unmolested by the Border Patrol. The Calexico headquarters of the strike were in a dilapidated two-story barn, cool and gloomy, with a resident flock of pigeons which cooed and peered down at the strikers moving about. On one wall there was a large polychrome print of the Virgin of Guadalupe, attended by votive flowers and candles. In her presence many problems were discussed and decisions made, such as the unexpected temptation of men pickets at the boundary posts who were propositioned by female wetbacks to dally a while in the darkness as the reward for a day's pass to the fields beyond. The solution to this was both prompt and decisive. The women of the local proposed, moved, and carried the motion that at every post there should be at least one female member of the union. The candlelight seemed to flicker the shadow of a faint smile on the face of the Virgin. Between crises of the 24-hour watches there were lulls during which the conversation turned from the immediacy of the strike to its more complicated depths in diplomacy, politics, trade unionism, international agreements, and the chronic poverty of Mexicans on both sides of the border. Working with the raw material of their own experience, the workers glimpsed their connection with more remote but equally vital realities heretofore unsuspected. Such discovery was the essence of morale; it lasted to the end of the strike, and beyond. I have never taught a college class or a graduate seminar in which the learning followed so closely on the teaching and both on the action.

Uppermost in these discussions were two topics and the position of the union with respect to them. One was the role of the braceros, the other that of the illegals. With respect to both, the union explained the daily developments and their meaning.

On May 31 one thousand braceros were in the Valley holding contracts that had expired. These men were being held for recontracting by the Immigration Service in spite of their illegal status. Throughout the bracero camps the word was passed that the association was the recognized agent of the U.S. Department of Labor with respect to the contracts. *Reconocimiento* ("official recognition") carried a heavy accent of status and authority. The other theme of the growers propaganda was that the strike had not been *reconocido* by either the drivers or the packers. *Des conocimiento* ("disavowal"), an even more heavily loaded word for all Mexicans, gave the psychological screw the final turn.

Nevertheless, the growers did not succeed in isolating the braceros from the union. Even before the strike began they had appeared at the union halls, asking for help in pressing grievances on wages, unexplained deductions, accident compensation, and meager earnings. The union leaflets publicized these complaints and invited other braceros to make them known, bringing supporting documents such as contracts and check stubs. Since the international agreement provided that the braceros enjoyed the right to elect their own representatives, the NFLU regarded the request for help in processing their grievances as such an election. Braceros were signed up as members and from that point the union submitted their grievances to the Department of Labor. In June forty braceros in the different locals had signed authorization cards. They became the source of detailed knowledge of the operation of the bracero program in the Valley, as well as of current information on conditions inside the ranches.

The Department of Labor lost no time in advising the union that it would pay no attention to these grievances, taking the position that "there is no provision in the international agreement for any nongovernmental agency or group to intervene in the cases of complaints filed against employers by Mexican nationals.''[194] And when word about them came back to management, clearly through the department itself, the complainers were threatened with deportation.

In spite of the department and the grip of the association on its decisions, it was often possible to correct the most indefensible violations of the rights of the braceros. In one case a crew of more than thirty men was removed from a camp after an epidemic of food poisoning. I found medical treatment for them and placed three of them in a motel room as witnesses. The Immigration Service sent three patrolmen to demand that I produce the complainants and to keep me under house arrest while they investigated whether the union was harboring persons who were remaining in the country illegally. That morning the association had cancelled their contracts, alerted the Border Patrol, and laid the foundations for a charge against me of a clear violation of federal law. Harrigan had lodged the complaint.

With the border police present in the union office I telephoned the Department of Labor in San Francisco and advised that from there I would accompany the patrolmen to the detention center. I refused to reveal the whereabouts of the three braceros until I had a guarantee that they would be held in the United States for a hearing on their complaints and until conditions in the camp were corrected. I knew that the Regional Office in the department would not welcome the press release that would follow, which I was already mentally composing. It agreed that the Immigration Service would hold the men, that their contracts would be reinstated, and that medical examinations would proceed immediately. I accompanied the patrolmen to the motel where I had lodged the three men.

In like manner the union collected back wages for braceros, tracked them to Mexicali where they had been deported without proper medical discharge suffering from serious injuries, confronted contractors who had abused men physically, recovered personal belongings that had been impounded by irascible foremen, and successfully sued one corporation for negligence in causing injuries to twenty braceros when the truck in which they had been riding had overturned.

These activities did not affect the strike, but each incident provided an opportunity to peel one more layer of the sophistry and pretense in which the bracero program was wrapped.

With respect to the illegals, union relations appeared even more inconsistent. Like the braceros, wetbacks often appealed to the union for help. Usually this happened when they were returning to Mexico voluntarily, hopeless and discouraged by the treatment they had received. On the most common complaint, unpaid wages, the illegals were assisted in filing claims with the labor commissioner in El Centro. Such a claim was presented on behalf of three men who had been arrested by the Border Patrol near Niland and forced to work for a rancher for one day under custody and then deported without receiving any pay. Affidavits were taken and presented to the ranking Immigration Service officer, who agreed to collect the wages due and pay the men and to issue an order prohibiting the practice. Since the complainants were always deported before being paid, daily contact with them was maintained where the union hung on the wire fence that separated the two countries a sign that said: Consultas - La Unión.

Through channels of communication like these, men exchanged information for services. They enabled the union to introduce into the grapevine, the principal source of information among illegals, explanations about the causes of the strike and appeals to refrain from working behind picket lines. The wetbacks were always eager to receive and distribute union leaflets on both sides of the border. Some of them applied for membership in the union on the mistaken belief that a union card would be honored by the Border Patrol as a credential for temporary residence. But the word was passed that wetbacks on the ranches and camps in the struck area would be treated as scabs.

From the point of view of the union the wetbacks could not be abandoned totally to the growers and contractors, however difficult it might be to maintain communication with them. The exploitation and social exclusion of the illegals foreshadowed the model to which all workers, including domestics and braceros, could be reduced. Manipulation of masses of wetbacks was the least defensible of the strategies of agri-business, measured by the institutional values of the larger society, Christian, ethical, and democratic. To repulsive economic abuses, difficult as they were to deal with, there was added a contagious social exclusivism, already deeply rooted in the labor movement of California. The promised land of collective bargaining that trade unionism was striving for held the promise of more income for fewer workers, the effects of technology, integration, higher wages, and better fringe benefits for those who survived the attrition. To protect it the border would have to become an unbreachable line of containment behind which a diminishing number of American workers could rest secure.

The situation in the Imperial Valley was a clue to the dilemma of the NFLU. There the economies of Mexico and the United States meshed, with labor bootlegging across the border a natural result. The mesh was becoming tighter, with American capital moving south into the Mexican borderlands and impoverished labor northward into those of the United States. The organization of domestic farm workers affected not only the interests of a comparatively small class of agricultural employers, but also those of two national social systems in which that class was entrenched.

On the strike front, it was obvious that the wetback was an employer's option of large magnitude, to be used or discarded, the choice requiring only that the governments of the United States and Mexico be cooperative. Some instances will illustrate the point.

In 1949 both governments agreed on a procedure by which illegals already working in the United States could "have their status adjusted," to make them available for contracting as braceros. In California this placed perhaps 40,000 illegals in the category of dried out wetbacks, between 4,500 and 5,000 of them in the Imperial Valley at the height of the strike. The Immigration and Naturalization Service refused to release the names of ranches on which illegals were apprehended, among them some belonging to the elite corporations, which maintained a regular transportation service from the border to replace deportees. At Calexico the Mexican Consul provided diplomatic facilities for instant conversion of illegals into braceros.

The Farm Placement Service played its customary role from the beginning of the strike. On May 25 it issued a report on the struck growers, stating that only 95 domestic workers had responded to the strike call.[195] The May 26 California Weekly Farm Labor Report out of the FPS office in Sacramento sent out a call for 1,300 melon pickers for the Imperial Valley. Chief Edward F. Hayes told a legislative committee that his staff had not been able to find a strike in the area. The service continued to send out calls for melon pickers into the middle of June.

The manager of the FPS in Calexico, Tom Finney, dovetailed his operations with the strategy of the association. He informed the union that when the harvest began bracero crews had already been contracted making it impossible to substitute domestics or enlarge the crews to give the latter work. When domestics applied for picking as crews, Finney referred them to the association or to distant and separate ranches, forcing their dispersal. This was described by the growers as the distribution of risks. Domestic workers who had served in the armed forces were denied job referral. Melon pickers were offered alternative placement as equal employment topping onions at the prevailing wage of 70 cents an hour approved by Finney's office.

Equally attuned to the strategies of Harrigan's association, the Mexican consul, Elias Colunga, did little more than rubber stamp documents in Calexico. On May 28 I informed Colunga by letter that braceros were being moved about the Valley under police escort, and I cited cases in which picket lines had been crossed. Since he did not respond the union organized a demonstration in front of the Mexican consulate, which was guarded by police displaying automatic arms. In the midst of the demonstration an employee of the consulate lowered the Mexican flag, refusing to talk to the demonstrators.[196]

Diplomatic maneuvers were taking place in the meantime. On May 31 Colunga, responding to an inquiry into the role of braceros in the strike, advised the Secretaría de Relaciones in Mexico City that fewer than one thousand workers had walked out, and that only fifteen ranches were affected.[197] The Secretaría also requested information from the U.S. embassy, which replied on June 6 that the strike had not been recognized by the Department of Labor.[198]

The Secretaría de Relaciones had apparently been more concerned over the situation than Colunga. It instructed the consul to arrange for the transfer of braceros out of the strike zone and to encourage the repatriation of illegals.[199] To clarify the press reports that circulated in Mexico City the NFLU asked the Department of State for release of the text of the notes exchanged between Relaciones and the embassy. The department replied that Ambassador O'Dwyer had lost the correspondence. If the Mexican government had in fact felt concern over the use of braceros as scabs, it was allayed rapidly. Colunga announced on May 8 that the braceros were not affected by the situation in the Imperial Valley.[200] The consulate general of Mexico in Los Angeles confirmed this statement on June 9, stressing the nonrecognition of the strike by the Department of Labor.[201]

Secure on the diplomatic front, the Imperial Valley Farmers Association was simultaneously moving in the regional office of the Department of Labor in San Francisco. During the six critical weeks from mid-May to the end of June when the harvest peaked and declined the keystone of the union strategy was clear: to compel the Department of Labor to enforce the terms of the international agreement and the individual work contracts negotiated under it. Those terms covered the conditions under which bracero employment could be authorized. Domestic workers were to be given prior claim to available jobs; mixed crews of illegals and braceros were prohibited; wages were to be leveled up to those of domestic workers. Harrigan looked to the department to resist compliance.

Even before the strike began the Department of Labor evidenced a lack of interest in carrying out its legal obligation to improve the economic opportunities of citizen workers. In April the department promised Mitchell that hearings would be held to review the complaints documented by the union. At the request of the department Mitchell made no moves to publicize such hearings. They were never held.[202]

Mitchell also understood from Assistant Secretary Creasy that in the event of a strike the braceros would be removed from the Valley; but when picketing started, the department advised that such decisions were administrative and not related to manpower problems. The department's regional office had already ruled that it would not grant the union an open hearing on violations of the agreement by O'Dwyer and Mets and other prominent Valley growers, letting these matters fall into oblivion with a limp promise: "We hope . . . to recommend improved control measures."[203] If, as the association claimed, federal officials had joined the Farm Placement Service in checking the effects of the walkout on May 31 and had verified that only ninety-five workers had struck, this information was never provided by the department to the union. On May 2 the regional office promised to begin inspections in the Valley to determine whether bracero users were hiring wetbacks also. On May 25 the strike was on and the inspections had not yet been made.

As of early June the union was not aware that the U.S. ambassador had assured the Mexican government that the Department of Labor had not recognized the strike. Mitchell kept pressing for the field investigation and a declaration that there was in fact a strike in progress. The department had been officially informed by the State Conciliation Service on June 8 that "a strike exists involving major work stoppage with picketing at Imperial Valley resulting from a labor dispute," and in response to a request from the union sent a conciliator to the Valley.

But the department was standing on a joint interpretation of the 1949 international agreement concerning strikes. Under this joint interpretation "what constitutes a labor dispute in the place of employment affecting the operations in which the worker is engaged is not susceptible of exact definition or delineation."[204] Setting aside the finding of the conciliators, made in accordance with California law, the department held to the policy that formal determination that a labor dispute exists "was to be made exclusively by the secretary of labor or his delegate."[205]

Accordingly, on June 9, with the harvest half over, the slow motion of the secretary with respect to the facts discovered a week earlier by the Conciliation Service continued. He announced his conclusion that there indeed existed a labor dispute in the Imperial Valley, and that he would take appropriate action under Article 32 of the international agreement. On June 13 a delegation of six officials from San Francisco arrived in the Valley. On the fourteenth and fifteenth the striking workers jammed the union hall in Brawley, bringing with them dismissal notices, affidavits, and other documentation relating to the massive layoffs of the previous weeks. The officials decided that the investigation should proceed ranch by ranch, even though the Imperial Valley Growers Association was the legal employer of all braceros in the Valley. The ranch-by-ranch approach brought the investigation to a crawl. According to a provision of Article 22 of the agreement, moreover, the department could prohibit the use of braceros only after it "finds that any job is vacant because the occupant is out on strike." It had taken the department three weeks to begin looking, and one more week to find the strike.

On June 25 the department ordered the removal of braceros from the farms of American Fruit Growers, Arena Company, and Western Fruit Growers. That day the *Brawley News* observed: "The removal would have little effect on their operations since the melon deal is practically finished."

Leaving nothing to chance the United States Employment Service, working through the regular machinery of the Department of Labor and the Farm Placement Service, certified another 1,500 braceros to replace contractees whose terms had expired during the course of the strike.

Convinced that the bracero tide had overwhelmed the strike, Mitchell called it off on June 25 "until next season." The NFLU had no political resources to match those of the growers in and out of government. It had no funds to take the Secretary of Labor to court on the legal issues that had been posed by the union. The State Federation of Labor had taken a limited view of its responsibilities to unionize harvesters whose condition it so deplored. It kept an observer in the Valley to report to Haggerty, who postponed appearing at a union mass meeting pending an invitation from grower spokesmen to meet with them to discuss the situation. Haggerty was indignant over the sudden termination of the strike, complaining that the news had come to him over the radio, that is to say, that he had not been consulted on the matter. He advised the NFLU to make no further requests for help, because the union was on its own in the Imperial Valley.

In retrospect the contrast between the employers' view and Haggerty's was not difficult to surmise. The agri-industrialists recognized that a small but aggressive farm labor union was in action. It could affect not only the wage scales but also the stability of their interlaced interests among themselves and with the Teamsters. Haggerty acted as if he regarded the strike as the hopeless effort of meanly equipped harvesters hardly distinguishable from braceros and illegals. Haggerty explained this when he appeared before the state legislators to support the Teamster agreement with the Associated Farmers in June; he declared that California was without question the bright spot in the nation in peaceful industrial relations because of this constructive policy.[206]

Imperial Valley — 1952

Mitchell called off the 1951 strike "until next season." The NFLU had completed a year of activity in the Imperial Valley, still reputed to be the most formidable stronghold of agri-corporatism in the state. The announcement signaled a truce until the next melon harvest, time enough to assess the lessons of 1951.

On the positive side it had again been shown that where farm workers had settled into stable communities, as in Arvin and Lamont, they were capable of organizing, willing to join a union, disciplined in the face of provocation, eager learners, militant on the picket line, and flexible tacticians. Standing on ground that was familiar, they provided the strength of numbers and of cultural and ethnic bonds that were readily transformed into union pride. They knew best the shady ways of the farm labor contracting system, the ingenious devices of the wetback underground, the infiltrating menace of the bracero system, and the tricks of false weights and short measures. They quickly recognized the most effective pressure points for union action, and were willing volunteers to carry the action themselves. Familiar with crew organization they readily adapted to team work on union assignments. They were deliberate rather than flamboyant in decision and action. Women were the equals of men on the picket line as in the fields and were more effective in confrontations with the police.

There were over a thousand families composed of people of this type in Calexico, El Centro, Brawley, Westmoreland, Holtville, Heber, Calipatria, and Imperial. But they were a landless folk, their residence dependent on jobs threatened by braceros and illegals. After the harvests in the northern counties a number of union families had failed to return, and the drift could become a tide. Others were delaying their return until January and February, concerned about the future intentions of the union. They sent word from Delano, Bakersfield, Soledad, or Fresno, paying their dues by mail, undecided. They saw favorable signs, such as the increase of field wages to 80 cents an hour. The fear of violent reprisals had gone. Nevertheless, the union had not been able to negotiate crew contracts for the next melon harvest. One year was not enough to convince the domestics of the Valley that the tactics of classic hedge-hopping, one-stop job actions of the 1930s that the NFLU had rejected were not more effective.

Before the winter of 1951 was over the NFLU decided to return and word to this effect went out. Mindful of the risks, the union made it clear that they would be taken. No union campaigns would be organized in the north. Word came from San Joaquin County, from Santa Clara, from

Ventura, and from Salinas that the braceros were everywhere and in large numbers. These factors went far to stem the migration out of the Valley. "Until next season" became a mutual obligation between the union and workers to prepare for a second encounter.

Mitchell's soundings of the Department of Labor officials in Washington were not encouraging. In December he submitted a documented memorandum to Undersecretary Galvin, reciting once more the hostile ways in which the Imprial growers had used the bracero program. Galvin did not respond. Mitchell again asked for public hearings. This time promises did not have to be broken because they were not made. Again Mitchell petitioned, on March 7, 1952, but the department made no move to review the scandalous record of the previous summer. In April the union requested lists of ranches to which braceros were being referred so union members residing in the Valley could apply for those jobs, a right which the department had never denied. The lists were "unavailable." Galvin finally explained to Mitchell that wage hearings would not be held because Congress had failed to appropriate funds to investigate the procedure of setting the prevailing wages written into the bracero contracts. The undersecretary did ask Mitchell to submit complete dossiers on the complaints that had been filed during the 1951 strike. Galvin said the department had no record of such complaints.[207] Mitchell passed the request to me which I rejected with the explanation that I was not the secretary's amanuensis. I had learned that "lost" files were a standard alibi among bureaucrats.

From my exchanges with Mitchell, by letter because telephoning was too expensive, I concluded that the department's officials in Washington and San Francisco had learned nothing and forgotten everything. Predictably, they consented to Harrigan's demands, allowing him to maneuver freely to continue displacing domestic workers—no hiring of crews, preferential hiring of mbraceros, and pay rates leveled down to the prevailing wage.

When the NFLU organizers returned to the Valley in the spring of 1952, locals had been replaced by braceros as irrigators and melon cappers. Local women had practically disappeared from the fields. Bracero crews were being contracted for melon picking at 70 cents an hour, with no guaranteed minimum of crates per trailer and no shed receipts. Dismissals of local workers who were subsisting on wages in field crops began in mid-April, advance warning that they would not be retained for the picking.

Lobbyists for the growers working in Washington had already improved their position in the matter of wetbacks. In 1952 Congress revised the immigration law, inserting two important provisions.

Harboring of illegals was made a felony, except that "employment, including the usual practices normal to employment, shall not be deemed to constitute harboring" (Section 274 [b], Public Law 414, 1952). It was also provided that "no officer or person shall have the authority to make any arrest for a violation of any provision of this section except officers and employees of the [Immigration] Service designated by the Attorney General." There was no opposition from organized labor to these provisions, and wetbacks came out of that session of Congress better protected than citizen residents. It was a large constituency; in the spring of 1952 there were over three thousand illegals in Imperial. Fearful that organizers would run afoul of these provisions, Mitchell ordered them to desist from citizen arrests.

As the 1952 melon harvest approached, the dismissals, which had been intermittent since early April, were stepped up by the larger growers. By the middle of May more than two hundred union men had been fired, principally by Western Fruit Growers, American Fruit Company, and Arena Imperial. The president of the Brawley local was again dismissed from his job as irrigator by River Farms Company. Other leading growers, like Danny Dannenberg and Fred Bright, turned down applications for melon picking. Finney, manager of the local Farm Placement Office, backed them. He wrote the union on May 28: "Inasmuch . . . as these men . . . are presently employed sacking onions at the prevailing wage of 70 cents per hour . . . which is comparable to that which they would receive at present in the cantaloup harvest, it would not be incumbent upon this office to refer them to work in the harvest of cantaloups."[208] In previous years the starting wage in the harvest had been $1.00 an hour, increasing to 25 cents per crate when picking became abundant. The 70 cent hourly rate had been set by the Department of Labor for braceros. These measures had the effect of drastic preventive steps against a threat that the association regarded as "a great disaster in the Imperial Valley and on down through Arizona and Texas."

Through May the union made no progress with the government agencies. On May 16 the regional office director in San Francisco, Glenn Brockway, told me that the responsibility for compliance with the international agreement lay entirely in the California State Department of Employment. A few days later I asked for a conference with Finney and his associate, Park, who merely informed me with cool neutrality that the growers would continue to insist on referring crew applicants to different farms; that new assignments of domestics would not be made to bracero crews already contracted; that the growers had agreed to distribute the risks of union action by diluting and dispersing union referrals; and that the appropriate referral route was through the association to the individual growers, who made the final decision on hiring.

Since the Teamsters and Packinghouse Workers had disregarded its picket lines, the NFLU attempted no further contact with them. Haggerty was not enthusiastic about renewed trouble in Imperial, and the vice-president of the State Federation for San Diego County, Osslo, was equally cool, murmuring about reports he had heard that the union had mismanaged the DiGiorgio strike. Like Haggerty, Osslo was irritated because the NFLU had not asked his approval to end the 1951 strike. After a round of dutiful consultations, performed unwillingly under instructions from President Mitchell, I decided that the melting point of organized labor in California in matters affecting the Associated Farmers and their allies was too low to withstand the heat of Imperial summers.

These matters were fully discussed in the nightly union meetings in Calexico, El Centro, and Brawley. Members from all over the Valley attended them. Decisions were being pondered by some two hundred men and women who were the network of communication and morale throughout Imperial. Among them were many veterans of picket duty and field operations. They talked gravely and confidently about the NFLU and its return. Even though I felt that we could not count on the labor federation, I was confident we could meet any contingency. As of May 15 the indicators were positive; the resistance would continue.

The basic strategy was agreed on. Union members would not accept referral out of melons into onions or any other field crop. The center of a strike would be the Brawley local. Rolling delegations were to hold meetings in Blythe, Yuma, and Coachella to simulate a large area-wide strike against all melon growers. In the Valley itself the action would be concentrated on the few big corporations that had done most of the firing of domestics. There was to be no strike relief because the NFLU had no funds, but gasoline would be provided for all union assignments. The central grievance would be the displacement of domestic pickers, with wages a secondary issue until union members were reinstated. All orders were to issue from Brawley and all locals were to be responsible for organizing teams to carry them out.

Rather than a formally declared strike it was to be a walkout, with immediate tactical responses appropriate to the many weaknesses of the NFLU at the moment.

The harassing tactics of the growers and the Farm Placement Service continued during the last week of May. Rejected melon pickers were referred by the placement office in Calexico and Brawley to onion fields fifteen miles away, from which they were laid off with little work. A group of thirty-six men and women, among them sixteen melon pickers who had been turned away, drove thirty miles to chop cotton and found on arrival that the employers preferred wetbacks. Another grower asked for a crew of pickers, offering to pay them nothing for standing by in case any braceros failed to report. Such contempt could be shown only by ranchers well supplied with a surplus of job applicants, guaranteed by the certification of braceros to fill the "labor shortage" previously declared by the Farm Placement Service.

When the 1951 strike was suspended the NFLU had paid off most of its $1,800 in debts. The national office had finished the year with a cash balance of $500. The locals in Imperial Valley had no reserves. There would be no financial assistance from the State Federation of Labor. Strike funds would have to come from small contributions by trade unionists, but such appeals could not be made until after a strike was under way. The NFLU team of staff organizers had dispersed, with Hasiwar assigned to organize strawberry farmers and sugar cane plantation workers in Louisiana. If there was to be any action in Imperial it would have to be by one national representative and the volunteer teams. As of the last week of May a hundred of these with strike experience could be counted on, most of them residing in Brawley. They carried union cards but were not paying dues. Their earnings clear of expenses on futile referrals averaged $5 to $10 a week. Many younger workers gave up the search for harvest work and sought jobs in the building trades. They continued to attend meetings, remaining on the union's records as melon pickers ready to return. The meetings in Brawley were attended by the regular two hundred, their morale bolstered by the presence of the NFLU.

From the first of May the union concentrated its efforts on locating crews of braceros and demanding that its members be referred to those jobs by the Farm Placement Office. Spotting such crews was costly; reconnaissance teams had to be constantly on the move over an area of more than four hundred square miles. I had repeatedly asked the Department of Labor to provide the union with the names of ranches certified for bracero melon workers and the number of men authorized. On May 8 the regional office finally agreed to allow union representatives to inspect such lists, but only at regional headquarters in San Francisco, six hundred miles away. The same lists were on file in Calexico, where they had been compiled in the first place. But Brockway, the regional director, could not forego another opportunity to show his contempt for the NFLU and his obeisance for Harrigan.

The firing of well-known union members continued through May. American Fruit, Western Fruit Growers, and Arena Imperial, the worst offenders, became the main targets of the union. On May 27 these growers refused an invitation of the Central Labor Council of the Valley to attend a meeting in El Centro.

On June 1 the volunteer teams of the three locals were placed on strike alert and the next day a strike vote was under way throughout the Valley. Nonmember farm workers voted to support a stoppage if one was called. In its June 2 press release the union named the employers who had replaced domestics with braceros and declared that to be the issue. By a vote of 8 to 1, authorization was given to me to call the workers out of the melon harvest;[209] I accepted this mandate with the statement that "the union proposes to meet this threat wherever it arises."

The volunteers fanned out over the Valley and the picking slowed down, not as effectively as it had the previous year, but its impact more visible because of the smaller target. Over a thousand union leaflets were issued daily. Organizers stopped at onion and cotton fields asking these harvesters to begin considering a general strike of all crops in the Valley, since the braceros were taking over these operations also. The union propaganda went straight to the point—the association had stepped up its plans for forcing all the resident families out of the Valley.

On June 5 the situation was normal for a crop strike, namely, with the union in the lead supported by a hundred active volunteers, perhaps twice that many ready to walk out, and many more watching expectantly.

Into a situation of that kind new tactics had to be introduced to tip the balance in favor of the union. It was decided to intercept on the roads the trucks and buses of contractors who were carrying wetbacks and braceros to and from work; the acceptance of braceros into the union; and the preparation of law suits against the state and federal agencies responsible for the certification of braceros.

The first step was the publication of a leaflet explaining state laws on minimum safety standards for farm labor buses and trucks. With this information in hand unionists made spot observations of the vehicles that assembled before dawn at the staging points of the major towns. It was a derelict fleet of cast-off school buses and dilapidated produce trucks that had been reconditioned with discarded lumber and canvas. The vehicles were usually without stirrups, seats, or cover. Into these rolling traps as many as fifty men were forced to ride standing, pressed against the side stakes. The accident rate for such vehicles in the Valley was notoriously high.

With the assistance of Tom Randall, AFL organizer, I induced the State Department of Industrial Relations to send special inspectors to the Valley to enforce the regulations. I provided them with the information gathered by the union volunteers under my direction, identified the chief assembly points, mapped the byways of the illegal wetback network, prepared descriptions and identification of the trucks of the leading contractors, and assigned union assistants to the inspectors.

The first road checks began late in May and continued through early June. Vehicles that were found in dangerous condition were ordered out of service on the spot. In one week twenty vehicles with a capacity of nearly a thousand persons were immobilized. Contractors were forced to double their facilities, install benches and stirrups, reduce loads drastically, and hire additional drivers. The unlicensed contractors moved out of the Valley, but the licensed ones had another problem. When a truck or bus was intercepted on the highway, union assistants noted whether there were illegals mingled with braceros. If so, the name of the employer was noted and the union filed a complaint against him for using mixed crews in violation of the international agreement. The growers had resorted to recruiting wetbacks exclusively through contractors, who could be disavowed in case of discovery. Also braceros were loaned freely among the certified growers, members of the association, and this, too, was a violation of the agreement. By shifting the responsibility for the loans to the contractors, the growers escaped liability for violations and injuries. Three of the major contractors in the Valley went out of business in the face of union pressure. One of them attended a union meeting to recant publicly, offering to join. I escorted him out of the hall with the advice that he leave the Valley permanently.

During the 1951 action a number of braceros had presented themselves at the union hall in Brawley to ask for help. They usually complained of wage shortages, overcharges for meals, and similar abuses. In 1952 more complaints of this type were brought to the union and I proposed to the strike committee that we enroll braceros in the local. There was some opposition at first, primarily because it appeared to contradict the position of the union on the bracero system. I pointed out that bracero memberships were not being solicited and that to reject the braceros would leave them without recourse since they had already appealed to the Mexican consul and the Department of Labor enforcement officer. As members the braceros could provide valuable information otherwise unavailable to us and they would agree to abide by union rules and instructions. I stressed that the effect of the bracero program was to split the workers into hostile camps, just as the wetbacks were pitted against both braceros and locals. It was agreed to admit braceros to the union on those terms.

This opened the way for a leaflet campaign among the braceros informing them of the difference in wages, such as the so-called beginning wage of 80 cents an hour for domestics and 70 cents for braceros. They were instructed on the computation of their daily earnings by the "pack-out system" at the sheds, which eliminated the trailer minimum guarantee the domestics demanded. In short the educational campaign was extended to the braceros sufficiently to assist those who approached the union with legitimate grievances.

As a morale stimulant the representation by the union of bracero members and the publicizing of their complaints had an immediate effect throughout the Valley. To further press the association and the Department of Labor I released a statement by Ezequiel Padilla, former Secretary of Foreign Affairs of Mexico, to the effect that braceros had a legal right, under the agreement, to join an American union of their choice. The statement had passed unnoticed and it was time to test the willingness of both governments to honor it.

The third tactic in the 1952 action was the preparation of law suits against the Farm Placement Service and the Department of Labor as malfeasant administrators of the international agreement. Mitchell had been making efforts in this direction in Washington, but I had come to the conclusion that Mitchell's friendly lawyers, who were serving without fees, were too far from the scene to appreciate the full import of the issues we were raising.

With the assistance of California attorneys the union prepared charges against several companies, the Farm Placement Office, and the Immigration Service to obtain a judicial ruling on equality if not preference in hiring domestics. Ultimately a law suit would have to be brought against the secretary of labor whose representatives in the Valley and in San Francisco were in open collaboration with the growers. Lack of funds prevented the filing of complaints and the union had to rely entirely on its field activity.

With the department failing to enforce the international agreement, roving pickets maintained intensive monitoring of crews on the major ranches. One of these, the Maggio ranch, was reported to be operating with a crew of two hundred braceros, among them an undetermined number of illegals. The next day a pre-dawn watch established that the illegals were commuters who crossed the border daily and were transported by company trucks to the job.

Charges against the company were filed immediately and on June 2 the Secretary of Labor determined that the Maggio Company had forfeited the right to contract braceros and ordered their immediate removal.

The same day at the Farm Placement Office the union offered a union

crew for referral to the Maggio operation. The company found itself at
the spear point of union pressure and concluded it could not complete
the picking unless it yielded. It agreed to hire the crew on the basis of a
verbal agreement that the pay rate would be 25 cents per crate with no
"bonus" withholding and a guarantee that the men would be hired until
the end of the picking. On their best day during the first week the
unionists earned $25, the most money they had made in more than two
years.

Typically, the Farm Placement manager, Finney, took cover behind
the excuse that the presence of braceros and illegals on the Maggio ranch
"had all been a mistake."

It was a moment of optimism in the strike. The psychological effect on
the entire Valley of seeing a union crew take over was obvious. But it
was presently shattered by an event that brought the situation to the
edge of violence.

On several ranches foremen had been appearing in the fields with
pistols at their belts. One overseer was making it known that he was a
sheriff's deputy and made the mistake of threatening to "shoot any
union son of a bitch on the spot." The crew stopped work immediately
and reassembled at the union hall in Brawley. With two of the workers I
drove to the field and verified the fact that two foremen were armed.

Back at the hall I telephoned Finney with the message that while the
union deplored fruit rotting on the ground its members would not work
under threats of armed employees claiming to be deputies. I told Finney
that I would appear with the crew at the field at the usual time the next
morning, that we would all be armed, and that our purpose was to pick
melons in spite of threats.

That afternoon Finney telephoned that he had talked to the company,
that it had all been a mistake, and that there would be a conference in his
office at ten the following morning to clear up the misunderstanding. I
attended the conference with two union delegates. It was agreed that the
sheriff's office would order all field personnel disarmed; he did and the
melon harvest proceeded, braceros and locals working side by side.

It was already June 11 and the situation was softening considerably.
Five more ranches hired union melon pickers on standard terms. Displacements ceased. American Fruit, Arena, and Western Growers reinstated all but eleven men whose cases were submitted for review by
the Farm Placement Office. The Maggio episode had also led to the
discovery that many growers, including O'Dwyer and Mets, were charging the cost of Twist-ems to the harvesters. Leaflets and meetings
followed with the result that these deductions were discontinued and the
Twist-ems were provided free to the workers. After these events, a

simple visit by a union organizer to a field to inquire how things were going and to talk briefly with his friends among the crew was enough to bring an offer to raise wages from the contractor. Unexpectedly two of the contractors were suspended when they were found by union watchers to be using mixed crews. The Department of Labor compliance officer began to respond to grievances presented to him, instead of ignoring them.

It was late in the harvest but the displacement process had been reversed. In mid-June Finney was superseded at the Farm Placement Office by a ranking member of Hayes's staff in Sacramento, who assumed control and made the decisions. Until the end of the harvest he performed as an effective grievance officer, verifying charges on the spot and exposing himself to the indignation of company martinets, one of whom threatened him with a shotgun.

As the melon harvest dwindled toward the end of June, union families began to move out of the Valley on their yearly round of migration, some of them bound for the melon picking that would start later on the west side of the Central Valley. The Brawley local shrank to a home guard of a dozen members with whom the NFLU would keep contact until the following spring. As there had been no official strike call, so there was no public announcement that it was over.

On the part of the harvesters, union members, and others, there was an expectation that the union organizers would return for the 1953 harvest. On the part of the NFLU there was no disavowal of this hope, nor was there a promise to fulfill it. As the harvests moved from south to north and back again the union was being drawn into a pattern of actions that appeared as futile as the insurgencies of the past. A total suspension of organizing would have greatly slowed down the momentum the union had been gathering throughout the state. But it would have given time to take stock of the realities underlying the events of the previous five years.

As a national organization, the NFLU was rationing its meager financial resources among organizers in Arkansas, Florida, Wisconsin, New Jersey, and Louisiana as well as California, raising the question of how long and to what purpose it could continue to challenge on such terms the most deeply entrenched agri-capitalist system in the nation. Nowhere in California had the character of that system been more sharply revealed than in the Imperial Valley. But the time for stocktaking was still a year off, and in the meantime the union responded twice again before returning for its final engagement in Imperial, first to the employees of the Schenley Corporation and then to the melon pickers of Los Banos.

Imperial Valley — 1953

In its organizing activities in 1951 and 1952 the NFLU had chosen to make the yearly melon harvest the spearhead of its strategy in Imperial Valley. The harvest, lasting less that two months, was short and vulnerable. To bring in the crop there were enough experienced domestic pickers who were familiar with cooperative organization as crews and who were long-time residents with strong family and neighborhood ties. Melon picking demanded skills and physical conditioning that placed them a notch above tomato pickers and onion toppers. They were cyclical harvesters making a living within a limited migratory pattern that provided them with peak earnings for the year. They were also part of a social pattern that enabled them to rally hundreds of resident farm laborers outside the union to their support.

Shunned by the State Federation of Labor and denied support by the Teamsters and Packinghouse unions, they had nevertheless openly challenged the Imperial Valley Farmers Association, the dominant economic and political establishment. In two successive encounters these workers, when given union leadership, had proved tactically equal to the combined powers of the association and its allies in the state and federal governments.

When the 1952 harvest was over there was no doubt that the antiunion alliance had not been broken, but it had been noticeably strained. These were some of the signs: The Associated Farmers sacrificed their cherished goal of a hot cargo law against all organized labor in return for Teamster collaboration against the NFLU. Brockway, the regional director of the Department of Labor, was beginning to cast the blame for the tarnished image of his own bureaucracy on that of the Farm Placement Service. The Secretary of Labor delayed but did not deny recognition of the union's charges. The department lawyers had fallen back on specious arguments, refusal to consider the evidence, and tricky delays to prevent the secretary of labor from appearing as, he was, an adversary in fact of the union. The Department of State had done no better. It pleaded administrative incompetence to conceal the diplomatic maneuvers of Ambassador O'Dwyer and Consul Colunga. Farm Placement Chief Hayes was forced to relieve Finney, the local administrator, who had demonstrated an alarming talent for bungling. The agents, attorneys, and administrators that the Department of Labor had sent to the Valley to investigate showed all the resolve of professional boxers sparring with their own shadows. Like the association, they avoided the forums of law and public opinion, relying on self-serving interpretations of their authority and the transparent device of losing from their files the mounting evidence the union was producing.

There was evidence, furthermore, that agri-business was not taking the union's actions lightly. It obtained the favoring amendments to the immigration law of 1952 regarding illegals. It demanded and received the pledge of Department of Labor officials that they exclude the union from the meetings in which the department received instructions from the associations. As will be presently shown, the industry prevailed over the state legistature to chastise the Conciliation Service for the performance of its duty. Moving without dissent from Congress, the state legislature or the governor, the Associated Farmers thoroughly destroyed any possibility that migrant farm workers could settle in the government labor camps.

To the NFLU the lessons of its first two years in Imperial were unmistakable. The most promising base for organization was an area in which domestic workers had settled in a cluster of stable communities. Legally and economically the bracero program could be proved to be indefensible and unnecessary. Farm workers were organizable. Cultural bonds could be sublimated with working class interests compatible with ethnic differences. Local leaders were waiting to be found and encouraged, taught, and stimulated by shoulder-to-shoulder action in the fields.

During the summer and winter months of 1952 the NFLU kept to the position that the action in Imperial had been simply suspended "until next season." It had not been defeated. But just as the strategies of 1952 had grown out of the experience of 1951, so those of 1953 would have to improve, taking into account those of 1952. Minimal support from labor organizations in the Valley would have to be committed. The State Federation of Labor could not be counted on. There would have to be a strike fund on hand before operations could be renewed. A full-time committee of volunteers would have to be provided with more than gasoline. The analysis of the melon "deal" would have to be completed months before the next harvest. Most important of all, preparations would have to be completed for action in the courts, with the necessary evidence in hand and legal briefs ready.

Theoretically these were the conditions required for continuing the campaign in July 1953. Practically, the union could meet none of them. Its return to the Valley was not an advance over the ground gained the previous year. It was a drift, caused more by the expectations of the workers who had stood the test so well and who remained far more confident than the odds against them justified.

All the events of the melon harvest season of 1953 were to show the effects of these two facts: that the union returned to Imperial with no financial or legal reserves and no institutional support; and that the growers and government agencies had closed ranks to complete the destruction of the union by administrative suffocation.

On February 14, 1953, American Fruit Growers gave notice of dismissal to forty domestics, including three union members, who were thinning melon plants, with only the promise that they would be called back in the future. The wage scale at the time was 70 cents an hour and the work force on the ranch consisted of three hundred braceros. The wages were lower than in 1952 for general field work. The following day River Farms Company dismissed thirty-five *locales,* among them three of the most reputable crew workers leaders in the Valley—Crescencio Pachuca, Jesus Yanez, and Ismael Gonzales. Efforts to reach the River Farms manager through the Farm Placement Office for an explanation were fruitless; he was out of town attending the Lettuce Golf Tournament, an annual social event of the Winter Garden. When finally reached, he explained that since there were only two days left of work it would hardly be worthwhile to reinstate the three men.[210] By the end of February over a hundred domestics had been fired. Eighty-eight of these workers were from four companies—American Fruit, A. W. Stern, Richmond Company, and Arena Imperial. Throughout the Valley there were more than five thousand braceros working short shifts.

The dismissals continued through April, the union keeping count and filing a complaint in each instance. On May 17 a Valley-wide field check established that more than 90 percent of the melon picking was being done by braceros. A few domestics were being used as pushers and pacesetters.

The register of dismissed and unemployed melon pickers at the union office grew as the harvest advanced. Nearly a hundred union members were on standby for calls from the Farm Placement Office that never came. Others gathered in idle groups on street corners and cafes in the *barrios* of Brawley and El Centro. Efforts to find work at the ranch gates had completely stopped, word having gone out of the FPS office that referrals would be accepted only from the association. The Farm Placement Service had completely abdicated to Harrigan.

Farm Placement Officer Finney had returned to his role and was playing it with confidence. He justified the dispersal of domestic crews on the ground that it distributed the risks of labor trouble, the position he had taken the year before. The system of loaning braceros was proper. His office had no open orders for workers from growers who were operating with braceros. Lists of certified employers were not available to the union. Domestics had no prior claim to jobs held by braceros.

Finney's confidence reflected the support he was receiving in Sacramento, San Francisco, and Washington. The State Department of Employment certified a labor shortage of more than 8,000 men in the Valley, on the basis of which 4,500 braceros were already in the fields. When pressed for detailed information the department answered that it did not know the exact location of the bracero crews because the distribution changed from day to day. Late in the season Hayes sent two agents to the Valley, ostensibly to make a thorough investigation of the protests the union was filing almost daily. These two, Geary and Park, made one contact with the union and were not seen again. Their investigation was over.

Neither was there any response from the regional office in San Francisco. Finney claimed that it was approving his decisions regarding dismissals and referrals. Around April 16 ranking officials of the Bureau of Employment Security, the State Department of Employment, and the Department of Labor held numerous conferences with farm employers in Imperial, of which the union learned after the fact from the newspapers. From these meetings there issued the statement that "the use of Mexican Nationals [braceros] has not depressed wages." The department had now completed the cycle of delay to evasion to misrepresentation to prevarication. Mitchell's continued requests for an explanation from Secretary of Labor Tobin were ignored.

The association refined its tactics. It set up, and Finney approved, two categories of bracero employers, active and passive. The active growers were those who were actually using contractees; the passive ones merely had been certified to draw on Harrigan's labor pool. It was from the latter class that braceros who were caught working with illegals or for unlicensed contractors were allegedly and illegally borrowed.

The 70-cent an hour prevailing wage for braceros was the wage for all types of farm operations and for all workers, domestic or alien. At these wages braceros were openly assigned to driving tractors, irrigating, packing, and other skilled operations. The thirty-one braceros registered as members of the Brawley local were abruptly moved from camp to camp, some as far as Borrego Valley, a part of the DiGiorgio property in a remote corner of the desert. Several braceros who had been injured in a highway accident and had joined the union for assistance in obtaining medical attention and lost wages were deported before their cases were heard. The Department of Labor field representative in the Valley made short work of all grievances of this type. He ruled, "The union may not represent the nationals directly before the employer, but only through the Department of Labor and the Mexican consul." The department had already filed bracero complaints transmitted by Mitchell into the basket of lost evidence. The Mexican consul, Colunga, had literally struck his colors.

As to illegals, they returned to the Valley in full force. They readily identified themselves as such to union men who stopped them in town or who visited them in the bush encampments ringing the Valley. The Department of Labor reclassified wetbacks from the former class of "nonlocal" to "local labor" of whom it found some 4,200 persons as of February 1953. The predawn shapeups of illegals in Brawley and El Centro were renewed, the shadowy shapes of men in huaraches and ragged clothing slipping silently through the streets long before the sun or the border patrolmen were in sight. Invariably many were left behind to steal back to their hideouts in back alleys. Living in perpetual concealment their bearing betrayed them, walking singly, close to available cover, their shoulders imperceptibly hunched, always scanning the street ahead, speaking to no one, startled when spoken to.

So familiar were these figures that I could recognize them at a distance of a hundred yards. Early one morning as I drove by the Border Patrol detention yard near El Centro I saw a group of them laying cinder blocks for a building, watched by an armed guard. I reported the matter to the building trades union office in town, which promptly sent a business agent to the spot. The men were wetbacks. The business agent protested, the men were removed, and the work went on at union wages.

In the closing days of the harvest more farm workers began to cross the international boundary into Calexico. These were commuters with daily passes, a labor reserve additional to the domestics, the illegals, and the braceros. It was the rehearsal for border crossings that became the so-called green card system, supplying a work force that would eventually extend deep into the interior of California.

Another omen was the appearance of unemployed packinghouse workers in El Centro and Brawley. Growers had begun to set up makeshift sheds in the fields, to which braceros were assigned as replacements of union men and women of Local 78, which had honored its contract with the shippers two years before and helped to break the harvesters' strike. These were white-skinned workers, native Americans whose turn had now come to join the ranks of the displaced. The business agent of the Packinghouse Workers Local, in a penitent conversation with me over a glass of beer, wondered whether his union had made a mistake in crossing the NFLU picket lines.

The growers were in neither a penitent nor a forgiving mood. After repulsing the efforts of the State Conciliation Service to persuade Harrigan to talk with Hasiwar, they set their statewide apparatus in motion to remove the service from the rural scene. Senate Bill 1619 was introduced in the 1953 session of the legislature, providing that the duties of the service "shall not apply to any labor disputes or work stoppages between or involving farm laborers and their employees." The bill passed the Senate by a vote of 22 to 7, but failed in the Assembly. The bill's sponsors also prompted their legislative friends to make pointed inquiries of the Director of Finance and the Attorney General as to possible usurpations of authority by the service. Warned of financial and legal reprisals, with a few friends, and nothing to match the lobbying power of agri-business, the service faded into a harmless liaison, rarely sought out by farm unionists, never by growers. An official declaration by the state that an agricultural strike existed no longer had any practical significance, even if the issue was the loss of jobs by domestics to braceros. The U.S. Department of Labor completed preemption of the authority of a state agency under its own interpretation of the international agreement, not subject to administrative appeal or legal redress.

All this was an example of how readily the political network of the Associated Farmers throughout California magnified the leverage of the local associations, like Harrigan's.

Since conciliation implied compromise of rights in conflict, and domestic farm workers had none in the view of the industry, there was nothing to conciliate. When the economic claims to work and wages consistent with the needs of domestic families were disposed of, the more intangible ones of residence and community were even less negotiable. By the fall of 1953 the abandonment of the working class *barrios* of field laborers in the Valley cities was under way. In three years over 150 families moved permanently to the north, their vacant houses occupied by illegals or razed to make way for bracero camps. In these ghost *barrios* the roots of the NFLU began to wither and die.

The Schenley Corporation Incident—1952

In the northern district of Kern County and adjacent to the town of Delano the Schenley Corporation owned and operated a 5,000-acre vineyard of wine grapes. The DiGiorgio Fruit Corporation also owned 5,000 acres of grapes in the vicinity. Both properties were located near the southern terminal of the grand canal of the Central Valley irrigation project.

For those inclined to notice the beauty rather than the economics of agri-business, the Schenley ranch looked like the classical country place of a corporate farmer. Fronting one of the busiest highways in the state, the vineyard stretched at eye level to the horizon, its crested hedges embroidered in the early spring with leafing canes stretched on wire trellises and rumpled in summer by warm breezes. A mile or so back from the highway stood the corporation warehouses, barns, and equipment sheds, overshadowing the cottages of the irrigators and field hands who lived in. The seasonal workers came principally from Delano, Pixley, Earlimart, and other neighboring towns.

It was not the harvesters but the irrigators of the Schenley place who turned to the union with their grievances. These began with the tolerable discomforts of living in a typical company town, complete with its own police and the right of management to inspect the rented premises at all times and to charge for butane and electric power. They ended, in the early months of 1952, with exasperated complaints concerning working conditions. Most irritating was the practice of the corporation of requiring more hours on the job than were paid for. An irrigator who worked twelve hours and noted the fact on his time card was credited with eight hours by his foreman, in keeping with the company policy of not recording more than sixty hours a week for an individual. Some irrigators were directed to turn in blank time cards to be filled by supervisors at their discretion.

The task of organizing the Schenley irrigators was assigned to William Becker, who operated out of the Bakersfield office of the union. The goal was to form a union local with stable irrigators and to move later into the seasonal work force.

In March 1952 the corporation began to lay off irrigators, among them several union members. Becker had signed up a majority of those who remained. Schenley refused Becker's offer of submitting the cards for verification. By a vote of 50 to 2 the members agreed to strike and the picketing began.

With the issue of wages muted, union recognition, working conditions, and a grievance procedure became the central demands of the union. Armed with affidavits that set forth the grievances, Becker submitted them to company officials, who refused to discuss them at all in writing and only at arm's length verbally. An appeal to the State Department of Industrial Relations invoking Article 923 of the Labor Code was rejected, on the excuses that no responsible company official had been involved in the dismissals; that the men had been discharged in the usual course of operations, thus disposing of the complaint of discrimination on account of union membership; and that the union could not prove its case beyond a reasonable doubt.[211]

Becker then proceeded to focus the pressures of organized labor not on the picket line, where they had not proved particularly effective, but in the subtler area of trade-union solidarity. Schenley had contracts with large international affiliates of the AFL, such as the bartenders and clerks unions. This approach was highly formalized and Becker followed it carefully. Sanction from the Kern County Central Labor Council was obtained. Locals of the carpenters, butcher workmen, building trades, and restaurant employees sent letters to company officials, and Schenley products began to appear on the "we do not patronize" lists of labor councils. In March the point was made that Schenley had accepted collective bargaining, acknowledging that all its distillations were processed, bottled, and packaged by union labor. By a natural extension backward in the production process it appeared reasonable that since its grapes were watered by union men they, too, should be under contract.

Becker, not temperamentally a man to carry a big stick, was nevertheless wielding a big idea, namely, that the channels of trade might be closed to Schenley products in thousands of bars, stores, and restaurants by the displeasure of sister unions. Haggerty, the secretary of the state federation, expressed his interest to the corporation. Matthew Will, member of the executive council of the AFL, did likewise. The clerks union of Los Angeles made ready to invoke its contract with regard to handling the products of which Becker was complaining; and General Secretary Ed. S. Miller of the bartender's union advised the corporation that it would be bound by its long tradition of honoring the unfair listing of the Schenley labels.[212]

Schenley officials stalled the negotiations through the summer, the local officials deferring to national officers who were absent on trips to Europe. Growers were threatening to withhold their tonnage from Schenley wineries if they yielded to the union.

Conceding on the issues except recognition, the corporation finally agreed to conversations, and early in June reinstated the dismissed irrigators, increased wages by 5 cents an hour, agreed to hear grievances, and consented to a wage survey in the area to provide a basis for possible wage readjustments in the future. It went further. Mindful of complaints that it had hired illegals as irrigators, the corporation ordered its foremen to desist, and to demand identification documents in case of doubt.

As often happens, those who have the fewest credits for the success of even a modest undertaking sometimes collect the most undeserved rewards. I had little to do with the Schenley strategy; nevertheless Mitchell instructed me to call upon a high Schenley official upon whom I was to impress the seriousness of the matter. I was cordially received in a suite of the St. Francis Hotel where I delivered my message, apparently with success. My farewell was even more cordial. My host presented me with a fifth of Schenley's most spirited whiskey which I carried in the crook of my arm through the lobby, wondering whether my future perquisites would be more valuable.

The Schenley operation caused ripples of anxiety in the corporation, one official lamenting that it was the most difficult problem he had ever been asked to solve. On the agricultural scene, however, it was not noticed, probably because of the discretion of all concerned. The support of organized labor had been effectively enlisted but the NFLU remained unrecognized. No permanent organization emerged. The workers were too few in number to support the costs of a local organization.

The Los Banos Melon Harvest—1952

On a comparably small scale but with different methods from those applied in the Schenley round, the NFLU provided support for the melon pickers who migrated seasonally into the Los Banos district in the northwest part of Fresno County. Many of them came from the Imperial harvest, moving on to the prune orchards of Santa Clara and the tomato fields of San Joaquin before returning south for the early spring planting and cultivation. They travelled in family groups, finding shelter in labor camps or pitching their tents in orchards and groves.

As the harvest got under way early in August there were some fifty pickers who had participated in the 1951 and 1952 actions in Imperial. Over half of them were members of locals of the NFLU. They were distributed in three labor camps and two camp sites, one in a roadside grove and another in an orchard near the main canal of the Central Valley irrigation system. To the east lay expanses of orchard and cotton plantings visible on a clear day from the high ground of the Los Banos melon fields and set off by the snow capped Sierra Nevada mountains. To the west, the barren, smoothly rounded crests of the coastal mountain range enclosed the magnificent panorama. This was the famous West Side in which the Southern Pacific Railway and other corporations held reserve blocks of thousands of acres.

The land sloped gently eastward, providing easy contours for gravity flow of water in ditches and furrows. Favorably exposed to the intense heat of the summer sun, the soil was suitable for melons with harvests that rivaled those of the Imperial Valley and Arizona. In the Firebaugh district the high yields of 160 crates per acre were surpassed by record yields around Mendota and Los Banos of 200 crates per acre.

The major grower-shippers of the area were the Sam Hamburg Company, with 1,100 acres planted in 1953; Azdherian Brothers with 1,400 acres; Brooks Cumming and Half Moon with 500 acres each, and Frank Coit with nearly as much acreage as any two of his competitors, 2,300 acres in 1957.[213] Sam Hamburg packed out more than 11,000 crates in one day. Out of his shed and those of his competitors 360 railway cars of melons rolled, their perishable cargo cooled and iced and moving according to precisely timed telegraphed orders. After the summer fever of the melon "deal" the economic temperatures of the area dropped to the more leisurely pace of dairy farming, sheep herding, cotton picking, and grain harvesting. Market sales of as much as $15,000,000 depended on the smooth torrent of cantaloups that descended between August 1 and September 15 from the sun-drenched uplands of the West Side.

The labor force in 1952 was dominated not by braceros but by wetbacks, of whom there were probably not fewer than two thousand available for picking. They were housed in camps tucked in the folds of the western hills, approached by country lanes on which buses such as those used by the Border Patrol could be seen miles away. These were the manpower depots of the multimillion dollar crop. They were regarded as necessary to the local economy as the precious water of the grand canal. The grower-shippers rated them as dependable workers. Local merchants thought them good customers. Welfare agencies were pleased because illegals did not apply for relief. And the local police approved of them as law-abiding persons.[214] With a geography propitious for concealment and quick flight, a community warm with sympathy and its out-of-the-way location off the main routes of traffic of the Central Valley, the Los Banos district enjoyed a privileged position among California's fruit bowls.

To operate a black labor market efficiently the grower-shippers relied on Mexican farm labor contractors. In the Los Banos area these entrepreneurs were particularly important as a buffer to the respected names of Hamburg, Brooks Cummings, and Azdherian, who could not be openly connected with the illegal traffic. Contractors refused to pass on to the shed operators the complaints of their crews. They told the workers once a week the estimated quantity of fruit that the ultimate employers, the grower-shippers, had rated as acceptable, and that was the basis of the weekly earnings of the pickers. The contractors' control in the camps was total and their accountability entirely a matter between themselves and the sheds.

How snug labor relations were in the area was shown by the following incident. Early in the 1952 season the Fresno office of the NFLU reported to the Immigration Service the names and locations of eleven camps that were supplying nearly 70 percent of the picking crews of braceros and illegals around Los Banos and Mendota. To put these complaints to rest the Hamburg Company agreed to refer domestics from Fresno. When these applied at the shed they were referred to field foremen, who advised the applicants that the crews were full but that they could stand by in case there was an immigration raid and a temporary shortage of pickers developed.

The grower-shippers did not entirely dispense with domestic harvesters, but merely reduced them to a calculated percentage of insurance against wetback losses. The terms of employment were based on what the illegals would accept. This meant that the domestics would be given no verified daily reports from the sheds. It also meant that the domestics would be mingled with the slower illegal workers, reducing the average earnings per man to a level that would discourage the locals from continuing in the harvest.

By the beginning of the 1952 picking the confidence of the growers carried them further. As the locals arrived they were informed that the wage scale would be 22 cents per crate, 3 cents lower than the previous year; that 2 cents would be withheld as a "bonus" until the end of the season; and that earnings would be compiled on the basis of packout at the shed, rather than field run measured by a standard trailer load. The shed operators automatically discounted 10 percent of the field run delivered by the pickers. Since it was to their interest and those of the contractors to further shorten the reported packout, the union pickers were well within reason in calculating that another 10 percent of their work was not paid for. This was close to the average discount that the NFLU had noted in the potato, tomato, and orchard crops.[215]

Alerted to these conditions by the first union members who arrived, I arranged to meet with them. I arrived in Los Banos after dark and located the camp where I would be less likely to be noticed. The orchard was in deep gloom. The encampment consisted of several shelters, patches of canvas roped to the trees and staked to the ground. I directed that all cooking fires be banked except one, around which some forty men, women, and children gathered for the briefing. In the circle were several who had led the volunteer teams of the Imperial locals. The older women said nothing but their role was decisive. They could hold back their men or encourage them, knowing the risks—loss of wages on which they were counting so heavily after the strains of Imperial, instant eviction if our plans were discovered, no other prospects of immediate work four hundred miles from home. The younger children slept, resting their heads on the lap of the nearest adult.

Decisions were reached before I left the camp at midnight. The crews were to work as usual. One of the women was to go to Los Banos to shop, where I would signal to her the date of our next meeting.

Three nights later I returned to the camp. I had spent the time canvassing the area in the early morning and late afternoon hours when I would be less likely to be recognized among the traffic of trucks and buses carrying field crews. I was able to see for myself the wetbacks at work, to locate the main camps from which they were commuting, to pick up in the bars and coffee shops the talk of the packing shed workers, who, like the members of the NFLU, had moved up from Imperial. I avoided the officers of the Packinghouse Workers Local 78, knowing that they could not be counted on for support, or even for prudence as to my presence in town. I asked our members to pass the word through the fields that I had been contacted but that I was busy in Imperial on assignment.

The strike plan was agreed to. In each of the five camps where union families were staying I appointed a camp delegate. There was to be no talk whatever of a stoppage. Neither the crews nor the families were to leave camp, the only exceptions being the five delegates, who with me were to issue all instructions. In each camp records were to be compiled of earnings based on estimates of crates picked by each man and the amounts withheld as "bonuses." During the stoppage, the camp delegate was to be in all respects the leader of the camp under my direction.

Between August 15 and 19, following my instructions, the union members sounded out the illegals in their crews as to their willingness to demand the standard wage scale per crate and elimination of the "bonus." When the soundings were favorably received the union men approached the contractors with requests that they arrange for contacts with the grower-shippers. All contractors refused. Among the illegals there was a division as to whether they would support the domestics in a protest. By that time we knew precisely where the main camps harboring illegals were located, who operated them, and how many men were in each.

At noon of August 19 the three men and two women camp leaders and I met in the public park of Los Banos for a picnic. With tacos and beer we relaxed in the shade of a tree to review in detail the strike plans. To the local police who drove by on patrol we must have looked like out-of-town farm laborers innocently occupied, possibly law-abiding wetbacks. We had parked our cars round about the neighborhood to avoid suggesting that a meeting was going on and arousing the interest of the peace officers in the license plate numbers. The picnic ended and we scattered. That night I registered at a motel for the first time since I had arrived. Our contact point was a well-known coffee shop at the north edge of the town.

According to the plan, the camp delegates polled all union members before midnight of the nineteenth. I checked all five camps that night and at 4:00 P.M., when the crews began preparing to leave for the fields, the stoppage began. The camp committee met me at the coffee shop; we chatted casually for a moment, and then separated.

With the camp leaders I called on two of the most important of the labor contractors and in the presence of their men I asked them to stay out of the fields until the union called them back, since the conditions we were demanding would benefit all of them. The contractors flatly refused to cooperate, saying that the growers were prepared to fire all domestic workers since there were enough illegals to do the picking.

We then spread the word that all illegals would be treated as strikebreakers and that the union would demand their removal from the area.

Years of experience with wetback strikebreaking now paid off. We immediately notified the Immigration Service, which by now realized that we were thoroughly familiar with the illegal traffic in the area and that we were ready to make a public issue of citizens arrests if it failed to act. The day the stoppage began border patrolmen moved through the melon fields and picked up a hundred men who had no documents. The *Los Banos Enterprise* lamented that they had "swooped down at the busiest time of the year" and had "really crucified our farmer friends this time."

The union committeeman scanned the fields on the morning of August 20, confirming my own impression that probably half the regular force was not picking. The domestics who were not members of the union were also staying in camp.

That afternoon wetbacks began leaving the area. They were spotted walking out of the camps toward safer havens. Promptly the union demanded of the State Department of Industrial Relations that it proceed against the contractors for illegal harboring of aliens. The previous year the department had said that it could take no action until the Immigration Service reported arrests in specified camps, information that the service had never been willing to reveal to the department or anyone else.

It was certain that the department would do nothing in this dilemma, but at least it placed the Farm Placement Service on notice not to refer domestic scabs to replace the illegals.

On Friday the twenty-first all sheds in Los Banos were shut down.

The packers stood idle at their stations, the loading platforms empty, the railway cars waiting with open doors for melons. The two largest wet-back camps were vacant. I had located two contractors to advise them that the following morning I would appear with union members to close their facilities. Exactly how we were to do this I did not know at the moment. I had already filed a complaint against one of them, a Mr. Dicochea, and had suspended two union members for breaking security.

At 3:00 P.M. on the twenty-first I was stopped by the police as I checked the sheds. I was not under arrest, however. The police were only bringing a message from the Sam Hamburg Company that it wished to meet with me immediately. I asked the police to run an errand for me also, to tell the Hamburg Company that the stoppage was under the direction of a committee of pickers representing all the camps and that the meeting would have to be with the committee and me.

An hour later we were assembled in Hamburg's office at the shed—Hamburg, the dispatcher, the shed manager, the camp committeemen, and myself. Through the window I could see the police car standing by. As the teletype clattered in one corner of the office and a battery of telephones rang on a desk we discussed the situation. Our terms for a return to work were as follows:

Restoration of the wage scale of 25 cents per crate; elimination of the "bonus," and substitution of the field run for the pack-out basis of payment to the pickers. Union crews were to receive every twenty-four hours a report on the shed run. Since the company negotiator readily agreed to discontinue mingling wetbacks with union crews, reducing the likelihood that shed reports would be manipulated, the issue was less important than the wage scale and the "bonus." It was agreed further than all "bonuses" withheld thus far in the season would be paid forthwith. The union agreed to issue a call that afternoon to all pickers to return to the fields on the morning of the twenty-second. I reported the terms of the agreement to the camps at once.[216]

After the strain of the three weeks of planning and carrying out the stoppage I needed a stimulant for my own morale, something trivial but priceless. As we passed out of the Hamburg shed I spoke casually to an idle packer, member of Local 78: "Tell the boys you all can go back to work tomorrow."

I left Los Banos relying on the verbal agreement and the ability of the union members to monitor their own performance as well as that of the grower-shippers.

Under the least advantageous of conditions a successful action had been completed. It had been swift and surprising. Something over fifty domestic harvesters had mobilized the labor force in support of the union's demands and had dealt effectively with the apparatus of illegal labor traffic. The scope of the strategy was limited to the capability of a small core, consisting of men and women experienced in strike tactics. The organizing skill of these unionists when the outcome depended on their own initiative was proved. If the grower-shippers had been prepared to move in bracero reserves the tables would have been reversed. Hopeful once more that they would do better on their home grounds, the pickers returned with their families to Imperial for the pre-harvest operations of 1953. What happened has already been told.

An Assessment—1947–1953

Before leaving California in 1952 to direct the organizing campaign in Louisiana Hasiwar had written: "This will be the end of a five-year stage of agricultural organization." But it was an end only to Hasiwar's assignment as director of organization in California; it was more like an interval to reconsider the NFLU in the light of more than five years of shocking contacts with agri-business.

The question was not whether the union had lost its nerve, which it had not, but whether it was capable of moving into a more effective stage of organization, a higher level of the historical process of which it was a part. The National Farm Labor Union, renamed National Agricultural Workers Union at its New Orleans convention of 1952, had achieved a national reputation as the obstinate challenger of rural social systems exempted from the law and the morals of Judaeo-Christian, ethical, capitalist, constitutional, and parliamentary society. It had become a union of perpetual protest with a record of nearly twenty years of organizing activity across the nation. Its followers in the fields were a people, black and white and brown, who had started with a total lack of experience in collective action. Its organizers moved from one part of rural America to another responding to "the calls of the disinherited," as Mitchell called them. Along that road they arrived in California, balked and confounded by factories in the fields instead of by plantations in the cotton.

It had come West as a union without doctrinaire slogans or handbook strategies, the successor of men and women who had been there before, armed with beliefs and courage. The agrarian revolution preached by the I.W.W. and the Communist campaigns of the 1920s and 1930s represented a state of mind of the revolutionaries rather than a state of the society in which they acted. If they failed in a torrent of violence and legal repression to raise the level of consciousness of poverty-stricken agrarian wanderers, they did succeed in heightening the visibility of the arena where their struggles took place. After that it was possible for union organizers to move openly in places like Imperial Valley, without risk of being tarred and feathered and beaten or escorted by armed vigilantes out of the county. Vigilantism gained more critics than friends, and agri-business resorted to provoking violence rather than initiating it.

Not bound by revolutionary goals, the NAWU pursued the more orthodox ones of collective bargaining, wage increases, the correction of the more glaring abuses, and even of gradualist improvements in housing and health safety. This had the important effect of disarming the red-scare propaganda of the Associated Farmers. It also allowed the NAWU to operate, until it could grow in strength, within the orthodoxies of trade unionism.

Whether those limits would ever permit the NAWU to apply the lessons of its encounters, it was too early to determine. At least it was face to face with the immediate realities of the life of farm laborers. To deal with them the union had established and maintained contact with harvesters in the important agricultural production centers: Bakersfield, Arvin, Lamont, Delano, Pixley, Fresno, Selma, Salinas, Soledad, Brawley, Calexico, El Centro, Earlimart, Porterville, Corcoran, Wasco, Firebaugh, Indio, Gilroy, Mendota, Manteca, Stockton, Tracy, Santa Clara, and Castroville. By the end of 1951 it had set up locals in twelve of these centers and had held its first state convention in the citadel of agri-business, Fresno, in January 1950.

The economic gains of the harvesters as a result of union action were consistent. Whether it was to prevent cuts in the pay scale or to raise it, union intervention had proved successful. Local affiliates were beginning to function in a network of information through area councils, a promising base for the local leadership which was emerging and which by the end of 1953 consisted of some one hundred men and women from the major ethnic groups, Mexicans, Blacks, Filipinos, and white settlers from the Deep South. Through them the NAWU maintained statewide distribution of leaflets and bulletins that neutralized the rumor-mongering of labor contractors. The ostentatious wage fixing conferences of the growers associations had been stopped by denunciation, wage ballots, walk-away tactics, different approaches to small and large growers, and caravaning.

The political operation of the NFLU in support of field activity was beginning to shape public opinion and to stir national interest. Mitchell and his friends in Washington induced President Truman to appoint a national committee to investigate living and working conditions among seasonal migrants, and its report in many respects up-dated the findings of the LaFollette Senate committee of 1942. Shortly thereafter the growers throughout the state, principally those of the Salinas Valley, set in motion a campaign to import Hawaiian laborers. The NFLU organized the opposition and the attempt failed. A research and information process had been simply conceived and carried out by which the locals gathered information which the union interpreted and released to a wide public to explain what was happening in the fields. If there was a theory underlying this aspect of the NAWU, it was that of action and research, two modes of experience acting upon each other to modify tactics and strategies as the union discovered more about the system it was challenging, its institutional allies, and its ability to deal with both.

Such capability was in itself a complex of factors. The union's goal was to discover out of its own experience the ways in which effective collective action could be organized and sustained among farm laborers.

By 1953 the union had come closer, more by accident than by design, to a theory of organization. The agrarian proletariat of California was composed, when the NFLU cast its lot with them, of some two hundred thousand adults of several ethnic groups and cultures. They were in the terminal stage of massive displacements in the Deep South and in Mexico, and to a lesser degree in Asia. The process had been going on for generations, hastened in the South by the Agricultural Adjustment Act and in the Southwest by the backwash of the Mexican Revolution. California became their ultimate haven. Originally all of them had been migrants, seasonal harvesters, wage earners, ethnic introverts, and cultural isolates. But perpetual migrancy seems not to be their natural condition. In time the migrants found in the migrant stream coves and backwaters beside which they could begin creating a semblance of community. Social nucleation, that among landless people that had been destroyed by plantation power in the southern states and by civil war in Mexico, began again.

Kinship ties, cultural compatibility, ethnic support, the chance to keep their young in school, the opportunity to buy a building lot or even a tent site in a windy dust bowl or a rocky wasteland for a few dollars made their first homes possible in the West, built from discards of every description. Thus the individual family found a place where it could reform. By stages the cinder block foundation replaced wheels, two-by-fours took the place of ropes, worn-out trucks were anchored permanently as additions to the house, canvas gave way to frame cottages and bricks.

Strung along ditch banks, on land that could grow nothing but poverty and along back roads that led to the main routes, the migrant families arranged themselves in a typical shoestring pattern. In time a node formed on the string where a church was built or where people met for the weekly auction of second-hand clothes and home furnishings. Around these nodes country towns began to form. Working families, with their automobile, jalopy, or rattletrap truck, described new circles of job opportunities, a centered mobility gradually taking the place of the social formlessness of migration. The shoestring thickened not in one place but in several, and these marked the location of the characteristic cluster of farm labor towns. Typical of the pattern was that of Delano-Pixley-Earlimart-McFarland, and that of Yuba City-Marysville-Gridley in the heart of the Peach-Bowl. These were small towns, with a population ranging from two to thirteen thousand. Taken together these country towns were the secondary units of a labor pool that tended to become less fluid.

This "settling out" process and its possible effects on union organization had been noticed long before the NFLU arrived in California. As Jamieson observed in his thorough survey of labor unionism in agriculture, in the 1930s labor organizers had begun stressing the importance of stable locals.[217] The trend in this direction had progressed sufficiently for the LaFollette committee to confirm that by 1942 "a large portion of the seasonal labor force maintains more or less permanent domicile and moves from job to job within the locality . . . mostly within a radius of some twenty-five miles of their abode."[218] The LaFollette findings were supported by the Tolan committee a few years later,[219] and the trend continued through the 1950s. It was estimated by investigators for a state legislative committee that in 1960 about 80 percent of farm laborers worked only in one area, within commuting distance of their homes. When I joined the NFLU in 1948, and after a statewide tour of all agricultural production areas, I reported to Mitchell that more than half of the harvest workers did not leave their home counties. The organizational base, Hasiwar wrote before he left California, was in those areas where a sufficient number of workers lived permanently to sustain an organization.

Not the rural town but the cluster had become, over a period of decades, the potential basis for a union. A group of such towns contained a working population of ten to fifteen thousand farm laborers.

Family and kinship ties had resisted the transplant from the original homeland thousands of miles away and many years ago. They had moved from bivouacs to shelters to camps to homes in a progression that removed them from the power of eviction of their employers. To the extent that their chief source of income remained family labor, social stability was reinforced. There tended to develop a specialization in skills but not so narrow that the skills of the general farm worker were lost. The crew system survived in such crops as melons, asparagus, and grapes. Ethnic groupings remained distinct, as with the Filipinos of Delano, the Blacks of Cottonwood Road, the Mexicans of Brawley, and the Okies of Arvin, yet they were sufficiently open to one another to avoid isolation.

These were the characteristics of an unfolding social pattern into which trade-union collectivisms could be woven. Its most important significance lay in the possibility of a change in the form of economic action away from the wildcat, hit-and-run methods that the I.W.W. had exemplified and that the Communist-led unions had not been able to outgrow. However unorganized, classes of men still possess a collective memory, and that of the farm workers of California was lively with recollections of strikes that dissolved abruptly in defeat, their leaders departed and their followers scattered.

It was now possible to adopt a union strategy and appropriate tactics based not on the pattern of a harvest but on that of a society still evolving. The number of workers residing within the cluster provided material and moral weight behind union demands. Their residents knew one another as well as they knew the fields and orchards of the district. A shorter distance between contacts and more frequent opportunity to maintain them were as important to workers as to union organizers. The news and information of a district lay in the daily observations of the working people, the task of the union being rather that of ordering, interpreting, and relaying back to its members what they were seeing and hearing. That it was more economical to settle and commute to work was as applicable to union organizers as it was to harvesters in the seasonal routines.

The product of more than half a century of drift of a people searching for the leftovers of an abundant economy, the resulting pattern was one that reduced the task of organizing to manageable proportions. California's agricultural production centers were distributed over a vast area, some six hundred miles from north to south and one hundred miles from east to west. In 1950 there were probably not fewer than eighty thousand harvesters and general farm laborers who represented the potential base for a union. Enough of them now lived within the clustered towns to provide access to every important farm region. In the short five years between the start of the DiGiorgio strike and the end of the Imperial campaign, the NAWU had begun to match a union structure to this pattern. It was tentative, but sufficiently discernible to indicate how it might look in the future, with its essential elements of locals, area councils, wage ballots, wage conferences, camp delegates, volunteer teams, crop committees, district organizers, a state federation, information and education programs for all levels.

This could only have been an intermediate stage in the goals of the NAWU, since it had nothing to say about the hazards of growth of a young organization. One of these was the imprint that established trade unionism might make on it. Another was that farm labor in the Southwest, notably in California, was vitally exposed to the pressures of the labor supply from Mexico, which could in no way be avoided. Eventually this would require a reexamination of the traditional exclusionary bias of a labor movement that had been build partly on ethnic agitation. Sooner or later the NAWU would have to decide whether to accept this tradition or state an alternative, with the additional problem that the international policies of the AFL, parent body of the NAWU, were already polarized, if not petrified. That the NAWU would ever be admitted to the high levels of policy making within organized labor amounted to a fantasy. Yet its future role in California would depend on it.

Intermediately the prospects were more encouraging. Self-supporting area councils could control the tactics of strikes and eventually apply the vigor of insurgency to the underlying realities of economic power and social monopoly. They had already proved better able to deal with the labor contractors, who represented an important tool of that power. They could provide a material base in the union halls such as the Union Acre of the Arvin–Lamont local. The small merchants of the rural towns catered to a farm labor trade, and their cooperation meant not only easier credit in strike times, but also a more sympathetic public opinion when tensions were high. Equally important was the experience of the union in all its actions up to 1953: the smaller farmers were themselves marginal dependents on the corporation control of agri-business. During strikes they could be neutralized by differentiating economic pressure between them. Coalitions were possible in such areas as legislation, research, water and land distribution. In the days of vigilantism, the small farmers had provided much of the mob pressure organized by the Associated Farmers. They were still available as extras for antilabor demonstrations before the state legislature.

It was through its own area councils that the union was able to gain support from organized labor. The central labor bodies were only one level removed from the rank and file, with which farm workers themselves intermingled through job mobility in both directions. These bodies had not entirely lost the initiative for organizing the unorganized that they once had, and to that extent the NAWU could continue to rely on sympathetic if not aggressive support. More importantly, it was the self-sustaining area federation of farm labor unions that had proved the most productive ground for volunteer organizers and effective education.

Thus situated at the end of five years of exploratory encounters, the NAWU now faced problems of a different order. It, too, now had to begin to stabilize itself, which was likely to engage it for another five years, if not more. Its principal asset was a theory for the intermediate stage—to organize the clusters of rural towns in manageable groupings in which local leadership could be trained. Centralization would have no role except to provide support in those areas of concern common to all districts, such as research, legislative advocacy, education, and financial assistance during strikes.

Standing in the way of those goals was the fact that membership remained highly unstable. With the passing of the harvests, farm labor income practically ceased and dues fell. In 1951 dues payments to the national office by all the California locals totaled only $2,646. On October 9, 1951, the national office had $528 on hand for all field operations and its own poverty-level overhead. Most of its assets were in the form of promissory notes on the future good will of individuals and organizations that had floated the NFLU for years. On that date Mitchell advised: "Shortly after the first we should receive an additional $1,000 to $1,500 in contributions and dues. We will prorate whatever amount of money we have and send you a check for as much as we can send you; however your check may be delayed for several days." Some of the organizers had been receiving supplementary salaries and expenses from the organizing fund of the AFL, but these were discontinued in July 1953. In California the State Federation of Labor struck the NAWU locals from its rolls for failure to pay per capita dues. The area council of the Imperial locals ended 1953 with unpaid debts of several hundred dollars. During the summer of 1952 the Western Division of Organization of the NFLU reached its peak of full-time representatives: Hasiwar, Becker, William Swearingen, and Galarza. In October 1952 the Fresno area office was closed, Becker had left, and Hasiwar was permanently assigned to Louisiana, where Mitchell hoped he would find immediate response and financial support from the sugar cane plantation workers. In what Mitchell called, with a cool flourish, "a shift of resources" from the Deep West to the Deep South, he wrote me: "It looks like you must hold the fort in California." That was on August 28, 1952.

But there were no forts to hold, only a handful of outposts in the cluster communities from which there could develop, under the most favorable conditions, a measure of strength. The grip of the grower-shipper associations had been shaken but not loosened. They remained entrenched in the federal and state bureaucracies, the boards of supervisors, the local police, the academic establishments, the advisory committees of various sorts, the rural press, the labor contracting system, and the lower judiciary. Any one of these levels of power, selectively or in concert, could be brought to bear on union organization.

Moreover, a long interval to take stock and consolidate what had been gained presented new problems. Immediate economic benefits to the harvesters would diminish, if not cease altogether. The absence of collective bargaining contracts would further cool the support of the State Federation of Labor. The stereotypes of migrant poverty would wear thin with a public unaware of the underlying changes that were taking place in rural California. And most importantly, the bracero system had become the central instrument of those changes.

IV: The Attack on the Bracero System—1952-1959

Agri-businessmen were never in the habit of formulating long-range theories about farm labor insurgency, at least not publicly. But from what they had seen in Kern County and Imperial they sensed that the age-old policy of keeping people on the move must be renewed by different methods. Farm workers were putting down roots from which a strong union could grow. To frustrate the danger, the industry realized that the roots must be cut, and perpetual mobility reintroduced as a way of life for harvesters.

This had, in fact, been the practical goal which agri-business had for decades pursued in three ways: the continuous replenishment of the illegal labor pool; the contracting of braceros; and the use of border passes by workers living in Mexican communities adjacent to the border.

How these elements of the farm labor market were aligned against the domestic workers had been fully demonstrated in the union actions beginning with the DiGiorgio strike. Of the three, the border pass system had the serious disadvantage of a short radius, the primary beneficiaries being the growers of the border counties, Imperial, San Diego, Riverside, and San Bernardino. As to the wetbacks, the union had shown that the logistics of the labor contractors on whom the illegals depended could be disrupted. Moreover, it was not a method that could stand in the long run the exposure of its evils.

Once the effectiveness of the bracero contracting had been proved and its respectability accepted by comparison with the traffic in illegals, a law was required. Public Law 78 was signed in July 1951. The law and the administrative practices that grew out of it provided (1) substantial public subsidies for the expensive logistics of recruiting and delivering Mexican nationals; (2) conditions for a partnership between agri-business and government agencies, notably the U.S. Department of Labor and the California State Department of Employment; (3) an administrative process that stripped domestic workers of recourse to protect their jobs and their homes; (4) a protective shield to the industry behind which it could de-stabilize the domestics; and (5) a rhetoric to disguise all these advantages to employers.

Public Law 78 became by the end of 1953 a weapon for all seasons and all crops. Its utility was shown in many ways, for example, the substitution of wage fixing by bureaucrats and diplomats for wage fixing by growers associations.

By the end of the summer of 1953 the northward retreat of the domestics from the border counties was under way. There were no caravans of refugees in dramatic flight, but a steady withdrawal of families from border areas where they could not compete for a living. As they soon discovered, there were no crops in the state where braceros were not present, bringing lower wages and harsher conditions of employment.

The possible foundations for a strong and effective union in the cluster towns were disintegrating. The vital question for the NAWU became whether to confess defeat and withdraw, or to remain in the fields, and if so, to what end?

Simply stated, the purpose was to examine at much closer range than before the operation of the bracero system; to use the information thus gathered in a persistent campaign of information and propaganda to discredit it; to throw light on corporate agriculture's infiltration and domination of government as an instrument to its ends; and to clear the way for future unionists to deal with the illegal labor market and the latent threat of the border pass.

In a fundamental sense the NAWU was committing for an indefinite period what little it had in funds and staff to throw light on the decision making process at all levels of agri-businessland that accounted for the multiple assaults against the domestic harvesters—the illegals, the braceros, and the border passers. During this search the task of building a union would have to be postponed, with the chance that it might not be renewed, even if the bracero system were, in fact, destroyed.

Neither could the NAWU announce publicly that this was to be its limited goal. While the domestic workers who still made up the core of the union fully understood the issue and placed it uppermost in their concerns, they nevertheless could not be led into limited actions without plausible goals of better working conditions, social security coverage, unemployment insurance, collective bargaining, and the like. To the trade-union movement of California, an anti-bracero campaign was bound to appear at first sight unrelated to the common objectives of organization as prescribed in the union organizing manuals. To the NAWU, with one staff organizer and as many unpaid volunteers as it could keep together, it meant following the braceros wherever their presence could yield knowledge of the multiple ways in which they were being used to destroy the domestic labor force. This was bound to create the impression, especially with the NAWU's few friends in the central labor councils, that a few forlorn agitators were again wildcatting around the state in pursuit of nothing in particular. If this was unavoidable at least it had the merit that the growers who were watching would think likewise. I wrote to Mitchell in 1951 that "we have to be fluid and that we had no choice but to be where the wetback and bracero tides were running the highest."

If organizing in California were ever to be renewed by the NAWU, the scattered teams of volunteer workers would have to maintain connections and broaden their experience in the course of the attack on Public Law 78.

The union had to take a major risk. It had to assume that if it succeeded in clearing the obstacles to farm labor unionism at least in this one vital respect, it would enlist more effective support from organized labor than it had in the past.

The northward movement of displaced domestic harvesters out of the Imperial Valley had begun before the spring of 1953. Forced to relocate, these families departed one by one seeking jobs and the opportunity to establish once more a permanent home. They scattered to Los Angeles County, Ventura, the desert ranches of Lancaster, and the cotton country of the southern Central Valley, as far north as the Salinas Valley, Santa Rosa, and the upper Sacramento farmlands. They still sought farm work as family groups, if it could be found, but the braceros were everywhere making jobs insecure even in agricultural districts four hundred miles from the border. They continued to pay the NAWU a tribute of confidence if not dues. As the volunteer organizers moved north the union moved with them.

With these limited objectives and a scattered band of members new locals were organized, giving the union nominal standing and a measure of presence in the fields. It reached from the southern end of the Salinas Valley through Santa Clara and San Joaquin counties to the upper Sacramento basin, and touched the western boundaries of Fresno County around Mendota and Los Banos. More than an area of organization, it was one of service and support provided by one NAWU staff organizer. The calls for help from the locals were intermittent but when they came they were urgent. Responding to them added little to the strength of the NAWU; but it sharpened resistance tactics and maintained contacts, keeping the union moving toward its target, Public Law 78.

The Salinas Valley—1952-1958

For a hundred miles parallel to the Pacific Coast a narrow trough of rich farm land separates the Gabilan and Santa Lucia mountain ranges. Through it runs the Salinas River, a sandy watercourse between gently sloping fields walled in by peaks that turn purple and gold in the setting sun. At its northern end the Salinas Valley is open to the Pacific winds, moistened by the fog. Where the Valley narrows and the velocity of the north wind increases, transverse rows of eucalyptus shelter the plantings of lettuce, carrots, beets, tomatoes, and other vegetable crops. The landscape is sparsely dotted with farmhouses and labor camps, and the towns, other than the city of Salinas, sit in a compression of intensive agriculture, at intervals of ten to fifteen miles along the course of the river. These towns—King City, Greenfield, Soledad, Gonzales, Chualar, and Castroville—were so many local labor pools from which the domestic farm laborers commuted to the seasonal harvests up and down the Valley.

News of the NFLU strikes in Kern County and Imperial was brought to the Salinas area by harvesters who came seasonally to cut lettuce and tie carrots. Others had abandoned their border homes and resettled, notably in Soledad and Gonzales. In Soledad a nucleus of union-minded *locales* joined the union as early as 1950, and with them volunteer organizers began to assemble a local.

The process was typical of what was happening elsewhere in the state. In Soledad Raul Aguilar and his wife, Trinidad, operated a small grocery store. Former farm workers, they were familiar with the problems of their customers and through them kept abreast of conditions in the local job market. Over their counter passed the talk of the fields and the camps, from which information about the union radiated to workers.

In Camp McCallum, a government farm labor center near Soledad, the union found another diligent volunteer, Jose Ayala. Fifty years in the sun had dehydrated Don Jose to the point where he was less than a hundred pounds of sinew, and a spare frame moved more by will than by energy. After the day's work in all seasons Ayala drove his ancient automobile the length of the Valley distributing union leaflets. In winter he assembled other tenants of the camp in his kitchen, the gas burners on his portable stove providing the only warmth. McCallum was already a refuge for families who had lost their jobs and their homes elsewhere.

By the end of 1950 there was a local in Soledad and another in Salinas. Between them, with a combined membership that never passed forty persons, they reached into every labor settlement from King City to Watsonville, a chain of towns with some two thousand resident domestic harvesters.

In several respects the organizing style that took shape in the Salinas Valley confirmed the strategy that had been foreseen by Hasiwar. There were enough domestic workers to sustain a central local with supporting affiliates throughout the Valley. The object was not to call strikes at random but to locate and organize a base. The Central Labor Council of Salinas provided a meeting room free of rent. Local merchants like the Aguilars, whose trade depended on farm laborers and packers, were enlisted in the campaign of public information concerning the effects of displacement of local residents. Union leaflets circulated throughout the Valley by hand, providing information on working conditions, the economy of the area, the aims of the union, and the labor strategies of the growers. The Salinas Valley seemed to offer displaced farm labor families a new foothold far from the more vulnerable border counties. In September 1951 the first state convention of the National Farm Labor Union was held in the city of Salinas, attended by 150 delegates from locals throughout the state. In one of the strongholds of agri-business the union unfurled its flag, a black eagle on a green, white, and red background.

Although the pace of organizing was deliberate and its aim unwavering, without the ability to protect the job security of domestic workers the union could not grow beyond a handful of members. The destruction of that security was the aim of the Salinas Grower–Shipper Association, representing the corporate interests of finance, production, warehousing, processing, transportation, and marketing of the area. The association still basked in the memories of vigilante violence with which it had suppressed farm labor strikes of the 1930s. Farm labor contractors provided large numbers of illegals, and managed many of the camps of braceros, for which the association was the contracting agent, recognized as such by the Department of Labor. As to the wetbacks the association did not take official notice of them, leaving the profits of exploitation and the risk of management to the contractors. It took the adamant position that it held contracting authority on behalf of member growers exclusively with regard to braceros and none to deal with the union collectively.[220]

Except for the occasional sweeps of the Immigration Service, the black market in illegal labor remained a major if disreputable asset of the association. In 1952 access to them was provided by many of the forty-three licensed farm labor contractors in the Salinas Valley, of whom thirty-three were Spanish surnamed. The mobile camps and hideouts were known to union members—hay fields where illegals slept in fox holes or barns from which they emerged before dawn to be picked up by trucks and private cars driven by growers and field foremen. In violation of government rules, wetbacks were mingled with braceros in crews from which domestic workers were excluded. Regularly domestic harvesters were referred by the Farm Placement Office to such crews and as regularly they were turned away with the comment "no work."

With illegals in plentiful supply the working conditions of braceros were determined by the association with considerable latitude, notwithstanding the written contracts. At the regular pay scale for field labor, braceros were assigned to pack lettuce, serving the packing rigs on wheels that were supplanting the town sheds. Around Greenfield, Soledad, and Gonzales local women were turned away. Men and women unable to find work moved from their homes to the cabins of Camp McCallum, a majority of whose residents were perennially on county welfare assistance. But even in these camps they were not secure, for into them the growers began to move braceros. Notices to vacate were served in order to make room for them. Since the braceros could not object to the withholding of "bonuses," contractors imposed them as a condition of employment of domestic workers, whose objection to the deduction provided an additional excuse for not hiring them. Braceros were also obliged to turn in their duplicate punch cards, depriving them of means to verify their earned wages. Many of them were loaned by the associations to contractors, who combined them with illegals, forcing wage scales down to levels that the braceros would accept only under compulsion and domestic laborers would not accept at all. Although the union did not reach a point where it was capable of organizing economic action to challenge these conditions, it resisted them in ways that did not risk pitting volunteer organizers against the association.

Information on wage shortages and false weights and measures was regularly distributed in all the camps, particularly where the illegals were concentrated. Where the union volunteers could document the frauds, the information was publicized to discredit the contractors who practiced them. They provided the connections through which illegal hiring was made possible, and their eventual elimination became a goal of the union. With their multiple tricks of deception, they represented a subsystem as deeply embedded in corporate agriculture as the braceros. Over time the tolerance of the illegal traffic by state and federal agencies would become public and notorious, and the political immunity of the system broken. The union began by enlisting the local merchants against the contractors who operated the camp commissaries with their special forms of price gouging.

The association contended that in the Valley there were few domestic workers with farm experience. A directory of local resident farm workers compiled by the union silenced the complaints of labor shortages with which the association justified its demands for braceros and it provided information for local referrals to the Farm Placement Office. The local farm laborers so difficult for the association and the Farm Labor Office to find were identified by name and address with a standing offer by the union to produce them. When the association began compiling black lists of "undependable" workers which by inference proved the superiority of braceros over domestics, the union exposed them as fabrications. No member of the union living in the Salinas Valley appeared among the "undependables" listed.[221] The aim of the association was to undermine morale by tactics of this kind, but the union checkmated them at every point.

Another weapon of discouragement was the serving on domestic families of notices to vacate to make room for braceros. Families seeking seasonal work were turned away with the excuse of "no vacancy." It was demoralizing to see a family's belongings piled in the street by the police on demand of a camp operator, usually a contractor employed by one of the corporate growers. In one instance the union moved the evicted family back to its quarters and publicized the case throughout the Valley. Temporarily the practice was stopped.

Although the braceros were clearly becoming a devasting economic weapon under the tight control of the association, it was important to avoid hostility between them and the local unionists. Here as elsewhere, it was necessary to observe how the system worked, not in general but in detail. The Salinas members agreed to admit braceros who brought legitimate grievances to the union's attention, signed membership cards, paid dues, and authorized the NAWU to act as their representative. Explanations of the terms of the bracero contracts were distributed and counseling services were offered to any applicant. The Soledad local particularly became the center of bracero contacts and the exchange of information with them. During the harvests of 1952 and 1953 complaints were filed, with supporting briefs verified by cancelled checks, punch cards, and other documents showing illegal deductions from wages for the use of blankets that were supposed to be provided free, inaccurate wage statements, refusal of medical attention paid for under group insurance, and wage scales below the prevailing rates set by the Department of Labor.

Every bracero grievance, after verification, was submitted to the Department of Labor through the local compliance officer who either made a *pro forma* investigation or ignored it. Hearings were consistently denied and the braceros were advised that joining the union meant summary deportation. In one instance union members took direct action. A young bracero had been confined to his cabin by a contractor for demanding more work and better wages. The young man was locked up and refused meals. He fell sick. His friends reported the matter and that night I went to the camp with three members of the Soledad local, broke the lock, and carried the bracero to an improvised bedroom in a garage, where he was cared for until he recovered.

Incidents of this kind made Soledad troublesome for the association, the compliance officer, and the contractors, but especially troublesome were the grievances submitted personally to the ambassador of Mexico in Washington by a bracero, Francisco Hernandez Cano.

Hernandez was one of a hundred braceros who joined the Soledad local after fruitless efforts to present complaints such as illegal deductions for blankets, medication prescribed and administered by row bosses, excessive insurance fees, unauthorized charges for carrot tie-wires, and denial of milk rations as punishment for insubordination. On the advice of the union the braceros prepared evidence, drafted a petition, and appealed to the Mexican consul in Fresno, who visited Salinas only long enough to reprimand the complainers and order them back to work. As an example to others, Hernandez, who wore his union button on the job, was summoned before the consul, the camp manager, and the compliance officer and advised that his contract had been revoked. He was ordered to pack his belongings and report immediately for repatriation. Instead he hastened to the union. I decided he should go to Washington instead and present himself at the Mexican embassy. Provided with a change of clothes, a bus ticket, and instructions, Hernandez left that night. To reassure his friends they were told that he had last been seen on the Fresno bus headed for Mexico. Mitchell received him in Washington as the representative of several hundred braceros in the Salinas Valley who had grievances pending against the association. In Soledad the union issued a release to the newspapers and a leaflet about Hernandez's mission. At that time the Soledad local had bracero committees in five camps.

Hernandez returned to Salinas with assurances from the embassy that his contract would be respected and that all complaints would be investigated. Orders came forthwith from the Department of Labor that deductions for blankets were to be reimbursed. An escort service for disabled braceros was set up to insure prompt attention at the clinics, and the prescription of general purpose pills for all complaints by camp bosses ceased.

By the end of 1953 the intelligence coming to the union through bracero members was more than adequate. Even the continuous transfer of men from camp to camp was ineffectual; braceros would travel by bus at their own expense on their days off to bring reports requested by the union, copies of contracts, check stubs, menus, notices posted on bulletin boards, payroll books discarded by camp flunkies, and medical bills. My title of Research Director of the NAWU was translated by the braceros as "el señor de los papelitos." At union meetings I explained to them and to the volunteer organizers how the "little papers" they brought me fitted as pieces of the mosaic of Public Law 78.

But the importance of investigating the bracero system as it actually operated from day to day, and the fact that the braceros themselves were the most effective agents for such an investigation, was overshadowed in the minds of the *locales* by the immediate threat to their own job security, the downward pressure on wages, and the deterioration of working conditions. Since the braceros were in effect a captive labor force, cooperation with them in economic actions was out of the question. It remained to be seen how such cooperation might be possible, in a way that would benefit the domestic workers themselves.

Such an opportunity was provided by the growers' charging carrot harvesters for the tie-wires—Twist-ems—which were covered with a strip of paper a quarter of an inch or more wide with the name of the grower printed in bright colors. The wires were sold to the harvester for 24 to 85 cents per thousand. A crate of carrots could cost the worker 25 cents or more. Occasionally a grower would provide the tie-wires without charge, but this was frowned on by the industry.

An expert carrot tier could be charged as much as $5 a week for tie-wires, depending on whether he was a domestic, a bracero, or an illegal. The charges were deductible from the weekly paycheck, and in some fields payment was in cash in advance. In the Salinas Valley harvest of 1952, the levy on wages of carrot harvesters amounted to more than $25,000. It was a production cost item that was passed on to the workers on the spot, as well as a forced contribution to brand advertising for the benefit of the grower.

All efforts to terminate these deductions had failed. They were justified as a traditional and common practice throughout the state, an approved way of discouraging waste by the harvesters. It had been so held by the Department of Labor in 1949.

In the harvest of 1951 and 1952 members of the union, domestics and braceros, documented the economics of the Twist-ems. Samples of the wires were collected, individual production and deductions noted, receipts compiled, and contractors queried. Growers responded by requiring cash payments in advance, discontinuing the giving out of receipts and changing work assignments. These evasions slowed down the monitoring of the harvest but they did not thwart the unionists.

With sufficient evidence in hand the union petitioned the attorney general of California to receive the evidence in the matter and to issue a criminal complaint, but it was his position that there was "no clean cut answer as to whether the practice was in violation of any statute. . . ."[222]

In December 1952 the NAWU filed a complaint with the State Labor Commissioner, supported by a brief to the effect that the deductions violated sections 226 and 450 of the Labor Code concerning work receipts. Deductions were in effect disguised wage cuts; some operators refused to reimburse workers for unused wires. No evidence had ever been presented that the deductions were necessary to prevent waste. In my brief I held that ancient practice could not legitimize a fraud. To emphasize these points and bring out the widespread nature of the violations, a similar action was started by the union in Santa Clara County.

In another parallel move the union submitted these grievances directly to the Mexican embassy in Washington, citing the provisions of the international agreement concerning deductions that supported the complaint. The matter was referred to the Secretaria de Relaciones Exteriores in Mexico City, which held it under advisement for eight months, forcing the union to issue a bulletin informing all braceros that their government appeared to have no interest in the problem. Like all union circulars, this one was sent in bundles to all locals in the state, and the Mexican government was notified.

When the labor commissioner called for hearings on the matter in August 1952 there were on file seven complaints for illegal deductions, documented as to the legal and economic aspects of the issue. By that time the commissioner's office was persuaded that the practices complained of were in violation of the Code.[223]

This exercise, not unlike that of one person riding both ends of a see-saw at the same time, succeeded. With information bulletins from the union circulating throughout California, with copies provided to the press in Mexico, it became more difficult for the Mexican government to ignore a practice, affecting its nationals abroad, whose legality was now being questioned. Consultations began between both governments. In April Secretary of Labor Durkin issued a rule that deductions for tie-wires violated the terms of the work contracts of the braceros, and in May a joint interpretation by both governments to this effect was concluded. Since this removed one of the economic advantages of hiring braceros in preference to domestics; and since it was unlikely that the labor commissioner would ignore the diplomatic reversal based on identical evidence; and with the further possibility that the issue for the union would now become one of gross discrimination rather than mere skullduggery by the growers and contractors, the deductions from wages of domestic harvesters also stopped.

It was now in order to file suits against the association, its individual members, and the contractors, for punitive damages as well as for injunctive relief. It was a pleasant prospect, but a hopeless one. Again the NAWU was forced to stop short for lack of funds. Financial assistance was denied by the State Federation of Labor, whose attorneys refused to plead so sensitive a case.

After 1955 the NAWU made only occasional contacts with the Salinas Valley domestic workers. The active volunteers, unable to find steady work, tagged as "*huelguistas*" or trouble makers, left one by one. Ayala returned to Mexico. Raul and Trini Aguilar gave up their grocery store and moved to Stockton. The volunteer team of the Salinas local dispersed to find factory jobs in San Jose and San Francisco. Thenceforth the association's domination of the farm labor market through extended use of braceros was uncontested. Between 1950 and 1959 seasonal farm work performed by braceros increased from 4 to 70 percent.

But even a 70 percent level of domination of the field labor market did not satisfy the association. In its view the domestics had to be discredited as well as displaced. A record must be compiled that would establish beyond doubt the poor stuff of which they were made and prove the wisdom of the Farm Placement Service and U.S. Department of Labor in certifying braceros on demand.

Hundreds of workers recruited from the skid rows of Los Angeles, the Central Valley, and the San Francisco Bay cities were induced to move in the Salinas area on promises of jobs. Most of these men were transported by contractors who did not in fact have work available. Since they could not pay for board and room in the camps they were turned out to wander in the city of Salinas, panhandling, and sleeping in the parks. Police arrested them as vagrants and drunks and crowded them into jails. Banner headlines completed the drama. It was an orchestrated farce intended to discredit the requirement that farmers exhaust all sources of native-born labor before hiring braceros.

All this occurred in the spring of 1960, the last time that the NAWU investigated the ploys of the Salinas Grower-Shipper Association. What stands out in the incident is the formidable array of public authority that could not prevail to uncover the facts and make them known. In March the affair was being investigated by the attorney general's office, the Department of Employment, the Public Utilities Commission, the Highway Patrol, the Board of Equalization, the Department of Industrial Relations, and the Monterey County Welfare Department. These agencies could not cope with the ability of the association to vilify domestic workers as a class and ultimately to pin the blame on the contractors hired for the purpose.

The report I submitted to Mitchell on March 28, 1960, on this affair was the last connection of the NAWU with the Salinas Valley.[224]

Opening Confidential Records

Under Public Law 78 domestic workers had the right to apply for and a prior claim upon work for which bracero hiring was officially authorized. The record of such authorizations should have been public and readily available to domestic laborers looking for work as close to their area of residence as possible. Wages for braceros were fixed as those "prevailing" for domestic workers; the manner in which such wages were "found" and their opportune publication was important to the local harvesters. The bracero contracts provided the same standards of work and the same scales of wages for them as were customary for domestics. This vital provision was written into the law to prevent the lowering of standards of pay and employment conditions for American citizens. Such contracts should have been open to public inspection in the agricultural communities into which braceros were brought. On all these and other equally important matters of information it became the settled practice of the U.S. Department of Labor, the California Farm Placement Service, and the growers associations to deny the workers access to the records, and the aim of the union to open them.

In the summer of 1950, when the union began accepting braceros so it could represent them in presenting legitimate grievances, the regional office of the Department of Labor in San Francisco was queried about the progress of such complaints in the department. There was no response from either San Francisco or the local compliance officer.[225] A year later the Farm Labor Office in Calexico was asked to supply copies of the lists of authorized growers certified for bracero hiring. These lists were filed in Washington, San Francisco, and in every Farm Labor and association office in areas where braceros were working. Legal counsel advised the California Department of Employment that such information was confidential under the provisions of the Unemployment Insurance Act, sections 97 and 100. The union was told, "The information you seek is obtained by the department in the course of administration" of the act.[226] Instructions were given to union volunteers elsewhere in the state and they began appearing at various Farm Placement offices requesting such lists.

Judging from the response to the union, there was consultation in the matter between the state and federal agencies who were legally required to give what the union was demanding. There was in effect an agreement in compliance with federal statutes that such lists were to be available to interested parties on request. This agreement expired in June 1952 and by common consent of the agencies was not renewed.[227] The state rule, favoring confidentially, took precedence over the federal statute, which did not. The data compiled by the Department of Employment related to the administration of a federal, not a state, statute, and therefore the restrictions alleged in support of confidentiality were irrelevant. The authority to release or withhold information lay with federal, not state, agencies. The Code of Federal Regulations, at Title 20, Section 602.8, mandated the release to interested individuals of job orders and wage offers on file in local offices.

The Farm Placement offices violated this rule regularly. When asked to explain, they were silent, except to warn the union that it did not even have the right to any public information posted on their bulletin boards. This was discovered when the union asked the Salinas office why it was posting calls for carrot tiers from other areas when there were local applicants for the work in every town in the Valley.

Confidentiality extended from the official files to those of the associations. There was in effect an "open order" policy which meant that the jobs to which braceros had been assigned in any area were to be regarded as continuing calls for domestic labor on simple application. B. A. Harrigan, Secretary of the Imperial association, refused a request for a meeting to determine what open orders he had on file. Local farm placement offices also refused to divulge such orders on the ground that they were "restricted information." This was in May 1953, when the displacement of domestic workers was at its height.

After two more years of persistent demands at every level of both federal and state administration there was slight progress toward open information. Starting in September 1956 state employment agencies were instructed to post "the number of workers which will be necessary to supplement the available agricultural labor force" and "the prevailing wage."[228] When the union secured the support of influential unions such as the Brotherhood of Maintenance of Way Employees, the Department of Labor moved the extra inch. On December 24, it advised that "to afford as much protection as possible to domestic workers, we will also make available the Authorization to Contract." When this concession was made, Public Law 78 had been in operation for five years.

The concession was less liberal than at first appeared, for it was conditional. These documents could be seen by union representatives only at the regional office in San Francisco, a day's travel from some of the areas in which the union was active. The same condition applied to the showing of membership lists of associations when they were the designated employers of braceros. Twice I made the trip from the Imperial Valley to see such lists since I was unable to obtain copies. The refusal of the local offices to provide the information continued.

But the NAWU had to reckon with the interpretation placed on these federal concessions by the state agencies. As of August 1957 H. L. Stewart, state director of employment, was still insisting that the law made such information confidential, and its disclosure a misdemeanor. To this he added that the constant movement of braceros from crop to crop made it impossible to report their exact number and location.[229] Not mere curiosity but an immediate means to test the effectiveness of the "open order" policy was the point of the union's demand. Stewart avoided it by explaining regretfully that his office did not "compile by counties" such information.[230] Continuing its statistical feints, the department offered to make the "necessary computations" of the "approximate total number" of braceros on written request from the union. These were skillful if transparent parries, all of them intended to widen the time lag between the hiring of braceros and the attempts of domestics to grasp the situation that was costing them jobs.

These responses were the result of consultations between state and federal officials in Washington and Sacramento, reviewed and approved by the highest legal and political authorities. The chief counsel of the Department of Employment carefully explained that the only change in policy contemplated was as to the release of county totals of braceros, which to the union was an interesting but not vital statistic. Still pressing its demand the union argued that the information sought was not obtained in the course of administering the state unemployment statute, but in the application of Public Law 78, a federal act.

To this argument the state's attorney general responded on August 1958: "The refusal to furnish the information you desire is not the result of any policy or position taken by the Director of the Department of Employment but rather is the public policy of the State of California as set forth by the Legislature."[231] Administrative discretion backed by legal advice was prolonging the exchange. The previous summer the department's attorneys had admitted that there was no judicial precedent or rule that clothed the lists in question with privilege such as was being invoked up and down the line.[232]

These ingenious responses were in contrast to the flat denials of 1950, and represented some progress toward open information. Lieutenant Governor Goodwin J. Knight gave an explanation: "The information you seek directly from local farm placement offices is not official at that point in the organization."[233] And Edward Hayes added, in correspondence with the union in August 1958, that he was guided in his policies by the attorney general and by the intent of Congress.

Throughout 1958 Hayes continued to rely principally on the unemployment act and also took certain precautions on a matter that was becoming increasingly touchy. In March 1958 he instructed the FPS local agencies to refer all requests for information about braceros to the central office in Sacramento; "We prefer releasing such information only through this office." A note of apprehension was creeping into his directives to the field men, who were required to report such inquiries by telephone. Not being acquainted with the unique methods of the union's volunteer organizers and their "papelitos," Hayes's apprehension turned into mild paranoia. He ordered that special locks be placed on files containing wage surveys, lists of members of grower's associations, local authorizations, and reports on housing conditions. The staff bulletin that gave these instructions included Hayes's order to "Destroy this notice when answered."[234] Later Department of Employment Director John E. Carr explained that this precaution had been taken because unauthorized persons were removing material from the files and that the security cabinets would protect the local office from suspicion of revealing "confidential information."

What gained support for Public Law 78 was the assurance, reiterated by its proponents, that braceros would be contracted only in the event of scarcity of domestic harvesters, and only for the duration of the need. The public credit of the system could be maintained only so long as there was no evidence that braceros were driving out domestics. Such evidence was being persistently accumulated by the union in the fields, and tenaciously ignored or evaded or concealed by the Department of Labor. It was my belief that the administrative records would confirm such evidence. What the union suspected the government feared.

Among the documents that came to light in the course of time was a confidential report on an investigation by one Lawrenson, ordered by the attorney general of California after the union had filed charges of fraud in the administration of the bracero health insurance system. Among other things in this report, growers associations' opposition to receiving applications by domestics for jobs held by braceros on the "open order" rule was explained: "a file of applications . . . would possibly reflect an untrue picture which would seriously hamper farm employers' efforts to import needed foreign workers." That the state agreed with this view was demonstrated by its unwillingness to receive such applications and its refusal to disclose the names and locations of ranches to which braceros had been certified. As the Lawrenson report phrased it, ". . . the current program of imported labor might suffer without justification through recorded registration." Such registration would have identified both the domestic workers who had been thrown out of work and the braceros who had taken their places. Hayes permitted a minimum of information to be published in the Weekly Report issued by his office on bracero employment; it was carefully screened to avoid "a certain danger of reporting facts beyond those appearing in the Report."[235] The growers associations demanded confidentiality of such records. "This was a time," said Thomas C. Campbell to a meeting of area managers of the Farm Placement Service in March 1958, "for caution and the utmost discretion in our contacts with the public."[236]

It was also time to raise the issue in Congress. The union asked for an inquiry by the subcommittee on government information of the House of Representatives, chaired by Representative John E. Moss of California.

The precedent for which the union had been waiting was provided in connection with efforts to force the Immigration and Naturalization Service of the Department of Justice to disclose information concerning the employment of Japanese workers imported into California. Fearing the mounting pressure of the NAWU on Public Law 78, the growers associations had begun to create a labor force of Asians to supplement that of the braceros. Initially this alien contracting program was administered by the INS. Since the importation of the Japanese was justified, like that of braceros, by the alleged shortage of domestics, the NAWU immediately requested the names of authorized employers and other related information.

At first the INS replied that "the internal records of the service cannot be made available to the public." I responded that the NAWU would appeal to Congress and that moreover I was prepared to make a public appeal for funds to test the authority of the INS in court. For whatever reasons, the service reconsidered its position and in March 1958 authorized the release of the information requested.[237] The Moss subcommittee had been persuasive in opening the records. Field reports from union members in the Salinas Valley continued in the meantime and it was this information that brought about a public hearing on the matter, and the termination of the Japanese contracting project followed shortly.

As the union proceeded with its appeal to the Moss subcommittee, it continued to file demands for information in various parts of the state and to press its own legal arguments for open records. Through attorney James Murray, the union notified the State Director of Employment of its intention to file an appropriate complaint, "to force the production of information concerning certifications,"[238] The reply from the director was gracious: "I do not have any objection to a suit being filed for this purpose."

On January 30, 1959, Representative Moss wrote the Department of Labor that he had been informed of the denial to certain trade union representatives of lists of employers of Mexican nationals and the number hired by each employer. After further inquiry by the subcommittee, the department began to yield, but not without continuing to cite directives and precedents in support of the traditional secrecy of its records. The state attorney general finally concluded that the information requested could not be withheld since it was not controlled by the state unemployment code. Division Notice Number 2189Q of October 30, 1959, confirmed this, specifying that the new rule applied to names and addresses of employees, the number of foreign workers and their utilization as farm laborers. Also released from confidentiality were the lists and authorization forms of growers in whose behalf the associations contracted braceros. All these could be copied by the public, but local officials were admonished to "make sure any attachments are removed, particularly correspondence from employers and memoranda from Central Office."[239]

In July 1960 the Department of Labor in Washington further agreed to make available immediately after their approval all joint interpretations of Public Law 78. In May of the same year the format of the Weekly Report out of Sacramento was modified to show "the approximate number of domestics required to replace foreign workers," indicating that the Farm Placement Service was moving at a snail's pace, but moving.

The documents the union had been attempting for nearly ten years to dislodge from restricted files were always specifically identified and their relation to the purported guarantees in Public Law 78 for domestics set forth. But it soon became clear that the forms on which such information was contained were merely the fringe of an intelligence system between agricultural employers and government agents. Exploration of this twilight zone depended upon the union volunteers. As time passed their number diminished, but those that remained became sufficiently experienced to pick up the clues that led the union to the private life of Public Law 78.

At the higher levels of policy making and decision, the administrative records were never published. How they were obtained is explained below and what they contained has already been told in *Merchants of Labor*.[240] It was a revelation of the private conferences between federal officials and grower representatives; of the diplomatic negotiations conducted behind closed doors; of the understandings between Mexican consuls and the departments of Justice and Labor to facilitate the instant reconditioning of illegals into braceros; of the exchange of information between the Department of Employment and growers as to union activity; of the financial benefits to the growers associations of bracero contracting; the exchange of money for especially designated braceros routed to favored growers, and of the profits of extortionate health insurance concessions approved by both governments.

For the NAWU the pursuit of this information was much like measuring a submerged iceberg; the lower depths of a captive public administration were difficult to plumb. The NAWU, nearing its end in 1959, did not live long enough to complete this task.

The Veto of Union Clearance

When Public Law 78 was enacted in 1951 there was in the U.S. Department of Labor a Bureau of Employment Security responsible for assisting American workers to find jobs and to stabilize their employment. A special branch of the bureau dealt with the placement of agricultural laborers, the object being to minimize migrancy by job information and referrals through a national network of farm placement offices. In their respective areas these offices were presumed to be reliably informed on demand and supply of harvesters. Theoretically a shortage of labor in any area was corrected by orders exchanged throughout the network. In California, local farm placement managers were responsible to the Chief of the Farm Placement Service. It was on the basis of their information that clearance orders were exchanged to facilitate the recruitment of harvesters into areas officially declared to be in need of supplementary manpower.

Structured in this way, the system had a number of features to commend it. On the organizational charts it represented a flow of available labor that could be directed rationally. Manpower floods or droughts, expensive and wasteful, could be avoided. Workers would no longer have to rely on false information circulated by contractors and crew leaders with resulting over-recruitment, lost time, wasteful travel, and depressed wages. The interests of the workers in steadier employment and those of the growers in timely recruitment were both happily served.

The order clearance process rested on the assumption that the local farm placement managers were familiar with and in fact utilized all the local sources of information as to availability of agricultural labor in their respective areas. Neither Congress nor the Department of Labor administrators ever recognized in this arrangement anything more than a technical solution to a vexing imbalance between the distribution of capital and of people. The more vital imbalance in the distribution of economic and social power in rural America was taken for granted. The formal structuralism of the employment security system was lowered into place on the old foundations. Absent from it were associations of landworkers, such as cooperatives or trade unions, through which the offer of labor could be institutionalized in favor of those who offered it, as those who sought it were institutionalized.

There was not only a lack of balance between the supply and demand of rural manpower regionally and nationally; there was a total lack of it between organized ownership and unorganized laborers.

The evolution of the Southern Tenant Farmers Union into the National Farm Labor Union and then the National Agricultural Workers Union was, in this connection, a case in point. In the southern states farm labor recruitment remained trammeled by legal restrictions and police surveillance to prevent the free movement of workers through self-organization. Mitchell sought a way out by attempting to set up arrangements with the Amalgamated Meat Cutters and Butcher Workmen so he could recruit southern sharecroppers and cotton wage hands through the STFU seasonally. There was already at hand the national employment security system, and Mitchell petitioned in December 1939 that it utilize the services of the NFLU in recruiting and placing farm workers. That the Department of Labor paid no attention to Mitchell's request plainly revealed the class limits of official structuralism.

In California this effort was renewed. In May 1950 William Becker wrote the State Department of Employment: "Will you let me know what procedure we can work out for getting the resident workers into jobs in their own areas first?"[241] There was no response, any more than there was to the letters addressed to local growers associations which were regularly certified for hiring braceros. This one-way correspondence continued until 1959. Occasionally similar letters were sent to local labor contractors, invariably with negative results.

Union demands for participation in the process of reporting available local labor were intensified in the spring of 1950. They resulted in a memorandum issued on April 25 by D. H. Roney, assistant chief of the Division of Public Offices and Benefit Payments of the State Department of Employment. It informed all local farm placement managers that "it is our responsibility to be absolutely certain that all domestic workers are given employment opportunities where such opportunities are available." Roney's instructions were to use "all available recruiting techniques" including labor unions. The instructions specifically referred to the National Farm Labor Union, whose representatives "were to be contacted and advised of the job openings and requested to refer any unemployed members to our office."[242] These instructions applied specifically to all orders "which involved Mexican nationals."

A list of the union's representatives in California with their addresses was submitted to the Department of Labor in Washington by Mitchell. It was transmitted to the Bureau of Employment in San Francisco, and then to the State Director of Employment in Sacramento, James G. Bryant, with instructions to contact the union in accordance with Bureau of Employment Security policy.

The Roney memorandum caused a tremor throughout Agri-business-land. The State Board of Agriculture, advisory body to the Department of Employment on manpower matters, denounced the instructions and requested that the department eliminate any reference to organized labor in the process of recruitment of farm labor or certification of braceros.[243] The new BES policy was attacked as a device to force organization of farm labor. The instructions should be rescinded, said the board, a position that was promptly supported by the Associated Farmers, the State Chamber of Commerce, Western Growers Association, the San Joaquin Valley Agricultural Labor Bureau, and the Agricultural Producers Labor Committee. C. B. Moore, managing director of Western Growers, bluntly told the Bureau of Employment Security: "We would like you to issue an order countermanding" the directive; he called it "the most brazen attempt we have seen to unionize an unorganized agricultural group."

Such suggestions, recommendations, or advice were in effect orders from agri-business to government, and they were promptly obeyed. Director of Employment Bryant declared that the federal government had no right to require the employment of domestic workers in preference to braceros and announced that he would comply with the recommendation of the board.[244] Rebuked, the U.S. Department of Labor made no move to assert the plain intent of Congress as expressed in Public Law 78.

Representative Tom Werdel, who was then playing a confidential role with Representatives Richard M. Nixon and Tom Steed in the preparation of a false congressional report on the role of the union in the DiGiorgio strike, intervened under pressure from the industry. Growers, Werdel said, "were very much stirred up. They came back here and the situation was eventually ironed out." Robert F. Goodwin, director of the Bureau of Employment Security, was also advised, as was Secretary of Labor Maurice Tobin. Don Larin, federal chief of the Farm Placement Service, reinforced the position by adding that there was not and never had been "any directive to clear with a union or other organization" in the process of determining how many domestic farm workers might be available.

On May 24 Roney issued a superseding memorandum explaining to local agents that "some confusion has arisen concerning the April 25 directive" and deleting from it reference to the National Agricultural Workers Union, but leaving general reference to labor camps, growers associations, Mexican settlements, and labor organizations. Of these only the growers associations were capable, as they had shown time and again, of matching their own bureaucracies with those of the state and federal governments.

The reference to labor unions "in general" in the second Roney memorandum was a particularly subtle technicality. On the advisory committee of the State Department of Employment sat three representatives of the State Federation of Labor with whom the department was theoretically in periodic consultation. They took no part in the scuffle over the Roney memorandum, allowing the recommendation of the Board of Agriculture to stand. No labor lobby was stirred to counter Werdel's moves in Washington. What the Department of Labor did not know about the availability of farm workers would not hurt the growers, and the value of ignorance proceeding with deliberate speed again became the norm of the Bureau of Employment Security.

Nevertheless, the growers associations considered it prudent to drive home their point that, listed or not, the union was not capable of providing workers. To accomplish this the close harmony between growers and the Farm Placement Service was once more demonstrated.

In June 1950 the Bakersfield office of the union received a call from the farm placement manager requesting forty citrus pickers. The union arranged for their transportation. The men waited all day for confirmation, but the order to clear them was cancelled because many of the crew were Blacks. The explanation from the growers was that Blacks were not likely to have had experience in that type of work, and that they were too corpulent to be accommodated in bunks designed for Mexican braceros.

Orders of this type were received throughout the summer of 1950. In

June the Brawley local was asked to send 150 melon pickers to Blythe. The union sent word to pickers who had already left the Imperial Valley under pressure from Harrigan's association, relaying the conditions offered, namely, wages of 65 cents per hour and no guarantees of housing. The wage scale in the area in 1949 had been the piece rate of 24 cents per crate. They rejected the offer, proving once again that "domestics simply will not do the hard stoop labor that braceros will accept." Again in July the association filed an order, transmitted by the Farm Placement Office, requesting 4,000 harvesters immediately, at 60 cents an hour, a scale guaranteed to assure refusal. With this groundwork laid Director Bryant was able to inform the Department of Labor in San Francisco of the many failures of the union to produce workers on clearance orders processed by the Farm Placement Service. This way the public officials and growers discredited the union as a reliable source of information on local manpower.

The game continued throughout the 1950s, the union responding to it no longer with the hope of securing work for its members on acceptable terms, but to discover as much as possible about how it worked. Union pressure at different points and times and places revealed some of those details. In the Lawrenson report of 1957, it was substantiated that the farm placement managers were opposed to the registration of local farm laborers. John E. Carr, as Director of the State Department of Employment, resorted to a familiar bureaucratic technique when on April 3, 1959, he stated that "a careful examination of the correspondence file does not disclose any offer of participation in planning by the union."[245] On the date of this reply the union had rounded out eight years of continuous offers to the department to cooperate in preseason registration of local farm workers.

Carr's misrepresentation showed the stonewall confidence of officials who could rest on the assurance of locked files and destroyed memoranda. Director Carr was conforming to an approved model. Previously, on August 21, 1956, Under-Secretary of Labor Arthur Larson had assured a correspondent, "The determination of availability or nonavailability of domestic labor is made after consultation with employers and labor unions who might supply the type of labor requested."[246] As to the employers the statement was abundantly true. As to labor unions it was a falsehood, in violation of Public Law 78, Section 503, paragraph 2, which read: "In carrying out the provisions . . . of this section, provision shall be made for consultation with agricultural employers and workers for the purpose of obtaining facts relevant to the supply of domestic farm workers and the wages paid such workers engaged in similar employment."

On paper, the clearance process relating to orders for farm labor through the Bureau of Employment Security was as neat as an organizational chart. It was compact in structure, resting on the inflated statistics of manpower needs compounded by growers through their associations and reaching its peak in the myth of workers consultation. It could not have been otherwise. Had the clearance system been administered to the ends mandated by law—the stabilization of employment of laborers under the best possible terms—the bracero system would have collapsed. Farm workers were reaching for the rising levels of living and work that the American promise held out to them; the NAWU was their agent in California; to make the clearance process work for them was its aim; to thwart it, the purpose of policy in the industry and in public administration.

Action in the Peach Bowl—1957-1959

As the pressure of bracero contracting became more intense on the domestic harvesters in the southern counties, those who did not retreat into the cities in search of industrial employment moved into the north central agricultural districts with which they had become familiar in the yearly cycle of harvesting. The Peach Bowl was one of these. Once a part of General John Sutter's extensive grants, the alluvial lands along the Feather River had declined as gold diggings and had become one of California's agricultural showpieces. Yuba City was its trading center, from which radiated miles of peach, prune, almond, and pear orchards. They seemed not so much cultivated as manicured, tended by an army of pruners, tillers, sprayers, irrigators, and pickers. Like all the agricultural bowls of California, this one had a touch of the luck of the Nile Valley, for it, too, was laved in turn by sun, Sierra rains, and the sweat of thousands of harvesters who came at high summer from all parts of the West. Here, too, before the coming of the braceros, farm labor families had settled out of the migrant stream in a cluster of towns like Yuba City, Marysville, Olivehurst, Gridley, and Live Oak.

But the braceros had come, and by 1957 they were crowding out the domestics, the old residents as well as those who had taken refuge from the southern districts. Displacement was already producing a drastic change in the labor force, wages were falling, and working conditions were reverting to the labor camp style of life. In the spring of that year braceros were pruning behind orchard gates posted No Help Wanted. Originally brought in only for the harvests, growers had begun to hold them over the winter slack as maintenance workers on canals, equipment, carpentry, and land preparation. A crew of ten seasonal workers who had been referred to Yuba City by the Delano Farm Placement Office was turned away after the long journey. Okies arriving in the area were refused access to the lists of open orders for braceros because the information was confidential. Six years had passed since Public Law 78 had been enacted, time enough for the familiar patterns to develop—a primary force of braceros supplemented by enough illegals to fill in, and a remainder of domestics willing to accept the working conditions, "take it or leave it." During the pear harvest of 1957 William Baird and Harry Mason, just arrived from Oklahoma and referred to the J. L. Sullivan ranch, returned to the Farm Placement Office with the complaint that they had been refused work. The explanation given them was that Sullivan did his hiring in Sacramento.

As peach season neared, the labor pool filled to overflowing forcing the seasonal migrants from the south and from out-of-state to find shelter wherever they could. They huddled on the banks of the Feather River, their bivouacs covered with the dust of trucks passing on the levee roads.[247] The police were less clement than the weather. Patrol cars posted No Trespassing signs and the families moved on, now in double jeopardy as vagrants and as trespassers. They parked cars and trucks under railway bridges for one-night stays, tramping by day from ranch to ranch looking for work. County health regulations were enforced to compel migrants squatting in abandoned shacks to move on. Parking space under trees could be negotiated with contractors who drove a hard bargain for lower wages.

The significance of grower control of the former government labor supply centers now became evident. The Yuba City center, with every shelter occupied by tenants falling in arrears on their rent or paying it out from their savings, was turning away applicants who spread blankets in the camp roadways. Thirty shelters that had not been used since the 1956 flood stood vacant in the camp. Whether to avoid responsibility for these conditions or to reward the management, the federal government transferred it without cost to the Sutter County Housing Authority, including title to the sixty-three acres on which it stood.[248] The farm center in Gridley, one of the most attractively landscaped sites in the state, regularly turned away migrant families.[249] Its fifty-two acres and dilapidated cabins had also been marked for retirement, consummated in the summer of 1959.

Union members, including some who had worked as volunteers in

Imperial and Salinas, were in the area by mid-May and called for assistance. Contacts with the Peach Bowl had not been totally broken off since Hasiwar and I first visited the area in 1950. The now familiar strategy of action research began. It was to be a self-help operation, since the national office of the NAWU had been closing its fiscal years with balances of as little as $1,800. Organizational expenses of the union throughout the nation at that time were hardly twice that much.

Throughout May union workers gathered information from the Woodland, Gridley, Oroville, Yuba City, and Marysville areas on wage rates, bracero employment, location of contractor camps, and sites where destitute migrant families were camping out. The regular participants in planning meetings numbered fewer than twenty members. The objectives of the campaigns were agreed upon: no general strike action, thorough briefing on the provisions of Public Law 78 relating to employment rights of domestics, assignment of one reliable contact in every camp, registration of applicants for picking, reports in writing on all contacts with farm placement personnel, no violence, friendly contacts with braceros and illegals, informal propaganda among local merchants on the basis of data furnished by the union, strict adherence to union instructions, collection of any wage records that could be obtained, and prompt reporting of bracero grievances.

Picketing was avoided. Instead the union directed "investigating teams" to the larger orchards, where they doubled as applicants for work.

Reports by domestics who had been refused work were sworn to in affidavits, sets of which were forwarded to Mitchell for presentation to the Department of Labor and to the governor's office, and for filing in the union's Yuba City office. In these affidavits Rose Jones stated: "I went to the California Farm Placement office every day since August 2, except Sundays. I asked for a job picking peaches but they told me there were no jobs." Affiant Clifton C. Ketchum swore: "On August 17, 1957, I had a lead . . . which was a dehydrator working. I went and asked for a job. They had eight or nine Mexican nationals there. The foreman said he had all the help he wanted." Vicente Cardenas, a man with a large family and many years experience as farm worker, stated: "I have gone to many ranches looking for work . . . I was told I would not get work because they were hiring nationals." Rock Lewis of Arkansas had left his home state after losing his 50-cent-an-hour tractor-driving job to braceros; in Yuba City he had been unable to pick peaches because the braceros had arrived ahead of him. James Roberts and more than fifty other domestics were laid off because braceros were available to finish the picking. By early July the union had more than two hundred authorization cards signed by unemployed pickers who had travelled from Arizona, Texas, Oklahoma, Arkansas, and Nebraska.

Among the applicants were many who carried union cards in other crafts and which they presented as credentials for temporary transfer to the NAWU. For the most part these workers were on seasonal lay-offs from industrial plants. To them harvest labor, if they could find it, was a welcome cushion for unemployment in their crafts. They belonged to such unions as United Mine Workers, Operating Engineers, Carpenters, Packinghouse Workers, Teamsters, Chemical Workers, and United Auto Workers.

The center of union pressure was the Farm Placement Office in Marysville, where bracero certification for the area was concluded. As a competitor with other means for recruiting domestic harvesters it stood lower than farm labor contractors, gate hiring by growers, and the skid row morning shapeup in Sacramento. But for bracero contracting its prerogatives were exclusive. It certified local shortages, determined the prevailing wages by crop activities, and registered the names of bracero users in its jurisdiction. Investigating teams sent by the union were told that information on the location of ranches hiring braceros and related data essential to the operation of the open order policy was confidential. The information, applicants were told, was locked in security files and could be released only on orders from Chief Hayes in Sacramento.

In mid-July the growers began responding to the union activity by defensive publicity and harassing tactics in the orchards. Information was released giving fictitious numbers of domestic workers allegedly busy in the harvest making high wages. Signs were posted outside the ranch gates, so that even entering the premises to ask for a job constituted trespassing. With braceros in plain view, some orchardists saved themselves the annoyance of turning down domestic applicants by hanging out No Help Wanted signs.

It should be emphasized that total displacement of domestics by braceros was never the aim of the associated growers. A minimum amount of token employment of citizen harvesters was important to their strategy. Skilled pickers were needed to set the pace of work. A few fabricated case histories of local workers making fabulous wages did require payrolls of real pickers, although they were poorly paid. The aim was to prove a drastic shortage, not a total absence of domestic labor. But this still left hundreds of harvesters to be disposed of. The method was harassment, practiced by field foremen who knew how to force domestics to walk off the job in disgust. Ladders were made scarce; buckets had to be shared; drinking water was placed in remote corners of the orchard; shifts from one orchard to another were more frequent; married couples were separated to work in different parts of the same orchard; young women were assigned work near bracero crews whose racy conversation was not welcome; box counts by checkers were delayed; children were not permitted to wait at the roadside while their parents worked; domestic pickers were started later and dismissed earlier than braceros; field sorting was required by exacting supervisors with an unusually sharp eye for off-grade or undersized fruit; orchards were muddy from irrgation the night before, making picking impossible; of a family group only the father was hired for the day; the traditional picking into canvas bags slung over the shoulder was replaced by picking into small hand-carried buckets; referrals from the Marysville office were to the more distant orchards; piece rates were leveled down to the bracero prevailing wage in order, as it was said, to avoid discrimination. The encouragement of industrial inefficiency was, by these devices, calculated to produce a disgruntled domestic labor with low productivity and high turnover.

There was another important reason for avoiding total displacement. The strategies of bracero hiring were determined by the largest orchardists, individuals or corporations that operated with hundreds of acres of plantings. The smaller growers were less favored because they contracted fewer men. Servicing them was not as lucrative for the association that acted as broker for all the users in the area. Small growers who needed three or four pickers could more conveniently pick them up in town or hire them at the gate. For these and other economic reasons, relations between small growers and harvesters were likely to be more personal, hence the utility of a marginal pool that remained open to domestics.

It was in Marysville that the empathy between the Farm Placement Service and the growers was most plainly shown. The growers were required to prove that they had engaged in active recruitment of domestic workers before they could be certified for bracero contracting. Proof was arranged in the following manner: In the early hours of picking days men and women stood waiting for a job call on the sidewalk in front of the placement office. Growers in passenger cars and pickup trucks cruised slowly by, singing out "Anybody want to work?" and offering wages at the bracero scale. After several passes with no takers, the recruiters would drive away, frequently with comments like "nothing but winos." This was accepted as active recruitment in full view of the farm placement staff. It documented the shortage of domestics and their unwillingness to accept prevailing work conditions.

The presence of the NAWU added a new element to the peach harvest of 1957 in northern California. Up to that time the bracero system had operated as a combined result of governmental complacency and grower rationalizations. The union set about probing into both. Investigation teams called frequently on Tollefson, the local farm placement manager. When domestic harvesters asked for work there or at ranch gates or in camps they asked knowledgeable questions about Public Law 78. Information on wage levels, housing conditions, market prices, violations of transportation safety regulations, and bracero allocations was disseminated regularly throughout the region by union volunteers. What only the growers association and public officials had known about the bracero system they were now sharing, involuntarily, with a large public of farm workers.

Unlike the labor resistance that growers had overcome traditionally, this one had a disconcerting quality. It was not aimed at production but rather at the political process that screened the braceros in and the domestics out. The Farm Placement Service and the growers sensed this and the collaboration between them tightened. State Director of Employment Stewart repeatedly insisted that the information persistently sought by the investigating teams in Yuba County was classified as confidential under the Unemployment Insurance Act.[250] When Tollefson yielded in some measure and gave out inconclusive figures on bracero employment in Sutter County, his chief, Hayes, publicly upbraided him and threatened him with prosecution for releasing classified information. Instead of referring domestic applicants directly to employers, Tollefson routed such referrals through the association, leaving to others the disagreeable responsibility of separating members of the same crew. At the association office domestic applicants had to promise to work diligently, accepting assignments anywhere in the area, no matter how distant, and stay on the job until picking was completed.

The service also purged its own ranks. Charles Eagan, a dispatcher in the Marysville office, had been heard mildly protesting against the denial of referrals to domestic applicants at a time when there were hundreds of braceros working. Eagan felt that "there was nothing I could do about it" except talk, but that was enough. He was suspended for two months on charges of neglect of duty, insubordination, and discourteous treatment of the public.[251] He had been on duty at the counter of the Marysville office during the critical days of the summer and his unusually candid admission of the charges the union was publicizing was a dangerous breach of Tollefson's security system.

At the height of the harvest it seemed possible to force an official government investigation of union charges made in public meetings and the news media. Up to that time the investigations made by the State Department of Employment and the Bureau of Employment Security had been conducted out of sight of the NAWU. Such had been the case in Imperial and the Salinas Valley. Assisted by a score of volunteer members, I moved to force an open official investigation.

First it was necessary to show the falsity of growers' claims that domestic workers were making exorbitant wages. In union meetings we reviewed the growers' propaganda of bonanza earnings. It was said that a highly skilled domestic picker could earn up to $40 a day on a pay scale of 15 cents per 40-pound box, the standard unit for delivered work. A union bulletin pointed out that this called for an eight-hour production of 266 boxes or one 40-pound lug every two minutes. With ladders in short supply, undersized buckets, time out for stacking boxes, selection of fruit by size and grade, placing and climbing the ladder as part of his time-and-motion requirements, such a picker, if he indeed existed, was not to be found by any of the union's investigating teams. The union leaflet presented this comparison side by side. According to worksheet estimates of the Department of Employment on preseason labor requirements, the average output per man day in peach picking was 1,800 pounds, the equivalent of 45 boxes.

Bulletins of this kind were distributed to every area in which the union maintained communications. The object was to counteract the customary announcements of labor shortages throughout the state, as well as recruitment by labor contractors based on such reports. By the union's estimates there were already enough domestic pickers in Yuba County to harvest the crop, and enough others registered with the various locals to provide additional harvesters if necessary.

It was also time to act on the ever-present problem of unlicensed contractors; there were twelve who had been identified and their camps located. A few unannounced calls by union volunteers sufficed to begin an exodus from the area, disrupting the principal source of illegals and the exchange of rented braceros among growers. At the Half Moon packing shed near Yuba City I paid a midnight call on a licensed contractor who was directing a crew of twenty braceros loading produce on freight cars; I advised him I would initiate charges immediately to revoke his license unless he placed an open order for as many domestics. The contractor broke camp before dawn. He was my cousin.

On another mission I observed a crew of braceros near Woodland who had been transferred to tomato picking through interchange between growers. There were forty men in the field, four of whom were loading. The contractor who was overseeing the operation was immediately approached with an offer to provide the same number of domestic laborers. He refused, saying that he could not pay above the bracero rate of 11 cents a box, that local pickers would not accept such a rate, and that there were not enough boxes for both domestics and braceros. The contractor was harvesting the crop for the Hunt Foods cannery which had bought it from Robert Stevens, the owner and staff assistant to Edward F. Hayes, Chief of the Farm Placement Service in Sacramento. The union inquired there and was told there was no connection; once the crop was sold to the cannery, the owner had no control over the hiring.

It was now the middle of August and time to begin releasing information to the press. Newsmen were invited to visit the area to examine the documentation that had been gathered and to visit the bivouacs of families in out-of-the-way places throughout the area, with union men acting as guides. Stories began to appear in the San Francisco dailies.[252] A committee of local businessmen in Yuba City and Marysville provided information on the condition of retail business in groceries, clothing, taxi services, home furnishings, and other small enterprises that depended on peak income at harvest time. The data showed that in both cities local business was in a state of depression, which the owners attributed to the transfer of wage income from domestics to braceros. The committee filed a statement with the governor's office and invited a public investigation of its complaints.

Since many of the migrant families idled by preferential hiring of braceros were Blacks, the National Association for the Advancement of Colored People was advised of the situation. An NAACP representative toured the Peach Bowl and interviewed families who had come to Yuba from as far away as Los Angeles. On the banks of the Feather River forty of them were cooking in oil cans on rock piles, in the manner of "jungle hobos." In a camp adjacent to an orchard twenty-five Black families were housed in ragged tents with dirt floors. There was one water faucet for all purposes and the toilet was an open ditch located a few yards from the camp. These facts were promptly reported to the NAACP by its own investigators.[253]

Throughout May and June frequent visits were made to the offices of the Northern California Growers Association, headquarters for bracero recruiting and allocation throughout Yuba County. These were informal calls on the staff or the manager, Charles Rhodes, who referred all inquiries to Farm Placement officials in Marysville. Until the premises were posted with No Trespassing signs, union members mingled with the braceros, recording complaints and making notes on the facility. The main unit was a stockade eight feet high; the braceros called it *El Corralon*, "the Big Corral," where they were assembled immediately on arrival from Mexico and where they boarded buses for their return. The corral had few amenities other than a tank of drinking water exposed to the blazing sun. It was also the open-air office of the *Casa de*

Cambio, where paychecks were cashed for a fee. In addition, it was used as a rest home for braceros who were convalescing from injuries or illness, a convenient substitute for medical services the braceros had already paid for through deductible compulsory insurance premiums. The corral had neither seats nor roof. Adjacent to it were the offices of the association, housed in a trim bungalow equipped with air conditioning and other comforts considered necessary for the hot summers of the Peach Bowl.

Like Harrigan's headquarters in Imperial, those of the Northern California Growers Association were the repository of the administrative records of the bracero system in the area. Without access to those records, as DeToqueville would have observed, it would have not been possible to reconstruct the processes by which the system worked. They were confidential, as carefully restricted as the copies that were filed in the locked cabinets of the Farm Placement Office across town. But more than locks and security rules protected the inviolability of these records. Also to be reckoned with was the power of the association's board of directors, which included Bruce Sanborn, a ranking officer of the DiGiorgio Fruit Corporation. His colleagues were the influentials of the region.

In due course Mitchell received a report on *El Corralon* and the association, complete with aerial photographs. The Mexican ambassador was advised. Inquiries were made at the Department of State, the Department of Labor, and the Department of Employment in Sacramento. For further evidence, one night when it was too dark for me to read the No Trespassing signs I removed the scrawled sign of the *Casa de Cambio*; it thereafter hung in the union office.

These preparations completed, Governor Goodwin J. Knight was requested on August 12 to meet with a delegation of NAWU members from Yuba County to receive evidence on the alleged shortage of domestic pickers. From George Meany, president of the AFL-CIO, Mitchell obtained a supporting telegram to the secretary of labor. The governor refused to meet with the pickers. Instead he sent Employment Director Stewart and Chief Hayes to investigate. Regional Director Brockway also visited the area for the Department of Labor.

On August 15 Knight informed the press that Stewart was "unable to find" such situations as had been described by the NAWU.[254] The consensus among all the investigators, state and federal, appeared to be that all was well in the Peach Bowl, since only 1,400 of the pickers out of the 3,000 at work were braceros. The Farm Placement Office in Marysville was broadcasting radio appeals for pickers proving, according to Hayes, that it was energetically on the job. New Pickers Wanted signs were posted at ranch gates. The day haul from Sacramento's skid row was shuttling 300 men each day. Unaware of the Eagan revelations, and refusing to read the union's affidavits, the governor stated categorically that every domestic worker who applied for work in the area was hired.

Determined to discredit the union, Governor Knight again stated on August 19, "Galarza's complaint is entirely without merit."[255] On the twenty-second Hayes's office, covering Knight's position, refused to divulge the figures on bracero recruitment and allocation in the Yuba area, holding Tollefson to strict account for the confidentiality of the records. Conclusively and on the basis of Tollefson's reports, the governor found that on August 30, with the peak of the harvest over, there was still a shortage of workers in the Marysville area.

It was now possible, putting these clues together, to reconstruct how an investigation of the union's findings with regard to the operation of Public Law 78 was conducted.

None of the state or federal officials who converged on Yuba County between August 12 and 15 indicated their presence to the union. None asked for on-the-spot verification of cases the union had documented of violations of the rights of both domestics and braceros. There was an intense exchange of information between the Farm Placement Office and the association, from which the union was excluded. None of the campsites reported by the union were inspected for the good reason that only the union knew their locations, and the governor could not ask union guides to assist his lieutenants. Federal officials made no effort to open Tollefson's files to check the veracity of Knight's denials. The local compliance officer, Lopez, was put to work checking alleged violations without once asking the union for evidence, so Lopez found all complaints uniformly without merit.

An unavoidable weakness of such an investigation was that the investigators could not claim credit for corrections made in response to public criticism. Such was the case with the joint investigation of the peach crisis of 1957. In the last few days of August more domestic pickers were hired, but it was important to avoid crediting the union for it. Some of the levee bivouacs were abolished, but not because sanitary accommodations had been provided for the migrants. The Big Corral was no longer a congestion of braceros waiting in the heat for transportation and the money exchange was abolished; but these disappeared quietly, to avoid raising questions of why they had existed in the first place, and proving the fact that they had.

Repentance in such cases does not indicate spiritual cleansing but rather a practical calculation of how little a system must give in order to remain unchanged. The small concessions made by the growers and public officials were covert and temporary and were based on a realistic assessment of the resources of the NAWU, too inadequate to enable it to hold its ground among resident harvesters in the region. The monitors would go away.

But the NAWU did maintain contact with a handful of members and volunteers in the Peach Bowl during the following two years, with intermittent information and training sessions. On this account it was still able to observe at close quarters the alleged great peach picker shortage of the harvest of 1959.

Applying some of the lessons they had learned in 1957, the associations of growers in northern California—Yuba, Yolo, Sutter, and Sacramento—continued improving on the bracero system. Their major aim was still to bring about a state of public alarm over a threatened labor shortage, the possibility of loss of the crop, and the urgent need for braceros.

In the course of my regular circuit of visits to all the union members north of Kern County I saw the familiar signs.

Early in August 1959 there began a carefully prepared publicity campaign with portents of an economic disaster for the Peach Bowl, with repercussions throughout the state. The harvest stood in grave danger of rotting on the ground unless braceros were imported in sufficient numbers and in good time. A $40,000,000 investment was at stake, 5,000 small farmers were threatened with ruin, and 70,000 cannery workers with idleness, all of whom depended on a crop of 900,000 tons of peaches on 46,000 acres in seven counties, of which the most important was Yuba.

In August 1959 the NAWU was technically still in existence but practically in its last throes. A new AFL-CIO affiliate, the Agricultural Workers Organizing Committee, was now in charge of organizing in the area. I stood by to assist the AWOC, analyzing the labor shortage that was being contrived in the classic manner. This is what I observed.

Hayes's office certified bracero contracts by the thousands for peach picking at 12 cents a box, 3 cents below scale of previous year, in Yolo and Yuba counties. Rejecting such pay, domestic workers left the area or refrained from making long journeys from other parts of the state. On August 14 the regional office of the U.S. Department of Labor obliged by raising the ceiling for bracero contracting for the summer to 37,500. New barracks for braceros were built as old shelters and cabins for domestic workers in the labor government camps were condemned. An official of Hayes's office visited the threatened orchards and was photographed for the media standing ankle deep in rotting peaches. Chartered buses unloaded hundreds of braceros, 4,800 certified on August 26, in addition to the 37,500 already certified. But even this was inadequate, so a committee of growers called on the governor admonishing him to speed up recruitment. Buses sent out by growers to the skid rows of Oakland and Stockton returned ostentatiously empty, there being no takers for peaches at 12 cents a box. Thirty newspaper reporters and editors were flown over the area in chartered planes to see for themselves what havoc recalcitrant, nonexistent domestic harvesters could wreak on California's most valuable fruit crop.

The scenario was too sophisticated and it moved too rapidly for peach consumers in the cities to understand it. On the spot, however, the underlying script was not difficult to read. Domestic pickers were being turned away from orchards; on August 19 over a hundred of them were left standing on the sidewalk after the morning shapeup in front of the Marysville Farm Placement Office. Braceros were in dominant control of jobs, but the blame for the rotting fruit was falling on the domestics.

Some hard facts, however, told another story.

As usual there was a preseason clash between growers and canners as to price and the tonnage to be harvested. The price offered by the canners fell from $65 a ton in 1958 to $50. Seven hundred thousand tons of cling peaches were ripening in the orchards. The growers demanded that at least 600,000 tons of them be bought by the processors, who countered with a figure of 532,000 tons. An agreement was reached for delivery of not more than 565,000 tons, leaving an expendable surplus of 135,000 tons.

To prevent the depression of market prices the surplus was disposed of by two methods—the "green drop" and diversion. The green drop meant that a specified percentage of bearing trees was not picked at all, the fruit being allowed to fall and rot on the ground. The remaining tonnage was still too large to stabilize prices at the agreed level, so 71,000 tons valued at three million dollars were diverted at the canneries for disposal as brandy, hog feed, public charity, and sewage. Peach production, like many other California crops, was regulated under a marketing order administered by a board of grower and canner representatives.

The green drop had nothing to do with the labor supply. But it provided a dramatic setting for the public relations of the system. A public inclined to regard the loss of edible fruits and vegetables as a calamity could find no fault with the massive hiring of alien labor to save the crop once it was officially certified that domestic pickers were not available. Unavailability could be guaranteed by simply lowering wages below the point of acceptance by domestics, whereupon the lower wage scale was set for braceros, who, according to the law, were guaranteed the same wages offered to citizen harvesters. To complete the delusion, at this point the cameras could again be focused on peaches rotting in the orchards. A touch of authenticity was added by farm placement officials who traveled from Sacramento to be photographed standing amidst the desolation of the green drop. Public relations had never before come so close to genuine rot.

To the south of Yuba the Peach Bowl levels imperceptibility into the Central Valley in San Joaquin and Stanislaus counties, also important peach producing areas. Unavoidably union activity during the summer of 1959 was extended in that direction, in the course of which I became acquainted with William Renner, compliance officer of the U.S. Department of Labor.

The Limits of Enforcement

Public Law 78, like all law that fixes rules and norms for social relationships, required continuous monitoring, powers of enforcement, performance control, and oversight. To these tasks there was assigned specialized personnel called compliance officers. They were the civil police of the bracero system, reporting directly to the regional director of the Bureau of Employment Security in San Francisco.

The enforcers of Public Law 78 and of the individual work contracts issued to braceros operated under the usual restraints of regulatory government. Their number was small, relative to the size of the territory to be covered and the number of braceros supervised. For the whole state there were probably not more than a dozen on duty in the fields at any given time. One officer was responsible for the entire Imperial Valley, another for Salinas, another for Santa Clara. Not being provided with secretaries, they spent much of their time receiving, reviewing, filing, and forwarding such documents as "manifests" of arriving workers, prevailing wage findings, and determinations of need. At one time they had been called Employee Service Representatives, but this had a ring of inconsistency with the duty of protecting the braceros from violations of their contracts. The title was changed.

In their day-to-day operations these officers roved in and out of the sensitive jurisdictions of local farm placement staff, managers of growers associations, Mexican consuls, the Immigration Service police, as well as the shadowy domain of labor contractors. Rarely did the economic interests or the bureaucratic claims or the prestige demands of these establishments regard themselves as supportive of the law. More often they represented cross currents through which compliance had to navigate.

It was in the interest of the associations to soften enforcement without resisting it outright. The compliance apparatus was, in fact, an asset to the industry. It was pointed to as proof that growers were under the strict supervision of a corps of dedicated agents who were ultimately answerable to the Secretary of Labor himself. For the compliance officer in the fields, the realities more closely resembled those of the policeman on his beat in any American city. As justice could be flavored with compassion, so enforcement could be tempered with permissiveness. Few enforcers could fail to be influenced over the long run by their daily contacts with association managers, behind whom there stood the organized power of the leading farmers of the district.

In one important respect the lot of the compliance officers was an odd one. Their immediate wards were thousands of individual braceros totally incapable of forming a constituency. For support the field officer had to rely entirely on his superiors within the departmental bureaucracy. Politically considered, his leverage outside the bureaucracy was nil. Protecting a bracero was, from this point of view, an act of piety, for which the only thanks was likely to be the ritualistic thanks of the Mexican worker: *"Que Dios se lo pague,"* May God reward you.

In some of the compliance areas enforcement was notably soft. In Yuba the local officer, Lopez, was never able to discover a single violation, even though the proof was at his disposal at the union office. In Imperial union complaints on behalf of braceros were investigated privately by the compliance representative, the grower, and the association. If the officer took notice of the union it was principally to report its activities to his superiors. In Salinas the enforcers stirred only when prodded by union complaints.

William Renner, compliance officer for Stanislaus and San Joaquin counties, was of a different stamp, proving to be a strict constructionist in line of duty. He went about it almost with zest, appearing unexpectedly wherever braceros were working and living. He had the use of a desk in the local Farm Placement Office where he could watch and be watched. Like all employees of his rank, he had access to the records of the San Joaquin Growers Association whose headquarters in Stockton were the staging point and control center of bracero distribution in the heart of the Central Valley. Here Renner was empowered to examine the most sensitive documents of all, the payroll records of the association members.

To all appearances, he represented the authority of the federal government in sustaining the mandates of Public Law 78 as well as the articles of the international agreement with Mexico. He had entree to the administrative precincts of the two institutions through which economic power and administrative authority was applied, the association and the Farm Placement Service. His vicissitudes soon showed that strict enforcement was disapproved of by the regional officers of the Department of Labor, his immediate superiors.

On October 8, 1957, Renner reported a visit to a camp of 370 braceros where he found garbage exposed, unsanitary drainage, and scattered rubbish so menacing to the health of the occupants that he recommended closing the camp until corrections were made. Technically, this was also the province of the inspectors of the California Health and Industrial Relations authorities, so in a sense Renner was stepping into another jurisdiction. A few weeks before, he had appeared at another camp with the Mexican consul from Fresno, pointing out violations with which that official had no opportunity to be familiar. Another report filed by Renner in San Francisco described how he had found 5 braceros in a packing shed in Tracy working for a well-known labor contractor at substandard wages and in unauthorized activities, such as handling trucks and sorting.

Over a period of months Renner's account of his activities to his superiors included payroll falsifications, hours worked but not reported, unauthorized exchanges of bracero crews among growers, wages set arbitrarily without determination of the prevailing rates, incomplete accounting to the braceros of wages due, overcharges for meals, exorbitant charges for busing to nearby towns, assignment of braceros as irrigators and other unauthorized operations, filthy and overcrowded camps, and braceros working after their contracts had expired.

On his inspection tours Renner did not hesitate to report labor contractors who were hiring illegals in mixed crews with braceros, a practice solemnly and frequently forbidden by the Department of Labor. In Renner's territory the traffic in wetbacks provided hundreds of such workers as a standby reserve to the bracero force. Some contractors were admitted to membership in the association, for which they acted as a buffer against the risks of surprise by the Immigration Service. Renner's denunciations of contractor practices were a firsthand account of how expertly the black market in brown harvesters dovetailed with the legalized exploitation of braceros.

It was in this connection that Renner incurred the displeasure of A. R. Duarte, the manager of the association. Renner had called upon a camp operated by Duarte's brother, and had found multiple violations. Braceros were not being provided with receipts for piecework. Their identification documents had been impounded. In an unusual signed statement, the men also complained of rough treatment and of short work days which left many with barely enough earnings to pay for meals.

Renner's address to his job and his candid reporting was, to say the least, unconventional. The conditions he was reciting were common throughout California, but noticing them and reporting them to higher levels were not. Each incident was like a thread in a rotten fabric which, if pulled too hard, might begin unraveling it. The threads led in many directions; to the widespread and illegal operation of contractors within the bracero system; to the partnership of reputable growers in camp ownership and management where braceros and illegals were housed under notoriously substandard conditions; to the setting of bracero wages by the association with *post hoc* approval by FPS Chief Hayes; and to the lucrative concessions for feeding and insuring braceros. There appeared to be only one compliance record like Renner's in the entire state, both unique and unwelcome to his superiors.

Renner's castigation began with charges by Duarte that Renner had falsely accused both his brother and him of unauthorized exchange of braceros. Renner was promptly banished from the association office amid personal abuse. That was on December 18, 1957.

A prominent vineyardist who had been adversely noticed in Renner's reports publicly denounced him as a communist. He was accused of having unfriendly relations with the Mexican consul. On the morning of December 23 while Renner was absent from his desk in the Modesto Farm Placement Office, on orders from Regional Director Brockway his official and personal papers were removed and sent to San Francisco.

The confiscation of the file was the culmination of disciplinary action that had started the previous May. It began with a guarded admonition to Renner from the regional Office: "We trust . . . [we] may be helpful to you in getting the whole picture of the program, rather than attempting to change it on the basis of individual cases as you may find them . . . Your actions should be tempered in such a way as to secure a better understanding between you and the growers." It was signed by A. J. Morton. Brockway's assistant.[256]

Since this came from the highest level of authority in the state, it may be taken as a statement of the enforcement philosophy of the U.S. Department of Labor which it expected all compliance officers to adhere to. Renner persisted in not doing so, he received another reprimand, dated December 18, concerning his "weakness." Renner was advised that he had been "unable to maintain and carry on satisfactory relations with the state officials and members of the public" and that he had failed to take corrective actions.[257] The references were unspecific but unmistakable. The state officials were those in command of farm labor affairs in the Department of Employment. The public was obviously the growers, contractors, and executives of the associations.

On December 20 Renner received a telegram from Brockway notifying him that as of December 23 he would be reported in annual leave status until officially notified by headquarters, pending personnel action. Renner had not applied for leave. He was dismissed on January 3, 1958. Robert C. Goodwin, who had authorized the December 18 reprimand, denied Renner's appeal of January 14, "I have carefully reviewed the records," wrote Goodwin. "Review has confirmed my belief that your separation was appropriate."[258] Renner was thirty days short of completing his probational period and qualifying for tenure.

Personally Renner did not have heroic pretensions. He went about his affairs with a simple stubbornness and a literal understanding that he was assigned to protect braceros from violation of their legal rights. To personal harassment he was able to respond. He sued his defamer and collected from him a settlement out of court. He had no trouble obtaining testimonials from the Mexican consul and employers as to the rightness of his official conduct. These credentials, however, carried no weight with Goodwin; the documents for his defense, had he been permitted one, were in Brockway's possession.

Renner returned to his home in Mexico with his family, leaving with me such papers as he kept at home and the communications that ended his career with the U.S. Department of Labor. Among these documents were copies of the minutes of Brockway's kitchen cabinet of grower advisors, the RFLOAC.

In the Valley of Heart's Delight —1958-1959

The history of domestic harvesters in California from 1952 to 1959 was not one of union organization but of relocation under the sustained pressure of the bracero system. Those who felt it most drastically were the Mexican *locales,* the most numerous ethnic sector of the farm labor force. The Filipinos remained a small, culturally compact enclave in rural society, with urban ties that were renewed during the winter lull in the fields. The Blacks accepted farm work mainly as a step toward jobs in the coastal cities, from which many returned to the farms during periods of unemployment. The Mexicans, because of their earlier appearance on the scene in large numbers, the availability of marginal land on which to settle, and their gravitation to stable *colonias* and rural *barrios*, became the chief objects of social de-stabilization. In their case what gave way was not only their place in the labor market and a standard of living one level above migrancy, but also a social fabric of familial and cultural relations that had remained typically Mexican.

Unlike the relocation of the Japanese during World War II, that of the Mexicans was prosaic. Families abandoned their old homes one by one, straggling northward in search of a new base. Through relatives or former employers or their own experience as seasonal travellers on the harvest circuit they sought, not to regroup again in communities, but in individual havens where work would be more plentiful than braceros. The West was still being conquered, no longer by military but by economic weapons, whose object was to remove those who stood in the way.

Following the sweep of the Imperial Valley beginning in 1950, a decade of silent evacuations of hundreds of families continued. Many turned to the Santa Clara Valley, where they had picked prunes, strawberries, beans, tomatoes, or apricots. As in their earlier migrations, they followed the cues of kinship and culture and occupation in towns and cities like San Jose, Gilroy, Hollister, Alviso, Sunnyvale, Mountain View, and Cupertino. These were not yet the magnets of industrial and financial growth and ubanism that they later became. There were still thousands of acres in orchards and vegetable farms that each spring carpeted the valley with blossoms from wall to wall of the surrounding hills. It was the Valley of Heart's Delight.

Santa Clara in the 1950s was becoming the spillway for population shifts southward from San Francisco and Oakland but there was a decade or more of farm work to be had. In search of it there came former crew leaders from Brawley, veteran irrigators from Blythe and Palos Verdes, pickers from Yuma and citrus workers from Santa Barbara. At first many of these neo-migrants thought of returning to their old homes, and tried it for a season or two; but the conditions that had forced them out had not changed and they had to take their chances for a new life in the Santa Clara Valley.

What they found was that the braceros were moving in also, contracted principally by the Progressive Growers Association, with headquarters in San Jose. They were appearing in the pear orchards around Hollister, the strawberry patches of Morgan Hill, the bean fields of Coyote and Milpitas, and the garlic spreads of Gilroy. Bracero specials even appeared as crew leaders, tractor drivers, and fruit packers in the sheds at the prevailing wage rate for field hands. The bracero crews were also slowly driving out the day-haul veterans from the Bay cities and the Texas regulars who came each year for the prune harvest.

Working and living conditions began to reflect this new state of affairs. Scenes like this one became common: One morning in the summer of 1958 domestic families—men, women, and children—were topping garlic sitting or squatting around the white heaps. Braceros were working among them, the advance crew of more who would follow later. That garlic toppers were having difficulties in finding shelter for the duration of the season was another omen. I visited these families in the following days and found them sleeping under the trees along the Pajaro River. One family had been given permission to occupy a white-washed chicken house behind a barn on condition that the family remain for fruit picking. Braceros were taking over the camps in the pear orchards of Alviso, and special facilities were set aside for them near Hollister and Gilroy.

The NAWU enlisted enough resettled members and old residents to organize two locals, one in Hollister and the other in San Jose. Their number fluctuated between twenty and thirty but the core of some twelve was sufficient to keep information flowing to and from the union throughout the Valley.

No union halls were set up, there being no funds for them. Instead the union assigned neighborhood stewards to collect dues, report grievances, contact arriving families, talk with braceros, and generally make it known that the union was present. During the winter I held meetings in the homes of members, seminars that turned into strategy committees for whatever action was indispensable during the work season. In these meetings I worked with maps, slides, and copies of documents such as bracero contracts and Farm Placement bulletins, relating them to the daily experiences the workers knew so much better than I and to the unseen workings of the system I knew so much better than they. I insisted that actions by the union be limited to the meager resources of manpower and funds to which it had been reduced. The benefits to these workers were immediate and visible, and they made it possible to observe the bracero system in the Santa Clara Valley.

During the pear harvest of 1959 a one-day stoppage was coordinated that promptly averted a wage cut. I appeared at the gates of a packing shed near Hollister where braceros had been assigned to take the place of the *locales*. The braceros were moved out. Teams of union volunteers monitored the country side, finding shelter for families found sleeping outdoors, one of them behind a screen of bushes in a cemetery near San Jose. In May 1959 I filed charges against a strawberry grower who had falsified the payroll records of nine braceros, replacement for domestics, with the result that the grower agreed to re-employ domestics. Our field research went into details, such as instructing braceros to find and deliver to me the fragments of duplicate punch cards they were entitled to receive at the end of each work day. Careless foremen tore them in the presence of the men, compelling them to accept estimates of the weekly work delivered instead of the units indicated on the cards.

The many ways in which information was gathered depended on surprising turns of events, and the twists of harassment of domestics continuously applied by growers and labor contractors. The Hollister local, by merely inquiring into the facts, prevented the substitution of small buckets for larger ones in pear picking, a device intended to discourage domestic pickers, provoking them to quit and thus create the shortage of manpower necessary to obtain a certification for braceros. Union men did not simply walk off the job in anger; they reported to the union and asked for help. Resistance to psychological degradation was part of the task. Such an issue was raised when a grower required that as a condition of employment domestics work at piece rates until they learned to pick properly, even though they were veteran harvesters.

The techniques of creating local labor shortages and undermining morale were by now standard operating practice among growers throughout the state, but it was necessary to discover whether they were being applied in Santa Clara, too.

They were. Pickers who appeared in work shoes or sandals were told that safety regulations now required that they wear leather boots. No such requirement was ever applied for braceros. Bean pickers accustomed to a daily pay-off were notified that wages would be paid only on Saturdays. The paymaster might arrive late in the afternoon; buses would depart from a pickup spot as much as an hour early; or the pickup point would change without notice. Domestic crews were assigned to clean up after braceros had gone over the field. Shortages of scissors suddenly developed on onion and garlic topping jobs, or the harvesters had to bring their own. With domestic bean pickers the procedure had been to move the sorting tables about as the picking progressed, to shorten the distance in carrying the full hampers and speed the work; with the coming of braceros, the tables remained stationary until the domestics walked off.

One of the most urgent calls for help that I received came after the union had gone out of existence. In August 1960 the Mexican consul in San Francisco broadcast over a San Jose radio station a message to braceros who had been complaining of short hours and low wages. Telling the braceros not to be discouraged by low pay, the consul referred to domestic workers, themselves Mexicans, as ne'er-do-wells (*malivivientes*) who buy a bottle of wine and then disappear. A letter-writing campaign was organized throughout the Valley, including one from me to the consul, of which several hundred copies were distributed out of Hollister and San Jose. The Mexican consul went off the air, and union members advised that they would deal with any public appearance of the consul. Had he come forward, he was to have been met with bottles of wine, empty ones.

The principal assignment of the union was, however, to monitor the Progressive Growers Association, a typical nonprofit corporation which negotiated for and represented the growers of Santa Clara. Association members were operators like garlic king Joseph Gubser, D'Arrigo Brothers, and Driscoll Strawberry Farms.

Of all the farm production areas in the state, the Santa Clara Valley was the least likely to suffer shortages of domestic harvesters. The process of displacement in the southern counties and the Central Valley deposited newcomers around the established *colonias* of Hollister, Gilroy, Morgan Hill, Sunnyvale, Decoto, and Union City. For most of them moving to these locations was an intermediate step out of agricultural employment. The Valley was an important fruit and vegetable processing center that provided jobs for thousands of cannery workers. Employment in a cannery gave access to the labor market of light manufacturing and the rapidly growing electronics industry. For the younger farm workers who had been forced out elsewhere this was the way up and off the agricultural ladder; but there were many for whom farm work remained the only available occupation, and these workers, discarded by the industry in areas that had been overrun by braceros, increased the local supply of experienced labor. As they resettled, however, they found that the only housing available to them was in refurbished barns, improved chicken houses, and remodeled sheds in the countryside and the marginal dwellings of growing *barrios* like East San Jose. Scattered over the spreading industrial landscape of the Santa Clara Valley they presented a special problem for the Farm Placement Service to locate and coordinate their recruitment. Less visible than ever, though more numerous, they remained marginal men, second-rate factors in farm production. As a class these rural Mexican families illustrated the process of social dumping into urban clots of poverty. In reshaping the demography of the state agri-business could thus transfer social costs of dislocation to city taxpayers.

The task of the NAWU in Santa Clara was changed by these conditions; it consisted principally of helping members to maintain their status as farm workers as far as possible. Here the orthodox guidelines of trade unionism had to be abandoned. There were a hundred men and women in the Santa Clara union, most of them nonpaying volunteers, a number too small to influence the yearly increments of families withdrawing to Santa Clara. The resident farm labor force was also overshadowed by the day-haul crews out of the Bay area skid rows and tenement neighborhoods, swamped by the summer migration of pickers from south Texas, and undercut by hundreds of braceros certified to the Progressive Growers Association.

Like its peers in other districts of California, the PGA represented an alignment of the wealthiest growers, those who had the most to gain from low wage rates and unregulated working conditions. They allowed the middling and small grower to participate in these benefits, creating a common interest and cohesion that was the basis of their political leverage on the State Department of Employment. It was they who certified the labor shortages in the first place.

The immunities of the association were shown in a number of ways. In 1959, for example, the local Farm Placement office had found a prevailing wage of $1.00 for pear picking, but PGA members continued to pay 90 cents an hour. The NAWU advised both domestics and bracero harvesters that they were entitled to higher pay, but the lower wage scale of the 1958 crops was maintained by some growers. It was not until June 1959 that the $1.00 scale was grudgingly accepted. The PGA was equally cooperative with strawberry growers for whom it contracted braceros. In May 1958 they were permitted, in consultation with the Bureau of Employment Security and the Department of Employment, to set their own sliding schedule of piece rates. Adjustments on the scale were to be made by the employers to meet the minimum requirements for daily earning of braceros and to prevent excessive earnings when the picking was heavy.[259]

Because it spoke on behalf of nine hundred grower members, the association did not hesitate to challenge the authority of federal and state agencies. This did not occur very often and was mainly over sensitive matters such as the examination of payroll records. Here a subtle element in farm labor politics could be discerned. Permissiveness by the State Department of Employment was held in check by the risk of disclosure, for which only the department could be held to account. And the risk of disclosure ran highest where the NAWU was if not active at least present.

This was the case in the Santa Clara Valley.

Through the union, complaints of domestics and braceros were filed in late August 1959 against a labor contractor who was a member of the association. The fact of such membership was itself a violation of federal regulations, but the point of the grievance was the systematic short weighing by the contractor's checkers. The forwarding of the complaint was slow, reaching the stage of field investigation by late October, by which time, the compliance officer reported, the harvest was over.

The association still had to deal with union members who applied for work and asked pointed questions over the counter at its offices in San Jose. For these applicants it developed techniques then current throughout the state. Some applicants were referred to growers who subjected them to harassment until they left the job. They were then reported as "hired and fired" with such explanations as would make them appear unreliable, incompetent, unstable, or cantankerous. These reports became part of a dossier that was forwarded to Hayes's office. But the harassment began at the counter itself when applicants were handed a questionnaire: "Have you ever been on welfare? Are you an agricultural worker? Are you now drawing unemployment insurance? Will you scatter trash and cans around the farm? How long do you intend to work? Do you know a worker can be arrested for taking tools or anything else that does not belong to him?"

My home in San Jose was under surveillance from outside by strangers escorted by association personnel, and inside by an attractive young woman posing as a newspaper reporter, who gained entry by asking me for an interview. Her only qualification for the undercover assignment was her striking good looks—I had to assist her to ask the right questions. She reported back that I was living in splendor on the dues of union members.

On October 16 I was cruising the Valley for bracero crews to locate ranches where union members could apply to the association for work under the open order rule. On a country lane a few miles from San Jose I noticed a painter at work on a neat cottage. There were several points of interest about the quiet scene, set back from the road in the shade of a row of arching elms. The painter was obviously a Mexican. He wore the typical clothing of a farm worker, not that of a professional craftsman. Nearby was a supervisor who was directing the work. At the curb there was a pickup truck such as those in which ranch foremen run about. There were farm tools in the truck. A short distance down the road I had just observed a large crew of braceros in a field I knew was operated by the D'Arrigo Company.

A second pass around the neighborhood enlivened my first suspicion that the painter was a bracero and that he probably belonged to the D'Arrigo crew. Acting on the hunch I went to a public telephone and called the compliance officer in San Jose. He appeared promptly and proceeded to interview the two men as I watched from a distance. In the seemingly trivial incident, the essence of the enforcement of PL 78 was being enacted. The compliance officer took notes as the two men answered his questions. The painter and his supervisor drove to the D'Arrigo field at a smart speed, and the compliance officer drove back to his office to record the incident. I proceeded immediately to file charges.

The complaint was submitted on October 16, 1959. The investigation went forward with unusual promptness, developing the facts that the painter, Luis M. Alvarez, was a bracero certified to the Progressive Growers Association and assigned to the D'Arrigo company under contract number L-3188588. On October 14, 15, and 16 he had worked at the house a total of fourteen hours scrubbing floors and painting. The payroll record had been falsified to show that he had worked as an irrigator at a wage of one dollar an hour. The supervisor, the occupant of the house, was a foreman for D'Arrigo. The NAWU specified four violations of the international agreement and demanded immediate withdrawal of the entire bracero crew of 137 men.

Floyd Behringer, the manager of the association by now had sufficient respect for the union not to attempt braving the uncomfortable situation. The NAWU had on file other charges of payroll falsification against members of the association. Behringer could not explain why braceros brought to Santa Clara to relieve a labor shortage were complaining of short work days or were being loaned for occasional moonlighting to fill time. He had withdrawn the notorious questionnaires after copies were circulated by the union. More and more braceros were bringing their complaints to the union on all manner of breaches of contract—unsanitary camps, incomplete pay records, impounding of identification documents, insurance overcharges, and physical abuse.

By the end of 1959 matters had reached the point where the NAWU was openly attacking the credibility of the state and federal regulators. In dealing with the D'Arrigo matter they chose a prudent course. Brockway, the federal strategist in these affairs, permitted the association itself to order the withdrawal of the D'Arrigo crew, proving that it was diligently carrying out federal policy of encouraging self-policing by employers. By this means also the several hundred members of the association were saved the loss of braceros they would have suffered had the association itself been held guilty of the violation. A confession was obtained from the foreman to the effect that there had been a misunderstanding and it was all his fault. Federal or state officials drew no conclusion from D'Arrigo's being able on 24-hour notice to replace its lost braceros with domestic workers hastily recruited in Santa Clara and Salinas, another area that had been certified as acutely short of local harvesters. D'Arrigo was then absolved by the association on the plea that the violation had been committed by a supervisory employee after repeated warnings from management. The incident itself was called a "misassignment"[260] and on these grounds the association asked for clemency on D'Arrigo's behalf.[261] The company, it was argued, had already been sufficiently punished by having to fall back on domestic workers to finish the harvest. In agri-business circles this was jokingly called "a fate worse than death."

Clemency was granted. Brockway accepted the resolution of the PGA board of directors to set aside any action pending against D'Arrigo. In a letter to the board dated November 4, Brockway pointedly said that his agency had not ordered the withdrawal of the bracero crew. On December 8 he assured the association in writing that no further action would be taken against the company, leaving it in good standing to hire braceros in the future.

The analysis of one particular case did not, of course, prove the corruption of the entire system. How many cases it would take to do so could be argued by statisticians. In any event, as Renner had been advised, what mattered was "the whole picture," not isolated examples.

But when the NAWU did turn its attention to the whole picture the result was as objectionable to growers and bureaucrats as a case study. The response was not clemency but an attempt at censorship. It arose in connection with the publication of *Strangers in Our Fields*.

The Affair of "Strangers in Our Fields"

Three years of intensive observation of the bracero system had been completed by the end of 1955, but the field notes up to that time related to conditions mainly in the border counties. It was time to survey its effects throughout the state to determine how far north and to what extent it was spreading. At that time the NAWU was so weak financially it was a question whether it would be forced to abandon California entirely. Mitchell obtained funds which enabled me to proceed with the survey. Several purposes were to be served, other than to determine to what extent the bracero system was becoming entrenched. The information in hand was to be brought up to date, based on interviews with braceros, published and distributed throughout the country. Presented with the experiences of the braceros in their own language, it was possible that the growers and government agencies would elect to challenge the material and thus bring the issue into the open.

I began this assignment in the summer of 1955 and assisted by union volunteers and correspondents located the major centers of bracero employment. Nearly 350 useful interviews were held in the camps from the Mexican border to Yuba City. The conversations were informal and usually took place in out-of-the-way places where camp bosses or police were least likely to interfere. Some of the camps were not guarded at night and in these the interviews became group exchanges of information. The men willingly produced work records, check stubs, copies of contracts, and any other documentation I asked for. I introduced myself formally as a union organizer (*representante del Sindicato Nacional de Trabajadores Agricolas*) and stated the object of my assignment: to let the American people know *como la están pasando*, "how they were getting along."

Mitchell arranged for the publication of the pamphlet *Strangers in Our Fields* under the auspices of the United States section of the Joint United States–Mexico Trade Union Committee affiliated with the International Confederation of Free Trade Unions. In the United States the Joint Committee was endorsed by the United Automobile Workers, United Mine Workers of America, the Railway Brotherhoods, and the AFL-CIO.

The report appeared in the spring of 1956 in an edition of ten thousand copies, addressing the subject, as the title page indicated, of "compliance with the contractual, legal, and civil rights of Mexican agricultural contract labor in the United States." The interviews were arranged into topical chapters dealing briefly with the most common concerns of the braceros—food, housing, transportation, wages, insurance, employer relations, medical attention, and contract enforcement. The pamphlet was illustrated with photographs taken on the spot and the eighty-page text had an introduction by Frank L. Noakes, chairman of the Joint Committee.

Insofar as translation permitted, the views of the braceros were reported in their own straightforward language. Some excerpts follow:

—　　"I worked four weeks in the pea picking. The best pickers made three or four baskets a day. We were paying $1.75 a day for the board. I made so little I owed the camp restaurants $5.00 at the end of the month.''

—   "We are installed in a barn occupied by the cows when we moved in.''

—   "Windows do not have screens. Mosquitos from the river possess themselves of the dormitory. You can get a little sleep when the mosquitos get tired of singing.''

—   "There was not enough work for everybody. That's the way it passes since we came. You work one day and the other no.''

—   "About twenty men in one bunkhouse were sick to the stomach from rancid beans. Some of the men got pills and some got strong purges. Some had to miss two or three days of work. They were charged for the meals for that time.''

—   "You hear everywhere that they will send us back to Mexico if we are not content with the situation.''

—   "The other day a motorcycle policeman stopped our truck and told the driver to put some seats in. The driver had to show his license. He said he would tell the patron to do it. But all he does now is go by a different road. He says it does not pay to put seats in because the picking is nearly over.''

—   "The contractor changes the wage without notifying us of the reason. One day we pick tomatoes by the box and the next day we pick by the hour. We don't know how much we pick by the hour or how much we pick by the box until we get our checks after fifteen days.''

—   "We noticed that the workers who complain get less work. They are transferred to the extra gang. This gang he says is for the loafers and the strikers.''

—   "The consul only talks with the contractor. He calls him on the telephone. The telephone is in the contractor's saloon near the camp. Among the people there is not one who knows how to use the American telephones. It does not make sense that the contractor would show us how to use his telephone so we could talk with the consul ourselves.''

—   "We named a commission of several men to speak to the company about the food and the shortage of work. But we had to break up the commission because there was a threat that we would be sent back to Mexico.''

My own conclusion drawn from the interviews was that in almost every area covered by the International Agreement, United States law, state law, and the provisions of the work contract, serious violations of the rights of Mexican nationals were found to be the norm rather than the exception.

Strangers provoked an extraordinary response from officials of growers associations, industry spokesmen, sympathetic politicians, academic watchdogs, and government agencies. But all this occurred behind the scenes and not until years later was it possible to discover the intensity of the reaction to the pamphlet. The intelligence network that reached every level of agri-business sounded with alarm and indignation.

On September 17, 1956, the State Board of Agriculture adopted a resolution addressed to Secretary of Labor Mitchell asking that "a well documented analysis and careful appraisal" be made of *Strangers*.[262] Copies based on this resolution with comments were distributed to newspapers and magazines. The *Bataan News*, a Filipino publication with grower connections passed it along to its readers. It said that *Strangers* contained both derogatory statements of Mexican nationals which had been proved contrary to fact and unfounded charges that the U.S. Department of Labor and the State Department of Employment were not properly fulfilling their obligations; these were damaging to successful cooperation between two friendly nations and a disservice to the cause of organized labor.[263]

The Associated Farmers renewed its attacks on the NAWU which President Charles S. Gibbs said "first showed its ugly head . . . at the DiGiorgio Corporation farm at Arvin!" Gibbs undertook to provide "some additional data so that you may have a complete history on Mr. Galarza and his activities."[264]

This history was provided by Regional Director Brockway, who instructed Hayes to prepare answers to the pamphlet. Brockway in turn received instructions from the Regional Foreign Labor Operations Advisory Committee composed exclusively of industry leaders and association representatives, among them a prominent procurer of braceros, J. J. Miller. On September 6, 1956, Hayes and Brockway met with Robert C. Goodwin, Brockway's superior, in Los Angeles to discuss the strategy of the rebuttal. At this meeting grower representatives were present. Farm Placement offices throughout the state were provided with copies of *Strangers* and instructed to gather responses from association managers and individual growers. A company that carried a large part of the health insurance of braceros was asked to cooperate. Hayes solicited documents from the files of the D'Arrigo company in San Jose and personally investigated suspected contacts between myself and the local FPS staff.

This mobilization of personnel and resources showed how sensitive the ubiquitous and diligent agri-business was in and out of government. The aim, Miller told Brockway, was to set the record straight on *Strangers*.[265] Hayes, in a deposition taken in another connection, declared: "Sure, I had it investigated. I had the documents proving the falsehoods and lies in it. . . . My office prepared the rebuttal."[266]

The materials collected by Hayes and his collaborators were assembled and filed with Brockway's office and from them a lengthy answer was prepared. Mimeographed copies were distributed throughout the network. These included the members of the State Board of Agriculture, Brockway's shadow cabinet of growers, Hayes's staff, congressmen, the Secretary of Labor, and the growers associations. It was a point-by-point denial of those parts of *Strangers* that were considered to be the most damaging and likely, in the words of deponent Hayes, "to destroy California farms."

The Associated Farmers organization was active in distributing the rebuttal. A copy was sent to Congressman Gubser, who found my report "a very biased and inaccurate pamphlet." In a flank approach to the subject, Gubser reviewed the files of the House Unamerican Activities Committee concerning Galarza, noting with regret that they "failed to show that he is disloyal."[267] It was the file that contained the results of the DiGiorgio strike investigation in 1949.

Gubser received from Brockway a copy of the rebuttal, which he passed on to the Reverend James A. King, S. J., Dean of the College of Arts and Sciences of Santa Clara University. The dean was not impressed by Gubser's comment as to possible disloyalty. Writing to Gubser on October 14, 1957, the Reverend King found my report "an additional argument that union agencies in the United States need national curbs to prevent them, among other things, from making irresponsible and subversive attacks on established society." The rebuttal itself did not impress the Dean either in the area of the arts or of the sciences. "What we really need," he wrote, "is a happy presentation written by a person with imagination and style of the opportunity presently furnished by California farm owners to the underfed and underpaid Mexican nationals who, to alleviate the hardships and sufferings which he and his family must endure under the socialistic Mexican government, come to California for a brief surcease."[268] The dean at the moment of penning these thoughts was in happy and imaginative company. He wrote Charles E. Gibbs on November 22, "Your letters arrived at the very time that Mr. Steve D'Arrigo was sitting across from me at my desk discussing the very people referred to in your letter."[269]

Not all of the activity was taking place in academic and political circles in California. BES Director Goodwin submitted a copy of the rebuttal to Noakes. The pamphlet, he wrote, was "a purposeful and misleading attempt to highlight in an unfair and misleading manner [particular cases] shrouded in anonymity and generality." It appeared to be Goodwin's criticism of both the case history approach and the whole picture. "We can expect," he wrote, "abuses by some individuals who will seek to cut corners," adding that "we have made important strides forward."[270]

Such a claim, itself shrouded in anonymity and generality, was of course the ultimate response in a prolonged cover-up of what was happening to braceros and domestics under Public Law 78. It dismissed the risky tests of due process—weighing of evidence, taking testimony under oath, confronting of witnesses including the members of the RFLOAC and other confidential advisories, summoning the braceros themselves, and verifying charges about payrolls and insurance deductions by an audit. In *Strangers* I had made statements that were denounced as scandalous, libelous, misleading, and false by the critics of the pamphlet. Proof of these charges would have been established only through a lawsuit with consequent risk of discovery of the truth by due process.

The Department of Labor was acting more prudently. An appeal from grower spokesmen in California to the secretary of labor that steps be taken to suppress the pamphlet was ignored.

In a second edition of *Strangers*, minor corrections were made concerning payroll records from information provided to Hayes by growers associations which had refused access to them while the original interviews were taking place. I made such requests as I travelled over the state, to check possible discrepancies in the information provided me by the braceros. To have allowed me to cross-check data on wages and earnings before publication of the pamphlet would have served the truth but not the employers.

Deceit in public affairs has the melancholy effect of denying its practitioners public credit as pragmatists or artists. Thus far the growers organizations had done their work effectively, and so had the officials of the state and federal agencies, in providing the technical attack on *Strangers*. The bracero system was becoming in some fashion a work of art that is to say, unreality commanding belief and approval. But when the plea for censorship failed, the Department of Labor not only did not claim due credit; it refused it. Goodwin wrote that "the files of the Department of Labor contain no instructions to the regional office of BES in San Francisco directing that office to give answers to statements made in *Strangers*."[271] Officials of BES swore under oath that they had no file on the pamphlet, nor had they distributed copies of the rebuttal.

They admitted that instructions to proceed with the document had been issued, but that they were confidential and privileged.

Total confidentiality, which had been the last resort of the department whenever its explanations fell apart, eventually broke down. I appealed to the House of Representatives, whose staff requested the record on the *Strangers* affair. Finally, in 1962 the department produced a purged file of fifteen of the documents it had claimed did not exist selected from privileged records. The rest were described simply as "not available."

Strangers remained uncensored and unimpeached. The combined efforts of agri-business and its collaborators in government to suppress the pamphlet were understandable, if futile. It provided trade unionists in harvest-related operations such as field packing and canning who were also beginning to feel the impact of bracero contracting with a nontechnical explanation of Public Law 78 and its flaws. The voice of agri-business was no longer the only one being heard: the NAWU was no longer its only critic. The usefulness of the Farm Placement Service was waning, its credibility fading and with it the effectiveness of its chief, Edward F. Hayes. The controversy over *Strangers* was a prelude to the crisis that removed Hayes from public office, de-stabilizing him into private life as an employee of corporate farming.

The Farm Placement Service Crisis

Two events marked the beginning of the decade that reversed the roles of farm labor unionism in California and the Farm Placement Service—the use of braceros to break the DiGiorgio strike in 1947 and the denunciation by the State Board of Agriculture of union clearance in 1950. The lesson of these two events for the National Farm Labor Union was that it had to reckon with agri-business power not only in the fields, but also with its influence on the state agencies whose decisions were controlling in the farm labor market. In the DiGiorgio strike a corporation not only broke the picket line with braceros but it was also able, as a condition precedent, to obtain a declaration of need for them from the government. These interfacings had been long in the making and had reached a high degree of effectiveness by the fall of 1947, when Local 218 struck DiGiorgio. This much was clear without looking beyond Kern

County. What remained for the union to learn, among the many things it did not yet know about its task, was that the political machinery of the State of California, at its highest level, operated to the same purpose as the local farm placement agencies.

It will be recalled that the coordinated campaign to force the Department of Employment to rescind the Roney memorandum of April 1950 was launched by the public attacks of the California State Board of Agriculture against the union. As the growers associations, farm bureaus, associated farmers, chambers of commerce, trade magazines, shippers, and processors joined the attack, the federal government itself retreated, folding, as I said at the time, like a half-cooked noodle.

Unable to resist the political onslaught, it was necessary for the union to set a course forced on it by these realities. I requested of Governor Warren that he appoint a representative of the NFLU to the Board of Agriculture.[272] The governor had designated this Board in 1949 as an advisory body to the State Department of Employment in matters relating to farm labor. There was also an advisory committee to the department, to which the governor had appointed, as a matter of custom, three representatives of the California State Federation of Labor. The Farm Placement Service was a subordinate agency of the department through which farm labor shortages were declared and bracero certification initiated. With such insulation the heat of a picket line could not reach the inner circle of grower power, for whom alien contracting under international agreements was becoming a permanent right.

The governor did not acknowledge my request. A single petition from a notoriously impoverished union was not reason enough for interfering with the agri-business establishment. Governor Warren approved the administrative design " to assure California agriculture that the Farm Placement Service could be an identifiable service that would receive full emphasis . . . thus utilizing an existing body functioning under state law." In its advisory capacity no limits were set for the State Board of Agriculture. And since the members of the board were the most influential spokesmen of the most powerful industry in the state, its advice was tantamount to an order in farm labor matters. Hayes never questioned much less crossed it. His control of the entire harvest labor market was assured by gubernatorial approval and his powerful advisors.

Thus shielded, the relations between Hayes's agency and the industry passed from mutual understanding to cordial collaboration. Staff planning conferences were attended by grower representatives "to share experience and knowledge and to discuss prospective operating policies and procedures in the light of identifiable problems."[273]

The man chosen for the pivotal role of chief of the Farm Placement Service was Edward F. Hayes. Once a manager of small business enterprises, he had carried out assignments as a staff member of the earlier Farm Production Council, a grower-dominated precursor of the FPS. He was acquainted with the ways of transferring publicly constructed farm labor supply centers to private ownership at bargain prices. As chief, he was an open and avowed antagonist of farm labor unionism. Throughout his tenure, Hayes remained a stockholder of the DiGiorgio and various other corporations that kept him in touch, as he expressed it, with the whole picture of industrial America.

Hayes, of more than medium height, was inclined to corpulence. He had a quality of cheerfulness that was not easy to escape, yet could be easily goaded to a temper when he was dealing with the farm labor union. As he went about the state he dropped in for lunch with hospitable gentry, like the DiGiorgios at Delano. He was a well-known and frequently sought consultant, available without charge to such clients as Western Growers Association, Associated Farmers, managers of growers associations, and the California Farm Bureau.[274]

Regrettably, Hayes reacted to the strictures of the NAWU as personal affronts. I had to remain silent when he testified that "Galarza never did a lick of work in his life." When pressed as to his personal knowledge of illegal lending of braceros among growers, he answered intemperately, "I don't know. I wasn't there. I was in Sacramento, . . . for Christ's sake. How should I know?"[275]

Rightly enough, Hayes held the NAWU responsible for the increasing leakage of his craft. He fell into the habit not only of not answering the union's requests for information but also of avoiding contact with union representatives he was investigating in the fields.

Hayes's services to the industry were not limited to certifying shortages and prevailing wages. The central office in Sacramento was the switchboard of grower information on union activities. It took no notice of thousands of illegals during the harvests, but facilitated their conversion to braceros, so that their number would approximate the labor shortages declared by him. Hayes approved the rule of the industry that domestic workers should serve time as apprentices "until they reach proficiency, so that the employers will gain confidence in the domestic worker."[276] He was referring to harvesters with years of experience behind them. As housing for domestics gradually was abandoned the Farm Placement Service merely lamented the fact and continued to certify braceros, admitting that such certification contributed to the housing scarcity for domestics.[277] When the union pressed the issue of open orders, Hayes began referring domestic applicants not directly to the job but to the managers of the association, who subjected the applicants to a standard treatment of degradation and frustration. With

Hayes's approval the associations kept dossiers on workers who had quit or been fired under harassment, using such records to screen out undesirable workers as much as possible. The associations emphatically denied they had anything to do with determining wages and Hayes agreed with them.[278]

These tactics were aimed at lowering the morale of domestic harvesters as much as proving that they were undependable. But it was a secondary role for the FPS. Primarily it remained as the certifier of need and the authorizer of braceros. Once this was done it remained only to find a prevailing wage level consistent with the advice and consent of the growers.

Until the mid-fifties Hayes did not hesitate to use his administrative powers to these ends. During the carrot harvest of 1958 in San Joaquin County, A. R. Duarte, the manager of the San Joaquin growers association, notified Hayes on June 9 that there was a short supply of domestics and that 750 braceros were needed. In view of the absence of a wage finding, Duarte wrote that the association itself had set the wage scale for tying. On June 10 Hayes approved certification for the number of men requested along with the prevailing wage already found by the growers.[279] Hayes also approved braceros for stripping grapevines in the Borrego Valley ranch of the DiGiorgio Corporation without bothering to issue a wage finding. Nor did he wait for a wage determination for the tomato harvest in San Joaquin in 1959 because the wage was a cent a box higher than the previous year and "they always approve our findings anyway."[280]

Hayes had no more difficulty with the governor than he had with federal officials. In April 1959 there was before the legislature a proposal by Governor Brown, recommending a minimum wage for agricultural workers of 90 cents an hour. Hayes prepared a secret report for the State Board of Agriculture and appeared with its members before the governor to ask that he delay submitting the proposal to the legislature. The union's request that this report be released to the public was not acknowledged by the governor's office, Hayes, or the board. The only thing that could be learned by outsiders was that the governor's advisors were opposed to tampering with the wage structure "in the light of the present carefully developed piecework rates." The union had sent the governor's office evidence that throughout the state a carefully developed wage policy was used to lower domestic piece rates to the level of Hayes's findings, and that these were in turn reduced to the even more carefully calibrated rates, prepared by growers associations, designed to prevent excessive earnings.

Under Hayes the wage philosophy of the FPS was consistent, if not altogether rational. Agriculture was exempt from the Taft–Hartley law, he argued. "We have nothing whatever to say about the wages of farm workers. . . . all we did was determine the prevailing wage," which coupled with certified shortages became the true wage for all. Hayes maintained, with an admirable aplomb, that there was no adverse reaction to his decisions from the union, or any desire on its part to interject itself into the wage reporting procedures.

Hayes's political services were as welcome to agri-business as were his labor policies. During the summer of 1958 the California State Federation of Labor mobilized its resistance to a referendum aimed at passing a right-to-work constitutional proposition. Governor Knight had publicly declared his opposition to the initiative, Proposition 18 on the ballot. Aggressively favoring it were the Associated Farmers and the Farm Bureau, the political grass roots of agri-business. As the Farm Bureau sought to gather a hundred thousand signatures in the agricultural communities, Hayes continued in his accustomed role of consultant to these organizations. If Knight regarded Hayes's role as politically disloyal, there was no indication of it. He probably did not. The right-to-work amendment legislation would have affected farm laborers as well as industrial workers.

Political currents that flow well below the surface can turn unexpectedly into rip tides. Something like this may have been foreshadowed by the *Strangers* affair and the failure of Proposition 18. The crisis of the Farm Placement Service approached in three stages, reaching its climax in the summer of 1959.

The years of intense activity in the Imperial Valley in 1951, 1952, and 1953 overlapped the administrations of governors Earl Warren and Goodwin J. Knight. Warren took public notice of the shooting of James Price and ordered an investigation, low key and soon forgotten. His role in the government camps transaction was noncommital. Knight's only response to the union's complaints out of Imperial was to assign William A. Burkett, an official of the Department of Employment, to investigate the employment of foreign agricultural workers. Burkett announced in January 1954, in a departmental press statement, that he was preparing to call witnesses from organized labor and grower groups. I was asked for and provided Burkett with evidence at a meeting we had in Los Angeles at his request. Nothing happened.

Such being the official climate in Sacramento, Hayes was able to ease his way out of difficulties such as the case of Chester Cook, a grower member of the Imperial Valley Farmers Association, against whom a complaint was pending by a CIO union representative for failure to hire domestics in place of braceros certified through the association.

Don Parks, Hayes's local representative for Imperial County, received the complaint from two U.S. Department of Labor agents. Parks informed Hayes. On Friday, March 4, 1955, about 4:00 P.M. Hayes telephoned J. J. Miller, whose role in the *Strangers* affair has been mentioned and who was a confidential advisor to Brockway. Hayes promptly informed Miller that "a serious situation exists in the Imperial Valley that not only involves the Imperial Valley but certainly . . . other phases of agriculture in California."[281] Hayes suggested that Miller immediately contact Keith Mets, president of the association and business partner of Frank O'Dwyer, brother of the U.S. ambassador to Mexico. Hayes indicated the need for swift action "to straighten out certain irregularities before the regional report is filed this weekend."

Miller acted at once. He first met with Harrigan, the association manager, and with him examined the records relating to Cook and his braceros. Before noon of Saturday, March 5, the irregularities were straightened out; Miller, Mets, and Harrigan called in Parks and Cook who talked with them on Sunday, the sixth. Miller was in charge of the meeting. Parks was grilled. He admitted he had made no personal investigation of the charges. He had, as he said, thoroughly familiarized himself with the records and referrals of braceros to Cook. He found the charges completely without foundation. Cook was given a clean bill of health and Parks was reprimanded. Miller himself, however, left on the record the statement that Harrigan had called Cook to instruct him to return his nationals as rapidly as he could replace them with qualified domestics, confirming at least one of the irregularities reported by Hayes.

The document from which the foregoing quotations are taken was sent by Miller to the RFLOAC in San Francisco, and was entitled "Report on investigation of non-compliance Imperial Valley." It was a succinct illustration of the policy of self-policing approved by the U.S. Department of Labor.

As indicated above, Hayes also supplied the State Board of Agriculture with another secret report in opposition to a state minimum wage proposal. It was part of the drumfire of attacks on the NAWU by the Farm Placement Service that continued for ten years. The union's response to the wage report was my May 9, 1959, letter to Governor Brown demanding that Hayes be removed. A collection of documents supporting recent charges published by the union accompanied the letter. It said in part: "these documents will persuade you the NAWU has ample justification for asking you to remove Mr. Edward F. Hayes. . . . In that happy event we would hope that none of the upper echelon officers of the service who have served Mr. Hayes's policies would succeed him."[282]

What happened in the inner circle of the Brown administration was never revealed to the NAWU. Characteristically, the office of the governor did not respond to the appeals, the complaints, the recommendations, the grievances, or the charges on record.

The pressure was deflected to the Department of Employment, where it took an unexpected turn. On June 4, 1959, John E. Carr, director of the department, announced plans "to strengthen our control over the Farm Placement Service." Thenceforth there would be "careful field work to see that the prevailing wage represents a level which will attract and retain domestic workers." As to the open order policy, Carr said, "Growers will be required to keep domestic workers continuously employed as a condition for bracero hiring." Carr also ordered that steps be taken to avoid adverse effects of braceros and domination by them of crop areas.[283] He admonished his subordinates to insist on gate hiring and the full use of day hauls to fill labor requirements and on hearing all complaints.

Carr apparently had gubernatorial approval to go still further. In his "Restatement of Policies" of June 4 he announced that the department would make internal adjustments in the administration of farm placement.

The adjustments that followed marked the end of the first stage of the union's long effort to bring the bureaucratic alliance with agri-business into the open.

Departmental charges were filed against a Farm Placement officer, William H. Cunningham, on August 1. On August 9 Carr publicly accused the service of turning away domestic workers in favor of braceros.[284] He stated, "We can't deny that mismanagement of the farm labor program does exist. . . ." Labor's complaints against the program were "for the most part justified." Carr's administrative ire mounted in a crescendo of suspense—"Those who richly deserve it are going to get it in the investigation of the farm labor program"[285]—and its finale was the demotion of Hayes from the post of chief to that of advisor to the director of the department. He was stripped of the authority to certify shortages of labor, approve bracero certifications, or find prevailing wages.

Carr's investigation went on. Cunningham was dismissed; Don Parks resigned; Hayes, declaring he had nothing to be ashamed of, said "They'll have to fire me."

It was unnecessary. On February 16, 1960, Hayes, too, resigned as advisor to assume new duties as manager of the Imperial Valley Farmers Association. Still defiant, Hayes, in his inaugural address as Harrigan's successor, lashed out at unions, do-gooders, and crusaders. In a new job but in an old role he assured his constituents: "We farmers are here to serve you."

Director Carr's drastic administrative changes ended late in November 1959, with a reprimand to twelve farm placement officers. Carr's successor, Irving H. Perluss, explained that the Farm Placement Service had lost its special status and was again in the regular line of operations of the department. From then on the department would "listen equally to the problems of all parties—employers, unions, individual workers, and community groups."

"Panic," as defined by noted psychiatrist Harry Stack Sullivan, "is the utterly unforeseen failure of something completely trusted and vital to one's safety."

The peach orchardists of Yuba County were in one. The week before his demotion Hayes had been busy certifying "supplementary" contractees to the Peach Bowl growers. To them the threatened halt in the certifications caused by Hayes's removal was a disaster and they reacted accordingly. The stress, of course, was on the certain loss of thousands of tons of fruit, valued at forty million dollars. Growers who had completed their harvests for the summer of 1959, and those who still had the fall and spring to plan their 1960 drafts of braceros, did not reach a helping hand to Hayes.

Panic in those who are genuinely possessed by it overcomes rationality. The peach panic was fictitious, its aim to create a political situation in Sacramento that at least for the emergency would mend the loss of Hayes. It would also test what Governor Brown meant on August 15: "I promise that the present administration will not rest until our farm placement program functions for the people it was created to serve—our domestic farm workers."[286]

But the administrative reform, even as the governor spoke, had already come to rest. Ripples of the panic had reached Hayes's successor in the Department of Employment, S. S. Goodman, who now stood next in line to bear the blame for the loss of the peach crop. The Associated Farmers echoed the dismal cries coming from the Peach Bowl, with the *California Farmer* angrily editorializing that "the crops were getting ripe and the Mexicans were two weeks late in arriving." Goodman yielded. On August 12, 4,800 braceros were certified for peach picking, on August 26, another 3,500 were authorized. The situation at the end of the month was viewed by the Associated Farmers as "a most favorable one." Carr's explanation of the FPS shakeup referred to perversion of the bracero program against the interests of domestic workers and to the professional laxness of some of the farm placement personnel. Of the two themes, the second was emphasized as the principal cause of Hayes's troubles. Reprimands and dismissals were based on formal charges of dishonesty, misuse of state property, accepting gifts from farmers, and falsifying expense accounts. The NAWU had never made charges of this kind; its unwavering attention had been fixed on a system of economic and political power, not on the peccadillos of individuals who served it within the bureaucracy. That was why I had written Governor Brown that in the event of Hayes's removal hopefully none of his close collaborators would replace him. But they did, and the lesson was plain: Individuals were expendable; power remained undisturbed.

On this appraisal, the 1959 crisis of the Farm Placement Service completed only the first stage of the NAWU goals in California. In the concluding sections of this book what this stage represented in the historical process of which the union was a part will be discussed. Viewing it in the dusk of Hayes's public career, the light of Public Law 78, also, was failing.

The Twilight of Public Law 78

The importation of Mexican agricultural laborers under officially approved contracts began as a temporary measure of national defense in 1942 and continued for more than two decades, drawn by new possibilities for exploitation of an indentured work force. As it advanced it infiltrated the regulatory functions written into the international agreements and Public Law 78 to the point where the important decisions could be made only with the advice and consent of the large farm employers. It provided a way for reversing the trend toward a nonmigratory class of citizen laborers who could in the long run become capable of organizing themselves. The bracero method proved superior to the historic strategies for manipulating the agricultural labor pool.

There was still another virtue to the managed migration of Mexican braceros, one that lay more concealed in the historical process. In the border lands of the southwest, especially in California, Texas, and Arizona, the economies of Mexico and the United States were intermingling, so that the relatively high living standards of the American workers made them increasingly less desirable as wage hands than the Mexicans, whose poverty the Mexican revolution had left unchanged. In the wake of the extensive reclamation projects of the United States government, cultivation of millions of acres of marginal land became profitable. The cost of labor inputs became a critical managerial problem for corporation farming, which gradually took over the conquered west. For fifty years or more a labor force of Mexicans flowed over the borderlands accepting levels of living and of employment that the American entrepreneurs found advantageous as compared with domestic laborers.

This type of agrarian proletariat was not satisfactory in every respect. Some migrants tended to settle down and learn the ways of Americans; the perennial wetbacks were even cheaper but hopelessly fluid and therefore quite impossible to integrate into the orderly subsystems of a modern farming industry. Midway between migrants and illegals a compromise had been worked out in the form of border-crossing permits, by which Mexican citizens could enter the United States to work, for a few hours or a few days, but this was satisfactory only to those employers near the border.

Ten years of employer experimentation with braceros concluded with Public Law 78, enacted in 1951 as the nearly perfect answer to these deficiencies. In a sense these were years of trial and error as growers made one delightful discovery after another. Like the sprinkling systems of mechanized irrigation, braceros could be turned on and off.

The seven years following the enactment of the law were those of consolidation, with the industry brushing aside the resistance of the NAWU, regarded by the Associated Farmers as "diligent but ineffective." The crisis of the Farm Placement Service of 1959 marked the turning point and the years from 1960 to 1964 were those in which the effect of the action research of the NAWU emerged. It was this last period that I call the twilight of the system. Like any dusk, this one had no sharp beginnings. It began with the documented attacks of the NAWU progressing as the ways of agri-business with workers were examined throughout the state. The prolonged cover-up came gradually into view, ending in a futile effort to save the system in December 1964.

The law had been launched on a flood of publicity and congressional oratory as the solution to a perennial farm labor shortage, an urgent measure of national defense, a form of economic relief for the poor of a friendly republic, protection for the wage levels of domestic citizen workers, and a school of democracy for all. A believing nation was persuaded, and any challenge to these claims by the NAWU through counter rhetoric would clearly have been useless. The power of publicity in the beginning was on the side of the industry. The only recourse was to document the imposture, however long it might take. As Director of Research and Education of the union, that became my assignment.

Over the years following the end of the DiGiorgio strike the search progressed. Out of it came a collection of statutes, ordinances, congressional hearings, bulletins, memoranda, international agreements, joint findings, resolutions, proceedings, petitions, newspaper clippings, and other evidence that had been committed to paper. But these did not wholly reveal how the system was actually working. Its tracks had to be found in the fields and followed with the help of the best trackers, the braceros and illegals.

Many of the records thus gathered were unconventional. They included copies of bracero contracts, payroll lists, piecework punch cards, notices of evictions, photographs, work sheets used by farm placement managers to determine labor needs, paycheck stubs, petitions of bracero crews for redress, sworn complaints, wage claims, lists of certified growers, cancelled checks, Farm Placement Service referral cards rejected and signed by field foremen, accident reports, head counts on skid rows, letters from returned braceros, and price tags from camp commissaries. From the fields also came a time book carelessly dropped by a contractor; strips of brown paper given to a bracero to bind a cut on his leg; a bottle of placebos distributed by a rancher on the job to treat headaches, stomach pains, diarrhea, hernia, sun stroke, fatigue, or nausea; a tomato lug larger than standard size especially for bracero crews, food invoices from a wholesale butcher to a camp commissary that regularly served braceros special dinners of sheep's heads and turkey necks. William Renner pulled out of a wastebasket a memorandum of a meeting in which prominent corporation spokesman met with officials of the U.S. Department of Labor and minutes of a meeting at which the department pledged itself to carry out the directives it received from the industry. In this odd and useful miscellany there was a crude cardboard sign from a camp where braceros were instructed to cash their paychecks for a fee, and bundles of slips that had been blown from a field where they had been used to mark task assignments for a crew of melon pickers.

Out of such stuff the reports to Mitchell were composed; these in turn became the press releases, statements, memoranda, and public presentations that he distributed to the press, congressional committees, financial contributors and other unions. In a few years the national office of the NAWU became the prime source of information on Public Law 78; the union propaganda was widely credited for its reliability as well as for its notorious advocacy of repeal of the law.

The task of on-site research of the system became easier as union volunteers grasped the importance of matters as trivial as the windblown *papelitos* discarded by unsuspecting employers and contractors.

When braceros reported that they were required to pay 50 cents a week rental for a television set in the camp, I suggested that they ask for receipts which the camp manager cheerfully provided. Braceros who were mildly amused at being classified as "loaners" notified the union volunteers who could then clock the movements of such crews and compute the lost time the men would have otherwise been paid for on the basis of contract guarantees. Three braceros, who had been ordered home by the association for disorderly conduct in a wage dispute, telephoned the union that they were sleeping in empty furniture crates as temporary quarters while waiting deportation. Union men verified the fact on the spot. Union sources also found that one association kept a sign at the camp gates restricting entry only to salesmen of a merchant with an exclusive concession. Notices were circulated informing the braceros of an arrangement authorizing deductions from wages to be paid to the Mexican Social Security Institute, through the managers of recruiting centers in Mexico, notorious centers of extortion. The association also, in the same office, both sold health insurance and collected irregular fees for delivery of bracero specials to favored growers.

In *Strangers in Our Fields* data of this kind were first published. The efforts of the growers, the U.S. Department of Labor, and the Farm Placement Service to discredit and suppress the pamphlet failed. Inner circles of Agri-businessland conceded that *Strangers* did contain "much valuable information."[287] *Strangers* went into a second printing for a total national circulation of fifteen thousand copies. A Spanish translation appeared in Mexico City, and the substance of its material appeared in the Congressional Record. In the fall of 1963 *Merchants of Labor* was published, copies of which were circulated in the House of Representatives during the final debates on the termination of Public Law 78.

As the controversy over *Strangers* went on, certain official investigations were taking place, out of public view. They showed the effect of the union's attacks, particularly of the disputed pamphlet. A technical study of bracero employment in the tomato harvesting in Santa Clara County contained the extraordinary information that the average total cost per day for braceros—housing, meals, and transportation included—was $1.80 per man day. Most associations charged the bracero $1.75 for meals alone. The Lawrenson Report of 1958 relating to these matters noted that referral cards issued by the FPS carried discriminatory markings as to nationality and color. Another report issued in 1959, the result of an investigation by Glenn Kaufman for the Attorney General of California provided official verification of what the union had been saying: that the recruiting center at Empalme, Mexico, provided a golden opportunity for extortion and graft. The Kaufman report was never released.

The evidence mounted, showing that the prevailing wage findings of the Department of Employment were fallacious; the low wages that were fixed for braceros had driven domestic workers out of the Imperial Valley; settlements offered to braceros for work injuries were below legal requirements and closed without the approval of the State Industrial Accident Commission; hernia injuries caused by lifting overloaded boxes to excessively high stacks were settled arbitrarily as non-occupational and compensation fixed on the basis of minimum wages earned; injured braceros were repatriated to Mexico with no provision for continuation of treatment, the San Joaquin Growers Associations falsified its payroll records; among the intermediaries bribed to obtain the braceros called "specials" there were Mexican consuls and officials at the reception centers in Mexico; interlocking management and profit taking existed between the operators of the compulsory health program and the concessionaires who boarded braceros.

The widespread support among Mexican contractors that the bracero system enjoyed at first had a great deal to do with its initial success, but it diminished as the benefits of collusion became more narrowly distributed. Some of the intermediaries had become favorites of the growers, even being permitted to become members of the associations, in violation of the law. The lesser contractors found themselves not only excluded from sharing the general exploitation of Mexican aliens but also unable to place domestic crews the growers no longer wanted. Bracero hiring also made inroads into the patronage of contractors whose close friends and relatives worked for them as checkers, drivers, time keepers, punchers, and camp managers. These assignments were taken over by bracero specials, often at the prevailing field wages but with the welcome transfer from the hard tasks of harvesting. The contractors began to feel the economic and social displacement which they had helped to inflict on the *locales*.

Agri-business was extraordinarily efficient in mobilizing its intelligence resources and its pressures in the face of a threat as specific as that of *Strangers*. It reacted swiftly to menacing situations such as the Renner and Cook affairs. It did not prove nearly so adept at grasping what the NAWU was intent upon during almost a decade. As long as the locals of the union continued to shrink and the union was less and less able to organize economic actions, the NAWU remained little more than a tolerable nuisance.

This assessment changed after the removal of Hayes from the center of bureaucratic control of the system. In 1960 the *California Farmer* was quoting growers to the effect that they were faced with threatening efforts of organized labor to eliminate the supplemental labor supply, or, as it said editorially, "They are going to murder the bracero program." Throughout California the associations resorted to strategems intended to improve the image of the system and to persuade grower members to mend their ways. Run-down bracero camps were spruced up as showpieces, photographed and advertised to belie the stories and pictures published in *Strangers*. The Limonera Company of Ventura spent thousands of dollars on vented heaters, central kitchens with the most modern equipment, and refurbished dining rooms. Even as the outside of the system was scrubbed an inner moral cleansing was attempted. The Northern California Growers Association required all members to sign a pledge that read:

1. I will diligently try to find domestic workers . . . and will hire any able-bodied worker they [the Farm Placement Service] send me.
2. I will place a Help Wanted sign on or near my ranch.
3. I will file all payrolls complete with numbers of hours worked by each worker.
4. I will pay the prevailing wage.

To the extent that genuine repentance is an admission of past sins this quadralogue of the new grower morality confirmed what Chief Hayes had not been able to find in his investigations.

In a similar vein the associations collectively adopted a code that did not come to light until after the publication of *Strangers*. It pledged all to meet payrolls promptly, provide drinking water in the fields, comply with state regulations on transportation safety, meet housing standards, and settle all grievances before the braceros were returned to Mexico.[288] A Department of Labor official commending it endorsed the code as "a well-prepared document."

As the associations exhorted, they pondered again an old idea, namely, the transfer of control of the bracero program to the U.S. Department of Agriculture.[289] Agri-businessmen felt a growing anxiety about the reliability of the Department of Labor bureaucracy, where the union pressure was centered. In spite of the "prevailing wage" manipulations of the FPS, farm wages were beginning to rise in some areas. A transfer, however, would have required some complicated manuevers in Congress and was likely to cause even more controversy. The idea was quietly dropped.

Incapable of recognizing the main objective of the union's campaign, the associations maintained an outward composure while the state and federal agents ignored or filed away the mounting evidence of violations. By 1958 the NAWU was carrying on an effective surveillance of the abuses widely practiced on braceros and domestics; in effect some fifty volunteers were doing the work that Hayes's staff and the personnel of the San Francisco Regional Office were being paid to do.

Not all the violations brought to light by the union could be ignored. Occasionally a response was unavoidable.

Such was the case of the death of a bracero, Vidal Lopez Silva, in Imperial on May 28, 1958. Lopez was driving a tractor in a melon field that was being sprayed with insecticide from the air. On one of its passes over the field the pilot of the plane failed to see the tractor through the cloud of malathion spray. The propeller of the plane wrenched the driver from his seat and dropped him, dead, sixty feet away. Within twenty-four hours the Department of Labor issued to the newspapers its report on the tragedy. It began by stressing that Lopez had not been employed as a tractor driver. (On the record braceros never were, since it was a violation of the law.) He had been driving the equipment as a favor to a friend. (Death did not result in the course of employment.) The U.S. Department of Labor "is ever vigilant," said the release, to enforce the exclusion of braceros from the operation of machinery.[290]

The report was based entirely on unsworn statements. The department did not ask for a coroner's inquest before issuing it. The payroll record of the dead man was not cited to determine why he was driving the tractor. No significance was attached to the presence of a worker in a field saturated with malathion dust. It was not determined whether Lopez was a "loaner"—newspaper accounts placed him on a machine not owned by his employer of record at the time of the accident.

On June 11 the NAWU issued a press statement on the basis of its own sources and asked for a truthful investigation. The union's report was never checked by the department. One of the witnesses it would have called under oath was the president of the Imperial Valley Farmers Association, Keith Mets.

The unprecedented speed with which the local compliance officer and the association and the dead bracero's employer coordinated their efforts to explain away the tragedy were understandable. The NFLU already had compiled and released a record of illegal use of braceros on farm equipment in Imperial, Santa Clara, San Joaquin, Yuba, and Fresno counties. The rate of injuries among braceros so employed was sufficiently documented to cause the state and federal agencies acute embarrassment. The death of Lopez Silva pointed to a prevailing practice, not to an exception.

Behind their cool demeanor, however, the associations were uneasy.

As I came to the end of my assignment the facts began to filter through.

In October 1956, A. R. Duarte, manager of the San Joaquin Farm Production Association, issued a circular to all members following a series of injuries to braceros in transportation accidents. "Unless violations which we know are going on are corrected immediately there is a good probability that we will not have the use of nationals." In November 1957, the manager of the San Diego County Farmers Association sent out an "important warning." He told his growers that they must employ domestic workers referred to them. In the Imperial Valley, after ten years of lassitude, the association's report contained these statements: "Domestic workers cannot be refused any jobs braceros are doing. To do so will cancel your certification to use braceros. . . . All members received copies of the new state laws regulating busses for hauling workers. These laws must be complied with or you are subject to . . . removal of your certification. . . . Organized labor is spending hundreds of thousands of dollars annually to oppose Public Law 78. The money is being used as grants to religious and welfare organizations. . . . Union activities in all California are carried on in every manner possible to oppose the use of braceros in California agriculture."

A sense of collective alarm was taking possession of agri-businessmen. Six years had passed since Harrigan's last encounter with the union, but he knew that the sins of Salinas or the Peach Bowl would be visited upon him, too.

The anxiety was statewide. In the Santa Clara Valley a major strawberry processor cautioned growers to comply with the 90 cent hourly minimum wage for braceros. In May 1959 the manager of the Progressive Growers Association, knowing it was being watched, pleaded with its members: "I'm telling you again, do not turn down domestic labor. Keep accurate records. If your nationals work ten hours don't be foolish enough to put down eight hours."[291] These warnings referred to the misrepresentation of work injuries as nonoccupational. In its December 15, 1958, bulletin Progressive Growers noted that "our nationals have had more hernias this year than in former years. . . . Our records show that most of the hernias happened among the nationals picking tomatoes. . . . These hernias are caused from lifting boxes of tomatoes." Union field checks showed that braceros were being required to stack full lug boxes weighing up to sixty pounds as high as eight to a stack, while the acceptable limit for domestics was six boxes. The bulletin went on to say: "We should also bear in mind that our Workmen's Compensation Insurance is exceptionally low because our accident rate has been low. . . . We have been receiving a large dividend from the insurance company that we always return to members which makes your cost of workmen's compensation insurance still lower.''

In the Peach Bowl union activity prompted Charles B. Rhodes, the manager of Northern California Growers Association, to issue a series of alerts. His circular of November 11, 1957, advised: "The situation has become so serious the program is in jeopardy" and demanded that all members sign the pledge of honest compliance or they would be dropped. Growers had been turning down domestic workers and Rhodes admonished them about it. In September 1957 he passed on to the membership a circular from the Department of Labor which referred to "your continued violations" of prohibitions against lending workers and payroll falsifications. A note of exasperation crept into Rhodes bulletin of April 10, 1958: "For gosh sakes do not turn down a domestic farm worker. I have orders to pull your crews if you do." These were the conditions that Hayes had not been able to find when he and Rhodes discussed the charges the union had published on those particulars.

Like the associations, the Department of Labor snubbed the NAWU, refusing to hold open hearings, denying administrative appeals, and avoiding giving any weight to the evidence the union presented. Closely watched by his powerful advisors, the members of the RFLOAC, Regional Director Brockway held that "braceros are a fact of life to which Americans must become adjusted."[292] Within the family, however, the department was forced to move from total permissiveness to remonstrance to exhortation and finally to enforcement.

Why the department began its slow progress toward the fulfillment of its duties was explained by Don Larin. Speaking to the RFLOAC in February 1957, Larin admitted that some of the allegations contained in *Strangers in Our Fields* about substandard housing were founded on facts. "Because of the pressure on the Department of Labor," Larin said, something had to be done "to clean up this substandard housing."[293] Thomas Campbell, of the State Department of Employment, admitted privately that conditions in Yuba County were as the union had reported them. Larin himself confirmed that thirty bracero camps had been found without potable water; there were housing units with dirt floors, thirty-six with no beds and others with no mattresses. Publicly, Larin was less precise, telling growers that "it is vitally necessary that we observe the integrity of the law and treaty regulations." Assistant Secretary of Labor Rocco Siciliano admitted to a congressional committee in August 1957 that thousands of complaints lodged by braceros were substantiated, some of them so flagrant as to require cancellation of eligibility.[294]

There were many large bracero camps, and many lesser ones, that were under observation by the union at one time or another. The worst were publicized by the NAWU, giving the Department of Labor no choice but to close them. In August 1957, 250 braceros were removed from the Gondo Camp near Watsonville. During the next two years as the union identified the growers who were the worst offenders the department cancelled their authorizations. Over 100 were cited throughout the state, some of them on personal instructions of Secretary of Labor Mitchell. The change of pace was noted by the Imperial Association, which was ordered to install heating units in bracero camps. "This has been in the regulations for years but has not been enforced in Imperial County because of our mild climate." Two years before, I had described a visit I made to a bracero camp near El Centro. It was midnight. Thirty men were sleeping in the field in bunks improvised with hay, one blanket to each man, and the temperature was fifty degrees.

Long reluctant to respond to the union, the department became increasingly sensitive, finally taking notice of the graft connected with specials. In January 1958 Robert C. Goodwin, federal director of employment security, recognized the widespread bribery in this connection and ruled that the department would no longer honor powers of attorney given to health insurance agents by growers to contract specials for them. The department revoked its authorization to Herringer Enterprises, prominent members of the Peach Bowl association, on charges of falsification of records, unsanitary housing, and illegal wage rates.

It should be noted that where the department could not ignore glaring disregard of the rules the transgressor's only penalty was the loss of authorization. But this, too, could be corrected. Braceros were borrowed: labor contractors were induced to manage clandestine pools of braceros into which growers in bad standing with the department could dip. The remedy for these evasions was to hold growers responsible in civil actions for monetary losses suffered by workers, as well as for violation of state statutes, conspiracy, and criminal negligence. There was enough evidence in the union's possession to file actions of this kind in Santa Clara County, Yuba, Imperial, and San Joaquin. But the NFLU had no funds for such litigation, and it could raise none among its friends in organized labor.

That the department was penalizing gross and notorious violations only to the degree that pressure compelled it, was clear from the tact with which it addressed the associations out of sight and hearing of the NAWU. The directives and memoranda issuing from BES regional headquarters in San Francisco were couched in gentle phrases—

"Please inform your members," "suggest that each association send a bulletin," "you are requested." This was the etiquette for dealing with persistent falsification, bribery, criminal negligence of state law, and airborne manslaughter.

Whether politicians would be willing to continue their support of a program increasingly in disrepute was the question on which the success or failure of the union's ten-year effort now hung. The system was now on the defensive, but still persistent. The Honorable Charles M. Teague, grower turned statesman, entreated the House Committee on Agriculture: "We must make the program respectable." In May 1960 this same committee suggested a diversionary tactic—to challenge the Secretary of Labor, who was proposing to use the Wagner–Peyser Act of 1933 to regulate wages, hours, and other conditions of employment of domestic workers. Congressman Poage polished the familiar rhetoric: "You are asking an impoverished industry to stand the cost of additional expense." Congressman McFall saw the situation apocalyptically: "The integrity of the American food supply is in the balance." Congressman Gathings: "If braceros disappeared from the scene we would not have something to wear on our backs." The issue in the congressional debates of 1960 was whether Pubic Law 78 would remain in force, and these were the best arguments that its more redoubtable champions could muster.

In the upper house Senator Hayden of Arizona offered to support a full investigation if Public Law 78 were extended. But the investigation was over, and the NAWU, in a petition with H. L. Mitchell's signature and mine, filed with Congress the most comprehensive bill of particulars of its many denunciations. The bureaucrats of the Department of Labor, the California Department of Employment, the growers organizations—none stepped forward to explain and justify what the union had made known. It was getting late for a rebuttal. State Senator James A. Cobey told the Commonwealth Club of San Francisco in December 1960 that "a climate for defeat of Public Law 78 was being established." State Director of Employment Perluss fourteen months later warned California growers that future availability of braceros was doubtful.[295]

Early in November 1963, the House voted 173 to 158 to approve the last one-year extension of the law. Former champions of the bracero system like Congressmen Sisk of California served notice that time had run out, and in August 1964 the *Los Angeles Times* accurately predicted, "There is no chance for another extension."[296] On December 31, 1964, Public Law 78 expired, fulfilling the hope expressed by Frank L. Noakes in his foreword to *Strangers* that Congress "would take long-overdue action to correct this situation."

Long before the end, the industry began to prepare for it. In the summer of 1963 Don Larin, in addressing growers at a farewell fiesta for braceros in Woodland, said, "This may be the last time we shall see you and have the opportunity to thank you for your labors in our fields."[297] In February of the following year the Council of California Growers announced that it would no longer support foreign labor importation but would concentrate instead on recruiting domestics. The State Board of Agriculture concurred.[298] Covering this retreat Hayes explained the increasing coolness of Congress as a case of jealousy and vindictiveness toward California, inspired by agricultural interests in the southern states, which had not been so well favored with braceros.

A last effort by Governor Brown to win a reprieve failed to win support. In November 1964 the governor put forward a compromise, a five-year phasing out of braceros by reducing their number 20 percent each year. He argued that this would prevent the interruption of the flow of produce from the fields, would allow time to study the changes that would be needed to induce domestic workers to accept agricultural employment, and would eventually eliminate dependency on alien contract workers. The governor had discussed his plan with farmers, union officials, government specialists, and academic experts before it was announced. He had not consulted the NAWU.

During the critical weeks preceding the final vote on Public Law 78 Brown's plan appeared to be gaining support. Unidentified labor spokesmen close to the governor were willing to consider it. The State Board of Agriculture thought it reasonable, and some of the liberal organizations that had been excoriated by Hayes as crusaders and do-gooders were inclined to accept it as a fair proposal.

The five-year phase-out would have been victory for the growers. It would have confirmed that there was indeed a critical shortage of domestic workers, and there would have been time to perfect new methods of manipulation.

Recognizing that only drastic opposition could prevent Brown's proposal from gaining momentum, I prepared for single-handed action. I wrote an open letter to the crusaders and do-gooders who had supported the NAWU over the years denouncing the idea. By this time the NAWU had gone out of existence and was now merged with the Amalgamated Meat Cutters Union. I had continued to borrow funds on my own account to pay off the NAWU debts, and with this money I prepared to assemble and deploy a team of former members to picket the governor's office, the State Federation of Labor, Mexican consuls, and selected growers associations around the state.

This proved unnecessary. By correspondence and telephone I succeeded in preventing public endorsement of the Brown proposal by prestigious liberals and church organizations known throughout the country for their sympathy with the rural poor. Puzzled and somewhat offended, they hesitated long enough to let the twilight of the system settle into night. By June 1965 there were fewer than one thousand braceros closing out their contracts in the United States, as compared with sixty thousand the previous year.

V: Labor Relations of the NAWU

It is now necessary to discuss the years 1947 to 1959 in the context of the American labor movement.

In the mid 1930s the southern tenant farmers banded into a union and black and white tenants and sharecroppers organized in a widespread insurgency against the wage exploitation of that followed chattel slavery after the Civil War. The need for outside support was urgent and the croppers found it among two sectors of American society, the liberal conscience of the nation and the trade unions of industrial workers. The protest became known as the Southern Tenant Farmers Union, which by the time Hasiwar arrived in California was changed to the National Farm Labor Union, renamed the National Agricultural Workers Union, all three organized on the model of industrial unionism—chartered locals, delegated councils, elected officials, affiliation with central labor bodies and state federations, membership dues, economic actions through strikes, and the other familiar characteristics of institutional unionism. The objectives of the NAWU were the traditional ones: bargaining and coverage under protective legislation such as unemployment insurance and the minimum wage.

The California State Federation of Labor

In California there was already a long history of concern if not of action among industrial unionists with regard to agricultural laborers. Between 1902 and 1910 the American Federation of Labor sent organizers into the fields and pledged itself to bring land workers into the fold of craft unionism. In 1903 an agricultural laborers local in Santa Clara County, was chartered by the Central Labor Council. These early efforts sought to create a pattern of organization for seasonal migrants amenable to continuous activity; in the 1920s it was thought that this could be done by establishing locals in the larger towns where these workers spent the winter in idleness and poverty. Some organizers felt the path to permanent and effective organization was the affiliation of harvesters with the packinghouse and cannery workers' unions that were forming in the middle thirties. Others propounded a single, statewide union of all workers in every agriculture-related job. A resolution to this effect was adopted by the California State Federation of Labor convention in 1935. Two years later the federation formally accepted the responsibility for the organization of farm workers.

Notwithstanding these concerns the history of agricultural workers in the state was influenced less by class solidarity between industrial operatives and harvesters in the cities than by racial tensions and ethnic differences. Farm labor was associated with aliens, and their place in labor history was marked by agitation against Japanese, Chinese, Filipino, and, less overtly, Mexicans. As industrialization progressed on the West coast, urban workers subjected to the cycles of boom and depression drifted to the fields for temporary jobs. From the farming areas there was a counter movement of men seeking escape from subsistence wages, mechanization, and a lower level of living presenting what the city unions regarded as a constant threat to organized labor. Said John F. Shelley, "The entire labor movement is weakened without a strong organization of agricultural workers."[299] Moreover, as labor leaders in the large cities like San Francisco and Los Angeles looked with concern at the corporate interests based in rural California, and the political structures they gave rise to, they saw that the opposition to this power was led by the militant leftwing organizers of the I.W.W., the

Trade Union Unity League, and the Union of Cannery Packinghouse and Agricultural Workers. Paul Scharrenberg, an early statesman of urban unionism, explained in 1942 to the LaFollette investigating committee that the goals of the State Federation of Labor were to help the harvesters obtain a little more to eat, and thus neutralize the soap box type of organizer, and to provide benefits to the employers also. Still later, as the federation became skillfully pragmatic in politics, it saw that demands for justice and a little more to eat for farm laborers could make them useful as pawns in the political game, exchangeable for concessions to the urban industrial unions.

In this context the NFLU made its California appearance. It was responding to the watchword of labor throughout the nation—"organize the unorganized." It had a dues-paying affiliated membership. Its first action, the strike against DiGiorgio, aimed at union recognition, collective bargaining, and wage increases, revolutionary aims in such an industry, to be sure, but commonplace ones in such a labor movement. In moving against DiGiorgio Local 218 had observed all the requirements of formal procedure, with signed authorization cards, a list of demands, elected representatives, central labor council approval and due notice. Members of a sister union, the Teamsters, joined in the strike. In calling the strike the NFLU could say in good faith that it had exhausted all avenues of peaceful negotiation. And when the union recited the miserable conditions of rural life in Kern County, it was merely recalling to organized labor what it had been saying for twenty years. The response of the affiliated unions in the state federation was sympathetic.

The foundations for this support were laid through the central labor councils, beginning with that of Kern County. The Fresno council raised a small sum to start off organizing in the citrus area of the Central Valley. In Salinas for a short time the Teamsters local provided desk space and use of a telephone, in addition to token contributions made by the labor council for organizational expenses. In the rear of the council's Labor Temple in Salinas the NAWU was allowed to use rent free the hiring hall, a small shed equipped with benches and a kitchen table. The councils were prompt to place farm corporations on their "we do not patronize" lists, a form of passive boycotting that did not go beyond appeals to their own rank and file. C. J. Haggerty, Secretary-Treasurer of the state federation, received Mitchell and Hasiwar cordially on their first visit in 1947.

During the DiGiorgio strike the federation contributed five hundred dollars a month to the union. There were other indications of welcome and encouragement. Haggerty detailed members of his staff to assist not only at DiGiorgio but also in the Imperial Valley, Fresno, and Salinas. They played an active role in the negotiations that led to the Schenley settlement. The Winery Workers Union joined the Teamsters in support of the DiGiorgio strikes. During the cotton strikes Haggerty authorized the financing of lawsuits against anti-picketing ordinances, carrying them to successful appeals in the higher courts. The federation's research library in San Francisco was available to the NAWU, and its bulletin from time to time carried reports of the campaign against Public Law 78. The federation remained critical of the bracero system throughout, with Haggerty demanding publicly that the secretary of labor hold open hearings and permit labor representatives to take part in the periodic negotiations with the Mexican government. In 1949 Haggerty said: "We do not believe that the U.S. Employment Service in this state is capable of contributing a point of view that would represent the best interests of . . . members of trade unions in agriculture."[300] When he learned from the NAWU that agreements had been negotiated without labor's participation, he expressed the fear that "the United States could be made an agent for the Associated Farmers."

The federation maintained its generally sympathetic attitude toward the NAWU, but it did not wholeheartedly accept it into its councils. The central labor bodies, notoriously weak financially, soon stopped donating funds for organizing harvesters, disappointed that the NAWU did not establish full-time local business agents to consolidate the work begun. By this time in the history of American labor the central bodies were no longer the driving force for organizing the unorganized. The authority and the funds to do this had become centralized in the hands of the secretary-treasurer of the state federation. In counties like Fresno, Orange, Imperial, and Yuba the councils operated in the strongholds of the Associated Farmers and the Farm Bureau Federation. The NAWU, their perpetual challenger, was not showing signs of settling down in stable locals. The politics of accommodation were uneasy at best, and the NAWU was not conforming to type. It insisted on picketing Mexican consuls, which irritated and puzzled business agents who could not understand the connection. With its overriding interest in the education of its members, the NAWU was prone to raise beyond the issues of low wages and the absence of contracts those of power, which accounted for both. The men of the local industrial unions in rural California had cleared openings in the backwoods of Agri-businessland, but they did not extend beyond the narrow circles of craft interest. Around them rural society was being transformed through technology, discarding thousands of harvesters who had no exit but to the crowded cities. The small family farm was falling before corporate agriculture. An economy of food scarcity and high prices was encouraged by law, making living more costly not only in the cities but in the country as well. The experiment in administered labor that the Associated Farmers was bringing to a successful stage appeared at first to be exclusively a form of anti-unionism in agriculture. In the long run it had possibilities of becoming an economic philosophy embracing all labor. California trade unionists were not looking that far into the future.

The circumstances under which the DiGiorgio strike ended contributed to the growing alienation of the NAWU from the state federation. Some members of the federations executive council were disconcerted, to say the least, by the publication of a congressional forgery in which the NAWU was attacked as the protege of communist fronts and which was signed by, among others, Richard M. Nixon. When DiGiorgio filed a multimillion complaint for libel, naming federation affiliates, they refused to join the union in resisting the attack. The suit resulting from the film *Poverty in the Valley of Plenty* became the conversation piece of labor officials around the state as an example of amateur unionism. Hasiwar's stock fell, Mitchell was avoided, and I became a diligent but ineffective man-about-the-state.

The monthly subsidy from the federation was cut off in July 1951, at which time the federation was spending $35,481 a year for the organizing expenses of its own staff and $5,500 to assist the NFLU. In 1953 the ratio was zero for the NFLU and $34,394 for the staff, of which $19,932 was for travel and related expenses of three members of the executive board.[301] The 1953 state convention did resolve that "the desirability of such support [for the NAWU] should be reaffirmed," directing that it should be left in the hands of Haggerty. He had already turned down a request from the union to continue financing the legal attack of the county antinoise ordinances, beyond the final donation of $1,000 for this purpose. "There is a limitation to what we can do for any one organization," Haggerty wrote. He estimated that the federation had spent $65,000 over a period of nearly five years aiding the NAWU.

The NAWU and the state federation went their separate ways after 1951. At that time the federation had an estimated membership of 1.3 million workers of whom 41 percent were in the transportation, warehousing, building, and retail trades. Out of some 3,500 locals, 25 were registered in agriculture, mining, and fishing. The prevailing wage scales under collective contracts in 1948 were indicative of the gap that remained between farm labor and industrial unionists. Average hourly earnings for construction workers in December of that year were $2.14; for farm workers, 70 cents an hour.

Wages measured only the economic distance between the two sectors of the working class, industrial and agricultural. The gap widened as the NAWU, failing to abide by approved standards of organizing, moved over the state tracking the bracero system and mounting limited actions in what appeared as a poor imitation of the hit-and-run tactics of earlier years. Its locals paid little or nothing in dues to the central labor bodies. It was winning no contracts. It did not cut an impressive figure in the ceremonials of the federation, such as the annual conventions. Its jurisdiction was doubtful, cautiously watched by the Teamsters and often flouted by the Packinghouse Workers, its picket lines ignored by both. Servicing, the true measure of a business agent, was provided by the NAWU not only to braceros but to illegals as well. None of this made sense to Scharrenberg's successors.

What the union thought were significant activities did not impress the leaders of organized labor. The documentation of the cottonseed monopoly was produced by the union, but it did not bring labor pressure to bear on the investigation the NAWU asked for. In the closing of the farm labor supply centers the mobilization of funds, personnel, publicity, and power were all on the side of agri-business.

The federation's position on these matters was decided by its top officers, little weight being given to the views of those most affected, the farm workers represented by their own union. In the long tradition of solidarity, as long as the NAWU locals remained affiliated with the federation the right to present their views with some expectation of support was assumed. But in this case it became increasingly clear that the ties between the federation, now a respected and influential institution, and a class of farm laborers, the domestics, were loosening. Association with a class that was being dispossessed by the design of agri-business, acts of Congress, and the consent of permissive bureaucrats was unpromising. The officers of the federation reported to the state convention of 1955 that the three remaining locals—247 of Bakersfield, 218 of Arvin-Lamont, and 213 of Fresno—had been suspended for nonpayment of per capita dues.

The suspension brought the political realities within the federation in line with those outside of it. The agricultural laborers' only hope of bringing to bear some leverage on the legislative and executive powers of the state was through organized labor. This was asking too much too soon of the NAWU, a newcomer in California. The NAWU carried no weight in the political process; the exclusion of farm workers from it was already a tradition.

Advocacy of state legislation relating to the welfare of working people was entirely in the hands of the federation's lobbyists in Sacramento, complemented by representatives of Teamsters and other special interests. Lobbying was costly. The NAWU could neither contribute to the expense of the federation's advocates nor maintain a lobby of its own. Bills presented to the state senate and assembly that affected vital interests of farm workers were compromised in the lobbying process. If the bills became law, those affected by them were in the position of third parties who were totally excluded from the final decisions. This was regularly the position of farm workers. Even before the bills reached the floor of the legislature, the assignment to the committee that was to conduct public hearings had already been made. From these decisions, too, the NAWU was totally shut out. Furthermore, the advocates of the federation in Sacramento promoted legislative programs representing their client's interests. The program might be a simple bill or an agenda embracing many areas of public policy. The details of such agenda changed from year to year, but the continuing goals were to add new benefits for industrial workers and to widen the coverage of those already established by law.

Each year the secretary of the federation presented to his constituents a summary report entitled *The Sacramento Story*. "In 1951," the *Story* said, "the California State Federation emerged from the session with historic victories in workmen's compensation and disability insurance." In 1955 organized labor made impressive headway in the social insurance program, the value of which was estimated at between twenty-one and thirty million dollars in additional benefits to industrial workers.

From time to time the federation included in its agenda legislative proposals regarding farm labor matters, which did not reflect major issues raised by the NAWU. On the whole, such proposals represented the federation's lobbying strategy of providing itself with counters that could be played in the bargaining process. These were modest indeed. The 1957 *Story* reported that the federation had won improvements in licensing labor contractors and the registration of vehicles used in the transporting of farm workers. Typically, in the 1959 session of the legislature labor and industry lobbyists agreed on Senate Joint Resolution 19 "calling upon Congress" to adopt minimum wage legislation for agriculture. Calling upon Congress was the ritual for dismissing the thorny controversies that the NAWU was provoking.

How the federation's lobby operated on these matters was described in the 1959 *Story*: "Not one measure affecting farm workers was passed that did not have the blessing of the dominant farm labor groups." The federation's officers were fully informed and currently documented on the NAWU's campaign against Public Law 78; but they did not offer any legislative remedies on that score. The State Board of Agriculture was a creature of the state, exercising arbitrary power over the Department of Employment. The chief of the Farm Placement Service, a civil servant subject to legislative oversight, was declaring farm labor shortages that had been proved time and again to be false. The legal authority of the State Conciliation Service to declare the existence of a strike was set aside without protest from the federation. Had the federation proposed to correct these abuses the chances of positive action by the legislature would probably have been poor; but they would have set in motion the public debate that was being so successfully muted by agri-business.

The federation's leaders were well advised, for once this happened, controversies would have disturbed the lobbying process in which the federation participated so skillfully. Haggerty described the situation: "months of intensive planning and negotiation . . . may be likened to a 120-day bargaining session, during which one premature move at any time could have destroyed the whole federation program."[302]

At the other pole of political power—the governor of the state—farm workers fared no better. The political crosscurrents that the NAWU was riding were clearly illustrated during Governor Goodwin J. Knight's campaign for re-election in the fall of 1954. The federation endorsed Knight after he had answered to its satisfaction the question of where he stood "on the vital labor issues facing us in California," as it was phrased by the California Labor League for Political Education. No issues were raised concerning the growers' offensive against domestic farm workers. Their evasion continued by common consent. Haggerty was at the height of his influence. He recalled: "Never in my years in Sacramento have I had a governor, Republican or Democrat, call me into his office, as Governor Knight has, and say, 'Neil, this is your bill. You write it. Tell me what you want in it, and I'll see that you get it.' "[303].

Gubernatorial courtesy was bipartisan. Governer Edmund G. Brown was in office when, through the persistent efforts of the NAWU, an investigation of the workings of the bracero system was made, resulting in the Kaufman report. Its contents were not only corroborative but explosive. The decision not to release it resulted from prudent inquiries among members ·of the legislature about its potential effect on their influential constituents in the rural areas.

The NAWU had established a reputation for credibility among journalists throughout the state. This confidence, added to the conflictive nature of the events in which the union was involved in the fields, gave the NAWU a consistently favorable press. Officers of the federation did not relish this. While "going to the newspapers" was not regarded as helpful by leaders of established unions, to the NAWU it was a vital factor in creating the climate of opinion necessary for the termination of Public Law 78.

When asked to help the union in the legal prosecution of the Twist-ems deductions in Salinas, Haggerty responded: "Before agreeing to furnish the services of the federation's attorneys I would want to go into this matter very carefully." The NAWU never heard from him again on the matter. The federation's attorneys had already rejected the union's appeal for help in challenging the validity of the bracero contracts. They were reluctant because the international agreements were treaties to which the United States government was a party, and for that reason challenging them would be a futile gesture.

Haggerty also decided it was inadvisable for the federation to con-tribute funds for the Tracy strikers whose picket lines had been broken under orders of Teamster officials. At the height of the NAWU's cam-paign to have Hayes removed, only the Los Angeles County Federation of Labor supported it.[304] While the NAWU attempted, wherever it went, to locate areas of possible cooperation with the small family farmers, the federation never went beyond resolutions, addressed to the small farmers "to work out a common sense program with the AFL's union of farm workers."

On occasion the federation went from avoidance of support on issues raised by the NAWU to endorsement of the antagonists of the union. One of these was Don Larin, deputy director of the Department of Employment in charge of farm labor. Larin was transferred from the Washington Bureau of Employment Security, where he had learned the intricacies of the bracero system. In 1948 he had a hand in the invasion of hundreds of illegals into Texas escorted by Department of Labor and Immigration officials.[305] It was Larin who ten years before helped to revoke the department's directive concerning union clearance on cer-tification for braceros. Larin sustained the FPS policy of breaking up union crews by referring their members to different farms.

Larin's appointment as deputy director required clearance with the State Federation of Labor. When consulted, Haggerty informed the governor's office that he "had no objections." The NAWU learned of Larin's confirmation from news stories. I wrote Haggerty on April 23, 1960, asking him to consider withdrawing his endorsement of Larin and making a public statement to that effect. Haggerty never answered and Larin stayed on to advise Hayes in the continuing collusion of Public Law 78. Haggerty was not alone in approving of Larin; the January 6, 1962, *California Farmer* said he had given "a heartening demonstration of a high order of public service under very difficult circumstances."

Where it was not a question of appointments or of positive action or of avoidance of risky positions the farm workers were dealt with as wards of the federation incapable of speaking for themselves.

Gubernatorial appointments to commissions and boards to study farm labor problems customarily included a spokesman for labor, usually the secretary of the state federation. Haggerty served under Governor Warren in this capacity. Ranking officers of the federation thus became a buffer between the farm workers and state government, sparing it the embarrassment of facing issues raised by the NAWU. It also insulated the union from information about the operation of the agencies that controlled farm jobs, legitimizing decisions that were plainly hostile to harvesters. And it raised one more barrier against interference with the legislative mechanism in Sacramento.

Where the wardship of the agricultural laborers was most clearly visible was in the governor's Advisory Council in the Department of Employment. Three of the council's seven members were appointed with the advice and consent of organized labor. In 1959 these three were C. J. Haggerty, Harry Finks, who lobbied against inclusion of farm workers legislation on housing standards, and C. P. Scully, general counsel for the federation. The council had no administrative powers, but its position near the director of employment brought within its influence functionaries like Don Larin and Edward Hayes. Between 1947 and 1959 there was no communication between the union and the council or any of its individual members in their official capacity.

In sum, this was the official recognition extended to the new statesmanship toward which organized labor had been striving since the 1940s, when Paul Scharrenberg moved from its ranks to the position of Director of Industrial Relations. "California," he claimed in 1948, "yields to no state in the matter of excellence of its labor laws." Governor Knight said of Scharrenberg that he had "participated in the progress of forty years" out of which had emerged the labor counterpart of the new industry, both joined in the common achievement of coast-to-coast abundance. In an address to the California Manufacturers Association delivered on October 25, 1957, Haggerty referred to "mature labor-management relations" which in California "are already ours." The high standard of living that had been achieved was the yardstick of success of private enterprise in the state. "Labor," Haggerty emphasized, "should accept fully the necessity for technological advancement and responsibility for increased productivity." He noted in an earlier report to the federation that labor had earned respect in many quarters "for our indomitable, uncompromising fight for the most exploited workers of America," referring to agricultural laborers.

Haggerty had reason to grow more confident. Labor repulsed the effort of employers to gain public approval of Proposition 18 for a right-to-work constitutional amendment. Having turned off the attack, he issued a public statement on November 7, 1958. "Now that this threat to democratic unionism has been vanquished, we are free to resume normal relationships with the business community of the state."

Haggerty also knew the private uses of statesmanship. Around that time he telephoned me to ask whether I would be interested in the post of labor information officer in the American embassy of Havana, for which he was willing to recommend me. I had travelled in Cuba as a representative of the Pan American Union years before. My response was that I preferred to stay in California. The termination of Public Law 78 was still several years away.

One of the marks of statesmanship is an appropriate rhetoric, and the federation had it. The February 3, 1954, issue of its news service carried this pronouncement by Haggerty: "The American Federation of Labor is under moral obligation to protect the living standards of all who work on our soil, regardless of race, creed, color, or national origin." This was in keeping with the note sounded years before in the convention proceedings of 1955, which declared that "agricultural workers . . . remain the forgotten step-children of our economy and the victims of inaction." In his 1957 Labor Day message Haggerty went back to the fundamentals: "We were founded to remove the outrages visited upon the men and women and children in the name of industrial profit." The Statement of Policy of the first California convention after the AFL-CIO merger, stated: "The plight of the agricultural worker is a moral and economic scandal requiring fundamental re-evaluation of all state and federal socioeconomic legislation enacted in the past two and a half decades which, by exclusion, has reduced the agricultural worker to the level of second class citizens."

The federation's August 29, 1959, *Weekly News Letter* loftily intoned: "Part of the nineteenth century has survived completely intact and untouched by collective bargaining and the legislative effect of unionism." To the progressing industrial unions this was a reminder of where they would still be "had organized labor remained too weak to win some measure of equality in bargaining with industry." The living reminders of that somber thought were the straggling ranks of the NAWU.

The International Brotherhood of Teamsters

The principal counterpoint to the struggles of agricultural laborers was the California State Federation of Labor, as indicated in the preceding section. No less important was the role of the Teamsters, unobtrusive at times and at others coming through with a staccato impact on the NAWU, as in the Imperial Valley and Tracy strikes.

Food processing, the industrial base of the Teamsters, began in 1852 in a commercial salmon cannery on the west bank of the Sacramento River near the state capital. When railroads made possible the large-scale overland shipment of canned fruits and vegetables, corporate food processing entered its modern period. Small plants gave way to the competitive advantage of the large ones. The figures for 1925 and 1961 tell the story of impressive growth. Peak employment in the vegetable and seafood canneries increased from 23,000 to 72,000, the value of the product from $181 million to over $1 billion. The plants were concentrated in Orange, Contra Costa, Santa Clara, and San Joaquin counties. By the middle of the century Cal-Pak, Libby McNeil, Heinz, Hunt Foods, Flotill, and Richmond Chase had become household brand names throughout America.

The understructure of this formidable industry lay, of course, in the fields where, from the 1920s on, radical unionists were carrying on the campaigns that the Industrial Workers of the World had begun. Their actions disturbed agri-business, dependent on the harvests, no less than the leaders of organized labor.

The leadership of the State Federation of Labor viewed with alarm and distaste the threat of soap-box organizers who did not fill the requirements of bona-fide trade unionism. In 1937 the organization drive to bring cannery workers into the ranks of labor began, the state federation supplying eighteen organizers, funds, and political support for the drive. It was swift, energetic, and successful, ending with the signing of a contract between the California State Council of Cannery Unions, affiliated with the Teamsters International Brotherhood and covering initially 65,000 workers. On behalf of all the major processors the contract was signed by California Growers and Processors Incorporated, a consortium which represented the united front of the industry. The Associated Farmers gave the historic event their blessing, approving the conservative and constructive record of the Teamsters Union rather than that of the radical Harry Bridges and the CIO.

The Teamsters, which became the most powerful union in the state, represented the most advanced stage of mature labor, with a quality of statesmanship, effectiveness in legislative advocacy, resources, and autonomy that some envied and others feared. With a solid base among cannery workers and drivers, the Teamsters guarded their jurisdiction as the fortress it was, always ready for sorties beyond into surrounding jurisdictions when time had ripened them for the picking.

In this the Teamsters were favored by certain trends in the nature of corporate agriculture and the rural society in which it was bred. Mechanization, the immediate product of technology, was driving harvesters from the fields, putting more of the means of production on wheels, the trademark of teamsterism. Even the traditionally fixed packing sheds were being mounted on mobile rigs, their lumbering profiles like warehouses on the move. Agri-business was rapidly catching up with other sectors of the national economy, integrating into itself the weaker partners of agriculture, the family farmers, while at another level the Teamsters proceeded with integrations of their own. As integration proceeded in farm production after the 1940s, similarities developed in the mental processes of agri-businessmen and the Teamster leadership. The higher levels, they were joined finally in what the American labor movement happily called the sweetheart contract, agreements arrived at in the spirit of affectionate compromise, by pyramided powers on both sides of the bargain.

Between these powers lay a still amorphous mass of harvesters, stereotyped as migrants, poor by definition, losing their little social stability step by step to the advance of the bracero system. As the domestics lost their moorings they tended to revert to the classic model of undesirables in whom the Teamsters had no interest. Typically, the contract signed with Visalia citrus growers in 1946 included "all employees except field workers." In October 1948 Teamster President Dave Beck, at a meeting called to plan the organization of the fruit, vegetable, and produce industries, sent out a message of straightline integration that stopped abruptly at the fields: "We want to go back to a certain point and organize . . . produce row so that we can control it from the packing shed . . . straight through to the consumer . . . . We will not organize field labor . . . . Our union will not accept that jurisdiction." Even though the cannery union, a subsidiary of the Teamsters

International Brotherhood, opened a direct line to the fields, Beck's organizers shunned it.

They had good reasons for this. The Teamsters held contracts with grower-shipper associations whose members were also employers of field labor. Low wages in the fields cushioned the costs of packing, processing, transportation, and warehousing. Organization of harvesters would have hardened the bargaining position of the employers against the Teamsters when their contracts were renegotiated. The labor pool that served the fields and orchards remained notoriously fluid. Teamster drivers depended on peak hauls during the harvests and field organization would only introduce another uncertaintly, that of potentially concerted action by the harvesters. Besides, their wages were lower by a wide margin than those the Teamsters had won in the other branches of the food industry, offering little incentive for costly organizing campaigns. Mechanization was making steady inroads into harvesting, demanding more skilled labor at higher wages, and thus creating the conditions which the Teamsters required for profitable organizing. The practical approach for them was to assimilate only those operations in which the harvesters attended the machines.

As to those field workers who remained "on the ground" the Teamsters were well advised of the problems of organizing them. Their official organ, the *International Teamster,* of September 1950, observed, "The Teamsters know as well as anyone how Western agriculture operates. Organizers in our craft have been active for many years and we all know what an uphill battle it is to get a decent break for the back-breaking toil required to harvest the many crops of the west."

The economic condition, the social status, the physical demands of their work did not, however, totally dispel an uneasiness in Teamster circles concerning field laborers. Clearly the NAWU was attempting to establish itself in the fields, at the initial point of production. Obstruction there meant loss of work to drivers, packers, and cannery employees. The concept of preventive organization was never absent from the Teamster's minds. Unions meant strikes and strikes meant stoppages. Since the Teamsters held the contracts with the cannery workers who packed tomatoes, "if they can organize the field workers they can prevent any stoppage at the cannery."[306] This Teamster observation applied to every crop that moved into processing.

Up to the 1940s prevention had been approached negatively. It consisted simply of combatting rival organizations that threatened to form behind the Teamster's back, or to keep such organizations firmly in the hands of the traditionalists in the AFL establishment. Left-wing unionism never ceased to hover over the fields, holding isolated footholds in packing sheds under contract with the United Packinghouse Workers of America, a CIO affiliate. Against this threat the federation served the interests of the Teamsters through the control of charters, the suspension of locals, and a rigid insistence on bona-fide unionism as defined by Haggerty's predecessors in the state federation.

In theory, the NAWU presented such a threat also, but the realists of the labor movement in California, like the Associated Farmers, never considered it serious. And when there was a possibility that it might indeed become effective, they, like the Associated Farmers, intervened from within the political establishment to impede its efforts, or simply abstained from coming to its aid.

The year that marked the beginning of the end of the NAWU, 1959, the Teamsters were hesitating between optional strategies, negative or positive prevention of organization. The *International Teamster* of June 1951 was ambivalent: "The Teamsters Union does not want to see the shameful conditions prevailing in the past in farm labor continued." The social consciousness that peeped through this statement had not appeared in Dave Beck's guidelines, but it clearly indicated an awareness of a potential jurisdictional area that could continue to be disturbed by outsiders. If these disturbances ever became threatening to the Teamsters, they would act.

During a strike directed by the United Packinghouse Workers, a Teamster organizer observed, "Watching the striking, picketing, and lack of organization the Teamsters decided to move in to protect their own people from unemployment and confusion."[307] Behind the confusion they discerned something else. Einar Mohn, a high official of the Western Conference of Teamsters, expressed it succinctly. Mechanization was proceeding at such a rapid rate that skilled workers would soon become "a backbone of the labor force." His union, he predicted, would move in on the farm workers in "a big way." The new men of the mechanized harvests "will be a nonmigrant labor force." And he made it clear that the Teamsters were still not interested in the ordinary farm workers.[308]

The "ordinary farm workers" who were thus to remain outside the fold were mostly Mexicans, more numerous than Blacks, Anglos, and Filipinos. The Mexicans, as the Teamsters were well aware, subdivided into domestics, braceros, and illegals. Concerning each of these the Brotherhood had well-defined feelings.

President Beck had expressed his views on the wetbacks in the *International Teamster* of March 1954. Beck said that because of "the dismal failure on the part of the Federal Government of policing the border . . . this country is being flooded with cheap labor." He regarded the traffic in illegals as a threat to "the economic health as well as the security of this nation." With the illegals themselves the Teamsters had only such contacts as would make their alarm and their repulsion more pronounced. The illegals infiltrated packing sheds under contract, abetted by the employers. They were permanent fugitives from the law, anonymous and totally unorganizable. Spanish was their only language. Usually bedraggled in appearance, socially and economically they stood even lower than "ordinary farm workers." By the tenets of mature trade unionism they could in no way be regarded as potential subjects for integration.

In contrast with the irreversible status of the illegals, the braceros looked somewhat more promising to the Teamsters, whose views evolved from hostility through tolerance to accommodation.

Of the bracero system the November 1, 1949, *Cannery Reporter* said, "We are opposed to this sort of international agreement to lower living standards in this country . . . a system that will bring Mexican nationals into a substandard area to compete with local workers." The system, the statement continued, offered the imported workers "nothing else but a share of the poverty and the exploitation suffered for years by the farm workers in general." Two years later the *International Teamster,* echoing these alarms, called it an evil of long standing in the State, foreseeing that they would eventually move into the canneries and processing plants. This was language prompted by experience. Braceros were already being found in the huge processing plants of the Central Valley and the coastal counties. And the Farm Placement Service was in the wings, ready, if called upon, to produce labor shortages in the canneries as well as in the fields, complete with prevailing wages drastically below those of the cannery unions.

In Teamster-controlled packing sheds, where they kept a running skirmish with the UPWA-CIO, there was at first a tendency to compromise on the bracero by omitting them from contracts with grower-shipper associations. Their dues were checked off automatically; they stayed out of the way in matters relating to policy and control. Moreover, the braceros were the instruments of the undoing of the NAWU—not a principal objective of the Teamsters but nevertheless an agreeable fringe benefit for them.

During the first five years of NAWU activity in California, Teamster locals had been generally supportive. On occasion there was even joint action between them and NAWU organizers, as in the DiGiorgio strike. In the Imperial Valley, until the NAWU's strike was disavowed by Beck, there was a possibility that through mutual support the beet fields might be organized, with the Teamsters taking jurisdiction of the drivers. Furthermore, a Teamster interest in the NAWU arose from the nagging presence of the CIO's UPWA, which had won contracts in numerous sheds in California and Arizona. For a time Teamster policy hesitated between the fear that the UPWA might approach the contested sheds through the back door of field organization, and the chance that the NAWU itself might some day be in a position to do likewise. The channels of communication established during the friendly years between the cannery unions and the NAWU on the whole served them more than the farm workers. Hasiwar and some cannery locals in the Central Valley for a time worked together through a joint committee on information, a reciprocal but not a mutually helpful arrangement. This interest in keeping abreast of undercurrents in the fields was pointedly expressed by Einar Mohn. In 1949, Becker, while on assignment to organize the Schenley Corporation vineyards, told Mohn that the union intended to picket the big ranch; Mohn responded testily that it was the first time the NAWU had advised the Teamsters before putting out pickets. Mohn stressed his interest in being kept abreast of other plans of the union. After Hasiwar left California I refused to maintain the joint committee; while it had lasted information of great value might have been passed back to the NAWU, but it never was.

Beginning in 1954 it was apparent that the NAWU and the Teamsters Brotherhood were on opposite courses so far as the bracero system was concerned. As the aim of the NAWU to repeal Public Law 78 became clear, the Teamsters began to move toward the industry's position on the issue. In 1954 I had reported to Mitchell my sense of this change, which I thought could end in outright acceptance of bracero importation. An early sign was the singular absence of Teamster statements criticizing the bracero operation that were coming from all the other sectors of organized labor. Another was the evident interest among Teamster circles in the disastrous effect that bracero hiring was having on UPWA locals. Still another was that the reports that the NAWU regularly circulated on the illegal and widespread use of braceros as tractor drivers never brought any reponse from Teamster representatives.

It was not until 1964 that reversal of Teamster policy concerning braceros was completed. On the eve of the termination of Public Law 78, Mohn said that growers did need braceros. His views, published in the *San Francisco Chronicle* on December 30, 1964, were a capsule of what Thomas Harris, analyst for the Western Conference of Teamsters in San Francisco, had stated a few days earlier in a public hearing.

Harris stated that the Teamsters had a direct interest in the prosperity of the agricultural industry. In related employment there were 500 field workers, several thousand drivers, and some 60,000 cannery and frozen food processing workers who were members of the Brotherhood. "Approximately one-quarter of the 270,000 Teamsters in California are directly dependent for their livelihood and well-being upon the prosperity of agriculture in California," Harris testified. Obliquely criticizing the industry for not having prepared for an orderly phasing out of labor importation, Harris went on to say: "the abrupt termination of the bracero program confronts our agricultural economy with a crisis which jeopardizes the economic security of some 70,000 Teamsters." Harris interpolated: "As for now many crops can neither be raised nor harvested solely by domestic labor." Crediting the Teamsters with "quite intensive and extensive experience in the organization of agricultural workers," Harris endorsed Governor Brown's proposal to phase out the program over a five-year period, which, Harris said, "would permit an orderly reorganization of the agricultural labor force."

The governor was coming close to one of those triumphs of consensus of which politicians dream. Between the state administration, unidentified officials of the State Federation of Labor, the most powerful union, and the Associated Farmers an agreement as to bracero importation seemed to be in the making. The NAWU disrupted it.

Harris's prediction of disaster for the agricultural industry was taken from the script of agri-business spokesmen. So was his assertion that the crops could not be harvested without braceros. In nearly ten years neither the U.S. Department of Labor nor the Farm Placement Service had been able to identify a single crop that had been lost because of a lack of labor, domestic, illegal, or contracted.

Three years before the Harris testimony was given, the Brotherhood was already working on a model for the reorganization of the agricultural labor force. This model was set forth in the contract negotiated in the spring of 1961 with the Bud Antle Company of Salinas, the largest lettuce grower and shipper in California. On its own acreage the company harvested 8,000 acres of lettuce and 1,300 acres of carrots, apart from what it produced on more than 3,000 acres of leased land. The company recognized the Teamsters as the bargaining agent for all persons employed by it in growing, packing, and harvesting agricultural commodities. It fixed an hourly minimum of one dollar for stoop labor with overtime pay after eight hours.

The Bud Antle Company had used braceros for several years before signing the Teamster contract. It had firsthand knowledge of the economics of the subject, as the Teamsters had of its strategic implications for the complete neutralization of the UPWA. The thinking of agri-business and the Teamsters became more alike, and the Brotherhood agreed "to assist the company in obtaining foreign supplemental workers for the Company in its harvesting operations." In the contract such supplemental workers were placed in a special category as follows: "Foreign supplemental workers are not subject to any term or condition of this agreement except as they may benefit from the wage provisions hereof and shall be governed solely by the applicable provisions of Public Law 78 and the Migrant Labor Agreement of 1951."

The system of administered labor, proposed by agricultural capitalists and served by a willing bureaucracy, now had the official endorsement of a powerful union.

The contract, a model of "sweetheart" negotiating, on the one hand clearly fixed the status of the few domestic workers who would be hired through the Teamsters hiring hall. On the other it created a special class of ordinary harvesters, the braceros, whose terms of employment were to be left to the sole discretion of the company.

Had this agreement been extended to the agricultural industry throughout the state, it would have been an adroit answer to the criticisms that the NAWU had been making for ten years. It pledged Teamster support in the recruiting of braceros in addition to those already available to the industry through the Farm Placement Service, the U.S. Department of Labor, and the government of Mexico. It closed the door on the possibilities for union representation of braceros, a principle recognized in Article 22 of the international agreement. Side by side with the wage scale agreed to for citizen employees, there would remain the prevailing wage declared by the State Department of Employment through Hayes's office, subject to the advice of the State Board of Agriculture. The number of braceros to be solicited with the approval of the Brotherhood would be determined by the employer, which in turn would be reflected in the labor shortages to be found by the Farm Placement Service.

In many respects, the Antle contract was the product of brilliant craftsmanship by both agri-business and organized labor at their most mature stage. To the company it meant a guarantee that it would "continue to have available . . . an almost limitless supply of good, stable, competent, and willing labor." So, at least, said Bud Antle official George H. Hobbs, addressing the Commonwealth Club in San Francisco in June 1961. It excluded a class of field workers defined as "farming or cultural personnel," that is "ordinary farm laborers." It protected the job security of 450 permanent employees and Teamster members, by keeping domestic harvesters under the discipline of the Teamsters and the braceros under that of the U.S. Department of Labor, avoiding what Hobbs called "abortive interruptions of work." And it was cheaper in comparison to what field labor might cost Antle under conditions that it could well imagine.

How closely attuned big business and big labor had become was manifested in the Hobbs address cited above, which paralleled the testimony of Harris already quoted. Hobbs also made these points: "The jurisdiction over the packing process was destroyed in one fell swoop. UPWA had been trying to regain its jurisdiction. They have caused both strife and strike. . . . To say we don't need supplemental workers is false. . . ." Hobbs also regarded the contract with the Teamsters as relief for the industry from "the search for qualified, willing, and able workers . . . among the culls of society—winos, vagrants, and wretches."

These were, briefly, the labor relations between the NAWU and the International Brotherhood of Teamsters, Warehousemen and Helpers between 1947 and 1959. It is now necessary to turn to those with the United Packinghouse Workers of America-CIO.

The United Packinghouse Workers of America

Standing midway between the fields and the canneries as an important source for farm-related employment were the packing sheds where fresh fruits and vegetables were sorted, trimmed, wrapped, boxed, graded, tied, packaged, cooled, labeled, and loaded. Isolated in the open country, as in the asparagus fields of the San Joaquin, or strung along railway tracks in important terminals like Los Banos and El Centro, they were the transfer points for millions of tons of produce moving to market in a hurry. Loadings from some of these larger packing terminals were counted by the hundreds of freight cars and trucks. With rare exceptions, the sheds were permanent structures fixed in the economic landscape of rural California, the center of the logistics that connected it with the national economy.

The men and women who served the sheds were skilled in the various specialties of their craft, mobile enough to follow the cycles of lettuce or cantaloups or grapes from one end of the state to the other, stable the rest of the year. With respect to the harvesters they were an elite, predominantly white, organized, and better paid. Getting a job in a packing shed was the next rung on the economic ladder for the field worker. From the assembly floors and loading platforms where trucks and railway cars were loaded the shed workers could look down on the field hands around them economically and psychologically.

Unions that began among harvesters inevitably fixed their attention on the sheds for these were the pivots around which organization could more easily begin. The temptation to "move into the sheds" was sharpened by the uncertainties, the costliness, the hazards, and the meager returns from field organization. In the shifting swirls of the agricultural labor pool the sheds were backwaters in which a stable union could be floated more easily. And as these advantages were compared with the dim prospects of the harvesting class of workers, the competition between rival unions for control of the sheds heightened.

This was the course on which the militant organizers of farm labor in the 1920s and 1930s moved through the California scene. Their unions began among the harvesters—the Cannery and Agricultural Workers Industrial Union; the Trade Union Unity League; the Confederación de Uniones Agrícolas Obreros Mexicanas; the United Cannery, Agricultural and Packinghouse Workers of America; and the Federation of Agricultural Workers Unions.[309] Led by Communist party activists these unions reeled and collapsed under the blows of vigilantism, legislative repression, police harassment, and armed citizen violence. In this succession the UPWA was in active control of many fruit and vegetable packing sheds when Mitchell and Hasiwar arrived in California. Its contracts were principally in Imperial and Salinas.

These contracts bound the UPWA to grower-shippers like D'Arrigo, Grower Shippers of Central California, Farley Fruit, and San Hamburg. The union was recognized as sole bargaining agent for packing shed employees exclusively. Field workers whose production moved directly into the sheds, often in sight of them, were not covered, in which respect the radical UPWA was conventional. Like the Teamsters' contracts with shed operators, the UPWA agreements contained "no strike" clauses by which they justified their violation of NAWU picket lines in Imperial. The Imperial Valley incidents placed the NAWU in identical relationship with both unions, representing a direct threat to the same growers and shippers with which they had agreements. Although as to the sheds UPWA and the Teamsters were openly competitive, UPWA gradually approached the Teamster position with respect to field workers, namely as a jurisdiction of last resort. The options of both unions were the same; the difference was that the Teamsters made their choice earlier, excluding field workers from the cannery contracts and from their agreements with the grower-shippers. In 1937 the state federation chartered the Council of Cannery Unions to organize shed and cannery as well as field workers. In the two decades that followed, therefore, the Teamsters had rounded out only two of the three jurisdictions granted them by the federation.

The UPWA had moved in the opposite direction and away from the radical tradition of its predecessors. Its affiliate in the Salinas Valley, Local 78, took the position in 1953 that "field workers ought to be in a union of field workers, and not in a shed workers' union." One of its officials expanded on the theme in these words: "A union which represents both field and packing shed workers must be careful in accepting wage formulas on hourly rates and productivity. A formula which will result in better returns to workers in the sheds may not work in the fields."[310] The UPWA theoreticians, like those of the Teamsters, shrank from the hazards of complete integration with harvesters.

In this statement there was a new dimension—technical structuralism as the basis of trade union philosophy had its limits. In the complexities of agricultural production these unions were no less disposed to keep field workers separate from the packers than the employers themselves.

On this level there was, however, a major difference between the approach of agri-businessmen and that of the UPWA. In abandoning the field workers, the union tacitly disqualified them as potential bidders for the benefits it had obtained for the packers and therefore made them inadmissible as partners against either the growers or the Teamsters or a combination of both. The growers, on the other hand, were already far along towards cutting the ground, literally, from under UPWA. The undercutting became noticeable in the early 1950s and reached its climax less than ten years later. Their weapon was the bracero.

Field packing of such produce as lettuce, carrots, and celery had become mechanized. It now moved on wheels and its attendants were braceros. They were put to trimming and packing, traditionally operations done in the permanent sheds by domestics. By 1953 in the Imperial Valley one thousand members of the UPWA had been displaced. Small knots of them stood on the roadside looking on helplessly as bracero crews took over, much as NAWU members had stood a few years before. Technology gave displacement another boost; lettuce could now be cooled in a continuous vacuum process that eliminated the icing of crates which domestics had been doing. As the lumbering packing rigs crept over the fields attended by thousands of braceros the sheds closed and sent their domestics home.[311]

The UPWA locals in California, which held some seventy-five shed contracts at one time, were overwhelmed. By 1958 they lost three thousand packing jobs. As the number of domestic packers dwindled, so did their wages. Earnings fell from a range of $1.40 to $2.05 an hour on piece rates to the 85 cents an hour straight time paid the braceros[312] and in some instances to as low as 75 cents.

By 1959 the situation could be described by the union's *Packinghouse Worker* as an uphill fight "to save the five thousand jobs of fruit and vegetable packers" in a struggle to hang on to the scattered outposts of its organization.

At this point the UPWA was reduced to tactics of desperation, too late to turn the tide. In Watsonville it struck in protest, gaining a momentary respite. A second strike was broken as bracero crews crossed picket lines, while police watched as they had in the Imperial and San Joaquin actions against the NAWU harvesters. These were the strikes observed by the Teamsters' business agent, who vowed to end such confusion in his own way. On one occasion members of Local 78 were reduced to pleading with braceros when they were used as scabs in another encounter. "Solo pedimos comprensión," the UPWA handbill read. But the plea for compassion was addressed to aliens who were in custody in a foreign land. Nor was the UPWA any more successful in its appeal to the Department of Labor, to which these events were familiar.

As its hold on the sheds weakened, the UPWA began to reconsider its position with respect to the field laborers it had so frequently disdained. In the citrus belt of Southern California the union once more saw the connection between different sectors of the same working class. It proposed to place picket lines on individual members of the Sunkist Growers, with which the UPWA was in negotiations. The association saw this, rightly enough, as a move in the direction of organizing the pickers. But it could also have meant that the UPWA was simply using the harvesters as leverage to secure the most advantageous terms in the sheds for the Sunkist packers. That had been one of the practical uses of field labor elsewhere and by others than UPWA. Similarly in the 1960 campaign to hold its contracts with lemon shippers in Ventura the UPWA made feints in the orchards; but when the contract was renewed, it did not cover harvesters and made no mention of braceros, who formed more than 80 percent of the field work force.

Hedging its options, the UPWA began a return to the fields. Its jurisdiction there having been confirmed by its parent body, the CIO, it announced a new campaign to organize field workers, along with workers in canneries, packing sheds, and poultry plants.

In the summers of 1954 and 1955 leaflets appeared in farm labor communities of Imperial and Salinas. One of them, dated March 21, 1955, announced: "UPWA–CIO is moving into a new stage—at the grass roots level." Addressing itself to the dominantly Spanish-speaking residents, the UPWA pointedly based its appeal on displacement by braceros—"Podemos conseguirles los trabajos en los campos." But as the UPWA fell back before the advance of the movable sheds in the fields, it proved helpless to restore its members to their jobs.

Throughout the state the UPWA sought to expand its base from the sheds to "the organization of thousands of field workers," as it reported to the CIO in 1954. It would be, announced the Salinas local, "a fight for jobs in the fields for resident workers . . . regardless of where the product is packed, and at union wages." Organizers moved through the Santa Clara, Salinas, and San Joaquin valleys, signing up unemployed field workers and promising that when new contracts were negotiated with regard to the sheds, field workers would be included. Consistent with its new policy UPWA representatives began to address their grievances to state and federal officials in the name of domestic field workers.[313]

As its thin line of resistance weakened, the UPWA never fully committed itself to the plight of the harvesters. It continued to sign contracts which did not cover field jobs. It publicized widely the promise to restore displaced Mexican domestics under its protection. The last contract it signed with Bud Antle Company covering trimmers and packers did not include the braceros in the fields. As a last resort some of the former shed workers, despairing of stopping the bracero tide, demanded that they be given first consideration for field work if the UPWA succeeded in organizing in the fields.

Compared to the single-minded course of the NAWU, that of the UPWA was opportunistic, undecided whether to provoke an open jurisdictional dispute with the NAWU, to ignore it, or to assume leadership on the bracero issue.

In the East and Midwest the UPWA was also losing ground as meat packers moved their plants to rural areas in search of cheaper labor. UPWA president Ralph Helstein was not optimistic about his organizers' ability to bring the field workers into UPWA ranks, and with reason. None of the courses being pursued by UPWA appeared promising. The Teamsters were holding in the sheds, waiting to pick up the remnants of their rival. Meanwhile, UPWA membership melted away. Members of NAWU locals did not respond to the belated promises of Helstein's organizers.

In the spring of 1952 I recommended to NAWU president Mitchell that he initiate an attempt to come to an understanding with Helstein, and he agreed. Nothing was done in that direction, however, and in 1954 I again recommended that a division of tasks be discussed. In July Mitchell proposed to Helstein that joint organizing be undertaken with a clear understanding that the NAWU had no interest in the sheds and that UPWA would discontinue its efforts in the fields. Helstein rejected this, partly, as he explained, because he did not think the NAWU could make any significant contribution to the organizational activities. A. T. Stephens, a vice-president of UPWA, made it clear that his union had no intention of recognizing the AFL's grant of jurisdiction to the NAWU. Mitchell fell back on the idea of persuading the AFL–CIO to set up a joint organizing committee of packinghouse and agricultural workers to be financed and directed by the national parent federation. The NAWU and UPWA were to be recognized as partners in the joint effort.

Still reluctant to accept a general agreement, Stephens proposed a limited experiment in joint action in the Salinas Valley for the summer of 1955. Second thoughts prompted him to stipulate that the NAWU match funds and manpower with the UPWA. Since the NAWU could do neither, the two unions continued on their separate ways. In July 1957, in view of the reverses the UPWA was suffering, I proposed to Mitchell that the discussions be renewed on a five-point basis: (1) agreement in advance on the farm districts where joint action could be undertaken; (2) recognition of the UPWA's jurisdiction in the sheds and the NAWU's in the fields; (3) a clear statement of both unions' organizational aims to be addressed to the workers; (4) NAWU recognition of the former job classifications of all the shed jobs down-graded by employers as braceros were substituted for domestic packers; and (5) limitation of the agreement to one year.

To these proposals Helstein was receptive. In a May 1, 1957, letter to AFL–CIO secretary–treasurer Schnitzler he expressed willingness to "sit down and work out a mutually agreeable program with the agricultural workers."

A memorandum of agreement along these lines was drafted and approved by Helstein and Mitchell on May 21, 1959. On June 5 Mitchell advised Helstein that the NAWU executive board had endorsed it. The memorandum stated that the immediate and limited purpose was to avoid differences between the participants in the organizing activities then going on in California. The agreement was not to be regarded as either a waiver or a relinquishment of any jurisdictional claims which either union might feel entitled to assert at a later date.

Again the officers of the UPWA had second thoughts and on June 10, 1960, Helstein wrote Mitchell: "We expect to exercise our rights under our charter, and we believe that it is clear that it includes field workers employed on farms throughout the United States. We shall assert our claim as vigorously as the situation may require. . . . In our assessment of the situation we feel that this [the organization of farm workers] can be done best through the full support of the AFL–CIO Organizing Committee. . . . The issue of jurisdictional claims, if any, can be resolved at a later date.''

Both union presidents had been careful to inform AFL president George Meany and CIO leader Walter Reuther; both favored direct negotiations toward a merger of the two unions in California, an unlikely prospect in view of Helstein's belligerent letter of June 10. Helstein was now telling Reuther that he wanted neither Mitchell nor Galarza in a merged union.

It did not help rapprochement when Mitchell filed charges against the UPWA for violation of the AFL–CIO no-raiding agreement, arising out of a Louisiana sugar workers' local's defection from the UPWA and the efforts of the UPWA to win it back. Mitchell welcomed the defection and proposed to Reuther that some fifty sugar locals throughout the country be reorganized into the NAWU. Stephens responded in a letter to Mitchell: "Let me make it clear . . . your organization has no business in the sugar industry." Stephens was angered when NAWU field representatives, including me, assisted UPWA locals, at their request, in a tense strike against Louisiana refineries, a gesture which could well have looked like a raid. In California, too, the UPWA detected signs in the NAWU of the old weakness of agricultural unions to drift into the safer harbors of shed organizing. Addressing a leaflet to the members of the Food, Tobacco, and Agricultural Workers Union, a lineal descendant of the old radical left, the then NFLU invited shed and field workers to join it. In response, FTA leaflets appeared on the DiGiorgio picket line, offering the members of Local 218 the leadership of "a truly militant union."

Even less favorable to an agreement between the two unions than the controversy over sugar workers was the attempt of the UPWA in California to hire me and several local NAWU officers away from Mitchell. In July 1954 Stephens invited me to change over and become director of organization for UPWA in the fields. I declined the offer on several grounds; I personally was not the proper channel to the executive board of the NAWU for such an offer; the UPWA was not proposing autonomy for field workers within its organization; the shed union had not demonstrated any skill in combatting displacement by braceros that the NAWU did not already have; and the UPWA had a negative record in NAWU actions like those of Los Banos and Imperial.

As the harvests came and went and both the NAWU and UPWA

wasted organizationally, it was clear that neither had much to lose because both were venturing less and less. In 1954 Mitchell expressed to Meany doubts that the NAWU could avoid withdrawing from California altogether; and Helstein's feelings about the future of his international became gloomier.

But during the summer of 1959 their calculations took an unexpected turn. Both now staked their hopes on the newly formed Agricultural Workers Organizing Committee. Undoubtedly it was this event that lay behind Helstein's letter of June 10 to Mitchell. The UPWA had reassessed the situation and concluded that within the AWOC it would do better than the NAWU.

The Amalgamated Meat Cutters and Butcher Workmen of America

The Southern Tenant Farmers Union entered the American labor movement by way of affiliation with the United Cannery, Agriculture, and Packinghouse Workers of America; this affiliation ended in March 1939 after Mitchell and his supporters split with the UCAPWA leadership, whose ties were with the Congress of Industrial Organizations. During the next six years the STFU held its own in the south, relying not on organized labor but on independent funds, encouragement, political counsel, and channels to a national audience. This became Mitchell's base, a loose sodality of sympathizers and well wishers moved by the oppression of the southern landworkers and the courage with which they were resisting it. When Norman Thomas, the socialist candidate for United States president, visited the scene and spoke to meetings of black and white sharecroppers, he drew the country's attention to the struggling union. Thomas's voice awakened the liberal conscience of the American people. Among them was a new sympathizer, Patrick E. Gorman, later to become the secretary–treasurer of the Amalgamated Meat Cutters and Butcher Workmen of America.

Mitchell's attempt to obtain a charter from the American Federation in 1940 was turned down. Five years later he tried again, sponsored by

Gorman, who enlisted the support of AFL president William Green.

The relationship between Mitchell and Gorman proved lasting. Gorman remained a sentimental socialist as he helped forge a union that eventually represented over 375,000 workers. As a practical way of assisting the STFU, Gorman's Amalgamated arranged to place unemployed STFU members in summer jobs with the Seabrook Farms of New Jersey, with which the AMC had a contract. Similar arrangements were made with the H. J. Heinz Company of Salem, New Jersey. Through them Mitchell's recruits went north to earn 70 cents an hour with guaranteed employment for the summer. In 1958 the Seabrook plan was still in operation, guided by a vice-president of the AMC, Leon Schachter, who also became a close friend and confidant of Mitchell.

Seasonal employment in the north helped but it did not remedy the chronic financial crises of the SFTU, and Mitchell from time to time received subsidies from the Amalgamated, prompted by Gorman and Schachter. A chasm separated the three men, standing as they did far apart, one in industrial America and the other in an unregenerate plantation society. Their fifteen-year dialogue was composed of sighs from Mitchell's end, and of promptings from Gorman and Schachter's, urging Mitchell to learn their ways and cross over into the better world of business unionism.

Gradually their ideas moved closer together. In 1947 Mitchell regarded California as the best hope of his union, but by 1955 he was disillusioned. He began to explore the idea of merging, or more accurately, submerging the NAWU with the Amalgamated. He approached Gorman in 1956 stating the goal—to organize the larger corporation enterprises covering all employees both in field and processing work. Gorman was well disposed, telling Mitchell: "We will be happy to help you to organize and will be about as happy as you if you succeed in the tremendous task you have ahead of you."[314] In October 1956 Mitchell appeared before the executive board of the Amalgamated to espouse the merger, and the board adopted a resolution creating a special agricultural department to work out the details. The plan was to be initiated by combining NAWU locals with those of the Butchers.

The AMC was already well into exploring a merger initiated through talks with officers of the United Packinghouse Workers of America. In October 1956 these negotiations broke down, less over jurisdictional issues than over the distribution of executive positions. Since the meat cutters had a much larger membership and a well-kept treasury they were in a better position to wait, which they did. As a matter of protocol, Mitchell advised Walter Reuther, who was to the UPWA as Gorman was to the NAWU, that he was negotiating with the Butchers. Meticulously,

Gorman on his part consulted George Meany, who responded that it would be perfectly satisfactory for such a merger to take place. These assurances were given in June and again in August 1957.

By this time the Amalgamated officers clearly had in mind taking over the official jurisdiction granted to the STFU and passed down successively to the NFLU and the NAWU. They could and did make a plausible case for absorbing Mitchell's union, having as evidence the years of financial support, of joint contracting for seasonal labor, and of Gorman's sponsorship of the admission of the southern sharecroppers into the House of Labor. Once this became an Amalgamated goal it was clearly their concern that the UPWA not encroach on Mitchell's territory. And as the Butchers could wait for ailing UPWA to come to their terms so could they be leisurely about annexing the NAWU.

Gorman was never willing to risk the Amalgamated's treasury in so bleak a field as farm labor organizing. He wrote Mitchell in July 1956 that "we may have a dues problem in view of the fact that agricultural workers are not in the better paid class." This was a craftsman laying the foundation, ever so gently, for rejecting Mitchell's request that in the event of a merger the Amalgamated create three posts to which Mitchell and two other NAWU officials would be named. Gorman told Mitchell: "We would be going into the red every month with three officers, if we were to guarantee their pay." Gorman made the suggestion that if two of the NAWU officers could get jobs elsewhere, "this may be helpful. . . ."[315]

Time favored the Amalgamated. The UPWA was losing plants in the East and Mitchell's membership was shrinking fast under the auspices of Public Law 78. Were the UPWA to rebound in the West and take control of the field labor in California, Gorman's calculations would be seriously affected if not demolished. On the other hand if the UPWA failed altogether the AMC would be rid of a competitor in the meat plants and hold a clear jurisdictional advantage as to agricultural workers.

Amalgamated's bargaining position was thus an almost immaculate example of business unionism, not only technically adroit but also sustained by the patience of those who can wait on time and improve it with power and a solid treasury. And while waiting, the Amalgamated was hedging in another respect. It had established working relations with the International Brotherhood of Teamsters for joint organization in areas where other jurisdictions might be lying unclaimed or weakly defended. Also, it had ended fifty years of contention with the Retail Clerks International Union over representation of retail market meat cutters, and it took in the Fur and Leather Workers International Union through a merger.

As time passed the NAWU was nearing exhaustion. Mitchell's efforts to keep locals alive in Arkansas, Wisconsin, Minnesota, New Jersey, Florida, and California were unavailing. As of November 1958 the monthly income from dues was five hundred dollars, less than half the National Sharecroppers Fund donation. A few AFL Internationals had been persuaded by Mitchell to make monthly contributions which totalled another two hundred dollars a month. Studying these figures, Mitchell was coming to the conclusion that the organization of farm workers depended solely on congressional legislation such as had favored industrial unions in the 1930s.

Mitchell well knew this was a long-term prospect, and in California even the short term was speedily coming to an end. The State Federation of Labor avoided the issue of right-to-work conditions in agriculture after it had repulsed the attempt to impose them on industrial labor in the state. The federation's 1958 and 1959 legislative programs took no notice of the NAWU, which by that time had almost totally abandoned organizing activity. Keeping the large ranches under observation, helping NAWU volunteers to find jobs in other occupations, updating the information that was the union's basis for attack on Public Law 78, and contending with state and federal officials occupied completely what little was left of the NAWU's resources in California. By midsummer of 1959 even these were exhausted and I borrowed two thousand dollars on a personal note from an old friend and supporter of the union, Gardner Jackson. Jackson remained until the end of the NAWU the most responsive liberal on the Washington scene and the most loyal friend of the union.

The American Federation of Labor— Congress of Industrial Organizations

Mitchell's first approach to the AFL in October 1940 was rebuffed, leaving the STFU executive board in confusion and desperation, according to the *Sharecropper's Voice*. As southern tenants and sharecroppers the members had learned to deal with despair better than with confusion, and with Gorman's support they tried again and succeeded.

When Mitchell approached the AFL for the second time in 1946 in the House of Labor there were already many mansions. None of them resembled the rundown cabins of STFU members or the corners of shabby hiring halls out of which the NFLU operated. Mitchell a southerner with the outward look of perpetual relaxation, saw nothing offensive in this. "Poor folks have poor ways," he said with a touch of literary elegance.

The chartering of the sharecroppers under a new name, the National Farm Labor Union, was greeted as a major event by the 1946 AFL convention. Farm workers, it declared, had been manipulated by communist front groups. By contrast the NFLU was, as the convention affirmed, a bona-fide free trade union. The granting of its charter was hailed as "one of the most significant steps in the growth and development of the AFL, symbolizing the oneness of our rural and urban economy." Under the NFLU, it was said, agricultural laborers were now ready to unite and bargain collectively.

Four months after its admission President Green agreed to place one of the NFLU's organizers on the AFL payroll at fifty dollars a week and expenses. The affiliated unions of clothing workers, butchers, seafarers, and pullman porters formed a consortium to give "Mitchell's boys," as they were sometimes referred to, five thousand dollars a year for two years. Thereafter Mitchell and his boys were addressed as "Dear Sir and Brother." The boundaries of the jurisdiction granted were set forth in a letter to President Green from Mitchell dated February 20, 1952, which said in part: "We understand that such jurisdiction does not include workers engaged in transporting, processing, or distribution of agricultural products. [It does include] all men and women who perform field work, operate or maintain farm equipment on or around a farm, ranch, or plantation in the U.S. continental North America, and adjacent islands." These vested rights continued when in December 1951 the seventeenth convention changed the name from the National Farm Labor Union to the National Agricultural Workers Union, to avoid confusion with the National Farmers Union, composed of small land owners mainly in the Midwest.

Through the years Mitchell had brought the southern sharecroppers and the western field hands if not into the mainstream of organized labor at least to its margins. President Green placed some California organizers on the AFL payroll, but warned Mitchell that such support could not be extended indefinitely. Mitchell's personal friends on the executive boards of important Internationals continued to respond to his calls for funds, which brought contributions of thirty thousand dollars in

1950. As an affiliated union the NAWU could, with the endorsement of the AFL president, make national appeals for strike funds when the need arose. Among labor's lobbyists there were a few who approached members of Senate and House committees on the NAWU's behalf. In this way Mitchell operated on Capitol Hill without a lobby of his own, sounding his old protests and denunciations in public hearings that were often reported nationally. In some measure all this countered the legislative advocates of the national agri-business in Washington, representing industries such as the Sugar Cane League of Louisiana.

All things considered, Mitchell had reason to accept the fact that organized labor paid heed grudgingly if at all to the plight of farm laborers. The years 1945 to 1955 were strained by the contention between industrial and craft unionism; and farm labor organization, such as it was, did not fit into either. The NAWU was too much a populist movement, a green rising that to many of labor's eminent leaders looked almost red. Organized labor's legislative agenda reflected the most urgent interests of the powerful Internationals, the national economic policies that affected them, the dilemmas of political action, and the endless crises of collective bargaining with the industrial giants. All of these created waves of maneuvering among which the NAWU bounced like a paper boat. It was reminiscent of the turmoil of President Roosevelt's New Deal during which labor's organizing committees used muscle and money to create within a few years new forces like the United Auto Workers. In the midst of these storms Mitchell was asking men powerful enough to checkmate industrial corporatism to pause and look at a universe strange to them, one without a handle of conventional forms of unionism. Socially, the farm workers and their representatives were permitted glimpses of how it might be for them some day, as at the AFL convention in Miami where Mitchell and I sought a brief audience with whoever would listen. We sat in the lobby of a luxurious hotel, watching the Who's Who of American labor in the flesh and hearing them paged by name and connection. We walked the sundecks among lolling Sirs like poor Brothers looking to be recognized.

But the important moments were not those of the yearly conventions. They were the rare occasions when the federation's president could be reached by telephone or talked to face to face. On these occasions it was George Meany who bluntly reminded Mitchell of the many years of the AFL had assisted the farm workers and the little progress they had made. Meany at times was inclined to believe that Mitchell was trying to impose unionism on people who did not really want organization, and even doubted that they could benefit from it. William Schnitzler, the secretary–treasurer, was of the view that the members of the AFL executive board were organizational experts and able to judge whether the NAWU had been effective.

Numbers seemed to justify these dim views. In 1947 the AFL had 7,500,000 members and the CIO counted 6,000,000. The nominal membership of the NAWU did not pass 5,000, with very likely less than one-fourth of them duespayers. In 1957 the AFL–CIO received per capita dues of $8,093,000; the NAWU that year reported an operating budget of $44,000, of which $6,000 was from dues, $13,200 from contributions by the National Sharecroppers Fund, and $25,000 from the Industrial Union Department of the AFL–CIO. Steelworkers were paying over $526,000 yearly per capita; the NAWU, $2,400.

If money talks Mitchell was only whispering when he submitted proposals for organizing efforts in the fields. At the time that yearly AFL contributions to the NFLU amounted to $15,000, Mitchell asked Meany to endorse an appeal for $250,000. Meany refused. His reasons were that farm laborers were not showing signs of wanting to be organized, and that the proposal was too much like a CIO operation. In 1953 when Mitchell asked again, Meany refused to appoint a committee to direct a campaign. Instead he agreed to give a subsidy of $15,000 for one year. In September 1954 Meany relented and approved a grant of $500 a month for five months to support a drive to organize rice mill employees in Louisiana.

The AFL proved even more parsimonious with its political resources than with its funds. High level AFL–CIO executives were appointed to federal positions with subcabinet and even cabinet rank, as in the U.S. Department of Labor. They made no attempt to support the farm workers from their positions of influence within the bureaucracy, where the agricultural industry had active sympathizers of the bracero system. Usually these functionaries demonstrated polite sympathy for their trade-union brothers, the harvesters represented by the NAWU. On occasion, however, their self-importance prompted them, as it did Assistant Secretary of Labor Creasy, to condone the secret diplomacy of the international agreements. Creasy, it will be recalled, went further with his claim that in those negotiations he was the representative of the American farm workers. This usurpation served the interests of the agri-business spokesmen who were taking part in the proceedings unofficially.

In Washington it was not pomposity but discretion that prevented political involvement of labor on behalf of farm workers. In the House of Representatives oversight of the bracero program remained with the Subcommittee on Equipment, Livestock Supplies, and Manpower of the Committee on Agriculture. The legislative history of the House clearly showed that the jurisdiction belonged in the Education and Labor Committee, a more favorable forum for farm workers. At my insistence this matter was raised with the AFL legislative advocates, to no avail. Year after year, the bracero system continued its havoc among domestic harvesters, shielded from congressional investigation at the critical control level of the legislative process, the subcommittee. A situation which industrial unionism would not have tolerated with respect to its own vital interests went unchallenged, because such a challenge would have cooled the many other irons that labor always kept in the legislative fire.

These were cues to the political process of which congressional strategies were only a reflection, and in which institutionalized trade unionism had won a place. Organized labor now had the only countervailing power in the nation that could compel organized corporatism to share created wealth with American farm workers. To keep and improve such a position, with its corresponding influence and prestige, became the central concern of the labor movement. Within the member unions that power turned self-serving as well as self-perpetuating. Its primary goal was to obtain more for those who were surviving the displacement of man by machines in the production process. For these lucky ones the only bulwark remained the trade union.

But for those who did not survive, trade unionism was also compelled for political reasons to offer some relief; this took the form of advocacy of remedial and protective legislation as a substitute for economic security no longer available through work. To the passage of laws on social security, housing, consumer protection, child welfare, services for the needy and the aging, and many other critical areas of social inadequacy or dislocation organized labor devoted considerable funds and sustained energy. Such advocacy affected millions of Americans who together made up a floating constituency that had lost its productive connections. Reflecting this situation the labor movement evolved into a counterpart of the welfare state and its clients. Among them were the farm workers, undifferentiated except when public clamor, awakened by the liberal conscience, raised doubts about the sensitivity of organized labor to the plight of sharecroppers, migrants, harvesters, and their economic kinfolk. In a sense, farm laborers were twice disadvantaged in American society: by themselves they were too isolated and unnoticed to bear any weight on the political scales, and organized in their own unions they were not admitted into the great brotherhood of labor.

The concept of the farm worker class as understood by most labor leaders and expressed by their decisions and actions resulted from these circumstances. Too poor to sustain their own unions, the farm workers required endless subsidies. In comparison with their meager per capita payments these donations represented chronic deficit spending. History showed that such grants regularly disappeared into organizational quicksands. Business unionism regarded the outlays for organizing campaigns such as those in steel and automobile manufacturing as investments that would eventually pay off in the form of substantial per capita dues. Farm workers had never paid off. Their union had never won substantial collective bargaining contracts. They lacked the economic clout of mass stoppages. They used such unorthodox methods of economic action as automobile caravans, nonviolent resistance, boycotts, and prayer. Theirs was neither a craft nor an industry, but a resistance of a folk of varied colors and cultures to the integrating appetite of modern corporate business. Their union, the NAWU, was controversial. And it was poor, indisputably, notoriously poor, so that although it was bold and courageous, by reason of its poverty it lacked both in dignity and weight.

The NAWU unfortunately came on the scene when organized labor was deeply divided by the conflicts between craft and industrial unionism. When this controversy subsided in the merged AFL–CIO, the old antagonisms polarized around George Meany and Walter Reuther. No important step could be taken on behalf of agricultural laborers unless both agreed to it. Any proposal had to be weighed in relation to their differences in outlook, social bias, political commitments, and internal alignments of power.

Reuther, who in 1946 became the head of the United Auto Workers of America with more than a million members, and later the recognized leader of the Industrial Union Department within the AFL–CIO, supported the NAWU independently of Meany. In his public addresses, he referred to the plight of farm labor more frequently and more fervently than any labor leader of his stature had ever done. Privately, he was, like Mitchell, an "old Socialist," but one whose keen appraisal of power and its shifting balances was not affected greatly by sentimental bias. Reuther was much more accessible to the NAWU and its friends than Meany. The UAW or the IUD could be counted on to contribute to strike funds needed by the NAWU, as during the Louisiana sugar cane strike of 1953. In February 1957, at Reuther's recommendation, the IUD gave the union five thousand dollars for organizational work and that June set up an organizing fund of twenty-five thousand dollars, payable monthly for a year.

A part of this grant was marked for California where the retreat of the domestics had pushed them from the southern counties to Santa Clara, Salinas, San Joaquin, and Yuba. Some of the ablest NAWU-trained volunteer organizers were now living along an irregular arc extending from Soledad in Monterey County through Hollister in Santa Clara, Tracy in San Joaquin, and Woodland in Yolo County, thence north to the Peach Bowl. After 1955, the strategy of the union was adapted to this pattern. It consisted of maintaining contact with the northern locals, increasing the pressure on the growers associations that dominated these districts, identifying the new locations where displaced domestics were regrouping, reaching them with union information, breaking the undercover alliance of the Farm Placement Service and the U.S Department of Labor with the growers, and preparing to try again to lay a regional base from which the NAWU could return southward again.

Reuther and the IUD officials with whom Mitchell negotiated the $25,000 grant could not have clearly understood the plans I had submitted to Mitchell, although my reports were lengthy and detailed. Not all of the fund was apportioned to California, but enough of it to stave off the collapse of the NAWU in the state. The first month's allotment from the grant included $250 to be paid to part-time organizers and $100 for legal services. My own salary was $400 a month; a substantial part of this was diverted to meet expenses not provided for in the modest budget.

During the twelve months beginning in June 1957 some fifty experienced volunteers were regrouped in four locals. After surveying the labor market of available domestics in five counties, the union concluded that it could call in and offer enough of these workers to provide sufficient manpower for any and all crops in these districts. Every major staging point of braceros was known to the union, and regular contact was maintained with braceros who continued to bring their grievances to the NAWU, as they had in Imperial and Salinas. Instruction and discussion sessions with the teams of volunteers brought some to the point where they could press grievances, file complaints, and confront state and federal officials, with help from me when necessary. Strikes were avoided except brief stoppages by which immediate but modest gains could be obtained. The area council structure was revived to maintain connections between the locals, and the union bulletin, *El Porvenir*, continued to circulate among farm workers throughout the state.

At the end of a year I recommended to Mitchell that he try to raise a fund of forty thousand dollars to be spent entirely in California to hold the northern ground. I proposed a larger subsidy for the organizing teams, the hiring of a part-time secretary, and the creation of an institute in San Jose for the more intensive training of the men and women who were like me, learning by doing. I recommended that I prepare and the NAWU publish a full-length documented account of the bracero system, immediately after which a full-scale attack on the Farm Placement

Service would be launched, to demolish it and make way for labor placement cooperatives, which were in fact already functioning through the local volunteer committees.

The final stage for the summer of 1959 was to be a thorough and critical review of the NAWU experience since 1950, as a basis for the type of organizing effort that Mitchell had been proposing for many years.

The forty-thousand-dollar proposal never materialized. As funds dwindled it became increasingly clear that Reuther had lost any interest he might have had in supporting the NAWU until it could become in its own right an effective union in the fields. He at first suggested and then demanded that the NAWU merge with the United Packinghouse Workers of America as a condition of continued financial support.

Early in November 1957, Mitchell met with Victor Reuther. Mitchell wrote Walter on the following day, "following consideration of matters affecting our National Union," that he understood the message brought by Victor to be that "the Industrial Union Department will not make any further contribution to assist in organizing agricultural workers beyond the present commitment of twenty-five thousand dollars unless the National Agricultural Workers Union merges with the United Packinghouse Workers of America."

The executive board of the NAWU then unanimously adopted a resolution stating that "in view of the difficulties of the NAWU with the leadership of the UPWA in the past, the NAWU would not consider giving up its charter with its clear jurisdiction over all agricultural workers in the United States and joining the United Packinghouse Workers of America."

In Victor's presentation of the IUD decision there was an element of depreciation vis-à-vis the UPWA which the NAWU board could not ignore. The Reuthers and their associates thought that "the Packinghouse leadership has the imagination with which to do things in a dramatic way so that public opinion is more effectively brought to bear on a given situation." Mitchell, recollecting the bitter struggles of the 1930s, and their own dramatic effects on public opinion, responded: "We are irrevocably opposed to joining the United Packinghouse Workers of America as long as that organization has its present leadership, which we are convinced is substantially influenced if not completely dominated by forces subversive to all that we stand for."

It was a total break by the NAWU with the power, prestige, and funds of the IUD, and it lasted until the NAWU disappeared. For Mitchell from that time on it was a matter of preparing to liquidate its only asset, a potentially valuable jurisdictional title. Reuther, for his part, held to the view that the NAWU had only chipped away at small segments of the agri-business monolith in spite of the twenty-five-thousand-dollar subsidy and other contributions to the NAWU. This was Reuther's analysis as of January 1959.

After the rejection of Reuther's ultimatum by the NAWU both Reuther and Mitchell entered on a course that for all their differences joined them in the preparation of an important event, the Washington, D.C., Conference of the National Advisory Committee on Farm Labor on February 5 and 6, 1959.

Mitchell, Reuther, and the citizens who joined the committee to stage the conference hoped that it would arouse public opinion sufficiently to persuade organized labor to provide funds for an organizing campaign equal to the demands of so large a task. But for Mitchell and Reuther the ends to be served were different: Mitchell's, to make one final effort to create, at long last, an effective union that could carry forward in its own name and under a recognized charter; Reuther's, to set the stage for the assumption by the UPWA of that task at which, in his view, the NAWU had so signally failed.

The Liberal Conscience

The revelations about the bracero system and the worsening conditions of the domestic harvesters based on NAWU reports continued. The leaders of organized labor could not ignore them. A documentary film, *Harvest of Shame*, was nationally televised on Thanksgiving Day 1960, the culmination of the stories that all the media had been carrying for several years. The American public was impressed by them and organized labor's eloquent resolutions, denunciations of misery and blight in the countryside, occasional strike donations, or calling upon Congress could no longer calm public opinion.

Once again the liberal conscience was stirring and it found operational form in the February 1959 conference. That event set in motion men and forces and interests acting for a brief time as active partners in history. Its nature and its role in American society, as illustrated in this instance, deserve more than passing mention.

This role, that Professor Charles Merriam called the general assent underlying government, operates through open channels of information and opinion which express a Christian ethic in a politically open constitutional society. To those ethical values abused minorities can appeal. It is an appeal over the head of arbitrary power by those suffering its abuses and incapable of resisting it by themselves. The respect and dignity due individuals become rights and dignities inherent in a productive role in society. Until they are so accorded they remain little more than claims upon the compassion of those who tend the ethical values of the general assent and its vital supports—civilizing liberties, constitutional representative government, education, and the free flow of information.

When the American national conscience stirs, it appears outwardly as an outraged protest, more or less intense against the abuse of a segregated group. It is an alarm signalling that a force is abroad which will threaten, if unchecked, those liberties in their general application to all. In this sense an alert society protects itself by coming to the aid of any abused minority within it.

What is not so clear is that the liberal conscience has no social discipline peculiar to its character and serving its purpose in the national life. It is a Fifth Estate, next after the press, that dissolves after a crisis, lying dormant and over-spent until the next one prods it into action. It little recognizes that because of its tidal effect it is the keeper of social morality and the guardian of justice, in an economic system that has little of either.

Some of the power of the liberal conscience lies in its idealization of the miserably exploited, for whom it arouses compassion. Its weakness lies in its inability or disinterest in helping class victims create their own collective means for resisting abuse and for changing the conditions that cause it. The liberal conscience drops the task when only half completed, its protégés still incapable of taking their rightful and responsible place among the free.

Those who have felt the sting of the liberal conscience sense this and by calling its active agents Do-Gooders focus attention on the half of it. When Edward F. Hayes was forced out of public office he railed at these liberals, not because they had done nothing but good, but because in their momentary action they had come close to destroying his power base and its instruments of class abuse. Of all this the Do-Gooders were only faintly aware when they assembled in Washington in February 1959.

Typically the liberal conscience in American life has acted through ad hoc organizations whose members are themselves not the victims of class abuse. One of these organizations was the National Sharecroppers Fund, created to support Mitchell's stubborn resistance in the South.

The NSF raised funds through a national network of institutions and individuals. Its yearly appeals provided a running account of life and labor among those the NSF called the disinherited. The NSF annual contributions began in 1933 and in one period of seven years its donations to the NAWU amounted to ninety-five thousand dollars. Based in New York City, the Fund's connections in Washington eventually led it to lobby before congressional committees and federal agencies.

Viewed by California's agri-businessmen the NSF was suspect. It was a target of the Tenney committee investigation of the DiGiorgio strike, initiated by the published charges of Joseph DiGiorgio that the union was dominated by communists. The committee report described the NSF as a "red front." As the principal source of citizen funds for farm labor unionism in the South and later in the West, the NSF was attacked for what it was—a lifeline that did not snap in spite of terror and defamation.

The means used by the NSF to arouse interest and raise money, apart from the annual appeals mailed to a select list of some twenty-thousand names, were the publicity media. It was a mesh of communications whose source was the workers themselves. What they knew and reported to the union required only verification and sorting to be passed on to organizations like the NSF, whose files were replete with the material for press releases, for columnists of the metropolitan dailies, conferences, and congressional hearings. Stimulated by publicity of this kind, an extensive literature about the disinherited accumulated ranging from popular accounts to scholarly studies. Over the years it became impossible to dismiss publications of this magnitude as mere do-gooding, and they created along with the advocacy of the liberal organizations the climate of opinion in which Public Law 78 was at last rejected.

The special forums of the liberal conscience were the congressional hearings, which usually took place in Washington. They were an important resource of the democratic process envisioned by John Stuart Mill: "the utmost possible publicity and liberty of discussion whereby not merely a few individuals in succession, but the whole public, are made to a certain extent participants in the government and sharers in the instruction and mental exercise derivable from it." The helping organizations issued their pleas and denunciations as they persistently appeared before House and Senate committees to refresh their awareness of the condition of the rural working class.

What the witnesses said became a part of the record, little of it producing immediate change but all of it adding weight to the prologue of the past. Among these the hearings of the LaFollette committee held on the West Coast in the early 1940s stood as a model. Into the record also went articles like Gladwin Hill's of the *New York Times* and Lester Velie's in *Collier's Magazine*. The record came to the attention of the presidency itself; Hill's stories moved President Eisenhower to observe, apropos of the traffic of illegals in the borderlands, that the exploitation of the wetbacks was accompanied by "a serious relaxation in ethical standards extending all the way from the farmer exploiters of this contraband labor to the highest levels of the federal government." When Hill made his field tour in southern California and northern Mexico to observe wetbacks and braceros, I took time out from the Imperial strike to travel with him.

The hearings, with their Fabian pace, left the structure of power unchanged in Agri-businessland, but they were nevertheless a factor in the work of organization. Just as terror in the South was held at bay and finally repulsed by the national publicity given the Southern Tenant Farmers Union, so armed vigilantism retreated in California. The early radicals, whose unions were finally destroyed and who were themselves sent to jail, cleared the way for the NFLU, so that its organizers could move into the bastions of Imperial Valley agri-business reasonably assured that they would not be tarred, feathered, mobbed, or shot down as their predecessors had been. Had they gone unnoticed the radical organizers would have changed nothing. Recognized, they left the scene with the only accomplishment possible to them, that of denting the cutting edge of class vindictiveness. To this the liberal conscience also made its contribution.

There were limits to the influence of the liberal conscience as there were to the good it was capable of. The reassurance felt by those who were carrying the struggle in the fields was genuine, but they were left barehanded to deal with the vested systems of landed property. The relaxation of morals at the highest levels of the federal government continued, so damaging in its effects that an entire agrarian class was dispossessed. Neither economic power nor political efficacy for farm workers was imagined beyond what the existing establishments were willing to permit. After a time dependency on liberal support could set in, as happened with the STFU. The coalitions between farm laborers and their urban defenders were always left incomplete. The drive of compassion, like all human emotions, is exhaustible. The crises waned, the moral pressure was turned off, and the destruction of the domestic harvester's unions continued. In a parallel case, Dr. Will Alexander, the Southern liberal, saw the Farm Security Administration decline and in the 1940s collapse as war-bred prosperity began and the public lost interest in the poor and dispossessed.[316]

Psychologically, the liberal conscience became fixed on one small sector of the agricultural laboring class, the seasonal migrants, those who lived on what Oscar Rumpf called the hurting edges of the world. Yet it was not these workers that the abuse of power by corporate agriculture was hurting most, as the NAWU had found out. The migrant worker was dramatized out of proportion to his actual role in western agriculture. Like the coal miners of Orwell's Wiggam Pier, the migrant became in imagery a sort of grimy caryatid upon whose shoulders nearly everything that was not grimy was supported. In 1958 interstate migrancy accounted for less than 3 percent of the peak labor force in California. Seasonal migrants who moved from crop to crop within the state numbered fewer than twenty-one thousand, 8 percent of the entire farm labor force, family labor and braceros included.

When Reuther notified the NAWU that the twenty-five-thousand-dollar grant would not be renewed, Mitchell and his friends recognized that this was a crisis marking the end of the NAWU's efforts, particularly in California. As a last resort it was again time to mobilize the liberal conscience.

In October 1958 the National Sharecroppers Fund announced the creation of the National Advisory Committee on Farm Labor composed of eminent Americans—Dr. Frank P. Graham, A. Phillip Randolph, Dr. Clark Kerr, Helen Gahagan Douglas, Mrs. Franklin Delano Roosevelt, Norman Thomas, and Dr. Maurice van Hecke. The committee began immediately to urge the AFL-CIO to do something about the deplorable condition of farm workers. The letters that George Meany received to this effect were numerous and prestigious. Gardner Jackson, who was an artist with the telephone, laced the country with calls and the NSF publicized the committee far and wide.

Within the AFL-CIO Walter Reuther supported the committee from the outset. The Industrial Union Department sent five thousand dollars with a letter from Reuther to Dr. Graham, chairman of the committee, encouraging him to proceed with "one of the most important items of American democracy's agenda." To George Meany, Reuther wrote on November 10, 1958, recommending that farm worker's problems be placed on the agenda of the Executive Council of the AFL-CIO.

When these preparations were complete, the National Advisory Committee announced that it would hold another hearing, this one under its own auspices. It lasted two days, February 5 and 6, 1959, at Washington, D.C.'s Mayflower Hotel, within earshot of AFL-CIO headquarters and of the national press. Its announced purpose was to encourage the organization of farm workers and to launch a legislative program on their behalf.

A succession of witnesses reviewed once more the conditions under which harvesters were working and living, in testimony that was some-times vivid, sometimes dramatic, sometimes prosaic, but always carry-ing a message to organized labor.

The conference and its hearing were a success. William Schnitzler, secretary–treasurer of the AFL–CIO, was present. What he saw and heard was the liberal conscience in its best form speaking through men and women of high standing in the Church, the arts, politics, and academia. Labor would often stand on the same side with them on issues affecting the welfare of the American people. Their influence with labor leaders lay in their willingness to believe that business unionism really cared.

Schnitzler was the keynote speaker of the last session of the confer-ence. He said: "This is the most shocking story of our time, . . . as horrifying and degrading as the sweatshop conditions . . . at the begin-ning of the century." He endorsed federal legislation for the strict control of farm labor importation. Moving closer to a commitment, he added: "We do not expect the National Agricultural Workers Union to carry out this heavy assignment on its own power. I am happy to report that after some months of study and consultation, we have formulated a program for an organizing campaign. It will be submitted for approval to the next meeting of the Executive Council."

Collaboration between Mitchell and Reuther had smoothed the way for the February conference. It also produced a document called "An AFL–CIO program to end 19th century poverty in 20th century rural America." The statement was approved by the council, which ordered a special assessment of one cent per member per month on all affiliates. The funds were to be applied to four objectives: (1) the abolition of foreign labor importation; (2) the passage of federal legislation to protect farm laborers; (3) a public relations campaign; and (4) an organizing drive in the fields.

The council also ordered that a director of organization be assigned "to assist farm workers in building their union." Out of these events emerged the Agricultural Workers Organizing Committee, the operating arm of the coalition that had been pledged at the Washington confer-ence. During the AWOC's brief and disastrous life it was to be revealed how power was working within the labor movement and how it finally rid itself of the embarrassment that Mitchell's boys had been causing it for decades. Its work done, the liberal conscience relaxed, once more an innocent bystander, its faith having moved a mountain. Or so it thought.

VI: Death of a Union

The Agricultural Workers Organizing Committee—AFL–CIO

Organizing committees were the expedient used by CIO international unions to organize the urorganized. With funds and manpower contributed by the Internationals their goal was to create new unions where none existed. The committees were temporary, giving way to regularly structured, dues-paying bodies appropriately chartered.

In the case of farm workers the situation was different. There were in existence in early 1959 two unions, the NAWU, chartered originally by the AFL, and the United Packinghouse Workers Union of the CIO. The parent bodies were not launching a campaign in new territory. Of the two unions the NAWU had its base exclusively among field workers. In California the UPWA drew its support from members employed in the packing sheds and processing plants of the food industry. The UPWA had not begun organizing efforts among harvesters in California until the mid-fifties, at which point it had no contracts or significant membership from this class of workers.

Both unions were in trouble, the NAWU in decline for reasons already explained, the UPWA losing ground in the California packing sheds and unable to gain a foothold in the fields. In the East UPWA strength was declining as the meat packing plants moved out of the Chicago area.

In this context the meaning of Schnitzler's statement to the Washington conference that the purpose of the AFL–CIO was "to assist farm workers in building their union" was clear. Mitchell took it to mean that the NAWU would receive such assistance, and Schnitzler had made a pointed reference to the inability of the NAWU to "carry out this heavy assignment on its own power."

In the light of later events, an important Executive Council omission was on the issue of jurisdiction, that of the NAWU now challenged by the UPWA. Helstein, in denouncing the memorandum of understanding with the NAWU, had left no doubt on this score. Schnitzler's commitment was to assist in organizing workers in fields to which the UPWA, as the council well knew, was now laying claim.

Reuther, in terminating Industrial Union Department financial help to the NAWU, made no secret of his motives. He had demanded as a condition of his support that the NAWU deliver its jurisdiction to the UPWA. In the continuing Meany–Reuther struggle, Helstein supported Reuther. Both of them saw that if harvesters could be organized on a large scale under the UPWA, its decline would be reversed and the IUD bloc strengthened. Reuther's support of the UPWA was consistent with his position as recognized head of industrial unionism in the labor movement. His financial contributions to the National Advisory Committee on Farm Labor, and his active endorsement of it within the Executive Council, could result in the abolition not only of poverty in rural America but also of the NAWU and in the consolidation of the UPWA's jurisdictional claim.

In sum, the commitments of the Executive Council, of which Meany was president and Reuther an influential member, were unequivocal; but each of the principals interpreted them according to his own interests. Meany's was a reluctant concession to a public opinion which he valued that had been strong on behalf of a union which he did not. In practical terms that meant that as soon as that opinion was placated Meany could return the NAWU to the limbo in which he had held it for so many years. Reuther's motive was to commit the AFL–CIO's financial resources to the campaign and to contrive that these redound to the benefit of the UPWA.

John W. Livingston, the director of organization of the AFL–CIO, a close friend of Reuther's and with him a participant in the struggle to organize the United Auto Workers, was instructed to proceed with the program. Casting about for a field director, he remembered Norman Smith, also a veteran of the UAW campaigns against the giants of the automobile industry.

Livingston observed the customary courtesies, consulting Mitchell on the Smith appointment. To Mitchell it seemed sensible. He had known Smith many years before as an organizer of Ford plants in the South. Smith became the third man in authority and the front line director of the AWOC.

At the time of his appointment Smith was a foreman at the Kaiser steel plant in Fontana, California. His view of the world around him, Agribusinessland, was explained in an address to the California State Federation of Labor: "For the past sixteen years I have been inactive so far as labor is concerned. . . . In some respects for sixteen years I have been more or less sitting on the moon. . . . For some peculiar reason our attempts to organize the field workers . . . seemed to have missed the mark. . . . As a director [of the AWOC] I don't know whether I would have taken it or not. . . . Labor should be interested because it is the moral, the right, and the decent thing to do. . . . My role in this thing is to build among agricultural workers a union that is so strong that by God they can take the things that are coming to them."[317]

Smith realized that he had been given an important assignment, one surrounded by a constant swirl of publicity and one in which he would stand at the intersection of the politics of industrial versus craft unionism, represented on the one hand by Walter Reuther and on the other by George Meany. He felt himself commissioned to reduce one of the last strongholds of anti-unionism in America, a task for which he was temperamentally and physically well fitted. His angers were sudden and volcanic, with the bull-necked will of the organizers who had established the beachheads of industrial unionism in its most violent encounters. His memory of them was vivid and his campaign ribbons were the scars he wore like chevrons on his scalp.

With distinct pride in his role, Smith held that neither Mitchell nor Hasiwar were professionals in his class, and of course neither was I. His loyalty to Reuther was strong, and he flushed with irritation when he spoke of Mitchell's rejection of Walter's generosity in offering salvation to the NAWU through a merger with the UPWA. To him Mitchell was an ingrate. Since I was present company I was spared these reprimands especially when, in moments of some mild disappointment, he confided that Livingston had given him no instructions on "how to do the job."

The staffing of the AWOC went ahead pending official appointment of its titular members. Since the program's purpose was to build the two unions, and the NAWU was relying on small donations to the national office and what I could borrow on personal credit, Reuther persuaded Meany to appoint me as field organizer on Livingston's staff as nominally assistant to Smith. I received my letter of appointment from Livingston on April 30, 1959, authorizing my salary and expenses, the use of a new Chevrolet Impala and instructions on mileage allowances, the filing of reports, and related matters. Like Smith, I, too, was puzzled on how to do the job. As approved by Meany my appointment had been cleared with Reuther on Mitchell's endorsement that I "would provide years of experience" to the program. On this and other occasions I was referred to as Smith's assistant, but with no precise duties or authority. My status as secretary of the NAWU and its director of research and education remained unchanged.

My most important colleague on Smith's new staff was Louis Krainock, whose past connections in the labor movement were close to the UPWA. Krainock was placed in charge of public relations but in fact became the administrative officer for Smith at the AWOC's Stockton headquarters. He regarded himself as a theoretician, giving much thought, as he phrased it, to finding the jugular vein of agri-business, upon which Smith could clamp his powerful grip. Next to Krainock came Henry Anderson, a trained sociologist with competence in research. A field survey he had completed at the University of California on the bracero system had been shredded and burned at the university on request of agri-business spokesmen and Department of Labor officials who were offended by it.

My instructions from Mitchell were to strengthen the NAWU in California with the harvester members Smith was to recruit in pursuance of the Executive Council's commitment, and from their dues to reconstruct the NAWU locals in the northern counties. To this end I introduced Smith to the NAWU volunteer organizers with whom I worked in the area and who were appointed to the staff by Smith on my recommendation. Through them Smith at once established connections with men and women who had spent the previous sixteen years on the hard ground of Agri-businessland in Imperial, Salinas, the Central Valley, Santa Clara, and Yuba.

On these points of contact, Smith set up a circuit of meetings, inspections, probings, and defiant appearances. Along the way he learned to distinguish beets from lettuce, peaches from apricots, and carrots from onions. As his nonprofessional tutors I and my fellow members of the NAWU introduced him to skid rows, viewed bracero camps, called on farm placement offices, and walked levees and back roads to places where migrants were camped, waiting for the bracero tide to recede.

The NAWU also provided Smith with the documented record of its resistance to Public Law 78 over the previous ten years, and of its encounters with the U.S. Department of Labor and the Farm Placement Service. I introduced him to the NAWU locals where Smith repeatedly explained his mission of bringing the full power of the AFL–CIO to their assistance. Presenting Smith, I stressed Mitchell's message that Smith was acting in the best interests of the NAWU. Smith asked me, and I agreed, to suspend the press statements I had been making about our findings on Public Law 78, on the sensible ground that to continue them would create the impression that there were two, and not one, organizing programs under way. In Washington Mitchell offered to distribute (through his own long-standing connections) the statements Smith was making as he began to feel his way into the bracero controversy.

During the first six months of his activities, Smith made it clear privately and publicly that he was the organizing agent for two unions. He wrote to the director of the State Department of Employment on November 4, 1959: "The Agricultural Workers Organizing Committee operates in the jurisdiction of both the UPWA and the NAWU . . . and has a representative interest in the domestic workers."

By the end of September 1959, Smith and his field men were in full stride. They opened AWOC offices in areas in which the NAWU had never attempted organization or from which it had withdrawn. He assigned paid staffers where the NAWU had maintained volunteer teams up to that spring. The AWOC was soon operating out of sixteen offices throughout the Central Valley, Santa Clara, and Salinas, with an advance post south at Oxnard. In Stockton, the headquarters of the drive, Smith rented a cavernous two-story building across the front of which he flung his shingle, a canvas banner fifty feet long and six feet wide painted with his challenge in bold letters. An organizing bulletin appeared regularly, and on the radio Krainock, the Voice of Agricultural Labor began to speak in regular weekly broadcasts.

The publicity illustrated a singular turn of Smith's organizing mind. The bulletin reported in detail on staff activities, assignments of personnel to various areas, the names of those training for leadership, and plans concerning the AWOC's intentions in the immediate future.[318] On September 2, 1959, before picking had begun, Krainock announced: "We shall be moving into tomatoes, there's no question about it." The schedule of action was published four months in advance, with Smith promising that "strikes will continue as new crops mature."[319] It was Smith's theory, as he explained it to me, that this was an effective way to throw the growers off guard because the AWOC was obviously putting out false leads, as would be normally expected of him. "Premature revelations of purpose," according to Gracian, "are never highly esteemed"; and according to Smith, rarely believed.

Equally disconcerting to me was Smith's view of the importance of skid row in his campaign. He was attracted by the daily shapeups of the state's most mobile transients. To him they appeared like those at the gates of eastern industrial plants he knew so well. On some mornings there were as many as a thousand men waiting in the early dawn for the trucks and buses along the row. Smith would rise at 4:00 A.M. to be on skid row with the earliest arrivals, moving among them, often recruiting members for the AWOC picketing. Smith came to believe that there he could organize the masses he needed to assault the gates of agribusiness. He felt so certain that by the middle of 1960 he was ready to move into the Oakland skid row, feeder of the day hauls into Santa Clara and the Central Valley.

Smith's basic tactics were the flying squads of pickets who would descend on a farm and keep it under siege while Smith and Krainock maneuvered for an opportunity to negotiate with the grower. By deploying these squads as the crops matured Smith was leading the AWOC back to the earlier days of the radical unions and to the tactics of job action of the Industrial Workers of the World. In rapid moves of this kind Smith challenged the growers of cherries, peaches, tomatoes, apricots, and pears, with threatening feints in the direction of lettuce, cotton, grapes, and asparagus.

On these quick sorties the AWOC challenged small growers and big ones, including the DiGiorgio Fruit Corporation, operator of the largest pear orchard in California, Dantoni's in Yuba. Smith made a minor thrust at the Peach Bowl in 1959 and a major one in 1960, during which he had to deal with police surveillance, braceros, litigation and injunctions, local farm placement managers, Department of Labor bureaucrats, and watchful Teamsters. The AWOC demanded pay increases, job security, bracero control, and union recognition with grievance procedures.

To the alarmed growers of the entire state the campaign of the AWOC, with Smith thundering over it, had the appearance of an avalanche. In its wake harvest wages were increased so that Smith could point with satisfaction to higher scales of as much as 20 cents a pail in cherries and 3 cents per lug in peaches. The AWOC came out of these encounters without collective bargaining contracts but with enough economic benefits to report progress to Livingston. Back in Washington he transposed these gains into membership figures and came out with an estimate of twenty-five thousand new recruits in the ranks of the AWOC, a figure which belittled even Mitchell's most euphoric pronouncements about the membership of the NAWU.

Tactically, the AWOC openly avowed its reliance on barnstorming in crop after crop. Strategically, it was less self-assured. Franz Daniel, assistant to Livingston and his direct liaison with Smith, and an organizer with a philosophical turn of mind, said in October 1959 that "we are searching for a formula," a refinement on Krainock's search for the jugular vein. Mitchell, who was the liaison of NAWU locals in California with Daniel and Livingston, felt that "Livingston wants to spend the next six months developing key men to carry out his formula," which according to Daniel was to "pull a switch and shut down the whole works." Krainock saw the problem of strategy as both anatomical and military. He estimated the labor force at 589,000 land workers whose organization was to be accomplished by cadres: "When we find the man with the following of 10 or 40, we fit him into the structure of the organizing committee now and the local union later. . . . Our cadres will be well trained and our army will be forming."

The role of the units that were to be the core of Smith's army became increasingly clear as his campaign moved into the fall of 1959. On the one hand, they were to be purged of NAWU elements; on the other, they were to develop into the new base for the UPWA.

The process of excluding the NAWU began after Smith felt himself sufficiently familiar with his task. It took a number of forms.

Smith, in meetings with his full staff, emphasized, "I am just the front man and Galarza [as assistant director] is calling the shots." However, he made all the important staff appointments without discussing them with me. When I raised the point Smith said that he was making these decisions to create a staff that represented the political spectrum of the AFL–CIO. I insisted that appointments be made on the basis of proven experience in dealing with the organization of harvesters under the circumstance then prevailing in California. He in effect dissolved existing NAWU locals by chartering new ones as affiliates of the AWOC. New membership cards were issued in place of those NAWU members were already carrying. Even though I was assistant director I had no direct contact with the new locals. Dues paid by new harvester members were impounded and placed in a trust fund, depriving the NAWU of them completely. One by one the trained volunteer organizers out of NAWU ranks were dropped. Smith was reporting new members in the fields but none in the sheds, a matter he refused to discuss in open staff meetings.

Nor, as assistant director, was I invited to staff discussions that Smith and Krainock held with the UPWA. I learned of these meetings later. Smith conferred, without notice or report to me, with state officials, notably with Don Larin, deputy director of the State Department of Employment, whose role I had exposed before Smith came on the scene. My discussion with Smith on this incident was not friendly, with me insisting in vain that he give an account of the meeting. Smith argued that Larin had been appointed by Governor Brown and endorsed by Haggerty.

About these proceedings I wrote Mitchell in November 1959: "The staff operations in California are now such that we know nothing of policy decisions and we are by no means informed about developments which have a very important effect on all organizing activities."

All this was obvious and Smith made no attempt to conceal or explain matters. Smith probably felt about me as his assistant director as he felt about Mitchell and Hasiwar—that he was dealing with an amateur organizer. The worst that I could assume was that he was carrying out instructions from Livingston. In any case, it was clear that our differences were becoming deep and that neither the NAWU nor I could fit into his schemes as to strategy for organizing or for candid dealing.

By the end of September Smith and I were antagonists rather than collaborators. I criticized his reliance on flying squads as inappropriate and self-defeating. I argued that reliance on skid row recruitment was a gross mistake, and explained why. Announcements of what the AWOC intended to do months in advance I characterized in language that Smith could understand; I told him he was "telegraphing his punches."

But it was with respect to AWOC dealings with the public officials that Smith went into one of his angers. My position was that in the chain of power containing domestic workers while the bracero system flooded the state the weakest link was the state and federal bureaucracy. I insisted that the attack I had sustained for years should continue; that legal action should be directed not at the growers but at the U.S. Department of Labor and the Farm Placement Service, and that the AWOC should also try to isolate the Mexican consuls and the Mexican government itself.

From this it was a short step to my criticism of the AWOC detente with the State Federation of Labor. I pointed out to Smith that none of the positions of influence that the federation had held in the state administration had ever been used positively to support the farm workers in strike actions or otherwise. The tutelary position, I insisted, into which the NAWU and its members had been placed by Haggerty was intolerable and his presumption as a spokesman for them should be disavowed privately and, if necessary, publicly. My arguments were based, I explained to Smith as he simmered, on a documented record that was at his disposal if he would use it.

His response in closing our last discussion of these matters was conclusive. "Ernie," he said quite slowly and with resignation, "you have to accept the Department of Labor and the State Federation as they are and try to survive under the conditions they lay down for you."

On October 13, 1959, I advised Smith that I was considering leaving his staff.

The list of our disagreements was not complete. I recommended and he rejected the enlistment of braceros in the AWOC, as the NAWU had done; Smith characterized this policy as immoral.

As the relations between the NAWU and the AWOC deteriorated, those between Smith's committee and the UPWA improved. From all indications, Smith was yielding to the promptings of Clive Knowles, organizing director for the UPWA, that he throw in his lot with the UPWA in the drive it was planning in Imperial, and to agree that all field workers would become AWOC members, with shed workers continuing to join the UPWA.[320] In April the AWOC began a campaign with UPWA organizers assigned to the AWOC for the purpose of organizing harvesters. When I asked Smith what this meant, he did not reply. Krainock's June 1960 bulletin announced that the AWOC was already marching forward with the UPWA. In November the UPWA was preparing to move into the Coachella Valley with similar intentions.

Late in December 1960 the long planned drive in Imperial began.

Krainock and UPWA field representatives appeared together to urge field workers to join the UPWA.[321] At these meetings no mention was made of the NAWU. Knowles was in Imperial promoting the organization of harvesters.[322] The leaflets distributed throughout Imperial were in Spanish and carried the name and address of the UPWA exclusively. Former members of the NAWU forwarded them to me.[323]

By the end of 1959 the AWOC bulletin was announcing that over four thousand of these "long neglected men and women" were dues-paying members of the union. The *Packinghouse Worker*, the national organ of the UPWA, was claiming successes in signing up field workers, reporting that more than five hundred of them had signed with the UPWA in Imperial Valley in December.

I questioned Smith about these appeals to field workers to join the UPWA instead of the NAWU. His response this time was authoritative. He demanded that the NAWU recognize the UPWA's jurisdiction and obey Reuther's wishes as to the goals of the campaign. It was the last of my exchanges with Smith. When I left Stockton he was aware of my opinion of his conduct and Reuther's.

On January 10, 1960, I wrote Smith: "I am therefore requesting that you notify Director of Organization Livingston of my resignation from the staff, effective on this date."

Throughout this period my reports to Mitchell stressed my concern that the NAWU was being cut adrift by Smith in favor of the UPWA. I rejected the complaint that my criticisms of AWOC's basic strategy and policies constituted sabotage of the AWOC, insisting, "as long as we hold jurisdiction we are entitled to be treated as equals with UPWA." Mitchell held to the belief, as late as July 1960, that I should ask Meany to be reinstated to Livingston's staff and that I remain within the AWOC to monitor its activities and to try to modify its course.

I was puzzled that Smith himself had never issued a statement confirming his instructions to assist the NAWU. What I was interpreting as ominous signs Mitchell was at first inclined to take on faith in Smith's fidelity to his original assignment. The new local committees that Smith was setting up did not disturb Mitchell, and he regarded the impounding of funds with little alarm. His instructions to me were that I should not make any public statements; he continued in his conviction that a settlement with the AWOC favorable to the NAWU could be worked out later. In May 1959 he could still write Gorman, with whom he was conducting negotiations on a possible merger: "If the campaign supported by the AFL–CIO is successful we will do all right." And even in October he was "unprepared to accept Ernesto Galarza's report that the AWOC is a new structure designed to replace the NAWU."

Nevertheless, Mitchell was mulling over my anxieties. In Washington he received assurances from the assistant director of organization, Franz Daniel, that the original agreement had not been changed and that Smith had not received instructions to build a new union to replace the NAWU. In July 1959, Mitchell wrote Smith: "We do need whatever gains are made reflected in the existing structure if the NAWU is to be preserved."

Seeing that Smith continued on the course I opposed, Mitchell wrote Smith on October 23, 1959: "It was our understanding that the California campaign was launched for the purpose of organizing field workers directly into the NAWU. . . . We should like to know your views on these matters and to know if you have instructions contrary to our understanding of the AFL–CIO's position."

Smith failed to reply to Mitchell, who then wrote to Schnitzler: "At this time we would also want to raise the question of the disposition of workers being enlisted in California. . . . As of this date our National Union has received no report as to the new members." Schnitzler did not respond.

That the NAWU had been given only a brief reprieve Mitchell learned on May 6 through a telephone call from Meany, who informed him that the Executive Council had decided to withdraw the charter of the NAWU and give it to the AWOC. The president of the AFL–CIO told Mitchell the reasons. Galarza had been putting NAWU locals into the Amalgamated Meat Cutters, and the AFL–CIO was acting to protect its investment of one hundred thousand dollars a year in the California campaign.[324] As to the investment, the figure was probably accurate. As to the transfer of NAWU locals by me, it was a total falsehood.

It should be noted that the AFL–CIO Executive Council decision had the approval of A. Phillip Randolph and Walter Reuther, on whom Mitchell had counted heavily for support.

The decision stunned Mitchell, and with good reason. The previous February Meany had heatedly rejected Mitchell's suggestion that Meany designate a successor to the NAWU as a way out of the situation into which the union was being forced. Mitchell was not commonly regarded as a member of the circle of labor leaders who now controlled the AFL–CIO, but he had been around them long enough to recollect ruefully how it had been in the former days. On June 13 he wrote Gorman: "I know that in the old AFL if a federation officer gave his word on a matter in most cases it was as good as if in a written contract. However we have a different labor movement today."

The action of the Executive Council was not properly an extermination but a liquidation, since the NAWU was still the legal possessor of a valuable asset, its charter. But it was decisive, and the scene in California emerged out of the fog of machinations that Smith was so inexpertly directing.

The official organ of the AFL–CIO printed on June 10, 1960, the announcement of the chartering of the AWOC with the declaration that "the Committee will accept into the AFL–CIO membership workers employed in the cultivation and harvesting of fruit and vegetable crops."[325] It also announced that the Executive Council had instructed the AWOC to establish branches of field workers which would operate as directly affiliated local unions of the AFL–CIO. In Stockton Krainock's bulletin reported that the charter would remain in effect "until, in the opinion of the committee and the AFL–CIO, a permanent organization should be established."[326]

Simultaneously with the lifting of the old charter and the lowering of the new one, Secretary–Treasurer Schnitzler made an important announcement. Up to this time Smith had operated on his own initiative, reporting only to Livingston. His staff had been, in effect, the AWOC. This anomaly was now corrected with the appointment of seven commissioners, Daniel V. Flanagan, regional director for the AFL–CIO in California; Franz E. Daniel, assistant director of organization under Livingston; Thomas L. Pitts, former Teamster official and successor to Haggerty in the State Federation of Labor; Henry Hansen, W. T. O'Rear, C. R. van Winkle, and Harry Finks, leaders of four central labor councils in the Central Valley. Smith was appointed chairman and secretary–treasurer.

Norman Smith and Louis Krainock had the new charter in hand by June 17, the date the *AWOC Organizer* carried the news. The intention to receive workers in cultivating and harvesting of fruits and vegetables was confirmed. In a signed editorial, Smith noted: "The greatest impact on us in the AWOC is the increased and expanded backing and support we receive from the AFL–CIO; the permanence of our organization, and our new ability to create branch organizations as these are needed."

In a separate paragraph Krainock, writing for Smith, delivered the sting: "We can now march forward with our sister union in the field, the United Packinghouse Workers, knowing that no jurisdictional conflicts will arise, that we are all pressing ahead together toward the common goals of social justice and economic equality."

I did not wait for instructions from Mitchell with regard to the action of the Executive Board of the AFL–CIO. To me it was an act of piracy, defined "to take over and use in violation of exclusive assignment to another, as a wave length." Or as a charter, Webster might have just as appropriately said.

On June 13, I wrote William F. Schnitzler, addressing him as Sir, omitting Brother:

> This is an illegal action on your part. . . . Under Article II, paragraph I, of the AFL–CIO constitution . . . it is the duty of the officers . . . to preserve and maintain the integrity of each affiliated union. . . . Article III, Section 7, unequivocally states that charters or certificates of affiliation shall not be issued to national or international unions, [or] organizing committees . . . in conflict with the jurisdiction of affiliated . . . international unions, except with the written consent of such unions. I also call your attention to the fact that . . . there was in effect an agreement between the NAWU and the United Packinghouse Workers of America on jurisdiction and cooperation . . . in direct compliance with the official policy of the AFL–CIO. . . . I realize that there has been an urgent policy on the part of the AWOC to turn over the control of the agricultural workers of California to the United Packinghouse Workers of America. When I joined the staff of the AWOC in April 1959 I did not know this. I was in fact led to believe that the purpose of the AWOC was to organize in our jurisdiction with the financial and moral support of the AFL–CIO in order to strengthen the National Agricultural Workers Union. . . . You may rest assured that I shall, in my capacity of secretary of our union, do everything within my ability to maintain the rights, the integrity, and the moral credit of the National Agricultural Workers Union intact. When these rights cease, it will be by the consent and voluntary action of the members and officers of the NAWU.

The executive board and the advisory committee of the NAWU met in Memphis, Tennessee, on June 26 to consider the crisis. Once more the elected spokesman and representatives of the land workers found themselves in confusion and despair. They came out of the meeting with a resolution declaring the AWOC a dual union, the worst heresy that unionism could commit. It characterized the action as illegal and a plain encroachment of the rights of the NAWU, requesting that the council rescind it. A formal hearing before the full Executive Council was requested; to this resolution there was no response.

At the peak of their accomplishments Smith and his associates had reasons to feel that they could now go marching forward toward social justice and economic equality untrammeled by the NAWU. A technical cloud over the new charter had been removed immediately before June 10 when Helstein wrote Mitchell that, on the basis of information he had, the Memorandum of Agreement of May 1959 was no longer in effect. The UPWA would assert its claim to jurisdiction over field workers. This notice was intended to remove from Schnitzler's path the embarrassment of having ignored the agreement, of which he had been aware all along. Smith was announcing that his leadership cadres were ready and "that we have the money to carry on the drive." He was claiming credit for the millions of dollars that the AWOC had forced the growers to pay in higher wages. The flying squad tactics were working.[327] He had successfully completed his detente with the government bureaucracies and the statesmen of the Federation of Labor. Personally Smith was in a position not unlike that of John L. Lewis, whose organizing committees had compelled huge industries to accept collective bargaining, carrying Lewis to the peak of his career.

With the money and power given him by the AFL–CIO Smith destroyed his sworn friends, the NAWU, but not his sworn adversary, the agri-business establishment. It regarded Smith as a hard-headed and businesslike professional and counted him a serious threat. Senator Cobey of the state legislature found after an investigation that the AWOC was "an organization activity trailing behind a rebellion against miserable conditions." Food processors whose canneries were threatened offered to raise funds to recruit nonunion harvesters and to assist by supplementing the Farm Placement Service staff, ever ready in such emergencies.[328] The Department of Agriculture set up an Agricultural Labor Problems Work Group to provide support to the growers. The County Agricultural Commissioners were instructed to keep the governor's office informed as to the problems of agriculture and to assist them in anticipating its difficulties, a task made easier by Krainock's announcements of strikes to come. Industry spokesmen like John Zuckerman of San Joaquin, an intense Smith watcher, were busy on the public relations front; to Zuckerman, Smith was a dues collector bent on destroying agriculture.

But it was through a lawsuit that Smith was first checked and finally stalemated by the growers. In the summer of 1960, the first full season for which Smith was prepared with his cadres and flying squads, court injunctions were harassing him. Growers Perry and Loduca obtained a temporary injunction, terming Smith's tactics a secondary boycott. Another grower was granted a restraining order prohibiting the State Department of Employment from finding that a labor dispute existed.

In this line of legal counterattacks the DiGiorgio Fruit Corporation finally delivered the decisive blow.

Smith's men had set pickets on DiGiorgio's Yuba operations in the summer of 1960. As a grower in its own right and as the recognized pacesetter of corporate agriculture throughout the state, DiGiorgio had the double interest of protecting its pears as well as its prestige. And it was Krainock who provided the opportunity.

On one of his public relations trips Krainock had learned of the short documentary film *Poverty in the Valley of Plenty,* which the Hollywood Film Council had produced for the NAWU to raise funds during the DiGiorgio strike in Arvin ten years before. DiGiorgio had sued the NAWU and its State Federation sponsors and had won a judgment for libel and a permanent court order prohibiting the showing of the film. Krainock called the film to Smith's attention without knowledge of the judgment and order, and they proceeded to use it at organizing meetings throughout the Central Valley.

The ever-alert intelligence service maintained by the Associated Farmers for the industry reported these screenings, and the corporation verified them and filed a complaint for libel—naming as defendants Norman Smith, H. L. Mitchell, Ernesto Galarza, and the Agricultural Workers Organizing Committee. This suit miscarried inasmuch as Galarza and Mitchell had had no connection with the showings, my own resignation from the Smith's staff having been submitted several months before. A second complaint, filed on September 13, 1960, went to trial. DiGiorgio won a judgment for $100,000 reduced on appeal to $60,000 plus costs, which was paid by the AFL–CIO—a heavy charge against Meany's investment in the California campaign.

At the time of Krainock's mischance there was pending in the Superior Court of San Francisco a counteraction by me against the DiGiorgio Fruit Corporation, prosecuted by my friend, attorney James Murray. I offered Smith my own files for his defense, but Smith countered with the suggestion that Murray serve as associate counsel to the AWOC, on condition that he drop out of my case. Murray did not do so, and the AWOC went on to lose the case.

Once before I had failed to enlist Smith's support in joint legal action against his adversaries. The U.S. Department of Labor had left my charges against the D'Arrigo Company of 1959 in such a state that I was prepared to bring a class action in court against the department and the company. Smith refused to finance such a suit against D'Arrigo, with which the UPWA had a shed contract.

Smith was losing his momentum in the fields. He decided to take part in the joint effort in the Imperial Valley to strike the winter lettuce crop. As indicated above, the UPWA was now recruiting harvesters, and Smith's support of his sister union was openly declared. The strike failed and Clive Knowles, UPWA leader of the strike, laid the blame on Secretary of Labor Goldberg for refusal to take prompt action to move the braceros working in the lettuce fields.[329] The Western Conference of Teamsters had announced previously that it would abide by its no-strike contract with the growers, who noted with satisfaction their refusal to assist UPWA. Smith retreated to the Central Valley while these events were pondered by Meany and the seven overseers of the AWOC. To the degradation of the DiGiorgio penalty of $60,000 there was now added the pain of $21,000 in legal fees and over $4,000 in fines imposed on the flying squads of the Imperial strike.

These assessments not only drained the $100,000 that Meany had approved for a year's operation of the AWOC, but also blighted Smith's prestige with his superiors. He now had to answer to the seven commissioners who, by their assignment, were empowered "to appraise and report the progress of the organizing campaign; to advise and assist Director Smith and his staff; to receive reports and examine records of finances; and to approve or recommend disapproval of operating committee action on policies." What they saw as Smith cut short his joint enterprise with Knowles was not impressive—no collective bargaining contracts, costs higher than dues collections, a humiliating and expensive lawsuit.

To the scars that Smith carried from his previous campaigns were now added those of his broken coalition with the UPWA. In the second DiGiorgio complaint the UPWA had been named as a defendant. A sworn declaration by Knowles enabled it to plead for and obtain dismissal. As declarant for the UPWA, Knowles swore: "Our union was concerned only with the organization of the workers involved in the packing and processing of fresh fruits and vegetables. . . . There was at all times . . . no organizational connection or any relationship between the UPWA [and AWOC]. . . . At no time . . . did UPWA authorize or request AWOC . . . to act on behalf of or represent UPWA."[330] The court was not aware of Smith's official statement to the State of California that he was operating in the jurisdiction of the UPWA.

From January 1961 what had been a decline for the AWOC rapidly became a collapse. Smith was ordered to cut his expenses to three thousand dollars per month. Field offices were closed and staff dismissed. UPWA organizers who had been carried on Smith's payroll went back to their own organization. An accountant arrived in Stockton to audit the campaign records. Krainock began to make overtures to the Teamsters to pick up the pieces.

Meany's interest in the AWOC cooled steadily throughout 1960. In February he had saluted the AWOC for having awakened the nation's conscience and in August the Executive Council appropriated another hundred thousand dollars, even though Livingston's figure of twenty-five thousand new members was revised to five thousand. By October Meany was considering dropping the campaign, or at least reducing the staff to a skeleton crew.[331] The spring of 1961 was uneventful and so was the summer until Meany's announcement that the campaign was over. Meany regretfully noted that only thirty-five hundred harvesters had joined the AWOC, out of a potential of two hundred and fifty thousand. The campaign had cost, according to Smith, five hundred thousand dollars.

The postscripts of disaster are melancholy or bright, depending upon who writes them. The Council of California Growers let it be known that "agriculture is not tearing down its forts because one band of marauders has been wiped out." A few weeks after Meany's announcement Smith swore he would stay at the task of organizing field workers as long as he lived and made an appeal to the central labor councils of the State Federation to support the continuation of the AWOC.[332] Krainock wrote his own epilogue in a different style. In February 1964 he announced the launching of an organization called the Agricultural Workers Union. Its joint patrons were Harry Bridges of the Longshoremen and James Hoffa of the Teamsters. By an act of true nobility, Krainock declared, the Longshoremen and Teamsters would give their support "with no strings attached" to assure that the new union would not be a dues collecting picket line union.[333]

Smith and Krainock, the agents of the high policy makers in Washington, had begun their campaign in May 1959; by the end of 1961 it was over in all but name. It had, in so brief a term, demonstrated its true intent as a design for the destruction of the National Agricultural Workers Union. Krainock's union was never heard from again and Smith disappeared from the scene, a brooding and perplexed man.

Meany's reasons for cutting off support were those of a prudent businessman. The investment was not paying off and his market analysis showed little hope of recovering it. But as the AFL–CIO took its financial losses Meany could record some results on the credit side. At long last, he was rid of Mitchell's nagging presence. One point of friction between him and Reuther had been eliminated. There was still the potential dispute between Reuther and Gorman of the Meat Cutters which could not have been viewed with dismay by Meany, since it would lie between two old socialists, neither of whom stood high in his esteem. And the campaign had lasted just long enough to prove to the liberal conscience that he and the AFL-CIO really cared.

For many years Mitchell had anticipated the end of his union by the process of benevolent neglect, not by a purge. What little there was left of the NAWU could still be salvaged: the NAWU could merge with their old friends, the Butchers.

The Merger

Conversations between Gorman and Mitchell about the possibility of a merger of the two unions had been taking place since 1956. As the AWOC's intentions unfolded the discussions reached the stage of formal negotiations, Gorman remaining cautious and confident while Mitchell, in a mood of quiet desperation, continued to press for an agreement.

Once the merger was agreed to by both sides, practical steps were taken. The first of these was my appointment by Gorman to the staff of the Amalgamated Meat Cutters, assigned to California, confirmed by Gorman in a letter dated April 22, 1960. My status was to be that of Special Organizer, somewhat above that of an apprentice and below that of International Representative. Gorman apologetically explained it this way: "You have just started working for our International Union with not too much in the making in organizing work." My salary was fixed at $125 a week. My briefing included a circular from Gorman: "We also suggest that as an Organizer for the International Union you remain away from controversial subjects."

Although I was now on the staff of the Butchers' Union, I remained as secretary of the NAWU and director of research and education. Mitchell supplemented Gorman's guideline. My task was to retain whatever membership the NAWU had in the state at the time. Its locals were to remain active and report to Mitchell, as they had regularly done in the past. I was to force Smith to place all field workers recruited by him into the NAWU, and I was to hold this new membership until the merger with the Amalgamated could be closed.

I was additionally instructed by Gorman to clear my activities with Max Osslo, vice-president of the Amalgamated for the western region and one of the vice-presidents of the California State Federation of Labor. My directives would come from the Chicago office of the Amalgamated. I was to make no public statements, and above all I was to be patient until the pending negotiations between the Amalgamated and the UPWA were concluded.

The central assignment was to protect the jurisdictional claim to field workers that the Amalgamated would receive by merging with the

NAWU. Leon Schachter, vice-president and Mitchell's closest friend in the Amalgamated, suggested supplementary instructions. I was to monitor AWOC staff headquarters in Stockton, establish friendly relations with the Amalgamated locals in California, maintain contact with the old NAWU members, try to influence the course of events generally, and reverse, if I could, the position of the government bureaucracies with regard to farm labor. This, and nothing more, was my assignment.

The part of it that was superfluous related to maintaining contact with the old members. If there was to be a merger they would have to be informed of every development in that direction. Since they had been told repeatedly and officially that the AWOC's assignment was to strengthen the NAWU, the obvious inconsistency between Smith's actions and that commitment had to be discussed in membership meetings throughout the state. It was necessary, also, to help the members who were losing hope of the NAWU's survival to find jobs outside of agriculture.

This part of my assignment was nearly overwhelming; and the order to clear with Osslo was distasteful. We were two bodies that repelled each other. He never responded to my reports or recommendations, partly, so I thought, because I was only a special organizer, and partly, I suspected, because I was a Mexican. He was the key official of the State Federation in the border counties, which included Imperial. Osslo was a member of the watchdog committee over Norman Smith. I was dealing with governors and bureaucrats as an adversary with access to the press, while Osslo necessarily was dealing with the same persons on the level of a statesman. My threat to take legal action against Schnitzler and the AFL–CIO Executive Board over the AWOC charter was clearly controversial and besides disrespectful.

As the merger talks progressed, Mitchell's primary concern was to hold his bargaining position with respect to the Amalgamated based exclusively on the charter he held from the AFL. Gorman's was more complicated but equally clear—to absorb the NAWU on the most advantageous terms; to use that jurisdictional right as a means of persuasion on the UPWA, with whom he was also negotiating; to avoid offending Meany; and to operate strictly within the protocol of the California State Federation of Labor.

The differences between the NAWU and the Amalgamated as to bargaining strength were striking. The Butchers were one of the powerful Internationals of the AFL–CIO and a model of mergemanship. The NAWU, by contrast, was in its usual state of financial exhaustion. Its income in January 1958 consisted of less than $500 in monthly dues and $13,000 a year from the National Sharecroppers Fund in monthly installments, not always paid on time, according to Mitchell. In July 1960 there were barely a hundred NAWU members in the Northern California locals. Smith had totally destroyed its effectiveness as an operating union. In August Mitchell wrote me the most dismal of all the accounts I had received from him on this score. The NAWU owed over $1,000 for printing, and $480 in per capita dues to the AFL–CIO. Premiums on life insurance policies of four hundred veteran members who had held the union firm in the south were overdue, and there was no money for the current salaries of the staff. "There is nothing much we can do but accept the decision of the AFL–CIO. . . . We can trade the charter to the Butchers for a job or two." Until the national convention of the Butchers confirmed the merger, any incident could spoil the negotiations. On receipt of a copy of my letter to Schnitzler, Mitchell telegraphed me: "Please do not make public statements. Don't put us or Amalgamated on the spot by newspaper attacks." In this Gorman was in full agreement with Mitchell: "Please don't write any more letters of that kind."

The options that Mitchell considered to save the union failed one by one. In May 1958 Haggerty flatly turned down Mitchell's appeal for financial help. The idea of resorting to the courts to sustain the NAWU charter crossed his mind. Smith was cold to the suggestion that a merger in California might be negotiated to include the UPWA, the NAWU, and the Butchers. Mitchell then considered chartering new locals in California directly in an open challenge to Smith. He also suggested that an Agricultural Workers Council be created in California, in which the NAWU would play the part of an equal. Gorman vetoed this idea as no longer necessary.

The Executive Board of the NAWU met in Washington on February 5 and 6, 1960, to consider the alternatives of a dignified exit out of the House of Labor. This meeting was called as a result of the message Mitchell had received from Victor Reuther and J. Philip Randolph to the effect that the AFL–CIO had decided to dissolve the NAWU in favor of a larger union if the California campaign was to be continued and eventually expanded throughout the nation.

As a result of the February meeting of the board, Mitchell wrote Meany on February 6 that the dissolution of the NAWU would be accepted on three conditions: (1) the AFL–CIO would commit itself to continue the California campaign until a national farm workers union was in existence; (2) that in the larger international union the identity of the farm workers would be maintained through a special department or division of agricultural workers; and (3) that the agricultural workers would be represented on the policy making board of the larger international union to which the charter would be surrendered.

The letter had interpreted the message from Reuther and Randolph as meaning that Meany had agreed to designate the larger international union that would succeed to the charter. Meany's answer was an indignant one, saying that he would not designate a successor and that the act of dissolution would have to be by the members of the NAWU themselves. Mitchell had outlined substantially these same conditions to Reuther in January 1960, resigned to the point of stating that if they were met it would not matter greatly which international union assumed the responsibility for the national farm workers.[334]

In an earlier day some consideration might have been given to calling another national conference in Washington to assemble the liberal conscience in support of the NAWU. But, as in February 1959, the National Sharecroppers Fund would have to play a central role, and the fund had already declared its position with respect to mergers, campaigns, recall of charters, and related events. Fay Bennett, secretary of the fund, wrote me in July 1959 that the fund was in a position of noninterference with AFL–CIO policies; that organized labor must assume directly the responsibility for agricultural labor; that the fund would have no part in my lawsuit against the DiGiorgio Corporation; and that it would restrict itself to public relations.[335] Her personal advice to me was to "work within the framework of organized labor and keep yourself in a position to try to influence its actions rather than to set yourself apart."[336]

One other unexpected option likewise failed on my account. Saul Alinsky, the noted radical and director of the Industrial Areas Foundation of Chicago, asked me to visit him in New York. At his expense I made the trip from Washington to learn of his interest in me for an assignment in California organizing in the fields. Alinsky said the foundation was prepared to spend a sum in six figures if I would accept. I answered that the proposal had merit but that since it affected the California position of the NAWU, and since I was the only representative there, the proposal would have to be made to the entire board. It was the only discussion we had on that or any other matter.

There were three approaches to the Amalgamated–NAWU merger other than Mitchell's, those of Walter Reuther, Meany and the Butchers. Their interplay forms the script of the last days of the NAWU. There is no need to discuss the UPWA in this connection, since it simply reflected Reuther's interests and judgment.

Reuther's position had been firmly explained to the NAWU on November 1, 1957, by Victor Reuther, Walter's brother and an official of the Auto Workers Union. At this meeting it was made clear that the Industrial Union Department, following Walter's instructions, would not extend its $25,000 grant to the NAWU unless the NAWU agreed to merge with the United Packinghouse Workers of America. The Executive Board rejected the recommendation, as explained above. Mitchell polled the board, and every member stated that he would not under any circumstances agree to work for the UPWA.

As the merger discussions with the Butchers progressed through winter of 1959 and into spring of 1960, Reuther's position remained unchanged. On February 5, 1960, Victor met again with the NAWU board in Washington. A subcommittee of the AFL–CIO Executive Council had decided to dissolve the NAWU. The NAWU was urged to work out an agreement with the UPWA. This course had the approval of Walter Reuther, based on the following considerations: the Butchers Union had no interest in field workers; they had spent no money and had no program; the UPWA, on the other hand, did have a historic interest in harvesters; Helstein had promised to set up a special department for farm workers within the UPWA; Helstein had on his staff organizers with recognized skill in this area; and finally the Industrial Union Department would subsidize a public relations program into which Mitchell could transfer out of active participation in union affairs.[337] On an organizational basis, the NAWU was told, it was desirable for only one union to represent both field and processing workers, and the UPWA had demonstrated a sincere interest in their welfare. Only if a merger with UPWA were accepted would financial aid for the California campaign continue.

Before concluding its February meeting the board voted to recommend to the membership that the NAWU be dissolved and that a suitable merger be negotiated. Mitchell was given the authority to arrange it.

On February 25 Walter Reuther and Helstein met with Mitchell and me at the Hay–Adams Hotel in Washington. Reuther reiterated his demands, offering a subsidy of fifteen thousand dollars a year for Mitchell's salary as public relations director for farm workers in cooperation with the National Sharecroppers Fund. He also made it clear that if the NAWU merged with the Amalgamated support for Mitchell from the IUD would end.

At this point Helstein was in a comfortable role. He advised Mitchell that the UPWA preferred to wait until the AWOC had fully organized the California harvesters and secured collective bargaining contracts.

On my return to California from the Washington meeting I was called to a telephone conference with Livingston and Franz Daniel, who urged me to accept Reuther's terms. I refused.

To Meany it must have appeared that the situation was slipping out of his hands and into Reuther's, for he called a meeting in his office on

March 8, 1960. Besides Mitchell and myself, Livingston, Daniel, Smith, and Schnitzler were summoned. Meany was blunt and to the point. He would not authorize direct charters to locals without NAWU consent. He categorically denied that he had made merger with the UPWA a condition for continuing the California drive. Directly he charged Mitchell with interfering in the California campaign to the detriment of the AWOC. He said that on this basis he had agreed that all dues collected from new enrollments of field workers be impounded until local unions had sufficient leadership to run their own affairs.

When my turn came to speak I made it plain that I opposed merging field workers with a processing union, because they were invariably traded off to protect the contracts of processing workers, and I cited cases where this had happened.

But the words that mattered in the meeting were not mine. They were Meany's. And he said, somewhat vaguely, that he might call off the California campaign. We knew where the AFL stood.

Through all this the Amalgamated strategy was twofold. Its first objective was to leave no doubt in Meany's mind that its claim to the NAWU charter would be vigorously sustained. Second, it would comply with Meany's demand that the NAWU not interfere with Smith's activities in any manner.

As to the first, Schachter let Mitchell know the views of the Amalgamated, that they, the Butchers, were definitely interested in the agricultural workers; that the NAWU should be strengthened by the AWOC; and that the Butchers did not propose to let the UPWA take the jurisdiction.[338] At a meeting of the National Sharecroppers Fund in January 1960, Schachter learned that Reuther and Randolph, after a discussion with Meany, were of the opinion that the NAWU could not organize farm workers, and that the UPWA was the logical union for a merger. Schachter telegraphed a protest to Meany who explained that he only meant that a merger was desirable, and that UPWA was the logical union.[339] At the meeting of the NAWU Executive Board of February 5 and 6, Schachter read a telegram from Gorman to Meany reiterating the Amalgamated's interest in farm workers. Meany responded by telephone to say that he had no power to recall the NAWU charter and that the NAWU could merge with any union of its choice.[340] Ever watchful that the prized international charter should not fall into Helstein's hands, Gorman advised Schnitzler not to issue local charters to agricultural workers, reserving that right to the Amalgamated.

In California the AWOC and UPWA's joint efforts in the fields were under surveillance by the Butchers. In the Imperial lettuce strike of early 1961, and after the NAWU merger had been completed, Osslo complained to Gorman, and Smith was ordered to withdraw, which he did, marking the beginning of the break between him and Knowles.

The Amalgamated was at the same time both opposing and courting the UPWA. This position Gorman had explained to Mitchell in 1956: "With the NAWU a part of our organization we will have a much better opportunity to press our claims for jurisdiction within the agricultural field."[341] Gorman regarded the field workers as a vast field for unionism, and he had Meany's repeated word that the Amalgamated would fall heir to it. Ralph Helstein was not taking personal offense over the Amalgamated's tactics. He wrote to Mitchell on January 10, 1960, "For many years our union has felt that a merger with the Amalgamated Meat Cutters was desirable. We intend to do everything we can do reasonably, with honor, to bring about such a merger."

Mitchell felt as late as September 1960 that all field workers then being organized in California directly by the AFL–CIO would also come into the Amalgamated. Gorman's pursuit of this windfall was tenacious, but it was a chase after a wraith. Even after Meany had advised him in the fall of 1960 that the closing of the campaign was under consideration, Gorman was telling Mitchell that he had positive assurance from Meany that the field workers signed up by Smith would be transferred to the Amalgamated.

In the jargon of labor, evasion of a difficult problem is called taking a powder. The Butchers, considering how smoothly matters were going, took a powder as to the AWOC campaign. In October 1960 Gorman explained to me: "When the AFL–CIO puts another $100,000 into a campaign and suggests only that we give the organizing committee a chance to do its own work, there isn't much we can do."[342] Gorman wrote me again in 1960: "If our $100,000 was doing the work instead of the $100,000 of the AFL–CIO we could paddle our own canoe . . . but inasmuch as not one penny of our money is being spent to organize farm workers, nothing is left for us honorably to do except go along with them." To Smith he wrote: "We have, in the interest of harmony, and in line with the promises and jurisdiction officially awarded us, decided to remain out of the California organizing program for obvious reasons." Gorman repeated this to the National Sharecroppers Fund.

As the AWOC tottered and the vast jurisdiction of field workers shrank from 500,000 (Krainock) to 25,000 (Livingston) to 5,000 (Smith) to 3,500 (Meany), Gorman revealed other subtleties about the Amalgamated's strategy. He explained to me in May 1961 what they were. "There isn't much we could have done about the situation in California. At least we can say that if the Teamsters sweep the state it wasn't our fault. . . . The AFL–CIO did not want us in the campaign. . . . We intended to continue to work with the Teamsters . . . and it could be that they will recognize our jurisdictional rights in the agricultural field . . . like we have with the Teamsters at the giant Seabrook Farms.'' In the meantime Gorman was assuring me that if the AWOC was abandoned the Amalgamated would carry on with its own program.

Only once did the Amalgamated feel any doubts as to Meany's real intentions, and this was when the NAWU charter was recalled and transferred to the AWOC. Gorman talked of legal action and a hearing before the Executive Council. But at a luncheon with Meany in July 1961, Gorman was assured that on completion of the merger twenty-five thousand people would come into the Amalgamated. Chartering the AWOC, Meany explained, was nothing more than a device to force Smith to spend twenty-five thousand dollars he had collected and im-pounded from field laborers. This at least was Gorman's account.

In one respect, the powder the Butchers had taken was particularly effective in their disposition of me as a junior organizer in California. They simply assigned me out. In May 1960 Schachter advised me to prepare to move to Texas to assist meat cutters who were having difficulties with illegals and border crossers. Mitchell suggested to me that I accept such an assignment, which I declined. I had not suspected that Schnitzler and Smith attached so much weight to my presence in California. In June both of them hinted to Gorman that if I remained where I was there would be no funds for the AWOC campaign to continue. The phrase was that I could not "continue in the picture." Gorman responded by assuring Schnitzler that "our man Galarza" was marking time with no intention of doing anything detrimental to the drive.

Gorman recognized that it was not a brave thing the Butchers were doing. In November 1960 he wrote me: "The courageous thing to do [would be] to start organizing, issuing our own charters. . . . Isn't it better for the AFL–CIO to do the job for us? . . . Abstention means only the State of California. The whole North American continent is a field.''

Gorman and Mitchell were reaching agreement on the terms of the merger, but Gorman was holding back because I was a defendant in the DiGiorgio action for libel against the AWOC. Gorman feared that in some manner the Amalgamated might incur liability. When I was se-vered from the complaint, this obstacle was removed. Since I was preparing to file a countersuit against DiGiorgio myself, Gorman in-structed me to use no Amalgamated funds because it was "matter affecting Ernesto Galarza only.''

In November 1959 Mitchell announced that the NAWU and the Amalgamated had agreed to negotiate a merger. In June 1960 the membership voted in favor of the merger and Mitchell proceeded to close with the Butchers in the final negotiations, which took place in New York.

By this agreement, dated August 2, 1960, the NAWU charter was transferred to the Amalgamated Meat Cutters and Butcher Workmen of America. The Amalgamated agreed to appoint one International Representative from the staff of the NAWU. A department or division for agricultural workers within the Amalgamated was established.

Since my signature as secretary of the NAWU was required I waited until I saw in writing that Mitchell had been assured of a staff position with the Amalgamated. Signing for the Amalgamated were Gorman and the president of the union, Thomas J. Lloyd. They acted pursuant to a resolution of the National Convention that read: "Whereas the Agricultural Workers Union has made valiant and dedicated but futile efforts to organize these workers [and has] made courageous sacrifices . . . the Amalgamated can and will put an end to the conspiracy of oppression."[343]

On August 10, 1960, Meany was notified by the Amalgamated that the merger was in effect.

With their new jurisdiction in hand, the Amalgamated assigned Mitchell to Louisiana to organize off-shore fishermen and rice mill workers. Plans were made for an organizing drive for field workers in other parts of the country, except California. Such a program never got under way.

The exclusion of California from the Butchers' paper plans was consistent with Gorman's careful attention to Meany's demand of full support for the AWOC. Field workers had always been by far the most difficult to organize in any agriculturally related industry. If the UPWA merged with the Butchers they would bring with them their packing sheds on the West Coast, at least those that survived the progress of mechanization and the infiltration of braceros. For Gorman it was in a sense a back door to California which could be opened by diplomacy rather than by field activity with domestic harvesters.

After the merger with the Amalgamated had been signed I made the last round of visits to all the locals in the Central Valley and the northern coastal counties. To those members I could not reach through meetings I sent reports on the events that ended with the merger. In them I expressed my strong belief that the Amalgamated would not go into the fields, and that it would not carry on the resistance against the bracero system in the manner that the NAWU had done. I also reported that the Amalgamated's chief representative in the state, Max Osslo, had personally complained to Gorman about my employment as a special representative, and that the Amalgamated was pressing me to leave California.

I was called to Chicago by Gorman to meet with Vice-President Harry Poole for a briefing. I was to return to California under the following conditions: no funds of the Amalgamated were to be committed to legal services to locals; I was to take no action that might be interpreted by the AFL–CIO as interfering with or reflecting on the AWOC; I was to clear all matters with Osslo; the AWOC organizing strategy was to be respected as laid down by Smith; decisions as to the AWOC were to be made by Livingston, Daniel, Smith, and Osslo. Poole commented at some length on the advantages of my accepting an assignment elsewhere, possibly in Puerto Rico, where I had spent a week on behalf of the Amalgamated after joining its staff.

On my visit to headquarters I had asked for the opportunity to present one item from my agenda. This related to the payment of six thousand dollars in outstanding debts of the California locals. The matter was never discussed.

On August 11, 1960, I informed Poole that I wanted to be relieved of my California assignment. On the sixteenth I wrote Gorman: "I am now convinced that it is impossible for you to see the situation except through the eyes of the AWOC." On August 25 Gorman wrote me: "Therefore as of October 22 we shall conclude that you will feel more satisfied not being with our International Union."

Gorman's personal sympathy for my lack of a job continued for several months, with offers to take me back for field organizing in any western state other than California. My response was unchanged: "The Amalgamated, by standing aside and giving its approval to Smith's course, has identified itself with the brutal destruction of the NAWU. Your critical judgment is in abeyance as long as Meany is paying the bill."[344]

VII: Preface to the Past

The past can be a compost pile of recollections of the disasters of the many and the triumphs of the few. In it anyone may dig out of curiosity to uncover some missing piece of lore, to fertilize a silting nostalgia, or to settle with faded chronicles a scholarly controversy. History practiced in this way can satisfy those who view the past as residue, as a post-mortem of successive epochs in which most men appear as subjects of history, not as its agents.

The past can also be prologue to those who are willing to learn from it. But to what purpose? To offer such minds a place and a role at the forward edge of the search for meaning where time, place, nature, culture, men and their conflicting interests and even disasters mingle to resolve their never-ending tensions.

Even more important is the sense and the will that, once a historical process is understood, a choice can be made as to one's place in its next moment, and the realization that the best history is that in which one has had an effective part. A mind placed at the forward edge of events and guided by knowledge uses the past, affects the present, and possibly helps form the future.

The action is where people are, and a place among them is the crux of everyman's search. Human society is an organized complex of settlements, among which men sort themselves into universes of commitment and communication and cooperation reduced to the human scale in which a man's grasp can equal his reach, physically and intellectually and emotionally. But in time these settlements become the foundations of social power. Gradually they reach out, absorb, integrate, merge, and acculturate other less vigorous settlements and distort if not destroy their human scale.

Within these settlements themselves—in America the Church, corporations, trade unions, government and its bureaucracies, the educational systems—the extension of power externally demands its concentration internally. When the tension created breaks, as it must, the settlements go into motion and become history. Social relations change, smoothly or violently; the movement slows to a stop, and history again becomes sociology.

Those who see and live the past as a prologue will to their discomfort discover that they have found the clue to the hoary dilemma of means and ends. They never can choose without considering values. In whatever settlement men find themselves by birth or luck, they will be in relationships with those who have had a greater or a lesser birthright or better or worse luck.

Power can be used to exploit these differences. However, it cannot operate openly and arrogantly, at least not in moral, Christian, democratic, parliamentary America. Compassion for the disinherited must be professed while power works under disguises. All the Watergates of its history show how irresponsibly America distributes power and how it pardons its abuse, *ex post facto*. Power is dressed in myths to make it agreeable to the requirements of a Christian democracy.

For those without power, there remains compassion. But compassion is not enough and neither is charisma, for compassion is exhaustible and charisma is a one-time, one-man thing. Each can be a social force at particular times and under special circumstances; neither can explain much concerning the historical process of which they are an incident, however brilliant and edifying.

In this tenor the closing section of this book is arranged. It is not an evaluation, which must be left to others. It does include some comments on how well or how badly the National Agricultural Workers Union did, what social myths surrounding agri-business it left in shreds as it died, and how the establishments of social power challenged by the union continued as before.

The NAWU: Apologia of a Failure

Before men could land on the moon, the combined scientific and technical knowledge of every discipline bearing on human travel into outer space, lunar orbit, and re-entry into earth's atmosphere and gravitational pull was exhaustively researched. In social science, too, important problems exist with respect to the intervention of one settlement into the realm of another and the negotiation of inter-social space.

These were the problems confronting the National Farm Labor Union when Mitchell and Hasiwar came to California, as Hasiwar put it, "to case the joint," to explore an intended organizing target. Their entry was effected by contacts with some central labor councils, state federation officials, and talks with the farm workers who had called them in. It was done in a matter of days for Mitchell and for Hasiwar over a period of several months in extended travel up and down and across the state. Hasiwar had been an organizer for the stationary engineers and electrical workers unions. Mitchell had organized and held together through the days of the plantation terror the Southern Tenant Farmers Union; through this he discovered and engaged the liberal conscience. Neither Hasiwar nor Mitchell was prepared to recognize and assess the social structure of Agri-businessland, and both of them had to learn of it through the encounters of the first five years, which ended when Hasiwar transferred to Louisiana.

Perhaps it was fortunate. Too much knowledge at the beginning might have been, more than a dangerous thing, a discouraging one. From October 1, 1947, when the pickets were placed in front of the DiGiorgio Farms, to August 2, 1960, when the NAWU was liquidated, was a period of continuous forced entry and discovery in the face of great odds—the denial of information by the Farm Placement Service, the conspiracy of the U.S. Department of Labor with representatives of Agri-business, the passive disinterest of the State Federation of Labor, the private diplomacy of the United States and Mexican governments, and the closed-circuit dealings of the State Board of Agriculture with the State Department of Employment.

As explained above, the task that Mitchell and Hasiwar had laid out for the union pressed on all these fronts, and by 1952 it had to be redefined and reduced if it was to continue on any level at all. For the next eight years it became a single-minded effort to lay bare in detail how the bracero system was operating and to apply that information to terminate it. This was done through what I have referred to above as action research.

The reduction of the original task, thus stated, oversimplifies other aspects of what the NAWU did during those eight years. For one thing, it was necessary to maintain, on scarce recourses, the connection between the union and the harvesters who had taken part in all the actions of the first five years and who had come to depend on it for information, guidance, and support. It was also necessary at all costs, even if the NAWU was to fail eventually, to maintain this connection in a manner that would not repeat the traditional pattern of unions disappearing after the final barnstorm. Finally, as the pattern of displacement of domestics, from which the union had drawn its members, turned into a retreat, it became necessary to establish a northern line along which their remnants could regroup and continue the attack on Public Law 78.

On these terms the NAWU both succeeded and failed. As an introduction to this assessment the nature of the labor force with which the NAWU had to deal must be considered and the extent of its territory taken into account.

In September 1959 there were working on all California farms 122,000 year-round wage workers, 34,500 seasonal harvesters who had come from other states intending to return there, 131,000 domestics residing in the work area or commuting to it, and 84,000 braceros. The domestics included day-haul recruits from over twenty cities, some of them more than a hundred miles from the area of employment; experienced illegals; braceros who had broken their contracts to become, as they called themselves, *libres* ("free workers"); youth on summer vacation; professional "bindle stiffs" who travelled the harvest cycle on railway cars or on foot; prisoners of county jails released to growers on what was called the "kick out program"; former field workers who returned to the fields when jobs were scarce in the cities; college students; and Filipinos who wintered in town. From 1949 to 1959 the number of persons in such a labor pool fluctuated, but the pattern remained.

To reach these workers NAWU organizers had to cover a territory roughly some six hundred miles long and eighty miles wide, within which were located the most intensely cultivated districts. This area embraced the ten largest counties in California, some of them larger than New England states. Organizing in the Central Valley often required trips of two hundred miles to hold a single meeting. Every organizer provided his own automobile or rode the buses. Compared to the deeply rooted and locally stable economic and social settlements of Agri-businessland, establishing durable locals over so much space was like trying to anchor pontoons in shifting tides.

Field workers, it was generally held by scholars and nonparticipating observers, were unorganizable. The structure and tactics of established trade unionism had failed for them. Such organization as was attained never consolidated its gains. A presidential commission concluded in 1951 that their cohesion was scarcely greater then that of pebbles of the seashore.

However, as a labor market it was not as unstructured as the experts believed. Within it there were many systems of recruitment and delivery of harvesters, whose variety gave the impression of hopeless confusion. It required a close look to notice that there were in fact many structures. Farm labor contractors as a class operated one of them. Ministers of the Gospel led their flocks on work days as well as on the Sabbath. The day hauls were a distinct and important source of manpower. Crew leaders who shunned the costs and responsibilities of contracting acted as advance agents for neighbors, friends, and relatives. The social clubs of the Filipinos were the economic face of a separate culture. Growers, especially the smaller ones, recruited in Mexico by correspondence. Operators of "flop houses" on skid row and publicans of various sorts connected men and jobs as an incident of their trade.

Among the conflicting interests of such recruiters the union organized locals sufficiently strong to take economic action in the most important crops, notably cotton, grapes, melons, and peaches. Nonorganizability implied, so it was said, psychological defects even more difficult to cope with than mobility; but the NAWU, on the scale that its resources permitted, disproved this also.

In the clusters of rural towns that became the pivots of organization, there were enough stable domestics to have formed a union of thirty thousand members in the late 1940s. Around these clusters local councils were formed; the circuit of travel for organizers was reduced with a saving of time and a reduction of costs. The leadership that responded was composed of men with local kinship connections and the social ties of family and church. The information they gathered day in and day out had only to be collated to provide the locals and their members with the indispensable facts for organizing strategies. The locals provided the first training ground for men and women who later developed into skilled negotiators. As the regular union staff dropped from five representatives to three and then to one for the entire state, the volunteers, occasionally paid stipends for travel, became the mainstay of the NAWU. The cadres that Krainock was seeking were already there when Smith opened in

Stockton, informal teams disciplined by their own experience, a growing confidence in their own understanding of the goals of the union, the nature of the economic system that confronted them, and the techniques of survival and resistance that they were learning.

Except for one half-hearted effort in Kern County to build the union more rapidly by drawing contractors and their ready crews into its ranks, the NAWU proved to be an effective competitor with them. Contractors stood in disrepute everywhere, their ambivalent roles of growers' middlemen in providing illegals and managing bracero crews adding to the disrepute of tricks by which they mulcted their crews.

The attack on Public Law 78 rested entirely on the vigilance of the local volunteers, their training in what the law, the contracts, and the international agreements provided as to the rights of both domestics and braceros. The union successfully prevented the appearance of class hostility against both braceros and illegals in a situation that fostered it. The increasing capability of the volunteers to confront the agents of the Farm Placement Service at any level drove them to concealment and hole-in-corner intrigues. When the records of the Department of Employment were finally opened for local inspection, the volunteers quickly became familiar with them and used them effectively. Grievances brought by braceros were attended by the volunteers, who became adept at using the work contracts to press the complaints and add to the union's knowledge on that score.

Although Norman Smith attributed the rise in wages to the pressure of his flying squads, as though it was unprecedented in farm labor history, the contrary was the case. With rare exceptions the NAWU was able to bring about such increases, sometimes by merely making the rounds of the fields at the peak of the harvesting. The immediate gain to the harvesters in the tomato harvest struck by the Tracy local amounted to 6 cents per lug box calculated on the basis of forty boxes to the ton and a harvest yield of thousands of tons when work resumed. Added to this was the elimination of the so-called bonus of 2 cents per lug and the additional benefit of fair weights wherever the union was active.

Without doubt such benefits redounded to the reputation of the union, but they did not build it. In every successful effort to prevent a wage cut, or to induce growers to raise rates of pay in order to forestall organization, the harvesters flocked to the union, but they did not join it in significant numbers.

Up to 1952 the union organized nine strikes, the first and longest of which was that of Local 218 against DiGiorgio. None produced recognition, and only the Los Banos action against the melon growers ended through negotiations. Immediately before a strike, membership usually

increased and remained at peak only during the action. Domestic harvesters attended rallies and paid dues for one or two months, quickly
moving on to the next picking and into the erratic drifts of the labor pool.
As other organizers had found long before, these actions owed much of
their effectiveness to the walk-away response to the exhortations of the
union, the uncertainty about the duration of the stoppage, and the
consequent loss of wages for entire families. The stay-away effect was
also stimulated through the distribution of strike announcements
wherever the union had members or active sympathizers. The illegals in
their way also responded to a strike. They left the area in fear that the
action would expose them more than normally to arrest.

Only the DiGiorgio strike lasted long enough to enable the union to
mobilize public support and financial backing from other unions. Since
the NAWU never entered these confrontations with reserve funds for
strike relief, they were costly as to emergency help to the strikers, many
of whom had no permanent connection with the union. Theoretically the
formal procedures observed by the NAWU before a strike, such as
obtaining sanction from the central labor body of the area, opened the
way for appeals within the labor movement for contributions, but with
the exception of DiGiorgio, official approval rarely was followed by
anything more than placing the resisting employer's brands on the unfair
list. Support for some of the actions was requested and turned down by
the State Federation of Labor. The harvesters regarded the union as a
militant one, not necessarily a credit in the eyes of labor's leaders.

Nonviolence was the standing order to all who took part in these
bursts of insurgency. It was a tradition from the days of the Southern
Tenant Farmers Union, when night riders raided union halls and homes
without provocation. Vigilantism had shown that union violence could
provoke wanton reprisals on the slightest excuse. By 1950 such violence
from the growers lay deeper under the surface, still potentially threatening but restrained by the image of civility that agri-businessmen were
trying to present.

That the NAWU found itself directing its most persistent attacks on
Public Law 78 against government officials rather than the growers
associations was a result of lessons learned beginning with DiGiorgio
and notably in the Imperial strikes. There it had become evident that
both the Farm Placement Service and the U.S. Department of Labor
were covert collaborators. The NAWU attacks on government officials
caused its alienation from both the State Federation of Labor and the
AFL–CIO. As the NAWU pressed on this front it also strained the
accommodation that the agricultural industry in particular and industrial
employers had reached with organized labor. By 1955 it was apparent

that as NAWU actions centered on Public Law 78 and isolated the government bureaucracies in Sacramento and Washington, the attack was not on individual growers or their associations nor even on the agricultural industry, but on the power system in which government was a permissive partner. In high labor circles coolness turned to a freeze and then to hostility that became open when Smith arrived to set up the AWOC.

I was never able to convince Mitchell that NAWU pressure should be greatest where that power was most abused—in Washington. In the national capital relationships had to be maintained routinely between lowly advocates and highly placed bureaucrats. Those who had favors to ask, and Mitchell had many, that would have been regarded as obligations in line of duty by the federal agencies had he been their peer, were dispatched, if noticed at all, with boredom. With a mildness that passed my understanding Mitchell held that bureaucrats like Robert C. Goodwin and Glenn Brockway, confidential consultants of agri-business, were the unfortunate victims of a political and economic system and that their lack of courage to defy it was understandable. If the bracero system was to be ended it would have to be done in the fields.

· In every action there was evidence that California's rural harvesters were not the only landworkers held in economic subjection by the corporate farmers. As a class, the smaller farmers had been the source of vigilante mobs and dupes of the propaganda that vilified farm labor unions as subversive. They were attached to agri-business not by sympathy but by fear. For crop loans they depended on banks that were financially related to and interested in successful large-scale operations. Cotton gins could hand out or call in such loans. Freight facilities could be rationed to small growers who paid above the prevailing wage or showed a certain preference for domestic workers. These farmers lived by the grace of the local consortia of money and influence, whose friends could tighten or relax grade inspections or housing codes. A coalition in that quarter was never seriously considered, much less pursued.

The traditional fixing of harvest wages by growers through their associations was brought to an end during the early actions of the NAWU in the Central Valley. The practice dated back thirty years or more and had become the orthodox way of leveling wages down, establishing a ceiling above which country gentlemen would not go. One of the most effective devices to end this practice was the distribution of wage ballots at the beginning of harvesting. The number of ballots returned was always high and gave the impression of extensive organizing that was not in fact occurring.

For defensive litigation the NAWU relied on the State Federation of Labor, which assigned counsel at its own expense to contest the county ordinances against caravaning. But the federation showed no interest in issues raised in connection with the operation of the bracero system. Nor would it respond to the request that it file actions related to agricultural employers' noncompliance with State Labor Code provisions for collective bargaining, from which farm employers were not exempt. Likewise the constitutional questions raised by the usurpation of authority of federal and state agencies failed to arouse the interest of the federation's legal department on which the NAWU depended. For the rest, occasional aid from friendly attorneys was volunteered, but this was insufficient to make sustained legal actions a part of the union strategy after the DiGiorgio strikes. This was the union's outstanding weakness, best demonstrated in DiGiorgio's easy court victory in its libel action of 1949. The class actions of a later time might have brought the U.S. Department of Labor to reconsider its behind-the-scenes role in the administration of Public Law 78 sooner, had the NAWU been able to retain attorneys. On the only occasion when federal officials were brought to cross examination under oath they came close to perjury in the cover-up of their connections with the *Strangers in Our Fields* affair. During all the years of the union in California probably less than five thousand dollars were spent on legal support.

After 1952 the union's reluctant friends in labor never tired of pointing to the diffusion of efforts of the single staff representative in the state. More than one central labor council complained to Mitchell that Galarza could never make up his mind to stay in one place. The business agent type of operator which was their model had no resemblance to what I was doing. The effects of displacement by braceros were felt earliest by the most active leaders of the NAWU locals. The best of them were removed by attrition, and with them disappeared the only means of continuing contact with the councils who had given support in the beginning.

In California there were special reasons for what the critics were complaining of. The national union itself was in a constant state of sprawl with its organizers. From 1936 to 1959 the STFU and its successors sent organizers into Alabama, Arkansas, California, Florida, Louisiana, Mississippi, Missouri, Texas, New Mexico, and Oklahoma. At one point Mitchell's plan for California was to enlist the central labor councils as the base of operations in the hope that they would provide essential services and financing. The roving assignment I had set for myself did not in any way encourage the councils to approve the idea.

Farm labor unionism, within the American Federation of Labor, passed through the three stages of the Southern Tenant Farmers Union, the National Farm Labor Union, and the National Agricultural Workers Union with a short interval (1937–1939) in the CIO. Covering a quarter-century of efforts in a dozen states, together they represented a search for a place in the American labor movement. Of the three unions, the NFLU for a time had the best prospects. This was the period from the beginning of the DiGiorgio strike until DiGiorgio's filing of the libel complaint and the settlement accepted by the State Federation of Labor on terms laid down by DiGiorgio.

At first the NAWU's goals disposed the leaders of the state federation and the central labor bodies to accept it. These were the traditional ones of representation, negotiation, collective bargaining, basic wage scales, grievance procedures, and fringe benefits. Combined, these aims pointed to a way out of reliance on legislative protection such as the minimum wage, of which it was said that it does not represent justice but the maximum limits of injustice which a free society will tolerate.[345] There was nothing in the union's stated organizational objectives to associate it with the early anarchist or communist unions or with any contemporary radical social philosophy.

The NFLU did not obtain contracts with employers. The Schenley corporation worked its way out of its difficulties with the union without any written agreements. In 1951 the Raisin Growers Protective Association negotiated an arrangement with the Fresno local that lasted one season. The Tracy strike ended because one grower accepted the pickers demands, starting a trend that other growers promptly joined; but there was only one agreement, a verbal one. Field stoppages sometimes compelled a contractor to settle wage and other grievances on the spot through negotiations by an organizer. The two-day strike of Los Banos was a stoppage of this type, and it, too, was resolved through a verbal agreement limited to the current harvest.

None of these met the standards for collective bargaining that organized labor in the state expected of a bona-fide union. When the NAWU came to be judged in 1960 by the Executive Council of the AFL they could truly say that the NAWU was a union without contracts.

In short, of the twelve years of the NAWU effort in California, in only the first three was there an overlap of what the NAWU was ready to strive for and what the state labor movement was willing to approve of. It was also the period during which the highest spokesmen of labor were willing to plead for the disinherited harvesters in the familiar compassionate language of the American liberals.

The second period of nine years was one of growing displeasure in the trade-union establishment over the NAWU attack on the bracero system and the governmental bureaucracies. The NAWU linked them with the whole apparatus of agri-business power in the society. The implied choice offered the NAWU by the state federation was a dilemma of the purest kind: Persist in your attacks on the system and be disavowed or allow the system to continue to destroy the economic class upon which you depend, the domestic harvesters. Itself already an ordained structure of power, organized labor could not accept a fundamental change in the power to which it belonged. This was why Osslo complained to Gorman during the short time that I was on the Butchers' staff because I kept going to the newspapers, saying I was carrying a chip on my shoulder.

In the 1930s the southern sharecroppers formed a trade union on the advice of Norman Thomas. It was a choice of desperation for Mitchell and his friends, setting a course that was to affect every major decision of the STFU, the NFLU, and the NAWU for a quarter of a century, ending with the sub-merger of NAWU into the Butchers Union. In sum, it was the ultimate rejection by organized labor of the long and often desperate search by American harvesters to find a place within the brotherhood of industrial unionism.

In 1949 I expressed to Mitchell my misgivings about the model the NAWU was still pursuing. I wrote him: "The business agent method will do more damage in agriculture than even in the industrial and service unions." What I saw in the following years in Imperial, Los Banos, Salinas, and Yuba confirmed repeatedly the dim prospects of ever organizing California's harvesters along this course. In the final analysis the unions in the packing sheds and the canneries would not have the courage, as Gorman so candidly admitted, to pay the costs and face the risks of helping to create autonomous unionism in the fields.

This was the mold into which the local leadership of the NAWU would eventually be cast, to conform it to the emerging labor statesmanship. "What we want," I wrote Mitchell, "is a mass that is strong not because it responds to centralized command, but because it represents many individuals effectively expressing themselves through responsive mechanisms of organization." The leaders who were emerging were men and women, Mexicans and Blacks and Okies and Filipinos who had not yet been transformed into functionaries. They remained workers who knew in detail the local conditions of production and whose social relations bound them in communities of their own, capable of generating self-protecting social power. That is what I meant by responsive mechanisms of organization. Mitchell had said the same thing about the roots of the Southern Tenant Farmers Union: "to concentrate on building a small nucleus of reliable members." In the course of twenty-five years the three unions relied less on this base and more on the support of organized labor, and it failed them.

As Schnitzler said in 1959, the harvesters could not be expected to cope without the resources for so immense a task. Their failures showed this time and again. In California caravans had to be disbanded for lack of funds. On the frequent occasions when the grower associations and labor leaders and government agencies exposed themselves to legal action, the union was unable to show that, in the courts, the system could be held in partial check, if not unhinged. This was the lesson of the DiGiorgio settlement of 1950. It took twenty years of investigation to lay bare the congressional intrigue that helped to break that strike.

But also to be taken into account in this assessment is that before the three unions could lift the nation's harvesters from poverty the unions themselves had to be raised out of it. This the American labor movement was not willing to do, except for an intermittent dole, grudgingly given, and eventually under terms of subservience. The donations were often given in good faith and out of genuine sympathy, perhaps even as installments due the liberal conscience. They did little more than keep alive the hopes of the rural insurgents that Mitchell was attempting to organize, the perpetually disinherited for whom labor could continue to show pity. In dramatic form this was the meaning of the Washington conference of February 1959.

That conference was a peak of commitment of organized labor power and the liberal conscience, both agreeing on a course that expressed a deep empathy for the poorest of the working poor in the nation. The events that followed during the next two years showed to what effect. Organized labor went on to destroy the union it was pledged to support. The union's liberal friends consented to that destruction by not passing over from the region of compassion into that of thought and action. The NSF nevertheless continued to donate funds so the NAWU could pay its debts in its final days, advising up to the end that it work within the system that was destroying it.

The NAWU from the beginning of its campaign against Public Law 78 had a certain bargaining leverage of its own, that those who were throwing money and power and influence on the scales against it relied heavily on concealment of how they were playing the game. In the long run, this could not work. The NAWU was more than an observer of events. The union itself was an event; or a long series of events, and it survived long enough to record them. There is no more interesting history than that in which one has taken part, and no better reward than the opportunity to write it.

The Myths of Agri-business

Social power operates on many levels. Whenever its actions affect other groups or individuals of society, it acts on the higher level of constitutional authority, and on a lower level of self-interest. Between the two there is the zone where competing powers meet, clash, and bargain. Depending upon the freedom possessed by each of the contenders the process moves up or down—upward to agreements, contracts, understandings, or simply accords that pass the legal and moral tests of constitutionality; or downward to the category of hoaxes, falisifications, official humbuggery, bribery, and cover-ups.

Social mythology lies in the middle zone. It can be likened to a screen of polarized glass. The insiders can watch the social scene from protective secrecy, while the outsiders are bemused and deceived by the images they see.

In agri-business there was something of all this. The myths were there from the beginning; but the bracero system, because of its drastic impact on a numerous class, the domestic harvesters, and because of the scale of profits it yielded, made it necessary to improve the techniques of distortion. The result was a line of false propositions that formed the closest thing to a philosophy of its business that the industry ever achieved. The most familiar of these propositions and a commentary on each of them follow:

—   *Agriculture is different from other industries in that it is subject to the uncontrollable laws of nature.*

The climate, the quality and variety of soils, the terrain, and the topography of California are a famous part of its lore. Corporate capital agriculture attracted by so favoring a combination of advantages, turned it into a bonanza of western agriculture. Agri-business used its political power to co-opt public funds to provide protection against drought and floods through the construction of dams and canals incomparable in America or abroad. Science, technology, and the state combined to give the fields of California a canopy second in its benevolence only to the famous California sky.

— *The land is owned and worked by dirt farmers.*

By the middle of the twentieth century, the small family farmer had been literally losing ground for fifty years. His place was taken more and more by the mobile speculators, the lessees of lands, and the buyers of crops whose investments were in capital equipment. Their concerns were more with the market than with the soil. A straightforward description of the prototype grower shows how distant the mythical small farmer was from the reality: "The farmer doesn't live off the land. If he loses it he is so heavily in debt he loses his land, his machinery, his house, and he and his kids are in the street looking for work."[346] The leading farmers of the state became the members of the State Board of Agriculture, the members of the kitchen cabinets of the U.S. Departments of Labor and Agriculture, the organizers of the cottonseed monopoly, and the liaison officers of the Bank of America.

— *California agriculture is not subsidized by government funds.*

This was a myth never qualified by the important exceptions. Crop subsidies of over $8,000,000 paid out of federal funds in 1957 went to the largest cotton grower in the Central Valley. Acreage reserve subsidies to cotton growers in eight counties totalled $7,480,000 in 1957. The cotton marketing program of that year was judged as "very successful" by the *California Farmer*. Seven and three-quarter million bales were sold abroad, "an expensive operation, with a U.S. government subsidy of 6 cents per pound and the American taxpayer footing the bill."[347] The 1959 subsidies to wool growers were $6,990,000, and to sugar beet producers, $8,942,000. For citrus and figs also there were successful years, in one of them $193,000 in payments to carry over a fig surplus.[348] In 1949 Marshall Plan donations enabled Great Britain to buy $2,000,000 worth of prunes and raisins, supplemented by purchase of another $2,000,000 worth by the U.S. Department of Agriculture. Even the cannery corporations qualified for subsidies because of their closeness to agriculture. They received loans of $4,216,000 to help tide them over a glut of canned goods that had forced them to live what was called a "hand to mouth existence."[349] Facing a drastic drop in prices because of an abundant crop, grape growers were bailed out by price supports that covered all or part of the selling price of nearly 80 percent of the state's exports to foreign countries over a period of years.

The largest subsidies were concealed in the water delivered from government reclamation and irrigation works. The per acre capital investment could be as high as $700, with water users in farming returning only $123, with the additional benefit of increases in land value from $500 to $1,000 per acre.

Even more concealed was the subsidy represented by the cost of the bracero system. Federal employees processed braceros in Mexico, supervised their transportation, sorted them out in reception centers, facilitated contracting to the growers associations, served as compliance officers, and officiated as consultants to agri-businessmen. These administrative costs amounted to over $100,000,000 between 1943 and 1958 funded by the Department of Labor under the provisions of federal law.[350]

— *California growers must be supplied with plenty of low-wage labor because they are highly competitive with producers of similar products in other states.*

Competition was one of the calamities that agri-business could not ascribe to nature. Nor was it based on the facts. The test of costs is in the marketplace, and in many crops Californians had virtually no competition. In twenty-four crops California farms delivered 50 percent of national production, asparagus with a 51.7 percent share at the bottom of the list and almonds at the top with 100 percent. These were the percentages of national production selected at random: peaches, 45.7; pears, 49.8; cantaloups, 52.7; lettuce, 54.0; tomatoes, 59.2; apricots, 83.3; garlic, 84.4; grapes, 90.6; walnuts, 92.2; prunes, 98.6; lemons, 98.8; figs, 99.1; olives, 99.8; and artichokes, 99.8.

Blessed by the weather, the climate, the soils, and the terrain, California growers were steadily pulling away from their out-of-state competitors, in accordance with the laws of economics that agri-business held inapplicable to their state. Between 1930 and 1950 the yield of fruit-bearing trees per acre rose by 65 percent, with comparable achievements in other major crops.

— *California growers pay the highest wages to farm labor in the nation.*

Without taking into account the wage rates paid to braceros or to thousands of illegals, the figures for domestic workers put out by agri-business were distorted enough. The wage payments made by growers through contractors suffered a toll taken by them, the extent of which did not show in the statistics. The data on which the industry relied so heavily was seriously flawed, and the conclusions drawn from it more in the realm of social mythology than of social science. These data, collected by the Department of Agriculture, did not include piece rates, a blank that was imaginatively filled by public relations. For statistical convenience piece rates were reported under crop reports, a practice which government agencies, the source of the data, questioned seriously. Composite rates included salaries paid to foremen, tractor driv-

ers, haulers, and skilled workers like irrigators and pruners. And as
braceros took over these operations, wage rates were commingled with
the mysteries of the so-called prevailing wage. In California there was
not even a rubber yardstick for these important data. The Division of
Labor Statistics and Research never compiled them on farm labor
wages, nor did any other state agency.

—   *The agricultural industry is too impoverished to meet the costs of
     business accounting.*

What agri-business could cull from official statistics it did not check
against its own information, for it had none. This point scored heavily in
the outraged protests against official red tape, time-consuming
questionnaires, and burdensome bookkeeping. Yet, insofar as the bracero system was concerned, growers were indeed capable of providing
numerous data. They joined associations that did the paperwork for
them. Thus it was possible to weather the blizzard of documents—
papers to be submitted at the reception centers, validations to be provided the regional office of the Department of Labor, and records to be
kept by the employer himself. A new variety of bureaucratese was
learned as growers submitted to powers of attorney, group health insurance contracts, authorizations for the use of facsimile signatures,
vehicle inspection reports, indemnity agreements, certified copies of
association charters, copies of by-laws, payroll forms, lists of officers
and directors, membership lists in triplicate, local authorizations, standard work contracts, receipts for disbursements, statements of earnings, social security benefits, food records, assignment lists, manifests
by which braceros were delivered by the numbers, and housing inspection clearances.

—   *Agriculture is peculiarly unsuited for collective bargaining.*

Behind this proposition were the assumptions that dirt farmers were
too individualistic, entirely lacking in the necessary organization to
engage in collective bargaining, legally impaired to do so, and
psychologically incapable of accepting it.

This was a myth that was neither pure nor simple, and it was untenable
on the facts. The grower-shipper associations were representative agencies with respect to braceros. The employer-employee relationships
between alien workers and growers were written in the international
agreement by a process of negotiations with bureaucrats and diplomats.
The outcome of these consultations up and down the line of Public Law
78 was a series of accords, agreements, and understandings—collective
bargaining, in short.

The associations were careful to distinguish between this process and that of dealing with domestic harvesters, contending that they were not authorized by their members to represent them other than with respect to braceros. Accordingly there could be no employer-employee relationship between them and domestic harvesters, even though the associations were chartered as "sole employers."

Nevertheless, there was collective bargaining between the same associations and processing unions. The Western Growers Association was bound by contracts with the Teamsters and Packinghouse Workers, the DiGiorgio Fruit Corporation regularly bargained with organized winery workers and teamsters, and so it went throughout the processing industry.

— *Harvest labor is unskilled labor.*

It was commonly asserted that field workers were unskilled and as such were well below the dignity of collective recognition. To be unqualified technically is the first step toward social exclusion and, if the public believed the myth, toward legal discrimination.

Field labor was a blur in which the details of field harvesting and the skills it required went unrecognized. To pick a ripe honeydew required a trained eye for the bloom of tinted cream, a sensitive touch for the waxy feeling of the rind, and a discriminating nose for the faint aroma of ripeness. In the asparagus fields, the expertness of the Filipino cutters was obvious to all but those who hired them.

— *A supplementary force of foreign contract labor is necessary to meet the shortages of domestic workers.*

As with the tale of high wages, so it was with that of the perennial shortages of harvesters from one end of California to the other.

Of all the myths of agri-business this was one of the most insistent. The alleged shortages were the deliberate effects of the wages growers were willing to pay, the level falling in direct relation to the number of braceros available. This number determined, other scarcity factors were applied. Housing for domestics was unavailable, the physical conditions of production were made more demanding, workers were screened by the Farm Placement office and rejected by growers or were accepted under conditions such as dispersion of crews, refusal to hire wives, separation of families, and other refined techniques of discouragement. The much publicized shortage of peach pickers in Yuba had all these characteristics.

The government agencies were ingenious in their own explanations. Governor Knight offered a classic short-cut between cause and effect. In response to criticism of the Farm Placement Service he said in August

1959: "The fact that a shortage of labor does exist in the Marysville area is substantiated by the recruitment efforts being made by the local office of the department through the use of radio and newspaper publicity." When the governor was not proving a shortage with noise, his acting director of employment, Goodman, was demonstrating how promptly a labor shortage could be corrected. On the morning of August 29, 1959, minutes after being asked, he ordered thirty-five hundred braceros on their way from El Centro to the peach harvest.

For public consumption Hayes's office regularly issued distressing statements about the plight of growers unable to find domestic harvesters. But Department of Labor assistants Keenan and Creasy believed it was impossible to predict the labor market for agriculture six or eight months in advance. Creasy, testifying in 1951, was explicit: "I do not believe that we should be called upon at this time to present with any degree of certainty the extent to which it may be necessary to supplement the domestic labor supply. The farm labor requirements as of a given time are affected by too many imponderables." Yet Hayes was making such predictions routinely. The invisible reserve of illegals, which in some seasons numbered over thirty thousand, was never taken into account.

— *Fruit and vegetables will rot in the fields unless braceros are available to fill the labor shortage.*

This mystification was double edged, intended to worry the consumer with possible price increases due to scarcity and to arouse his sympathy for an industry that was trying valiantly to keep the life line of America, as publicists were fond of calling it, adequately supplied. In any season crops rotting in the middle of a harvest could be photographed and released to the newspapers on call. The press releases deplored shortages of domestics with sidelong criticisms of bureaucrats who were delaying consignments of braceros. But there were reasons for the waste other than shortage of manpower. The peach green drop was an officially commanded destruction of edible fruit to get rid of unwanted production with a minimum of expense. Conservation and not destruction was penalized. And for the purposes of the myth, such fruit was highly photogenic.

Peaches could be attacked by rot on the branch, as in the Yuba harvest of 1958, or the fruit could fail to meet the minimum requirements of the canneries. A heavy run of fruit could clog the canneries, which would send back to the fields produce they had contracted for but could not process for lack of facilities. This fruit, too, could be dumped ostentatiously. And when the growers could not come to terms on price with the canners, they withheld deliveries long enough to bring them to reason. There were consequently different kinds of waste—waste by legal command, waste due to acts of nature, waste to relieve gluts in processing, and waste for bargaining purposes. The purposes of the myth of labor shortages made none of these technical distinctions, and any one of them could serve for panic publicity.

— *Braceros do not lower the wages of domestic labor because they are paid the prevailing wage.*

This served the farm employers and state and federal bureaucrats equally well. For the associations it was wage fixing in another form, accomplished not in local meetings of association members but by diplomatic negotiations in distant places. The field data on which the wage prevailing for domestic harvesters was "found" was, in the final analysis, the same unacceptable wage offered to domestic workers at the Farm Placement offices. This became the scale proposed by the American negotiators to their Mexican counterparts when the international agreements were renewed.

The prevailing wage became the predetermined wage of an administered labor force, the braceros. As this level dropped domestics left agriculture. Hayes's proficient subordinates found that in some instances it was not even necessary to make wage surveys, accepting instead the rates set by the directors of the local growers association.

— *The bracero program is strictly supervised by government agencies in compliance with the individual contracts, Public Law 78, and the international agreements.*

Rarely was a labor system so solidly buttressed with law, administrative regulations, contracts, and an agreement with the force of a treaty as was the bracero system. The Larin doctrine of both the U.S. Department of Labor and the California State Department of Employment was that the associations should do their own policing, thus relieving the enforcement officials from that unpleasant task.[351] When violations were egregious and the complaints were supported by evidence, the regional office simply advised the violators to do better the next time. In this class were the numerous cases of injured braceros who were returned to Mexico without a medical release. Sometimes these men were returned immediately and sometimes often a period of convalescence in the compounds of the associations, such as the corral of the Northern California Growers Association in Yuba. In July 1956 the regional office, aware that the NAWU was publishing these facts, issued a circular to all employers admonishing them to desist.[352]

—   *The compliance agencies do not take sides in disputes between
     domestic workers and employers.*

This was not a virtue claimed so much by agri-businessmen as by
bureaucrats playing the role of umpires. Such was the position taken by
Hayes and the federal compliance officers. The evidence to the contrary
was overwhelming and was to be found in the minutes of the meetings of
agricultural employees and the staff of the regional office. Here the
position of the federal government was candidly though confidentially
revealed. The federal administrators agreed not to hold such meetings
with farm workers and not to issue regulations without the prior approval of the associations or to permit union representatives to appear in
closed hearings in which accused employers were present. The regional
office notified the NAWU in May 1958 that the union's demand to be
heard in open hearings violated normal investigating procedures. From
this it was a short step to restricted files and special rules of evidence
applicable only to harvesters. Assistant Secretary of Labor Newell
Brown explained this in a letter to Mitchell on February 5, 1958: apropos
of a complaint I had filed over the rejection of a NAWU crew by a
grower who at the time was using braceros exclusively. "Unfortunately," Brown wrote, "at the time of the investigation our field representative was unable to determine which of the parties was telling the
truth. We frequently develop in an investigation diametrically opposed
statements and conflicting evidence." I was one of the witnesses and I
had forwarded to Mitchell the signed rejection card that had been issued
by the local Farm Placement Office.

The mythology of agri-business had prestigious endorsers in
academia, like George L. Mehren, director of the Giannini Foundation
at the University of California, Berkeley. To him the migrant seasonal
workers were drifters who were "shockingly unreliable on the job."
Raising wages "would probably make things worse." Dr. Mehren believed that bracero employment did not drive wages down. Asked if he
had talked to workers or labor representatives, he responded that he had
gathered his information from growers. In academia the consolations of
ignorance were no less comforting than those of philosophy.

Prologue to the Future

Around the time that the NAWU appeared in California the economic and political establishment called agri-business reached an advanced stage. The term itself was coined to describe a process that had been at work since the conquest of the West by American arms. The United States government conceded the vast public domain thus created in huge blocs to private ownership. Immense portions of these lands provided the foundation of corporate agriculture, which through the decades adapted to its own ends the scientific knowledge, the technological advances, and the administrative structures of a swiftly changing society.

Agri-business, in its own eyes, was the apotheosis of business as the principal business of rural life. The formidable success of free enterprise in catering to the needs, the comforts, the luxuries, and the caprices of those who could afford them, and in tempting the desires of those who could not, gave it credit as the most efficient provider of incalculable wealth, the model of the American culture. Around it national integration was taking place, and something like its traits and values appeared in all the expressions of the national life style. In education it might have been called pedo-business, in creative expression arti-business, in the keeping of peace at home and abroad, milito-business. In the provision of food or fiber, it was agri-business, preceded by more than half a century in the wheatlands of the middle west, where already in the 1880s farming was conducted on the scale and with the techniques of a railway corporation.

As new words and phrases follow new social forms of action and organization, "agri-business" became a part of the American language, being defined by Henry Schacht, an agri-columnist, as "the term coined to describe modern agriculture's interdependence with business—the fertilizer companies, feed manufacturers, trucking concerns, machinery manufacturers, hardware dealers, lumber companies, and all the many others who make up the business complex supporting the world's greatest and most productive system of agriculture."[353] Omitted from this list were the electric power utilities, the banks, and the universities.

Considered as an integral part of the complex, the production process on the land came to be regarded as a "manufacturing operation," as the Petaluma *Courier* called it on October 28, 1955. Alan T. Rains, executive vice-president of United Fruit and Vegetable Association, described it succinctly: "We buy raw material, and we produce as any manufacturing plant does."[354]

The technical and psychological identification of food production and its managers and owners in these terms was fulfilled by the 1950s. In 1946 Dean Hutchinson of the University of California characterized California's new farming class as both agricultural-minded and business-minded: "They need to be. They work with properties involving the use of much capital; they handle large sums of operating cash; they make substantial expenditures." W. B. Camp, the Kern County land owner, agriculturist, merchant, breeder, and associate in the organizing of the planting cotton seed monopoly, stated the matter in unvarnished language: "The farmer is a capitalist . . . (who) must not be considered a separate and special class of American society."[355]

At last, after a long detour through the Jeffersonian beginnings of rural America, the risks and the toil of homesteading, and the dreams of family farming of Elwood Mead's engineering projects in the Central Valley, the business of agriculture became business. Agri-businessmen, as capitalists, had joined "The world's most successful vehicle for the production of wealth, the economy of the United States."[356] That the foundation of this success was the exploitation of manual labor was recognized in the 1881 report of the Maine Board of Agriculture, which contained this statement about the new farmer: "It is in the employment of many laborers and in the accumulation of profits of those many laborers that he builds up his income." Standing at the center of the complex was the agri-businessman, a country gentleman of great expectations.

Those expectations were temporarily disturbed by the repeal of Public Law 78 but the power that had negotiated the bracero system for more than twenty years remained unaltered.

The best of the land was still under corporate control through ownership or leasing. It found ways to skirt the 160-acre limitation on ownership of lands irrigated with federal water. Corporate farming held the choicest sections of over seventeen million acres of irrigated soils in 1958, and another seven million were in sight. The major question was how to extend the reach of agri-business. California was already laced with canals and ribboned with freeways, tying the smallest communities and the largest cities into one continuous distribution system. "Give us an unfettered market, and watch us go," pleaded the *California Farmer*, the voice of the industry.

The coordination of local interests remained under the direction of the area grower-shipper associations, their jurisdictions assigned roughly by counties. Had landmark monuments been erected to mark their locations and range of influence they would have identified the establishments of power in rural California and the memorials of successes like that of association leader Bruce Church of the Salinas Valley, who borrowed $3,000 and parlayed it in a few weeks for a return of $100,000. Coordination of the associations in all their common interests worked through statewide cooperatives like Sunkist Growers, Sun Maid Raisin Growers, Diamond Walnut Growers, and many others. Politically, coordination was assigned to lobbying and publicity councils of which the Agricultural Council of California became the prototype. Since the directors of the local association, the commodity groups, and the councils were the same or closely related persons, they in effect formed a family of power. And since these same persons were also the select collaborators of the State Department of Employment and the U.S. Department of Labor, sitting with them in consultation on policy, the family now became an extended one, with kinship ties to all levels of public administration. To agri-business the vision of the future was both exciting and prophetic. Robert W. Long, a banker's expert, exclaimed: "Wouldn't it be the coup of the century if control of the food supply should rest in the hands of the few?"

Other coups were already being accomplished. The elimination of the family farmer and the domestic hand harvester was merely one aspect of the overall integration required by the large concentrations of capital. In 1958, the California Packing Corporation owned and operated ninety plants in twelve states, sold annually $325 million in products, and had an interest in ninety-eight thousand acres of land. The process was vertical and horizontal. Chain stores became partners in mass production, mass purchasing, and mass distribution, with tight scheduling for all operations. Growers, processors, and shippers made the system monolothic and creditworthy.

The market position of agri-business improved as rural California was invaded by an unprecedented urban overflow. A growing population placed at the door of agri-business a market of over twenty million consumers. Over half of the agricultural production was sold within California for civilian consumption, and 60 percent of the canned tomatoes and 175 railway cars of lettuce per month were sold to the United States armed services. Agri-business could also count on a fair share of subsidies for crops subject to cyclical distress, like cotton, prunes, and grapes, and lemons. The markets, too, were well on the way to integration.

As to the use of Mexicans for stoop labor and other menial services, agri-business was no worse off in 1960 than it had been in 1947. The extensive borderlands remained open for the passage of illegals and border crossers, and possibly for the braceros again when political conditions might be more favorable for another Public Law 78. There was enough leeway in immigration policies and laws to fill the chronic "shortages" of manpower. The wetbacks continued to be regarded as a police problem rather than the effect of a national economic policy that kept the Mexican people within the orbit of American capitalism. There was not, in 1960, any indication that agri-business would lose these incalculable assets.

The political coalitions that agri-business had formed through decades were not under stress when the NAWU was liquidated. The Department of Employment, to be sure, was renamed the Department of Human Resources, but the issues that the NAWU had raised remained—the usurpation of administrative authority, the immunity of state and federal officials from accountability, the exclusion of harvesters from decisions that determined the character, size, and uses of the labor force.

From another quarter, organized labor gave agri-business little reason to worry. Industrial labor in the state had gained security enough from the economic system to shrink from questioning the system itself, as the NAWU had done. Finally, academia remained as it had always been— credulous instead of inquiring, gilding the common myths of agri-business with its prestige, cooperative to the point on one occasion of burning writings that had displeased the powerful. Courses on agri-business appeared at Harvard University in 1952 and were being intro-duced on state campuses, preparing managers who would complete the tasks of total integration.

The base of agri-business as the union found it in 1947 was reduced by the action of the NAWU in one respect only: the bracero system was terminated. Time came to an end for the NAWU on August 2, 1960; it remains only to complete the assessment of its brief passage through history.

It cleared the way for those who might later continue the watch over alien contracting in the manner of Public Law 78. From the borderlands agri-power was still able to call up the hosts of illegals driven by poverty from Mexico, and of border crossers, a secondary reserve no less numerous. To these the NAWU did not address itself. The union's 1952 convention considered the illegals as Mexican citizens alienated by the same forces that were integrating Mexico into the capitalist model at all levels. Obviously American industry and agriculture would continue to entice border crossers north for work or to move capital south to exploit the Mexicans at home.

The question remained: was the NAWU a failure or a success? It was a success only as to the role it played in ending the bracero system.

Some thought that even the failure of the NAWU was useful because it kept before organized labor the image of how it might have been for all the working class. This sentimental view of the fate of farm laborers missed the point. In agriculture, as in manufacturing, technology and mechanization were slowly reducing the base of organized labor, expelling from the process of production those who had become obsolete, inefficient, and unnecessary. Removed from the production line the union brothers became ex-brothers, more numerous than those who were permitted to stay on and live by their labor. As the ratios changed, the discarded had to move again, not to other productive work but to welfare rolls and the ghettos of decaying cities. This is what happened to farm workers in California.

The short view of this, of course, was that greater numbers of human beings had to be dropped out of production in order to distribute the wage capital among fewer workers, whose incomes could now be levelled upward relative to those of industry. This was the strategy of the Teamsters throughout, exemplified by "sweetheart" contracts. As the circle tightened around the harvesters no collective bargaining could restore them to economic citizenship.

With loss of citizenship came loss of faith. Collective bargaining could not restrain the attrition of the ranks of labor, so those who dropped out of its brotherhood lost, along with their paychecks, the sense of community that active membership had provided them. The retooling of an industry never reinstated them; it merely recycled them into unemployment and its despairs. Declassed, they could only look from the outside at an establishment, their union, in anger and frustration, the rejected partners of a broken faith. All this, too, happened to the farm workers of California.

For the harvesters these experiences were terminal, but for others they were prophetic.

In the 1930s the concept of the labor pool—three workers for every available job—was the accepted model for a labor market only in Agri-businessland. In 1970 there were labor pools of teachers, engineers, scientists, tool and die makers, clerks, printers, meat cutters, and even junior executives. The national obsession with technology, as Sydney J. Slovich pointed out, also produced a neurotic rejection of political ideas and social interrelationships.[357]

More subtly and with profounder consequences the fate of the NAWU adumbrated the infection of American society noticed by President Eisenhower. The bracero system was a cover-up of agri-business in partnership with government, or more accurately, of government as the junior partner of agri-business. That class attrition in America is possible was demonstrated through the twenty-two years of the bracero system. This also, the California farm workers had experienced.

The promises of the American spirit were (1) freedom, the equal chance to choose among the many possible options to live a creative life; (2) liberty, the effective and accomplished pursuit of these choices; (3) democracy, the opportunity to live in a society in which freedom and liberty can be enjoyed by all; and (4) community, the ultimate commitment to maintaining those social settlements in which persons of whatever condition can effectively preserve and defend freedom, liberty, and democracy. These, too, were denied to the farm workers of California. To achieve them their struggle goes on.

Notes

1. Sanford A. Mosk, *Industrial Revolution in Mexico* (Berkeley: Univ. of Calif. Press, 1950), p. 4.

2. Howard Kester, *Revolt Among the Sharecroppers* (New York: Arno Press, 1969), p. 24.

3. C. H. Hamilton, *North Carolina Agricultural Experiment Station Report,* September 1953.

4. *Sharecroppers Voice,* May 1935.

5. *Sharecroppers Voice,* July 1935.

6. Nels Anderson, *Men on the Move* (New York: DaCapo Press, Inc., 1974), p. 255.

7. *Sharecroppers Voice,* April 1935.

8. Report of the Select Committee on Migration of Destitute Citizens. U.S. House of Representatives (Washington, D.C.: Govt. Printing Office, 1941), p. 27.

9. Bureau of Labor Statistics, 22nd Biennial Report, 1925-26, p. 116.

10. Special Commission Report, February 1934.

11. California State Federation of Labor, *Proceedings,* 1938, p. 84.

12. Fresno *Bee,* 12 March 1949.

13. Fresno *Bee,* 22 March 1950.

14. Claude B. Hutchinson, *California Agriculture* (Berkeley: Univ. of Calif. Press, 1946), p. 406.

15. California State Board of Agriculture, Statistical Report, 1914, pp. 4, 5.

16. 27 Cal Reports 2, p. 570.

17. Robert W. Long, *Western Water News,* September 1969.

18. California State Board of Agriculture, Statistical Report, 1914, p. 151.

19. Hutchinson, *California Agriculture,* p. 421.

20. California State Board of Agriculture, Statistical Report, 1914, p. 148.

21. Bank of America, Selected Economic Data on the California Economy, September 1964, p. 38.

22. *California Farmer,* 11 April 1959.

23. Judges 1:15.

24. Special Committee Report, Imperial Valley, 1934, p. 8.

25. Ernesto Galarza, *Merchants of Labor* (Santa Barbara: McNally and Loftin, 1964).

26. *Congressional Record,* June 1951, p. 7322.

27. *Congressional Record,* March 1954, p. 2367.

28. California Farm Bureau Federation, 33rd Annual Meeting, 14 November 1951.

29. New York *Times,* 26 March 1950.

30. California Wage Stabilization Board, Memorandum by G. L. Rice, 23 October 1951.

31. Letter from Robert L. Sessions, Imperial Central Labor Council, 4 March 1954.

32. Letter from Mexican Consul Pesqueira, 5 March 1954.

33. Wagner-Peyser Act, 48 *U.S. Statutes* 1731.

34. Report on Migration of Destitute Citizens, p. 113.

35. Letter from E. F. Hayes to H. Hasiwar, 3 September 1948.

36. Farm Placement Service, *Annual Report,* 1957.

37. *Western Grower and Shipper,* February 1960, p. 39.

38. Letter from E.F. Hayes to James Murray, 8 April 1953.

39. Farm Placement Service, *Annual Report,* 1955, p. 68.

40. H. W. Stewart, 1958 Preseason Planning and Training Meeting, 19 March 1958.

41. *Farm Placement Service Bulletin,* No. 139, 29 January 1958.

42. J. J. Miller, Report to the Agricultural Section, California State Chamber of Commerce, 5 December 1958.

43. Cobey Committee Hearings, 1960, p. 212.

44. Farm Placement Service, ES-229, July-December 1956, pp. 6, 8.

45. Farm Placement Service, Preseason Farm Labor Market Report, January-June 1959, p. 2.

46. E. F. Hayes, *Agricultural Life,* Vol. I, p. 7.

47. Fresno *Bee,* 1 September 1951.

48. Minutes, RFLOAC, 17 May 1956, p. 18.

49. *California Agricultural Code,* 1949, Sec. 1192.

50. Yolo County Farm Labor Association, Incorporation papers, 20 June 1951.

51. Tulare County Farmers Association, Inc.

52. Petaluma *Courier,* 28 October 1955.

53. *California Agriculture,* 1950, p. 12.

54. Hearings. Select Committee on Migration of Destitute Citizens. U.S. House of Representatives, 76th Congress, 3rd Session, 1940, Part 6, p. 2474.

55. Stuart Jamieson, *Labor Unionism in American Agriculture* (Washington D.C.: U.S. Department of Labor, 1945), p. 139.

56. *Farm Bureau Monthly,* October 1959.

57. *Western Fruit Grower,* July 1960, p. 17.

58. *Western Grower and Shipper,* March 1959, p. 52.

59. *Western Grower and Shipper,* 2 October 1961.

60. San Francisco *Examiner,* 19 May 1959.

61. Circular letter, Santa Clara County Farm Bureau, 6 May 1959.

62. *Fortune Magazine,* November 1938, p. 109.

63. Hank Strobel, Address before the Commonwealth Club, 24 October 1951.

64. *Brawley News,* 27 September 1953.

65. Fresno *Bee,* 9 September 1959.

66. *Western Fruit Grower,* July 1960, p. 17.

67. *California Labor Code,* Sec. 1773; charter of the City of Los Angeles, Sec. 425.

68. *California Labor Code,* Sec. 150.

69. Farm Placement Service, *Annual Report,* 1950.

70. Tracy *Press,* 15 January 1951.

71. "Some farmers [in Madera County] have torn down their old housing for seasonal workers saying that abuse of this housing resulted in prohibitive costs to maintain standards demanded by the state." Farm Placement Service, *Annual Report,* 1951, p. 30.

72. "A small vineyardist with 40 acres of early table grapes needs 20 pickers at peak. If family housing must be provided, he would have an investment of $100,000 in housing, which he will use for only 40 days per year. A typical vineyard with buildings has a market value today of at most $2,000 per acre, or a total of $80,000 for 40 acres." Leland J. Yost, Migrant Labor Hearings, Senate Bill 1129, February 1962, Vol. II, p. 413.

73. Fresno *Bee,* 7 April 1948.

74. Farm Placement Service, *Annual Report,* 1951, p. 30.

75. San Francisco *Chronicle,* 14 September 1960.

76. *San Joaquin County Farm Bureau News,* April 1957.

77. U.S. Department of Labor, Employment Service Circular, Letter No. 892, 6 June 1958, p. 3.

78. Bakersfield *Californian,* 24 February 1951.

79. U.S. Department of Labor, Employment Security Review, February 1960, p. 21.

80. *Imperial Valley Press,* 10 February 1961.

81. *California Farmer,* 20 February 1960.

82. Los Angeles *Times,* 6 August 1948.

83. *Wall Street Journal,* 12 January 1961.

84. *Imperial Valley Press,* 10 February 1961.

85. Saul K. Padover, *The Complete Jefferson* (New York: Tudor Publishing Company, 1943), p. 64.

86. In 1976, by redefining a farm as a unit whose annual production sold at a minimum market value of $1,000, the department reduced the total number of farms in the nation by 500,000.

87. *Western Grower and Shipper,* September 1961, p. 4.

88. Fresno *Bee,* 10 November 1951.

89. W. B. Camp in *Who's Who in Kern County, 1940,* p. 39.

90. *California Agricultural Code,* 1947, Sec. 952-52.

91. Fresno *Bee,* 13 January 1951.

92. *California Farmer,* 10 October 1959.

93. Bakersfield *Press,* 13 November 1949.

94. San Francisco *Chronicle,* 15 August 1952.

95. *P. G. and E. Progress,* March 1961.

96. California Annual Farm Labor Report, 1950, p. 1.

97. *Code of Federal Regulations,* Vol. 20, Sec. 602.17, Revised, 1 June 1961.

98. San Francisco *Chronicle,* 6 December 1960.

99. Special Investigating Commission, Imperial Valley, 1934, Report, p. 14.

100. Farm Labor Newsletter, U.S. Department of Labor, 13 February 1953.

101. Joint Interpretation, 1949 International Agreement, U.S. Employment Service *Information Bulletin,* 1949, p. 16.

102. Joint Interpretation, 1949.

103. Agricultural Section, California State Chamber of Commerce, December 1958.

104. Hearings, 1951, p. 57.

105. California Farm Bureau Federation, *Monthly,* January 1960, p. 2.

106. Letter from E. F. Hayes to H. Hasiwar, 17 August 1949.

107. *Brawley News,* 30 January 1954.

108. *California Farms,* 4 August 1956.

109. Cobey Hearings, Part A, p. 26.

110. Minutes, RFLOAC, 17 May 1956, p. 4.

111. *Congressional Record,* 5 February 1952, p. 814.

112. *La Opinion,* 2 May 1958.

113. Letter from Newell Brown to Frank L. Noakes, 3 June 1959.

114. Minutes, RFLOAC, 9 November 1954.

115. *Congressional Record,* 8 June 1953, p. 6404.

116. Modesto *Bee,* 29 October 1952.

117. Minutes, RFLOAC, 9 November 1954, p. 3.

118. Ibid., p. 5.

119. Hearings, Series D, 1951, p. 27.

120. *Western Grower and Shipper,* February 1962, p. 33.

121. *Congressional Record,* 2 March 1954, p. 2362.

122. Brief of the Western Growers Association before the State Industrial Commission, San Francisco, Calif., 30 March 1960.

123. Farm Labor Newsletter, U.S. Department of Labor, 13 February 1953.

124. *California Agricultural Code,* 1949, Sec. 1190.

125. *California Statutes,* 1947.

126. Jamieson, *Labor Unionism,* p. 103.

127. *Fortune Magazine,* June 1965.

128. *California Farm Bureau Monthly,* February 1961.

129. Marysville *Appeal-Democrat,* 9 September 1959.

130. Davis McIntire, *Labor Force in California: A study of Characteristics and Trends in Labor Force, Employment and Occupations in California,* 1900-1950 (Berkeley: Univ. of Calif. Press, 1950).

131. Letter from the Division of Labor Statistics, California Department of Industrial Relations, 22 October 1974.

132. Assembly Committee on Agriculture, Alan G. Pattee, Chairman, Report, 11 April 1969, p. 1.

133. Western Growers Association, January 1961, p. 11.

134. Farm Placement Service, *Annual Report,* 1951, p. 11.

135. *Imperial Valley Press,* 3 February 1961.

136. Western Growers Association, April 1959, p. 15.

137. *Congressional Record,* 30 June 1951, p. 7717.

138. Final Report, Governor's Committee, 1951, p. 287.

139. Bakersfield *Californian,* 10 February 1958.

140. *California Blue Book,* 1950, p. 84.

141. San Francisco *Chronicle,* 26 June 1949.

142. Letter from H. Hasiwar to Joseph DiGiorgio, 21 September 1947.

143. DiGiorgio Fruit Corporation, Report to the Stockholders, 1960, p. 3.

144. Bakersfield *Californian,* 13 November 1949.

145. *Congressional Record,* 22 March 1948, p. 3289; see also Press Release, NFLU, 2 October 1947.

146. Los Angeles *Times,* 9 November 1947.

147. Bakersfield *Californian* 10 November 1947.

148. Bureau of Employment Security, *Employment Security Manual,* 1961, Part II, p. 2435.

149. Complaint in unlawful detainer, *DiGiorgio Fruit Corporation* v. *Juanita Herrera,* No. 2068, 22 November 1947.

150. *A Community Aroused,* Special Citizens Committee, Kern County, December 1947.

151. California State Federation of Labor, *Weekly News Letter,* 29 October 1947.

152. *California Grange News,* 28 February 1948.

153. Associated Farmers, News Release, 2 February 2, 1948.

154. Los Angeles *Examiner,* 9 February 1948.

155. Los Angeles *Examiner,* 10 February 1948.

156. Bakersfield *Californian,* 19 February 1948.

157. *Congressional Record,* 22 March 1948, p. 3287.

158. Ernesto Galarza, *Spiders in the House and Workers in the Field* (Notre Dame, Indiana: Univ. of Notre Dame Press, 1970).

159. Bakersfield *Californian,* 10 May 1950.

160. Circular notice issued by potato growers and packers of Kern County, 25 March 1949.

161. Fresno *Bee,* 4 September 1949; Press Release, NFLU, 7 September 1949.

162. Fresno *Bee,* 26 September 1949; Press Release, NFLU, 26 September 1949.

163. Delano *Record,* 27 September 1949.

164. Fresno *Bee,* 24 September 1949.

165. Fresno *Bee,* 4 October 1949.

166. NFLU, Bulletin, 2 September 1949.

167. Letter from H. Hasiwar to U.S. Department of Agriculture, 10 October 1949.

168. Legislative Joint Commission on Farm Labor Housing, 1949, p. 32.

169. House Committee on Agriculture, Report on Farm Labor Camps, 80th Congress, First Session, Report No. 1008.

170. California State Federation of Labor Convention, 1947, *Proceedings,* p. 342.

171. Marysville *Appeal-Democrat,* 14 August 1957.

172. Marysville *Appeal-Democrat,* 26 June 1959.

173. Fresno *Bee*, 17 March 1949.

174. Bakersfield *Californian,* 28 March 1950.

175. *Payne* v. *The United States of America,* 269 Fed. 871,873.

176. Letter from Paul Prasow to Local 300, NFLU, Tracy, 10 August 1950.

177. Conference Notes, San Francisco, 15 June 1950; H. Hasiwar, E. F. Hayes, and representatives of State Department of Employment and U.S. Department of Labor.

178. Letter from Howard J. Wilson, Secretary, Tomato Growers Association, 23-N, 23 November 1951.

179. Tracy *Press,* 10 September 1951.

180. California Wage Stabilization Board, Memorandum by G. L. Rice, 23 October 1951.

181. *Saturday Evening Post,* 5 June 1954.

182. Niland Ninth Annual Tomato Festival, 1949, p. 6.

183. *Imperial Valley Press,* 22 May 1951.

184. *Western Canner and Packer,* April 1951; *Congressional Record,* 1 May 1951, p. 4707.

185. *Ultimas Noticias,* Mexico, D. F., 28 January 1951.

186. Letter from G. Brockway to H. Hasiwar, 12 March 1951.

187. Letter from H. L. Mitchell to H. Hasiwar, 17 May 1951.

188. *Imperial Valley Press,* 24 May 1951.

189. *Imperial Valley Press,* 17 May 1951.

190. *Imperial Valley Press,* 31 May 1951.

191. *Brawley News,* 24 May 1951; Los Angeles *Times,* 25 May 1951.

192. *Imperial Valley Press,* 24 May 1951.

193. *The Packer,* 16 June 1951.

194. Letter from A. J. Norton to NFLU, 29 May 1950; letter from A. Figueroa, Compliance Officer, to Galarza, 4 May 1953.

195. *The Packer,* 16 June 1951.

196. *Imperial Valley Press,* 6 June 1951.

197. *Novedades,* Mexico, D. F., 31 May 1951.

198. *Imperial Valley Press,* 8 June 1951.

199. *Novedades,* Mexico, D. F., 31 May 1951.

200. *Imperial Valley Press,* 9 June 1951.

201. Bakersfield *Californian,* 9 June 1951.

202. Letter from H. L. Mitchell to Galarza, 19 April 1951.

203. Letter from G. Brockway to Galarza, 13 March 1951.

204. Joint Interpretation, 1949, p. 19.

205. Bureau of Employment Security Local Organization Manual, Amendment No. 14, 4 April 1960.

206. *Imperial Valley Press,* 22 June 1951.

207. Letter from H. L. Mitchell to Secretary of Labor M. Tobin, 24 April 1952.

208. Letter from T. N. Finney to NAWU, 28 May 1952.

209. *Brawley News,* 4 June 1952.

210. Letter from Galarza to T. N. Finney, 22 February 1953.

211. Letter from the California State Department of Industrial Relations to NFLU, 13 August 1952.

212. Letter from E. S. Miller to Ralph Herzfeld, 20 October 1951.

213. *California Farmer,* 9 November 1957.

214. Los Banos *Enterprise,* 29 August 1952.

215. Los Banos *Enterprise,* 29 August 1952.

216. Los Banos *Enterprise,* 29 August 1952; Fresno *Bee,* 29 August 1952.

217. Jamieson, *Labor Unionism,* p. 116.

218. LaFollette Committee Hearings, 1942, Part 3, p. 306.

219. Hearings, Migration of Destitute Citizens, p. 2474.

220. Letter from Jack Bias to NFLU, 27 September 1951.

221. Compilation by the Salinas Grower-Shipper Association.

222. Letter from Roxanna Oliver, Acting Labor Commissioner, to Galarza, 13 March 1953.

223. Letter from the Labor Commissioner's Office to the NFLU.

224. San Francisco *Examiner,* 15 March 1960.

225. Letter from H. W. Stewart to NAWU, 23 August 1957.

226. Letter from G. Brockway to NFLU, 5 May 1952.

227. Letter from U. S. Department of Labor to NAWU, 24 December 1957.

228. Letter from U. S. Department of Labor to NAWU, 18 July 1957.

229. Letter from State Department of Employment to NFLU, 13 November 1951.

230. Letter from H. W. Stewart to Galarza, 13 August 1957.

231. Letter from State Attorney General to NAWU, 18 August 1958.

232. Letter from J. Murray to H. W. Stewart, 3 February 1958.

233. Letter from Gov. G. Knight to NAWU, 12 March 1958.

234. *Farm Placement Service Bulletin,* No. 147, 5 February 1958.

235. Minutes, Area Managers Meeting, Farm Placement Service, 23-24 April 1958; see also *Farm Placement Service Bulletin,* No. 147, 5 February 1958.

236. Minutes, Area Managers Meeting, 19-20 March 1958.

237. St. Louis *Globe-Democrat,* 14 April 1958.

238. Letter from J. Murray to Acting Director Goodman, State Department of Employment.

239. State Department of Employment, Division Notice No. 2189Q, 30 October 1959.

240. Galarza, *Merchants of Labor,* pp. 123-24.

241. Letter from W. Becker to State Department of Employment, 25 May 1950.

242. Instruction from D. H. Roney, Assistant Chief, Division of Public Employment Offices and Benefit Payments, State Department of Employment, 25 April 1950.

243. Fresno *Bee,* 16 May 1950; Berkeley *Californian,* 16 May 1960.

244. Visalia *Times-Delta,* 16 May 1950.

245. Letter from J. E. Carr, Director, State Department of Employment, to D. Anderson, 3 April 1959.

246. Letter from A. Larson, Undersecretary of Labor, to F. Bennett, 21 August 1956.

247. San Francisco *Chronicle,* 18 August 1957.

248. Marysville *Appeal-Democrat,* 14 August 1957.

249. Marysville *Appeal-Democrat,* 15 August 1957.

250. Letter from H. W. Stewart to Galarza, 13 August 1957.

251. Marysville *Appeal-Democrat,* 3 August 1959.

252. San Francisco *Chronicle,* 24 August 1957.

253. Report of the National Association for the Advancement of Colored People, San Francisco, 29 August 1957.

254. San Francisco *Chronicle,* 15 August 1957; letter from Gov. G. Knight to Galarza, 15 August 1957.

255. San Francisco *Chronicle,* 19 August 1957.

256. Memorandum From A. J. Norton to W. Renner, 21 May 1957.

257. Letter from G. Brockway to W. Renner, 18 December 1957.

258. Letter from R. C. Goodwin to W. Renner, 14 January 1958.

259. *Farm Placement Service Bulletin,* No. 154, 1 May 1958.

260. San Jose *Mercury,* 23 October 1959.

261. Letter from PGA to Department of Employment, 29 October 1959.

262. California State Board of Agriculture, Resolution, 17 September 1956.

263. *Baatan News,* 5 October 1956.

264. Letter from C. E. Gibbs to Rev. J. A. King, S. J., 25 October 1957.

265. Minutes, RFLOAC, 16 November 1956.

266. Galarza, *Spiders in the House,* p. 163. These statements appear on p. 11 of the deposition.

267. Letter from C. S. Gubser to Rev. J. A. King, S. J., 22 October 1957.

268. Letter from Rev. J. A. King, S. J., to C. S. Gubser, 14 October 1957.

269. Letter from Rev. J. A. King, S. J., to C. E. Gibbs, 22 November 1957; letter from C. E. Gibbs to Rev. J. A. King, S. J., 20 November 1957.

270. Letter and memorandum from R. C. Goodwin to F. Noakes, 26 September 1956.

271. Letter from R. C. Goodwin to Galarza, 12 March 1964.

272. Fresno *Bee,* 23 May 1950.

273. H. W. Stewart, Statement of 19 March 1958.

274. *Farm Placement Service Bulletin,* No. 56, 9 May 1956.

275. Letter from E. F. Hayes to W. Becker, 30 June 1950.

276. *Farm Placement Service Bulletin,* No. 56, 9 May 1956.

277. Salinas *Californian,* 4 March 1960.

278. San Francisco *Examiner,* 2 August 1959.

279. Letter from A. R. Duarte To E. F. Hayes, 10 June 1958.

280. San Francisco *Examiner,* 22 April 1959.

281. Confidential Report on Investigation of Non-Compliance, Imperial Valley, J. J. Miller to U.S. Department of Labor Regional Office, San Francisco, Minutes, RFLOAC, 11 March 1955.

282. Letter from Galarza to Gov. E. G. Brown, 9 March 1959.

283. California State Department of Employment Restatement of Policies, 4 June 1959.

284. San Francisco *Chronicle,* 9 August 1959.

285. San Francisco *Examiner,* 3 August 1959.

286. Stockton *Record,* 15 August 1959.

287. Comment of Ivan A. Wood, Manager, San Diego County Growers Association, to RFLOAC, 1 October 1956.

288. Minutes, RFLOAC, 16 November 1956.

289. San Jose *Evening News,* 23 March 1960.

290. *Imperial Valley Press,* 29 May 1958.

291. Progressive Growers Association, *Informacion,* 18 August 1959.

292. San Francisco *Monitor,* 1 July 1960.

293. Minutes, RFLOAC, 1 February 1957.

294. San Francisco *Chronicle,* 19 August 1957.

295. San Jose *Mercury,* 18 February 1962.

296. Los Angeles *Times,* 16 August 1964.

297. San Francisco *Chronicle,* 18 February 1964.

298. *California Farmer,* 15 June 1963.

299. California State Federation of Labor, Conference on Agricultural Unions, 27 February 1937.

300. Letter from C. J. Haggerty to U.S. Department of State, 16 March 1949.

301. California State Federation of Labor, *Proceedings,* 1953, p. 123.

302. California State Federation of Labor, *The Sacramento Story,* 1955.

303. Gladwin Hill, *The Dancing Bear* (Cleveland, Ohio: World Publishing Company, 1968), p. 143.

304. Los Angeles *Citizen,* 1 May 1959.

305. The border breakthrough of illegals is described more fully in Galarza, *Merchants of Labor,* p. 49.

306. San Francisco *Chronicle,* 23 August 1973.

307. *California Farmer,* 16 June 1961.

308. San Francisco *Chronicle,* 30 December 1964.

309. Sam Kushner in *The Long Road to Delano* (New York: International Publishers, 1975), Chapters 4 and 5, gives an account of the early strikes of farm workers in California under the leadership of the Communist Party.

310. Statement of J. Ollman, official of the United Packinghouse Workers of America, March 1960.

311. Los Angeles *Daily News,* 12 February 1953.

312. Report by A. T. Stephens, Vice-president of UPWA, 19 February 1958.

313. Complaint of Clive Knowles, international representative, to J. E. Carr, 5 March 1959.

314. Letter from P. E. Gorman to H. L. Mitchell, 12 January 1956.

315. Letter from P. E. Gorman to H. L. Mitchell, 10 July 1956.

316. *Collapse of Cotton Tenancy,* edited by Edwin R. Embree and Charles S. Johnson (Chapel Hill: Univ. of North Carolina Press, 1935).

317. California State Federation of Labor, *Proceedings,* 1959, pp. 72-74.

318. AWOC *Organizer,* October 1959-June 1960.

319. San Francisco *Chronicle,* 11 June 1960.

320. Kushner, *The Long Road to Delano,* p. 111.

321. *Brawley News,* 28 December 1960.

322. *Imperial Valley Press,* 30 December 1960.

323. San Francisco *Chronicle,* 25 December 1960.

324. Memorandum by H. L. Mitchell, 6 May 1960.

325. *AFL-CIO News,* 10 June 1960.

326. AWOC *Organizer,* 17 June 1960.

327. Ventura *Free Press,* 4 April 1960.

328. Stockton *Record,* 12 August 1959.

329. *East Bay Labor Journal,* 31 March 1961.

330. Sworn Declaration of Clive Knowles, San Joaquin County Superior Court, 29 May 1961.

331. Letter from P. E. Gorman to Galarza, 21 December 1960.

332. *East Bay Labor Journal,* 4 August 1961.

333. San Francisco *Chronicle,* 27 February 1964.

334. Letter from H. L. Mitchell to Victor Reuther, 27 January 1960.

335. Letter from F. Bennett to Galarza, 26 July 1960.

336. Letter from F. Bennett to Galarza, 26 August 1969.

337. Minutes, NAWU Executive Board, 5-6 February 1960.

338. Letter from H. L. Mitchell to Galarza, 19 May 1959.

339. Minutes, National Sharecroppers Fund Executive Board, 22 January 1960.

340. Minutes, NAWU Executive Board, 5-6 February 1960.

341. Letter from P. E. Gorman to H. L. Mitchell, 30 November 1956.

342. Letter from P. E. Gorman to Galarza, 25 October 1960.

343. Amalgamated Meat Cutters and Butcher Workmen of America, *Proceedings,* 20th General Convention, 20 June 1960.

344. Letter from Galarza to P. E. Gorman, 8 November 1960.

345. Arthur J. Goldberg, quoted in *Labor in a Free Society,* Michael Harrington (Berkeley: Univ. of Calif. Press, 1959), p. 115.

346. Statement of Charles Cooper, Executive Secretary, San Joaquin County Farm Bureau, 19 June 1959.

347. *California Farmer,* 17 August 1957.

348. Fresno *Bee,* 10 May 1949.

349. San Francisco *Chronicle,* 11 August 1949.

350. Compiled from Hearings on House Resolution 6287, 85th Congress, First Session, 1957.

351. Minutes, RFLOAC, 1 February 1957.

352. Memorandum from N. H. Lueck, Secretary, Bureau of Employment, 11 July 1956.

353. San Francisco *Chronicle,* 8 October 1961.

354. Marysville *Appeal-Democrat,* 27 January 1958.

355. Bakersfield *Californian,* 22 April 1955.

356. *Western Grower and Shipper,* December 1958, p. 34.

357. Sydney J. Slovich, San Jose *Mercury News,* 9 November 1969.

Recommended Reading

Agricultural Workers Under National Labor Relations Laws. Fred Whitney, Ph. D. Urbana, Illinois: University of Illinois. 1948. 32 pp. Deals with some aspects of the question: Why did the U.S. Congress fail to include farmer laborers in the coverage of the National Labor Relations Act of 1935 and subsequent legislation of this type? Reviews legislative reluctance and its interpretation by administrators and the courts. The iceberg of economic and political interests of which legislatures, administrators, and courts are the tip is left for other scholars to expose.

"Analyzing Labor Requirements for California's Major Seasonal Crop Operations." Margot Wakeman Lenhart. *Journal of Farm Economics*, Vol. 37, No. 4, November 1945, pp. 963-75. Illuminating introduction to the science of statistical guesswork and mathematical inflation of labor shortages in California agriculture, the critical factor in agri-business manipulation of the farm labor pool.

Agricultural Labor in the San Joaquin Valley. The Governor's Committee to Survey Agricultural Labor Resources. Sacramento, California. 1950. 60 pp. Report of a survey carried out under the chairmanship of a prestigious representative of the banking branch of agri-business. Among its recommendations there is one to use the Agricultural Extension Service, traditionally the little brother of agri-business, to educate agri-businessmen on the philosophy of better treatment of farm laborers.

"American Agricultural Wage Earner." Lawanda F. Cox. *Agricultural History*. April 1948, pp. 95-114. The subtitle of this suggestive article, "The Emergence of a Modern Labor Problem," should be noted by students of the subject of this book. The article, brief but meaty, places the California experience against a broad background of the nationwide evolution of farming as a business and the transformation of the "hired hands" into an agricultural proletariat. The article is also a reminder that the confounding of workers and cattle goes back nearly a hundred years. In 1886 the California State Agricultural Society was talking about "nomadic herds of farm hands."

California Farm Labor Force—a Profile. Advisory Committee on Farm
    Labor Research of the Assembly Committee on Agriculture.
    State of California. Sacramento. 1969. It is less disturbing to
    view the California farm labor force in profile than full front as
    McWilliams, Anderson, London, and Acuna do. In this official
    document the profile is weighted with tables and charts and
    accented with analytic summaries and occasional highlights
    such as the datum that median earnings of all California farm
    workers in 1965 were $753, and some 74 percent of all farm
    workers earned less than $2,000.

California Annual Farm Labor Report. Farm Placement Service. De-
    partment of Employment. Sacramento. 1959. 53 pp. Farm labor
    presented in a miscellany of statistics, comments, and opinions
    by farm employers, with data on mechanization and other tech-
    nical changes in agricultural production, photographs, news-
    paper clippings, and logistic data on migrants by seasons of the
    year, demand forecasting for pickers, and congenial views of
    agricultural society as One Big Family. There are occasional
    glimpses of the familial relations between the Farm Placement
    Service and agri-businessmen.

California Housing. Division of Housing, Department of Industrial
    Relations. Sacramento. 1954. 83 pp. One of the side effects of
    the political reform movement led by Hiram Johnson was the
    creation of the California Commission on Immigration and
    Housing in 1913. In the course of the next forty years the
    pioneer efforts of the commission to ameliorate the living condi-
    tions of farm laborers were gradually inhibited under successive
    administrations of conservative and liberal governors. This was
    the period during which agri-business was maturing in Califor-
    nia.

California Unemployment Insurance Code. State of California. Sac-
    ramento. 1957. Legislative action on behalf of the human dis-
    cards of business, whether industrial or agricultural, may be
    said to be a record of meticulous exclusion. As an example, this
    code devoted nine sections of one chapter to a detailed defini-
    tion of farm labor as nonemployment for the purposes of un-
    employment insurance, excluding such tasks as weeding, pick-
    ing, cultivating, chopping, bundling, milking, leveling and ir-
    rigating. Sooner mosquitoes could pass through a metal screen
    than a farm worker through the eye of the Code.

California's Farm Labor Problems. Senate Fact Finding Committee on
    Labor and Welfare. State of California. Sacramento. 1961. 326
    pp. Also identified as the Cobey Committee Report, from its
    chairman, State Senator James A. Cobey. A mass of statistics

and innumerable threads of human action are reduced to order, mostly by graphs and tables but also by rigorous objectivity to avoid entaglements in social morality. As the process is sterile so is the conclusion melancholic: ". . . under these conditions . . . it is doubtful . . . that . . . improvement in the lives of farm workers . . . seems probable of achievement through unionization."

Deposition of Edward F. Hayes. January 22, 1963. Superior Court of California Civil Case No. 503735. A deposition taken by plaintiff in *Galarza* v. *DiGiorgio Fruit Corporation.* A confessional view of a public servant in charge of farm labor placement for the State of California. Hayes was at this time a stockholder of DiGiorgio Fruit Corporation, Libby McNeill, Southern Pacific Company, and numerous other members of the agri-business family. This document reposes in the Stanford Library collections.

Factories in the Field. Carey McWilliams. Boston: Little Brown and Company. 1939 edition. The pioneer survey of the history of farm workers in California, viewed in the context of the evolution of agri-business. Chapter 13 summarizes the great strikes of farm laborers in the 1930s; Chapter 15 introduces the study of attempts at farm labor union organization in the state. The method is historical enlivened with journalistic skill. *Factories* deals with an aspect of American society intermittently neglected by historians and journalists.

Farm Labor Contractors in California. Mimeograph of an otherwise unpublished draft submitted by Bruce Allen to the State of California Department of Industrial Relations. No date (1948?). A careful survey of an important control factor in the farm labor market of the state. Contains detailed data on the operation of the farm labor contract system and analytic comments on its weaknesses from the point of view of statutory regulation of contractors considered as employment agents. In the nature of the assignment this study emphasizes the operational aspect of the system rather than the exploitive.

Farm Labor Fact Book. U.S. Department of Labor. Washington, D.C. 1959. This survey might be regarded as a handbook of farm labor in the United States, and the economic structure of agriculture of which the labor force was a part, with data on wages, earnings, migration, and the importation of foreign laborers, especially from Mexico. Contains stimulating hints for further inquiry into the nature of American agriculture, such as the United States government requirement of higher working and living standards for foreign contractees than for domestic workers.

Farm Labor Housing in California. Partial Report of the Joint Committee on Agriculture and Livestock Problems. California State
Senate. Sacramento. 1949. Continues the examination of the
problems of farm workers and livestock. The fine print is worth
reading. One passage explains why agri-business preferred captive housing and why it took over the government farm labor
camps in 1949: ". . . families residing on the property of the
operators and subject to the selection of an experienced foreman are usually dependable and loyal. They will behave themselves. . . ."

Farm Labor Organizing. National Advisory Committee on Farm
Labor. New York. 1967. 68 pp. A brief history of farm laborers
in the last half century, from Hawaii to Louisiana. The epic
struggles of plantation "hands," sharecroppers, and wage migrants are briefly told in this highly compressed and sympathetic
recital by an organization of citizens. Viewed as in a concave
mirror the image of American economic democracy in the fields
shrinks noticeably.

Farm Labor Program. Report Number 1642 of the Committee on Agriculture, U.S. House of Representatives, 86th Congress, 2nd
session. When this report was submitted, the Mexican bracero
program was already in serious disrepute with the American
public, except stockholders in agri-business corporations. The
report recommended extension of the program until June 1963.
It is a capsule of congressional inability to perceive the evils of
the bracero system.

Guide to the Microfilm Collection of the NAWU. Editions of the Southern Tenant Farmers Union 1934–1970. Microfilming Corporation of America, 21 Harrison Road, Glen Rock, N.J. 1971.
Description of sixty reels of microfilm containing the papers of
the SFTU from January 1935 to December 1970. Contains six-
page introduction, a list of the principal organizers of the union
during this period, an index of persons and organizations referred to in the papers, and itemization of the accounts in the
STFU archives that were not microfilmed.

"Immigration, Migration, and Minorities in California." Moses Rischin.
Pacific Historical Review. Vol. 41, February 1972, pp. 71-90.
The history of California is viewed as a centenary drama of
migration from all quarters of the nation and all corners of the
world. The odyssey was dramatic for the Anglos, but traumatic
for the Chinese, Filipinos, Japanese, and Mexicans. Rischin
discusses the peculiar racism of the superordinate white majority somewhat as Professor Galbraith treats the Mature Corporation. Both are viewed as a promise of adult civil human relations.

Labor Code. State of California. Sacramento. 1959. There are 7 Divisions, 24 Parts, 87 Chapters, and 8,100 sections of codified legislation dealing with the protection of the California proletariat. Some provisions deal with such matters as farm labor contractors. The heart of the Code is Section 922, which reads in part: "Government authority has permitted and encouraged employers to organize in the corporate and other forms of capital control. . . .Therefore, it is necessary that the individual worker have full freedom of association, self-organization . . . and representatives of his own choosing to negotiate the terms and conditions of his employment. . . ."There is not a single instance of farm workers trying to organize for the purposes of Section 922 during the twentieth century that has engaged the aggressive support of organized labor or of any administration of the state government.

Labor Relations in Agriculture. Varden Fuller. Institute of Industrial Relations. Berkeley: University of California. 1955. Professor Fuller ranks with the California scholars who are best documented on the subject of this brochure. The editorial comment on this short treatment is made by another authority in the field, Dr. Clark Kerr. "The author concludes that the imbalance of organizational power is more likely to be upset, if at all, by legislative action than by self-action on the part of agricultural workers." In the view of this author the imbalance of organizational power is not likely to be upset if there is not self-action to upset the imbalance in economic power.

Labor Unionism in American Agriculture. Stuart Jamieson. U.S. Department of Labor. Washington, D.C. 1945. It is easy to miss the sweep of this monograph and its importance for the understanding of the history of farm labor in the United States. A documented compilation of sources available at the time of writing on the efforts of farm workers to organize from the close of the nineteenth century to the mid-1940s. There is an austerity of style in the treatment of the early modes of Agri-business violence in the suppression of striking Mexicans and others in the 1930s and 40s.

Long Road to Delano. Sam Kushner. New York: International Publishers. 1975. As the foreword properly and modestly indicates, Kushner's book is an outline of the efforts of agricultural laborers in California to organize themselves into unions. In time, heavy research such as has been published about the rural proletariat of eighteenth-century England will flesh the outline. Meanwhile running narratives like this one, a sympathetic and refreshingly non-objective field report by a participant journalist, will serve as trestles where bridges are still wanting.

Louisiana Story 1964. The Sugar System and the Plantation Workers. Robin Myers. National Advisory Committee on Farm Labor. New York. 1964. 40 pp. Like the *Sorrow Song in Black and White* this is a pamphlet in memoriam of a broken strike in an unbroken cause. The sugar plantation system against which the strike was called by the National Agricultural Workers Union is described in broad strokes. There is a clue in the statement that "the strike was against a whole system of society." It suggests that in the long run, if farm workers keep striking, eventually the system itself will come into view.

Major U.S. Corporations Involved in Agri-Business. Agri-business Accountability Project. Washington, D.C. 1973. Mimeographed. 72 pp. Described by its authors as a directory of the major U.S. corporations that are financially and managerially related to the national food industry, whose sales volume in 1970 was approximately $120 billion. The compilation shows the connections of national and international agri-business in production, processing, transportation, marketing, wholesaling, and related activities of food, seeds, fertilizers, pesticides, and feed.

Merchants of Labor. Ernesto Galarza. Santa Barbara: McNally and Loftin. 1964. Subtitled "An account of the managed migration of Mexican farm workers in California 1942-1960," this essay describes how the traditional labor pool of harvesters was transformed into a rational control system by substituting alien contract workers for domestics. Migratory labor, with its many unpredictable factors, was stabilized over a period of more than twenty years. The process of reshaping the farm labor market from a condition of drift to one of management and its effects on national policy, bureaucracy, and diplomacy is the subject of this book.

Mexican Contract Nationals in the Imperial Valley. National Agricultural Workers Union. Washington, D.C. 1953. Mimeographed. 32 pp. After the DiGiorgio strike, the most severe test of the union's organizing capability developed in the Imperial Valley in 1952 and 1953. Strike action failed to break the uncompromising opposition of the Imperial Valley Farmers Association abetted by the partisan maneuvering of employees and officials of the Farm Labor Service and the U.S. Department of Labor. The view of the operation of the Mexican bracero system is very close and detailed in relation to the union's activity during strikes. Stanford University Farm Labor Collection.

Mexican Nationals in Agriculture in the U.S. Statement submitted by the National Agricultural Union. (1952) Unpublished but available at the Stanford University Farm Labor Collection. A brief

analysis of the bracero program separated into its chief components: certification of need; effect on wages; displacement of
domestic workers; noncompliance; and administration. Details
the operation of a system of labor exploitation implanted by
government as observed by organizers who dealt with it at first
hand.

Migrant Farm Worker in America. Committee on Labor and Public
Welfare. United States Senate. Committee print (1960) and
Senate Report No. 1225 (1962). One of the most thorough inquiries, after the LaFollette hearings of 1942, of farm labor and
probably one of the least consequential in the long series of such
congressional documents. The investigation, chaired by
Senator Harrison A. Williams, was conducted with scope and
sympathy. Only of reports such as this can one say that American farm labor has a congressional history.

National Farm Labor Union in California. Donald Grubbs. Stockton,
Calif.: University of the Pacific. 1972. Mimeographed. 26 pp.
As an effort to fill the gap in the coverage of the period from 1947
to 1960 in the history of farm labor in California, this might be
rated a sketch. It is based on documentary sources, mostly
those records of the union now deposited in the special collections of the University of North Carolina. In so brief a treatment
the question: Was the NFLU a success? is left unanswered.

North from Mexico. Carey McWilliams. New York: Greenwood Press.
1968. A reprint of McWilliams' classic study of the Spanish-
speaking people of the United States from the point of view,
quoted in the foreword, of this ethnic group which was "living
competitively in . . . subordination with respect to some other
people. . . ." The "some other people" emerge clearly and are
finally characterized as those forces, institutions, and attitudes
that typified the expansion of the United States empire west-
ward. The concept of the Borderlands, which McWilliams
utilizes, clarifies the past and has important implications for the
future.

Occupied America. The Chicano's struggle for liberation. Rodolfo
Acuna. San Francisco: Canfield Press. 282 pp. Professor Acuna's text deals in detail with the history of this ethnic group in its
competitive subordination to "some other people" commonly
designated by Chicanos, in their more amiable moods, as
"Anglos." Professor Acuna is centrally concerned with cultural clashes, the heritage of violence, the legacies of hostility,
and the omission of the Chicano from the history of Man in
America. This is a book for those who wish to understand many
of the themes and manifestations of the militant Chicano mind.

Organizability of Farm Labor in the United States. Alexander Morin. Cambridge, Mass.: Harvard University Press. 1952. 102 pp. An overview of agricultural economic data of the principal farm areas of the United States in relation to the status of farm laborers and their capability for union organization. The familiar main themes of the subject are touched upon—migrancy, mechanization, the perennial gap between agricultural and industrial wage rates, and strikes. California is indicated as one of the places where union organization is most likely to succeed when "rural workers accept their identity as a group," and where they attain "a degree of awareness of their permanency in agriculture."

Partial Report of the Joint Committee on Agriculture and Livestock Problems. Part III. *Information on Various Labor Camps.* Senate of the State of California. No date (1949?). Documents relating to farm labor camps established by the federal government in various agricultural areas of California to stabilize the supply of seasonal laborers. The multimillion-dollar investment represented by these camps was liquidated at bargain prices in favor of agri-business with the effect of further stabilizing its control over migrant workers. In the process an incipient form of organization of the workers was also destroyed.

Policy Resolutions. Third Constitutional Convention of the AFL-CIO. September 1959. AFL-CIO. Washington, D.C. 1960. By 1959 reference to farm workers, their plight and startling inferiority of economic status vis-à-vis industrial workers had become ritualistic in the proceedings of AFL-CIO conventions. In this compilation the reference is sandwiched between a passing lament for the family farmer and a call for the regulation of foreign labor contracting. Farm labor organization was not included among the priorities indicated for the national labor movement's action.

Poverty in the Valley of Plenty. Ernesto Galarza. A report on the DiGiorgio strike. NFLU. Washington, D.C. 1948. 9 pp. Like the press releases and reports issued by the union during the strike, this one was written for propaganda purposes among the friends and supporters of the union. Unlike most other such reports it is a somewhat polemical mix of facts colored with the natural bias of a union organizer. In retrospect, this sort of public relations, sustained during fifteen years, might be described as the persistent termiting of the more decayed portions of the agri-business woodwork.

Recruitment and Placement of Farm Laborers in California 1950. Special report of the Joint Legislative Committee on Agriculture

and Livestock Problems. Senate of the State of California.
Goodwin J. Knight, President of the Senate. Sacramento. 1951.
Demonstrates the traditional difficulty that California legislative bodies and their agri-business constituencies have had in
differentiating between farm laborers and cattle.

*Report on the Farm Labor Accident at Chualar, California, on Sep-
tember 17, 1963.* Committee on Education and Labor. U.S.
House of Representatives. Washington, D.C. 1964. 66 pp. The
collision of a farm labor truck and a freight train left thirty-two
Mexican braceros dead along the tracks of the Southern Pacific
Railway near Chualar. The accident was the product of a whole
social system, which may explain why a swarm of local, state,
and federal investigators who examined the horror withdrew in
silence, except Chairman Adam Clayton Powell of the House
Committee on Education and Labor, who authorized the preparation of this report. Includes identification of data sources and
list of the dead.

Revolt Among the Sharecroppers. Howard Kester. New York: Arno
Press. 1969. 98 pp. The author, an ordained minister graduated
from Princeton University, joined the protest of the southern
sharecroppers in the mid-thirties. He observed and reported the
terror organized by the cotton planters that failed to break the
Southern Tenant Farmers Union. He diagnoses the economic,
social, and political callousness of the New Deal and the mass
eviction of the people whose fate Kester reported. Its qualities
of subjectivity, sentimentality, and humanness present a commentary on one of the least glorious aspects of Franklin D.
Roosevelt's several administrations.

Sacramento Story. "Labor and the California Legislature." California
State Federation of Labor. San Francisco. 1951, 1957, and 1959.
Annual reports to the federation secretary–treasurer C. J. Haggerty. A summary of the triumphs and defeats of organized
labor as the legislative watchdog for union labor. Not before,
not during, and not after the years covered by this record was
there anything noteworthy to celebrate or to lament so far as
agricultural laborers were concerned. The watchdog only occasionally barked for them, but not very loudly.

So Shall Ye Reap. Joan London and Henry Anderson. New York, 1970:
Thomas Y. Crowell. 208 pp. The title of this book alludes to its
predecessor, *As Ye Sow* by Professor Walter R. Goldschmidt
(Harcourt, 1947), which provides an oblique view of agri-
business by describing the community effects of family farming.
Anderson was for a time on the staff of the Agricultural Workers
Organizing Committee in the early 1960s and writes as a

sociologist capable of historical perspective. Joan London, daughter of Jack London, a skilled author in her own right, fought a terminal illness to complete her share of this collaboration with Anderson.

Sorrow Song in Black and White. Vera Rony. Southern Regional Council. Atlanta, Georgia. 1967. Pamphlet, 40 pages with short bibliography. Reviews sympathetically the struggles of farm workers to organize from the founding of the Southern Tenant Farmers Union in 1934 to the beginning stages of the Delano movement in the mid-1960s. Provides a quick look at labor unionism in the Louisiana sugar cane plantations during the early 1950s.

Spiders in the House and Workers in the Field. Ernesto Galarza. Notre Dame, Indiana: University of Notre Dame Press. 1970. In history it is the context of an event that must be pursued to the limits of available knowledge if it is to radiate meaning. So it was with the publication of an item in the Congressional Record of March 9, 1950. The piece was a purported "report" of a congressional committee fabricated for and signed by three Members of the House including Richard M. Nixon. The hoax succeeded; it broke the DiGiorgio strike, stopped a union organizing campaign, postponed the end of the bracero system by ten years and set the stage for a detente between agri-business and agri-labor.

Union Labor in California. Department of Industrial Relations, State of California. San Francisco. 1960. 35 pp. The statistical, tabular approach to farm labor history can be productive for scholars, albeit by obliquely suggesting questions, not by answering them. This report is an illustration. Statistic: "Union membership in California totaled 1,741,000 in July 1959." Question: "Why, in a state with a powerful trade-union movement, was a feeble farm labor union quietly destroyed in July 1959?"

Violations of Free Speech and Rights of Labor. Report of the Committee on Education and Labor. U.S. Senate. Senator Robert M. LaFollette, Chairman. Part 3. Washington, D.C. 1942. pp. 153-405. This is only part of the voluminous report of the celebrated LaFollette Committee investigation of "the disadvantaged status of unorganized labor in California's industrialized agriculture." For thoroughness and breadth this report has never been surpassed as a documentation of the apparatus of control by agri-business, its historical roots in patterns of land ownership, and its ideology of the corporation in overalls.

Welfare and Institutions Code. State of California. Sacramento. 1947. Some aspects of California's drama of migration, emigration, and racial minorities are documented in codes like this one. The Golden State in time took notice of the very considerable residue of human poverty that its successive rushes and booms left in their wake. State charity became unavoidable as a prudent husbanding of resources and a concession to the demands of the economically deprived. The code has touches of poetic insight, such as its description of the cyclical lack of jobs, wages, shelter, and food of the farm laboring class as "seasons of repose."

Index